THE ITALIAN STALLIONS

THE ITALIAN STALLIONS

HEROES OF BOXING'S GLORY DAYS

STEPHEN BRUNT AND THE WRITERS OF *SPORT* MAGAZINE

===

INTRODUCTION BY THOMAS HAUSER

===

FEATURING PHOTOGRAPHS FROM
THE *SPORT* COLLECTION

Published in the United States of America by Sport Media Publishing Inc.,
Wilmington, Delaware, and simultaneously in Canada.

For information about permission to reproduce selections from this book,
please write to:
Permissions
Sport Media Publishing, Inc.,
21 Carlaw Ave.,
Toronto, Ontario, Canada, M4M 2R6
www.sportclassicbooks.com

Cover design: Paul Hodgson / pHd
Interior design: Paul Hodgson / pHd
Front cover photo of Rocky Graziano: The *SPORT* Collection

ISBN: 1-894963-03-2

Library of Congress Control Number: 2003114043

Printed in Canada

The articles from *SPORT* included in this book are reprinted exactly as they
originally appeared in the magazine. Many words and phrases commonplace
in the middle years of the 20th century sound peculiar or, in the occasional
instance, perhaps even offensive today. However, it was determined that
altering the original language would diminish the accuracy and, ultimately,
value of the strong historical context contained in the articles, and should
therefore be avoided.

To those tough, resilient men who employed their fists in a frantic bid to scale society's ladder and whose exploits are celebrated on these pages, and also to those who utilized more mundane implements—their typewriters and cameras—and whose work for *SPORT* magazine set a standard for sports coverage that was ahead of its era.

SPORT

Rocky Marciano speaking at the banquet honoring him as *SPORT* magazine's Man of the Year, March 1955

CONTENTS

WHEN BOXING
MATTERED

BY THOMAS HAUSER

In 1922, Jack Dempsey was heavyweight champion of the world. Babe Ruth was patrolling right field for the New York Yankees. And Knute Rockne was the head football coach at Notre Dame. But as "the Roaring Twenties" were blossoming, a wave of xenophobia was sweeping America.

The previous year, Italian-born anarchists Nicola Sacco and Bartolomeo Vanzetti had been tried and found guilty of killing two men in a Massachusetts payroll robbery. Despite substantial evidence of their innocence, they were later executed. Also in 1921, Congress passed legislation that sharply curtailed immigration to the United States. Much of the impetus for this legislation came from anti-Italian sentiment. Shortly thereafter, Benito Mussolini marched on Rome and formed the fascist government that would be forever identified with his name.

It was into this world, in 1921, that Thomas Rocco Barbella was born. He was joined in 1922 by Guglielmo Papaleo, Giuseppe Berardinelli and Giacobe LaMotta, and, in 1923, by Rocco Francis Marchegiano. Ultimately, these five men would become known as Rocky Graziano, Willie Pep, Joey Maxim, Jake LaMotta and Rocky Marciano. They would win world championships as professional boxers. And in doing so, they would shape the way in which America viewed the Italian-American community and also the manner in which the Italian-American community viewed itself.

Boxing belongs to the underclass. When the Irish came to America in large numbers, John L. Sullivan was their standard bearer. In the early 20th century, the Jewish ghettos of New York gave rise to Benny Leonard and Barney Ross.

Giuseppe Carrora emigrated to the United States from Sicily with his parents. Fighting under the name of Johnny Dundee, he won the junior-lightweight title in 1921 and, a year later, the world featherweight crown. Dundee was regarded as the first of the great Italian-American fighters.

Italian-American champions born in the United States followed in Dundee's wake. Frankie Gennaro and Midget Wolgast won the world flyweight title. Battling Battalino and Petey Scalzo held the featherweight crown. Sammy Mandell and Sammy Angott ascended to the lightweight throne. Tony Canzoneri reigned as featherweight, lightweight, and junior-welterweight king.

These men represented the struggle of first-generation Italian-Americans born in the United States who were trying to fight their way out of the ghetto. And they fought at a time when boxing truly mattered.

In the first half of the 20th century, boxing and baseball were America's two national sports. On Saturday afternoons, hundreds of people would go to Stillman's Gym in the Bronx just to watch the fighters train. At one time, there were 22 fight clubs in New York City; each one in a different neighborhood. And unless someone was boxing an opponent from another part of New York or had risen to world-class status, he fought guys from his own neighborhood. There was no such thing as bringing in an opponent from out-of-state for a four-round preliminary fight.

Fighters were connected to the community in a meaningful way. People in the neighborhood knew

Left: J. Edgar Hoover (in hat) ringside for Tony Canzoneri's fight against Frankie Klick, 1935

them and saw them on a regular basis. And for Italian-Americans, boxing had special meaning because there were few Italian-American heroes on a national scale.

Fiorello LaGuardia was elected mayor of New York in 1933, but Italian-Americans were largely excluded from the high councils of political power. It wasn't until Lyndon Johnson designated Anthony Celebrezze as Secretary of Health, Education, and Welfare in the mid-1960s that an Italian-American served in the president's cabinet.

Meanwhile, Angelo Bertelli starred on the gridiron for Notre Dame. Hank Luisetti excelled in basketball for Stanford. And of course, there was Joe DiMaggio. But the sport that was most open to Italian-Americans was boxing. Willie Pep reigned as featherweight champion for seven years. Joey Maxim won the light-heavyweight title and is in the record books as the only man to knock out Sugar Ray Robinson. Rocky Graziano and Jake LaMotta captured the middleweight crown.

LaMotta is an icon today because of the movie *Raging Bull*. But in his heyday, his standing within the Italian-American community was a complex matter. LaMotta was born to Italian immigrant parents on the Lower East Side of Manhattan. After a brief sojourn in Philadelphia, his family moved to the Bronx. LaMotta attended Public School 55 and got as far as ninth grade. Then he was sent to a juvenile detention center. Subsequent to his ring career, he spent six months in prison for a conviction on charges that he operated a cocktail lounge for purposes of prostitution.

LaMotta wasn't the only "bad boy" among Italian-Americans in boxing. Rocky Graziano had dropped out of school after fifth grade and resided in correctional institutes for six of his first 20 years. Drafted into the United States Army during World War II, Graziano then spent 10 months in military prison for going AWOL and assaulting an officer.

Willie Pep had been arrested for illegal gambling. Joey Giardello, who later reigned as middleweight champion, also spent time in prison. But to his neighbors, LaMotta's crime, the one the community reviled him for, was worse than any of the aforementioned offenses.

In 1947, LaMotta signed to fight Billy Fox, a Philadelphia light-heavyweight with a record of 48-1, and 48 knockouts. The "Bronx Bull," as LaMotta was known, was the number-one middleweight contender. He had never been knocked out. On the afternoon of

the fight, the odds jumped from even money to 12-to-5 in Fox's favor. Madison Square Garden was completely sold out. The fight, as LaMotta later admitted in testimony before Congress, was fixed. Fox hit him with unanswered blows for four rounds. Finally, the referee halted the bout.

LaMotta had committed the ultimate sin. People had believed that he was an honest fighter. His neighbors were certain that he would always do his best. Now that belief was gone. Men and women who worked hard for their money, neighbors who had known him for years, had bet on him and lost. He had betrayed them.

Nineteen months later, LaMotta won the middleweight title, but he was an unpopular champion. Many fans disliked his abusive personality. Others despised him for having thrown the Fox fight. *Newsweek* described him as "more hated than any other two champions." W.C. Heinz wrote an article entitled "The Most Hated Man in Sports" that closed with the words, "Jake LaMotta will go into the books as one of the most unpopular sports figures of all time."

But as a counterpoint to LaMotta, there was Rocky Marciano.

Marciano was embedded in the consciousness of Italian-Americans in the same way that Joe Louis lived in the hearts of his people. Born in Brockton, Massachusetts, the son of an immigrant shoemaker, Rocco Marchegiano left high school during tenth grade. For a while, he worked in the same shoe factory as his father; but he couldn't stand being indoors, so he took a job as a landscape gardener and then went to work clearing land. In 1943, he was drafted into the United States Army. Two years after World War II ended, he turned pro. In 1952, Marciano knocked out Jersey Joe Walcott to become heavyweight champion of the world. Four years later, he retired with 49 victories in 49 fights.

There had been an Italian heavyweight champion before Marciano. But Primo Carnera, who wore the crown for less than a year in the mid-1930s, was mob-controlled. Many of his fights had been fixed, and there came a time when the public knew it.

Marciano was the real thing, and he reigned at a time when the heavyweight championship was the most coveted title in sports. It was also a time when the sports media was very different from today. Fans got most of their information from newspapers and magazines. The fights themselves were experienced by attending in person or by listening to the radio. On occasion, they were witnessed on a new medium called television. And for the most part, reporting on athletes was innocent in the extreme.

Thus, Ed Fitzgerald wrote in the pages of *SPORT* magazine:

"All the boys from Brockton identified themselves with their champion. His victories became their victories. They rejoiced that success hadn't taken Rocky away from them. He still lived among them. Rocky is a neighborhood kid who married a neighborhood girl and who thinks the old hometown is the greatest place in the world. Rocky's social activities are confined largely to entertaining friends and relatives at home or making the rounds of their houses, and to the Ward Two Club and the Seville Council, Knights of Columbus. The priests and nuns of St. Colman's parish where he worships call on him again and again to serve as a model for their lectures to the neighborhood kids."

The profligate womanizing that marked Marciano's life went unreported. So did other instances of anti-social behavior. And for Italian-Americans, Rocky Marciano became the ultimate status symbol; in part, because he was seen as the stereotypical Italian-American.

To the community, Marciano was "one of us." Joe DiMaggio had a passport to a higher level of society. DiMaggio was the essence of style and grace, but DiMaggio was aloof. He gave the impression of being above it all and on a level that other Italian-Americans could never reach. DiMaggio married Marilyn Monroe. Marilyn Monroe would not have married Rocky Marciano.

There were several Italian-American champions after Marciano. Carmen Basilio's parents emigrated to the United States from Italy. Basilio's father became an onion-farmer in upstate New York. Basilio became the welterweight and middleweight champion of the world. Joey Giardello followed suit as far as the middleweight title was concerned.

But assimilation and upward mobility were ending the glory years for Italian-American fighters. And while there have been fighters who mattered a lot during the past half-century—Muhammad Ali foremost among them—boxing as a sport has receded in the public consciousness.

Still, a final look at Johnny Dundee, Midget Wolgast, Frankie Gennaro, Sammy Mandell, Tony Canzoneri, Battling Battalino, Sammy Angott, Petey Scalzo, Willie Pep, Rocky Graziano, Joey Maxim, Jake LaMotta, Carmen Basilio, Joey Giardello, and Rocky Marciano is in order.

The term "champion" has been devalued in recent years with 17 weight classes and four world sanctioning bodies. But these men were true champions. And they were tough. Their composite record reveals 2,101 professional fights, many against world-class competition, often against one another. Yet in 2,101 professional fights, they were knocked out only 44 times. Discount the inevitable late-career knockouts by removing 48 fights from the end of their composite record, and the totals show a mere 26 knockout losses in 2,053 fights. That's extraordinary.

Want more? In world championship fights, these 17 men compiled a composite record of 77 wins, 36 losses, seven draws and one no contest. In 13 of the 15 years between 1945 and 1959, at least one of them was involved in *Ring Magazine's* "Fight of the Year."

And one final note. Sugar Ray Robinson is the gold standard against which all other fighters are judged. Four of these men (LaMotta, Maxim, Basilio, and Giardello) beat Robinson.

But statistics can be cold and hard, so let's give the final word to another Italian-American fighter. Vito Antuofermo was born in Italy and came to the United States as a child. During a career that lasted from 1971 to 1985, he had 50 wins, 7 losses, and 2 draws. Antuofermo was as honest as a fighter can be. Strong, plodding, always moving forward. His curse was that he cut easily. Time and again, his face betrayed him.

In 1977, the great Carlos Monzon retired as middleweight champion. He was succeeded by Rodrigo Valdez, who gave way to Hugo Corro. On June 30, 1979, Antuofermo won a 15-round decision over Corro to capture the 160-pound crown. Antuofermo's first defense was against Marvin Hagler. It was a foregone conclusion that Hagler would win. Except, at the end of the bout when the judges' scorecards were tallied, Antuofermo had retained his title on a draw.

"Sometimes I wish I could have fought against those guys," says Antuofermo. "You know, against guys like Basilio, LaMotta, and Graziano. It would have been an honor to get in the ring with them and to test myself against them."

Antuofermo is part of a tradition; Italian-American champions who share a common bond dating to a time when boxing truly mattered.

CHAPTER ONE

THE EXODUS

FROM ITALY WITH LOVE – AND DESPERATION

BY STEPHEN BRUNT

Men fight for money because they have to, which is true now just as it has been true whenever and wherever the sport of professional boxing was allowed to flourish. Always there have been exceptions, gentleman boxers and schoolboy boxers, drawn to the sport or led to the sport convinced that it's a character builder, middle class kids who have never missed a meal somehow attracted to a meaner life. And some, violent by nature, have found in organized fisticuffs a socially acceptable outlet for their anger.

But what separates boxing from other games that people play for pay is that it isn't much of a game at all. It is real and primitive and unsparing. There are no teammates to fall back on. There are no technological advantages, no hardware at all beyond padded gloves and tape. There are rules, but none that do much to protect fighters from harm, since harm is the point of the exercise. Instead, boxers are stripped to the waist, deserted in the ring by their trainers and supporters, left to fend for themselves against someone who desperately wants to hurt them. There are no time outs, there is no place to hide, and several of the most fundamental characteristics of a civilized society—compassion, restraint, mercy—are suspended for the three minutes that make up a round.

To play that game, to not run away, to not surrender, to be hit and ignore the pain, to hit another human being and then, seeing them hurt, hit them again, requires a person very brave and normally a person very desperate. The sport's structure is designed to swallow the willing quickly. In boxing, you don't have to earn a place on a team, you don't have to progress through a system, you don't need a university scholarship; you don't even have to be very good to start. Pass a physical examination, demonstrate basic skills, and someone will pay you to fight tomorrow—not much, but something, and in cold, hard cash. At the bottom of the great capitalist pyramid, those willing to take that step do so almost invariably because they can't wait, because they have mouths to feed, because they have no alternative, because they're poor.

When the professional sport of boxing made its first inroads in the new world in the late 19th Century, a vast pool of potential labor was already waiting. Of the immigrant waves that landed on North America, some sought religious or political freedoms denied in their homelands, and many were lured by free farmland in the wilderness for homesteading. The Germans and Scandinavians, especially, made their way west to make new lives for themselves in relative isolation. It's no surprise, then, that few of their number turn up in the early annals of American boxing. By and large, they didn't have to fight their way out of despair.

Other immigrants, though, were pure economic refugees, most notably the Irish, driven from their home by poverty in general and the potato famine in particular. Or they were members of persecuted minorities, like the Jews, who would at times find the new land not much more accommodating than the old. Many of them came too late for homesteading. Instead, they became workers, settling not in the boundless

Left: Carmen Basilio, 1955

wilderness but in the urban centers of the eastern seaboard. It was there, from poverty, from the ghettos, that the first great American boxers emerged. They were led by a flamboyant, sports superstar who crossed all cultural barriers, who achieved fame as no other athlete had before: the heavyweight champion John L. Sullivan. He was ethnically Irish (as was his first marquee opponent, in the last of the great bare-knuckle fights, Jake Kilrain), and soon the Irish fighters would be joined by Jewish boxers, especially in the lower weight classes: an Irish-Jewish bout was every match-maker's dream, playing on the rivalries of two communities that often came together, less than amicably, in daily life. African-American fighters were also part of the mix right from the beginning, for the same socio-economic reasons. Though some would be given the chance to win championships, most would face insurmountable barriers ascending the hierarchy of boxing just as they did everywhere else.

You won't find many Italian names in the boxing records of the late 19th and early 20th Century, but that certainly doesn't mean they weren't there. It takes a little detective work to learn that Lou Ambers was really Louis D'Ambrosio; that Sammy Angott was Samuel Engoti; that Young Corbett III was Ralph Giordano; that Young Zulu Kid was Giuseppe Dimelfi; that Fireman Jim Flynn was Andrew Charlione; that Jack Sharkey was Giovanni Cervati; that Packey O'Gatty was Pasquale Agati; that Johnny Dundee was Giuseppe Carrora; that Sammy Mandell was Samuel Mandella; that Midget Wolgast was Joseph Loscatzo; that Pete Herman was Pete Gulotta; and that masquerading as Irishmen and Jews they were world champions who called Italy home. To understand how they got there, and why the disguise was necessary, requires a short glance at Italy's turbulent history in the 19th Century, and the resulting mass migration, one of the largest in the history of the planet.

Before 1860, the quite small numbers of Italian immigrants who came to North America tended to be from the country's north. Many of them were relatively well off, and arrived with job skills, to be absorbed easily into the American melting pot. The Italian Revolution led by Giuseppe Garibaldi, which culminated in the country's unification in 1870, drastically altered those migration patterns. Though they had supported Garibaldi, the poor peasants of the Mezzogiorno, the Italian regions from south of Rome—Abruzzo, Molise, Campania, Basilicata, Apulia, Calabria and Sicily—found themselves cut off from political and economic power. They were treated as second-class citizens in their own country, and endured an unbelievable series of plagues, including a cholera epidemic that killed 55,000 people, an earthquake, a tidal wave, and the spread of the plant disease Phylloxera, which destroyed most of their grape vines.

Not surprisingly, many southern Italians decided to leave—in total, a third of the entire population. First they headed for other parts of Europe, then Latin America and Brazil—though the latter became less desirable after a Yellow Fever epidemic killed 9,000. After that, the preferred destination, and future home of 4.5-million Italian immigrants, was that great land of opportunity and equality, the United States of America. In the beginning it was mostly young men who made the long, often perilous journey, some of them seasonal laborers, many of whom returned to Italy when their work was done. (By 1914, one out of every 20 Italians in Italy had been to America at least once.) Italian immigration was only slowed by restrictions imposed by the U.S. in 1924, and then by the fascist government of Benito Mussolini, which prevented its citizens from leaving.

Though most were peasant farmers in their homeland, by the time they came to the United States the homesteading opportunities were gone. Like the Irish, they settled largely in urban areas, but unlike the Irish, they didn't speak the language. As the most recent arrivals, the new Italian-Americans took their place at the bottom of the food chain, stereotyped as stiletto wielding gangsters, or as bomb-tossing anarchists (witness the scandalous trial and execution of Sacco and Vanzetti). They faced bigotry, they faced violence both from other, more established immigrant groups and from the burgeoning, bigoted American "nativist" movement. Living in Italian-speaking urban ghettos, consigned to menial labor (when there was work at all), they were forced to claw their way up from the very bottom.

This is the world—in his case, Lower East Side Manhattan—so vividly described by Jake LaMotta (with Joseph Carter and Pete Savage) in his autobiography, *Raging Bull*:

"What I remember about the tenement as much as anything else is the smell. It's impossible to describe the smell of a tenement to someone who's never lived in one. You can't just put

your head in the door and sniff. You have to live there, day and night, summer and winter, so the smell gets a chance to sink into your soul. There's all that dirt that the super never really manages to get clean even on the days when he does an hour's work, and this dirt has a smell, gray and dry and, after you've smelled it long enough, suffocating. And diapers. The slobs who live in tenements are always having kids, and naturally they don't have the money for any diaper service, so the old lady is always boiling diapers on the back of the stove and after a while the smell gets into the walls.

"And the food you eat when you're poor. All it does is keep you alive, and it has a smell, too, because it's food like corned beef and cabbage, or food that's cooked in heavy grease, the smell of it cooking goes all through the building.

"And there was the heat in summer, when I'd try to spend all the time I could out in the street or on the roof or the fire escapes, and the cold in the winter. It seemed like I was always cold in winter when I was a kid. Being on home relief doesn't do much to keep you warm. Everything piles up on you when you're poor. The super in the building doesn't give a damn and God knows the landlord doesn't, and you call City Hall and get some clerk who doesn't give a damn either because he's on civil service and what the hell difference is it to him if you're freezing your ass off. It's not hurting him any. So winters I remember wearing as many clothes as I could and staying in bed as much as I could, or in the kitchen, which was about the only room in the house that was even halfway warm, unless the old man was in a foul temper like he was a helluva lot of the time, and then the kitchen was off-limits to any kid with a grain of sense in his head.

"And the rats! What's a real tenement without rats? Not the kind of rats you probably know that run if they hear a sound. These were rats as big as goddamned alley cats, and if you meet them at night you got out of their way. You could hear them at night, too, in the walls, squealing and slamming around, afraid of nothing. Zoccolas, we called them, which is Italian slang for a dirty vicious whore."

In the old country, sports would have been regarded as a waste of time, a distraction from the work necessary for daily survival. In America, though, where street violence became a way of life for many, some Italian-Americans naturally made the leap to boxing. It says something that even in that sport, the refuge of those with no other alternatives, a whole generation of Italian-American fighters was forced to adopt other names, other identities, in order to subvert racism and appeal to the ticket-buying audience.

It wasn't just boxers, though. Arguably the first great Italian American athlete in the United States was a baseball player named Francesco Pezzolo, who took the name Ping Bodie (Ping being the sound the ball makes when it's struck by a bat). He played for the Chicago White Sox and for the New York Yankees, where he was for a time Babe Ruth's roommate: "I don't room with the Babe," Bodie explained about his famously social teammate. "I room with his bags." It wasn't until 1917 that the first Italian ballplayer turns up with an Italian name—Tony Defate, of the Detroit Tigers. Eventually, though, the Berras and Rizzutos and Lazzeris and, especially, DiMaggios, took their place among the greatest players in the great American game.

Of the Italian-American boxers who fought under adopted names, the greatest was probably Johnny Dundee, who was born in Sciacca, Italy in 1893, and immigrated to the United States as a child. The "Scotch Wop," as Dundee was not so subtly nicknamed, began fighting in New York City in 1910. In 1913, he was given a crack at world featherweight champion Johnny Kilbane, but the fight ended in a 20-round draw. Kilbane kept his distance after that, while Dundee fought on, mostly in "no decision" fights, including a long series against the great Benny Leonard.

In boxing, the opportunity to proudly compete under the athletes' true family names was longer coming than it had been in baseball. A few Italian fighters did reveal their real identities in the 1920s and 1930s: Mike Ballerino, a junior lightweight champion, Battling Battaliano, who held the featherweight title, Frankie Genero (who Anglicized his name from Frankie DiGennera), a flyweight champion, Fidel LaBarba, who was featherweight world champ. The best of that group was undoubtedly Tony Canzoneri, who was born in 1908 into a first generation immigrant family in Slidell, Louisiana, near New Orleans, and then moved to Brooklyn, New York. Canzoneri won the state amateur bantamweight title as a 16 year old—though he weighed only 95 pounds, competing in a 118-pound weight class. He turned professional in 1925, and in 1928 won the world featherweight title. He had fought two world championships before he was 20 years old, and by the age of 22 was a two-time world champion. At age 23, he was considered the best fighter, pound for pound, in the world. When his career wrapped up in 1939, after 175 professional bouts, Canzoneri had also claimed lightweight and junior welterweight crowns, the third fighter in history to win world titles in three weight divisions, and came within a hair of winning a fourth championship as well—he fought to a draw with Bud Taylor as an 18 year old when challenging for the bantamweight title.

Along the way, Canzoneri met 18 world champions, and many of the greatest fighters of his era: Bushy Graham, Johnny Dundee, Sammy Mandell, Jackie "Kid" Berg, Barney Ross, Lou Ambers, and Jimmy McLarnin. He was stopped only once, in the final bout of his long, distinguished career.

The most famous Italian fighter of that early era, though, wasn't Canzoneri, and wasn't an immigrant, but was instead a man straight from the old country who would come to be widely regarded as a sad cliché, the embodiment of how the business of boxing can ruthlessly exploit its athletes. Primo Carnera was a native of Sequals in Northern Italy who grew up speaking the Friulian dialect, the son of a worker in that town's famous mosaic business. Even as a teenager, he was a physical anomaly, a 6-foot-6, 260-pound giant in an era when even heavyweights rarely tipped the scales at more than 200 pounds. Carnera was bigger even than George Foreman or Lennox Lewis.

He left school after the third grade, with only a limited ability to read and write, and eventually moved to Le Mans, France, where he lived with an uncle and worked as a manual laborer. Carnera's size, though, soon turned heads, especially among those who might take advantage of the gentle, naïve Italian peasant. By age 21, he was touring with a circus as "Juan the Unbeatable Spaniard," taking on all comers in boxing, wrestling or weightlifting. Carnera wasn't a natural athlete, and he certainly wasn't an aggressive, violent man. His sheer size, though, was such a huge advantage that he nearly always came out on top. It was while with the circus that Carnera was discovered by Paul Journee, a former French heavyweight champion who soon delivered him to Leon See, a journalist and manager of fighters. See would later write a book—*Le Mystere Carnera*—detailing how he built Carnera's record with a series of fixed fights in Europe. Carnera "won" 14 of his first 15 bouts in 1928 and 1929—the only loss coming to Franz Diener on an unscripted foul. Then, according to See, he arranged for a pair of bouts against the American heavyweight contender Young Stribling, one in London, one in Paris. Carnera won the first, on a foul, and lost the second, on a foul, with both results pre-determined, for

the first time with Carnera's knowledge.

That set the stage for Carnera's much-publicized arrival in the United States in 1930, beginning with a first-round knockout of Big Boy Peterson in New York City. In the U.S., his management was quietly transferred to a couple of mobsters, Bill Duffy and Owen Madden. But the strategy remained the same: barnstorming across the country, winning fight after fight by quick knockout, and stirring skepticism among the American sports press, who suspected (correctly) that the fix might be in. Carnera did have a few real fights, even in the early stages of his careers: he beat George Godfrey on a foul in 1930, lost a decision to contender Jimmy Maloney the same year, and then returned to Europe where he beat Paulino Uzcudun in Barcelona. In 1931, he lost a tough 15-round decision to future world champion Jack Sharkey, and followed that up with a decision victory of Kingfish Levinsky. In 1932, a long string of Carnera wins was punctuated by losses to the tough Canadian Larry Gains, and to Stanley Poreda.

Though widely ridiculed in his own time, and especially after the fraudulent nature of his early career was exposed, there are those who claim now that Carnera was better than his tarnished reputation suggests, that he became a reasonably skilled boxer, and that he was never quite the same after he knocked out Ernie Schaaf in February, 1933. Schaaf, who it would later be revealed had entered the ring with a blood clot on his brain, died a few days after the fight.

Nevertheless, in his very next bout, Carnera knocked out Sharkey with an upper cut in the sixth round to win the heavyweight championship of the world, just the second European (after Bob Fitzsimmons) to hold the belt. No one has ever claimed that the result was anything but legitimate.

Carnera defended the title twice, against Uzcudun and Tommy Loughran, before taking the fight that would unfortunately come to define his career. Facing hard punching Max Baer at Madison Square Garden, Carnera was knocked down 12 times in 11 rounds, enduring both a terrible beating, and the humiliation of watching Baer mock him and imitate him, much to the delight of the crowd. The devastating loss was seen as definitive proof that, despite winning the title, Carnera had been an invention, a fraud, a "hoax"—as *The New York Times*' columnist Arthur Daley cruelly dubbed him when he penned the fighter's obituary in 1967.

The Baer fight was the effective end of Carnera's

boxing career. He continued to fight through 1937, a period notable only for his sixth-round knockout loss to the new heavyweight sensation, Joe Louis. From 1938 to 1944, Carnera was inactive. During the war years, he lived in Sequals, and appeared in a series of Italian movies. After the war, he fought five times, losing the last three to an Italian fighter named Luigi Musina.

Soon afterwards, the story of Carnera's brutal exploitation, capped by the fact that he'd been left nearly penniless despite his success in the ring, became widely known. Best remembered today is the Hollywood version of his boxing life, *The Harder They Fall*, starring Humphrey Bogart as a corrupt sports writer, with the names and situations slightly altered. Carnera sued for libel because of the way a character clearly based on him, pathetic Toro Moreno, was depicted in the movie. He lost.

In the 1950s, Carnera would devote himself to a sport to which he was in many ways more suited: professional wrestling. There, he was wildly popular with audiences, traveled the globe, and won a 'world championship.' He also appeared in films, usually in near silent bit parts, ranging from the sublime (*On The Waterfront*) to the ridiculous (*Hercules Unchained*). In 1953, like millions of his countrymen before him, Carnera became an American citizen. In 1967, he returned home to Sequals and died there, largely of symptoms related to alcoholism.

While Carnera was in many ways a throwback to the days before the great migration to the United States, the Italian fighters who came after him, during the 1940s and 1950s, were very much the vanguard of a new, hybrid culture. They were the children, in some cases the grandchildren, of the original Italian emigres. (Because Italian immigration had been severely curtailed from 1924 on, there had been no new waves from the old country.) Raised in the cities, many as poor and desperate as their forefathers, but more comfortable with the language and much more assimilated into society, they were ready to help create a new image for the Italian-American. Fighting under their own names—or, in some cases, anglicized versions of their own names—and earning a reputation for stand-up toughness, for their unwillingness to quit, they made the idea of Italian boxers synonymous with courage, heart, and thrilling, blood-and-guts entertainment.

Not coincidentally, the rise of the new breed of Italian *faitature*—the immigrants' term for prize-fighters—coincided with the beginning of the World War II. The war was a watershed moment for Italian-Americans. Regarded with suspicion as potential fascist sympathizers, with some interned as though they were the enemy, half a million nonetheless joined the U.S. forces and fought with bravery and distinction overseas. Out from the ethnic ghettoes, slowly but surely integrated into all aspects of American life, Italian-Americans would make their mark in the arts, in business, in politics, in the intellectual and academic realms. But as is the case with most immigrant groups, that stamp would first be most obvious in the world of sport, and especially in the sport of boxing.

Fans love a compelling story to go with their athletic heroes. They love to root for the underdog, for someone born without advantages, without superior physical gifts, who still manages to succeed against the odds. It is the defining myth of America, after all, the Horatio Alger tale, that anyone from anywhere can become anything they choose. And it would be embodied in the Italian-American fighters, who grew up in dire poverty, and rose to become heroes, to become champions of the world.

Perhaps the best of those stories was also one that cut slightly against the grain. The man born Rocco Barbella certainly wasn't a sympathetic figure as a kid: in fact, he was a hood, a thief, a tough guy who bounced from reform school to prison. And when, during World War II, he was released from custody to join the U.S. Army, he went AWOL, was charged with desertion, court-martialed, and in the end dishonorably discharged after spending a year in the stockade.

Still, when he stepped into the ring under the name he originally adopted to avoid the military police—Rocky Graziano—the fans loved him instantly, and by the time his career was finished, Graziano had been transformed into a beloved figure, admired both for his ferocity in the ring and for his winning personality—so much so that enjoyed a second career in film and television. It sure isn't every Italian ghetto kid who gets to sit back and watch Paul Newman star in the Hollywood story of his life.

Graziano was born on the Lower East Side of Manhattan on New Year's Day 1921, but grew up in Brooklyn, not far from Coney Island. He and his brother Joe were the only two of the first seven Barbella children to survive past the age of two months. His early life was poor, troubled, and violent. His father was both a former fighter and a nasty drunk who tried to push his two sons into the ring. His mother, worn down by an abusive husband, and by the deaths of children in infancy, turned to alcohol as well, and eventually would be confined to a mental institution.

"Except for me, we were a very respectable family," Graziano wrote in his autobiography (with Rowland Barber), *Somebody Up There Likes Me*. "I was the only wild one. My mother's people had all been honest, legitimate Italian-Americans.

"Both my father and my mother were born in New York City. Both their families—the Barbellas and the Scintos, my mother's family—come originally from near Naples, Italy. They were all Napoletan—or like we pronounced it, 'Noppily-don.'

"My father, Nick Barbella, was the middle son in a big East Side family. His father I can remember only vaguely. He was a tall man with a huge mustache who drove a horse-drawn hearse for an undertaker. I remember seeing him sitting up there high in the open seat of the black hearse, wearing a black derby, his mustache sweeping out of both sides of his face, driving along and talking in Italian to his skinny, gray horse.

"All the men in the family were called something 'Bob', that being short for Bobbella, the way our name got pronounced in the city. I always been 'Rocky Bob' to my old friends. My father was 'Nick Bob' . . . Before he got married, Pop fought almost 70 professional bouts as Fighting Nick Bob, around the neighborhood gyms and clubs. He was a good welterweight—never no contender, but right up there. Before he went into the ring when he was 18 years old, Nick Barbella had been a wild kid too, just like his son Rocco was turning out. I didn't know until many years later, but before he begun to fight, he never took a job, hung around the poolroom, and began to steal a little bit here, there . . . Then he became a fighter and stopped stealing. Then in 1916 he met Ida Scinto and stopped fighting."

Young Rocco was done with school after grade seven, and long before that had been identified as an incorrigible street punk, destined for jail—according to at least one of those who dealt with him as he bounced around the legal system, destined for the electric chair. When he became too much for his parents, Graziano was sent to live with his grandparents in the old Italian neighborhood of Manhattan.

"The center of it all, the center of the world, was the East Side," he wrote. "The East Side meant to me where the Italians lived, from First Street up to Fourteenth Street, from Third Avenue almost over to Avenue A. The Italians were the only real people in this world. Everybody else had something queer about them and you called them by filthy names you heard the older kids use."

It was clear from the very beginning that Graziano could fight: on the street he was merciless, and nearly unbeatable. But his dream was to be a hood, a mobster, a thief, not a fighter, and he initially resisted all efforts to redirect his aggression towards the ring. When he finally put on the gloves as an amateur, he approached his opponents exactly as he would have in a street fight.

"Every fight was the same. I just come out to kill the bastard opposing me. If he hit me, I got wild like an animal. I get it in my head he's going to make a monster out of me, with puffed up eyes and a busted nose. Anybody do this to me, I'm going to break him in two. Knee in his balls, thumb in his eyes. Grab him by the back of his neck and smash him with a right. Sometimes the referee warned me about fighting dirty. What the hell do I care about the referee?

"I got the crowd screaming like a bunch of frigging madmen every time I take after a guy with my blood boiling and my right swinging like a windmill. I got the crowd screaming and that's money in the box. I got my opponent bleeding in a heap on the canvas. No matter what any referee wants to say, I am the winner, ain't I.

"I give them what they want."

Graziano finally decided that professional boxing was a better option than going back to prison. But by then he was AWOL from the U.S. Army. Discovered at Stillman's Gym, and placed under the tutelage of the great trainer Whitey Bimstein, he pulled the name Graziano out of the air when he was booked for a fight on an army base, and thought it might be a bit too risky to appear there as himself. The military caught up with him eventually: Graziano was court-martialed, spent a year in custody, and was dishonorably discharged. And then his life turned around.

Boxing has certainly broken many men, left them physically and emotionally shattered. It is economically exploitative in the extreme, the only professional sport that operates entirely according to the cruel dictates of the market. But occasionally, it has also provided salvation—a chance for those who had none, a lifeline for those who otherwise would have wound up in jail, or worse, a place where poor boys with no hope can become rich and famous with their fists. And because it's an unforgiving game, because there are no nights off in the ring, boxing imposes a discipline on its participants, a cycle of training and fighting, that mandates a particular order in lives, like Graziano's, that otherwise would be adrift.

There was nothing in Graziano's past to suggest

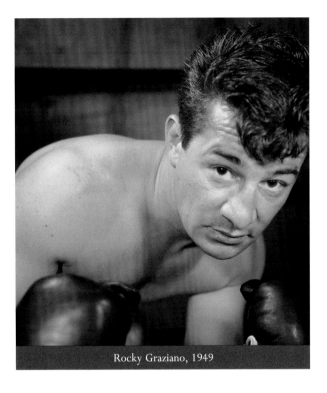
Rocky Graziano, 1949

anything other than a long, downward spiral. Instead, he reinvented himself as a fighter, and the fans loved him, because he so clearly gave his all in the ring. His style was crude but effective, all power punches, precious little defense, with his great right hand the equalizer. The difference, though, between a career as an exciting preliminary attraction and someone who rose to the very top of the sport was Graziano's enormous heart. Understanding how hard life could be, willing to endure pain for a reward, for salvation, he just kept on punching. His first breakthrough came when he savagely knocked out Billy Arnold in three rounds in 1945. Next, there was a win over welterweight contender Al "Bummy" Davis. In two, non-title fights against the reigning welterweight champion Freddie Cochrane, Graziano twice came back when trailing after nine rounds to knock out Cochrane in the tenth. Those matches established him as a solid box-office attraction in New York City, and as the number one contender for Tony Zale's middleweight title.

When they were matched for the first time in 1946 at Yankee Stadium, it was easily the biggest middleweight fight of all time—and the beginning of a trilogy that would define Graziano forever in the public imagination. In total, their three fights lasted just 15 rounds—with seven knockdowns—featuring some of the most

thrilling action in the modern history of the sport. In their first fight, the champion Zale came back from an early knockdown to stop Graziano in the sixth—the first time Graziano had been knocked out in his career. The rematch in 1947 had to be shifted to Chicago Stadium, because Graziano had lost his New York license for failing to report being offered a bribe before a meaningless match that was subsequently cancelled.

Zale-Graziano II is remembered still as perhaps the most savage fight of all time. Even watched in grainy black and white, it is startling in its brutality.

"This was no boxing match," Graziano wrote in his autobiography. *"It was a war and if there wasn't a referee, one of the two of us would have wound up dead. Today I still can't look at the pictures of that Chicago Stadium fight without it hurting me and I get nightmares that I am back in the ring on that hot July night and I am looking out through a red film of blood."*

Graziano's left eyelid was sliced open in the first round. In the ugly, one-sided third round, he was knocked down, then battered around the ring by Zale, all but out on his feet. Seeing the fight now, in an era when much greater efforts are made to protect fighters, it is impossible to believe that the referee didn't step in and stop the fight to save Graziano from further punishment.

"Then I got a second wind, like a breeze of cool air come from heaven and I sucked it deep in my lungs and I felt new

strength tingle down my arms and legs and I yelled that I was going to kill that stinking rat bastard and I tore into him and never stopped," Graziano remembered. "I hit him until both my fists go numb. I hit him until he can't hit back no more, he can't hold his hands up. He sways over and I grab his throat and straighten him back up and hit him. He sways again, and I belt him up straight.

"Somewhere a bell must have rung and I must have gone to my corner to get the blood wiped off but I don't remember.

"I am back out there in the sixth round, and he is helpless and I am ripping him up and tearing him apart. I'm breaking every bone in his body. I'm stoving his head in and punching his guts out. I don't even know any more who I am killing, whether it's a cop or a guard or somebody who ratted on me or Tony Zale or who.

"Suddenly there is a sharp whack across my face. My good eye comes into focus. I am standing in the middle of the ring in the Chicago Stadium and twenty thousand people are going crazy. I have been trying to belt out Jack Healy, who is out there with me, and it is Whitey Bimstein who slapped me and who is saying, 'Rocky! Rocky! Come out of it! Rocky, you're the world champion.' "

After they announced to the crowd the name of the new middleweight champion of the world, Graziano yelled into the microphone: "Hey, Ma—your bad boy done it!"

That was the peak, and really, for Graziano that was the end. In their third fight, this time at Ruppert Stadium in Newark, New Jersey, he was knocked cold by Zale, and lost the title. His managers sent him on the road after that, exploiting his popularity with fans, putting him in a series of easy fights that Graziano won with absolute predictability. But the fire wasn't really there anymore—he was wealthier than he'd ever imagined, married, a father, comfortable. The anger that had driven him in the ring was gone. There would be one last brief moment of glory—he knocked down the great Sugar Ray Robinson before being knocked out himself in his last championship fight—and then a meaningless loss to TV creation Chuck Davey.

"Whatever the poison was inside of me—whatever I picked up from the tar on the streets and roofs, from the oil scum of the East River, from the rats that crawled through the Tombs, from the blood-caked rubber hose in the station house, from the bedbugs of the reform schools and the cans and the guard-houses—whatever it was, I had beat it out of me in the boxing ring. I didn't need to fight anymore."

Instead, he spent the rest of his life playing a character called Rocky Graziano—a tough looking but funny and kind-hearted caricature that debuted on the *Martha Raye* show (Graziano was regularly cast as the comedienne's boyfriend, who she called "Goombah"). In late life, like so many other fighters, he suffered from memory loss. Graziano died in 1990.

Where Graziano was transformed by boxing from angry hood to a lovable, nearly comic character, his old friend from the neighborhood, Jake LaMotta, achieved no such deliverance. The irony is that LaMotta wanted that kind of acceptance so badly. But where Graziano fell into his second career in show business, LaMotta actively tried to make the transition from fighting to acting and stand-up comedy, with limited success. And where Graziano's mythic image is paired forever with Paul Newman's, and the sanitized, Hollywood version of his life, *Some One Up There Likes Me*, LaMotta's will forever be synonymous with Robert DeNiro, with the mean, raw and brilliant world of Martin Scorcese's great film *Raging Bull*, perhaps the least romantic movie biography ever made. "Even Hitler loved his dog," LaMotta once said, when asked about the film version of his life. Scorcese and DeNiro's LaMotta lacked even that single, modest virtue; he was both a great fighter and an angry, pathetic, masochistic, wife-beating creep.

The two middleweight champions, though, were far more similar than the cinematic version of their lives might suggest. Both were born in the Lower East Side Italian ghetto of Manhattan to immigrant parents—though LaMotta left as a child for Philadelphia, and later moved to the Bronx, hence his original ring nickname, the Bronx Bull. Both lived with violent, abusive fathers, and beaten mothers. Both Graziano and LaMotta grew up to be petty thieves. (LaMotta spent much of his young adult life mistakenly believing that he had killed a local bookmaker during a mugging.) Both were renowned street fighters, who fought each other, and also collaborated in crime. Both were sent to a state reform school as teenagers, where they renewed acquaintances, and where both were formally intro-duced to the sport of boxing.

LaMotta, though, at least initially made the trans-formation to straight life earlier. Encouraged by a priest who understood his potential, he went straight from reform school into amateur, and then professional boxing. Like Graziano, he was crowd-pleaser, an action fighter who would take three punches to land one, though in fact, LaMotta's talent was more polished, and his ability to slip away from the full power of punches was underrated.

They never fought each other, though they were signed for a match after Graziano had lost the title, and LaMotta had won it—the fight was called off when Graziano broke his hand in training, and was never rescheduled. In the end, their public images parted ways because of a decision LaMotta made in 1947 that he was never able to live down, at least in the eyes of the American public. Graziano may have been a punk, and he may have gone AWOL from the U.S. Army during World War II and he may have been court-martialed, but as far as anyone knows, he never threw a fight.

LaMotta, by his own admission, under oath, did. In 1947, having built a reputation and ranking as the number one contender for Zale's world title with a series of impressive wins, LaMotta found himself mysteriously shut out of the championship. Even his victory over Sugar Ray Robinson in 1943 in their second fight, Robinson's first loss in 121 bouts as an amateur and professional, wasn't enough to make the match. That was because, as LaMotta would later explain to the Senate Anti-Trust and Monopoly Subcommittee—better known as the Kefauver Committee after the senator who headed it— he had steadfastly refused to hand over his management to someone connected with organized crime. Though the Mob has always existed at least around the fringes of the sport, the period from the late 1940s through the 1950s is regarded as the time when that influence was most overt, through connections to the dominant promotional organization of the era, the International Boxing Club. There were undoubtedly other fixed fights during the period, and other under-the-table deals. None though, was better documented, more notorious. And no other fighter, no other athlete was ever described as LaMotta was by the sports writer Jimmy Cannon: "probably the most detested man of his generation."

What's been lost in the scandal, in the film, in the other black marks on LaMotta's personal life (after boxing, he would serve prison time after being convicted of encouraging a 14-year-old girl into prostitution), is just how talented a fighter he was. No mere brawler would have been able to hand Ray Robinson his first loss as a professional. The other five times they met, LaMotta came out on the losing end—including their final fight, when Robinson stopped him in the 13th round to claim the middleweight title. But to have one

win and a couple of very close losses to the man widely regarded as the greatest pound-for-pound fighter of all time, in his prime, certainly counts for something.

And when, after dumping the fight to Fox with a pathetic, passive performance that absolutely no one believed, he was finally given a title shot against the great French champion Marcel Cerdan, LaMotta rose to the occasion. Cerdan quit on his stool after the ninth round, claiming a shoulder injury, and Jake LaMotta was champion of the world.

"The noise was so loud you couldn't hear yourself think. It sounded like it would lift the roof off the joint, and the aisles were filled with people, and my brother Joey jumped into the ring, and then the seconds, and they threw their arms around me, yelling and screaming and pounding, and the cops piled up there all around the ropes to keep these jokers from climbing in, and the bell kept gonging away for silence till it quieted down so the announcer could get the overhead microphone again:

"Ladies and gentlemen . . . Marcel Cerdan is unable to answer the bell fore the tenth round . . . The winner and new middleweight champion of the world . . . Jake LaMotta!"

That was the peak. There was to have been a rematch with Cerdan, but he was killed in a plane crash while returning to the United States. The planned match-up against Graziano was cancelled and never rescheduled. LaMotta instead lost a non-title fight to Robert Villemain, and looked awful in the process. He then defended the title against Laurent Dauthuille, who had earlier beaten him in a non-title fight, and was far behind on points before scoring a knockout win with 13 seconds left in the 15th round. After that came the last dance with Robinson—"I fought Sugar Ray so much, I wound up with diabetes," LaMotta used to say in his nightclub act—and though he fought on, it was there his boxing career effectively ended.

LaMotta tried to follow Graziano's lead and build a career in show business, first as an actor, and then as a stand-up comedian. But where Graziano made an easy transition to playing a warm, funny version of himself, LaMotta had more difficulty exorcising the demons of his past. In large part, that was because he could never entirely leave the rough world of his childhood behind.

"From as early as I can remember, I didn't want to trust anybody," he acknowledged in *Raging Bull.* *"You trust a guy, pretty soon you find that he's using you to give you a screwing. You trust a dame, pretty soon you find out she's giving you a different kind of screwing. But if you don't trust anybody, or make sure that basically you don't give a good goddamn about*

anybody, you're safe. If a guy sells you down the river, it's your own goddamn fault, you got only yourself to blame. So what if a dame does go off with someone else, there's always plenty more of what she's got. Just don't trust anybody, anywhere, anytime."

With Graziano and LaMotta, Italian-American prizefighters had ascended to near the top of their game. But the greatest title in the sport—the greatest title, arguably, in all of sport—was by definition beyond the reach of a couple of 160-pounders. That last step would instead be taken by an immigrant shoemaker's son whose family story mirrored millions of others, and who would come to embody so many of the best qualities of his people. "There was much of the transplanted Italian peasant in (Rocky) Marciano," Jerre Marigione and Ben Morreale wrote in their book *La Storia*. "Patience, a capacity to absorb punishment, loyalty to friends and relatives, and the ability to survive and endure."

Marciano's father, Perrino Marchegiano, and his wife Pasqualena, came to the United States shortly before the World War I, in the midst of the Italian immigrant wave. They found a home in the industrial northeast—in their case, in Brockton, Massachusetts, a local center of shoe manufacturing where Marchegiano could ply his trade from the Old Country. He had hardly settled in his new home when, in 1917, he joined the United States Army and returned to Europe to fight in World War I. Marchegiano was caught in a German poison gas attack, and came home a semi-invalid, impairing his ability to support his family. The Marchegianos were working poor, living in a cold water clapboard house in Brockton's own Little Italy, when their son Rocco was born in 1923. He was a big, strong boy who was encouraged to fight in informal kids' boxing matches, who built his arm and shoulder muscles stirring the

Checking out Rocky Marciano's bicep, 1953

contents of his grandfather's wine vat. But baseball and especially football were the games that really attracted him: he was paid a few bucks to play center for a semi-pro team, and had a brief tryout as a catcher with a Chicago Cubs' farm team, where an old arm injury cost him any chance of advancing further. When he entered the U.S. Army in 1943, Rocco Marchegiano had never trained as a fighter, or competed in a serious, organized boxing match.

Stationed in England during the war, he had a few, unofficial fights, and then on returning to the United States, while still in the service, he began to compete seriously for the first time as an amateur. In 1945, he went all the way to the finals of the National AAU tournament, where he lost a three-round decision, but knocked his opponent unconscious a few seconds before the final, saving bell. In 1947, Marchegiano quietly had his first pro fight—he used the name Rocky Mack—and was paid $35 for a three-round knockout. He still wasn't convinced that boxing was his future, but on leaving the Army, the best job the high school dropout could find was working on a construction gang for 90 cents an hour. So Marchegiano returned briefly to the amateurs—his one pro fight under an assumed name having apparently gone unnoticed—and then finally turned professional for real in July 1948, under the training of Al Goldman and the management of crafty Al Weill.

Though at the advanced age of 24 he was still a raw novice, though he had no idea of the fine points of boxing (and especially, of defense) four years later the man re-christened Rocky Marciano was the heavy-weight champion of the world. Goldman certainly refined his technique, and helped him to understand the physics of power-punching, but that rapid rise to the top, and the remarkable record Marciano would compile over his career—49 fights, 49 victories, no defeats, a slate unmatched by any heavyweight champion—were the pure product of natural power and heart. Marciano faced a physical disadvantage in most of his fights: at 5-foot-11, 185 pounds, he wasn't a big man for a heavyweight, and his short reach left him forever fighting through punches to get inside. He accepted that punishment without taking a backward step, he fought through his own pain, often through a mask of his own blood, and methodically chopped his opponents down. Such was Marciano's punching power that he could spend the early rounds of a fight battering an opponent's arms and shoulders, knowing that

eventually the guard would drop, and he would be able to move in for the kill.

Most of Marciano's early fights took place close to home, against an undistinguished list of opponents. He knocked out 23 of the first 25, nine of those in the first round. Stepping up in class in 1950, he struggled to a hair thin 10-round, split-decision win over slick Roland LaStarza, a fight in which Marciano's shortcomings against a gifted boxer were exposed. It was a learning experience, and before the end of 1951, he had polished off contenders Rex Layne and Freddie Beshore, before predictably knocking out the aged former champion Joe Louis, in the sad finale of Louis' career. By 1953, Marciano was regarded as the champion in waiting. But when he finally got his shot against Jersey Joe Walcott, to that point the oldest man ever to hold the heavy-weight title, he found himself outboxed, outpunched, and bleeding profusely through 12 rounds. In the 13th, Marciano connected with a perfect short right hand, one of the few clean punches that Walcott absorbed in the entire fight. The old champion slipped to the canvas and was counted out and, for the first time, there was an Italian-American sports hero to nearly match the great DiMaggio.

Marciano's title reign lasted just six fights, strung over three years. He destroyed Walcott in their rematch, then finally gave LaStarza another shot, and stopped him in eleven rounds. In 1954, he beat the former champ Ezzard Charles by unanimous decision in a grueling, bloody bout, and then knocked him out in eight in the rematch. The next year, he knocked out the Englishman Don Cockell in nine rounds, then suffered a scare against the great light heavyweight champion Archie Moore, knocked down and almost out before coming back to stop the challenger in round nine. That was enough for Marciano. Only one other modern heavyweight champion to that point—Gene Tunney—had retired with the belt and stayed retired. Only two—Tunney and James J. Braddock—had ended their careers with victories. And none, from the sport's earliest incarnation in the 18th Century, had retired undefeated. Marciano was, at that moment, widely regarded as the greatest heavyweight of all time, and he had no obvious challenger on the horizon. Through the late 1950s, he resisted overtures to come back and fight the man who succeeded him as champion, Floyd Patterson, claiming that he already had enough money in the bank, and understanding how unfortunate comebacks had altered the legacy of so many great champions past.

Today, defining Marciano's place in the heavyweight pantheon makes for a lively debate. Much has been made about the quality—or the lack thereof—of Marciano's opposition. "Rocky Marciano couldn't carry my jockstrap," Larry Holmes said—unwisely, undiplomatically, but some felt not inaccurately—after he lost the title to Michael Spinks, preventing him from tying Marciano's record of 49 wins without a loss. In a staged "fight" between Marciano and Muhammad Ali, filmed just before Marciano's death in a plane crash in 1969, a computer gave the win to the old champ by knockout, but most fans today couldn't imagine that result—or that Marciano would have stood a chance against modern giants like Lennox Lewis. What the tale of the tape can't measure, though, and what old fight films and records can't convey, is the size of Marciano's heart, the desire born of his hardscrabble background, the indomitable will that none of his contemporaries found a way to stem.

Thanks to Graziano and LaMotta and Marciano, the predominant image of the Italian-American fighter is one of a two-handed, all-out brawler. But there were artists as well. Roland LaStarza, who gave Marciano the most difficult test of his professional life the first time they fought, which later earned him a shot at the title, was a slick-boxing defensive master. He was never quite good enough to win a title, at least in the Marciano era, but he would have been a tough test for any heavyweight in history because of his consummate skill.

Certainly the greatest stylist of his era, and arguably one of the most unique talents in the history of the sport, was the featherweight champion Willie Pep—born Guglielmo Papaleo in 1922 in Middletown, Connecticut. The 5-foot-5 Will o' the Wisp, as Pep was nicknamed, started fighting as an amateur in 1937, where he went 62-3, and won state flyweight and bantamweight championships before turning professional in 1940. Twenty-six years and 242 fights later—

including stints in both the U.S. Army and Navy during World War II, and a six-year retirement—Pep finally called it quits, with an unbelievable record of 230-11-1. Pep won the first 62 fights of his career, and later enjoyed a streak of 73 victories in a row. Those numbers are unmatched in the history of the sport.

He is also famous for once having won a round without throwing a single punch. That came against a southpaw named Jackie Graves in 1946. Before the fight, Pep told a few sportswriters what he planned to do, and called the round beforehand: the third. In those three minutes, he did everything possible in the ring except throw a punch in anger, and still when they checked the scoring afterwards, Pep had carried the round on all three cards.

Willie Pep, 1953

"If Willie had chosen a life of crime, he could have been the most accomplished pickpocket since the Artful Dodger," Red Smith wrote in the *Chicago Sun-Times* in 1955. "He was the only man who ever lived who could lift a sucker's poke while wearing eight-ounce gloves. In action, he's a *marvel*, and in the record books he's a downright hoax."

Though his style, a mixture of feints and a dancer's footwork (and occasionally, of sneaky power) was unique, his story fits right in with those of the other great Italian-American fighters of his time. "My parents were from the other side, as we Italians say," Pep wrote in one of his memoirs, *Friday's Heroes*. "My old man was from Syracuse in Sicily, and he couldn't read or write in English. He was a construction worker and things were pretty tough during the Depression."

Pep was a little guy who learned early that he couldn't face bigger guys head on and survive. Instead, he perfected the art of self-defense—but unlike so many slick boxers who do their best to avoid contact, he would also become a fan favorite, a star of the sport's early years on television.

The greatest moments of Pep's career came in a four-fight series against his nemesis, Sandy Saddler. The featherweight bouts were remembered both for the excitement they generated and for producing some of the dirtiest prizefighting ever to take place under the Marquess of Queensberry's code.

They met for the first time in 1948, with Pep on that 73-fight winning streak, a year after he'd survived a plane crash that looked like it might end his career. Along the way, he'd won the world title, lifting the belt from Chalky Wright in 1942 without ever once hurting the champ. Then Pep had completed his war service, and fought mostly non-title fights against all comers in what seemed like every state in the Union before coming face to face with a fighter who couldn't be fooled. Saddler had a long reach and refused to be bamboozled by Pep's unusual style. "I started out feinting as usual to get a feeling for him and he ignored it completely and waded in and caught me cold," Pep remembered. "I was completely surprised. He knocked me down twice before the fourth round and then he stopped me."

The inevitable rematch came in 1949, one of the first big fights to be widely viewed through the new medium of television, and a classic by any definition: in 1981, *Ring Magazine* named it one of the top ten bouts of all time. This time, Pep built an early lead over Saddler, and then found a way to hang on. "I was thinking and jabbing well and keeping him away with good right hands and then tying him up. I had him off balance most of the time but he was desperate now and kept swinging with those long arms of his trying to end it all with one punch. But I had him mostly off balance, only a few of his shots were really hard. He tried desperately but he couldn't put me down. I had my title back."

Nineteen months later came the disappointing third installment of the series: Pep hurt his shoulder in the fight, giving Saddler the title back. That set the stage for the finale, a fight widely regarded as one of the dirtiest of all time. "It was a real brawl, like the old time bare knuckle days, with wrestling, heeling, eye gouging, tripping, thumbing—you name it," Pep remembered. "A lot of writers thought that we should have both been thrown out." The referee let the shenanigans continue, and Saddler finally emerged victorious in the ninth round. There ended Pep's career on the world stage (aside from a knockout loss to Hogan "Kid" Bassey in 1958) but it would be another 15 years before he'd finally say goodbye, permanently, to the ring.

The Golden Era of Italian-American fighters really ends with the career of Carmen Basilio, the son of an onion farmer who was born in Canastota, New York, now the home of the International Boxing Hall of Fame, in 1927. His rough, tough, aggressive style and willingness to endure pain hearkened back to the glory days of Graziano and LaMotta. By the time he got a shot at Kid Gavilan's world welterweight title in 1953, Basilio was five years into his career, and already had 10 losses and five draws on his record. That's the mark of a working fighter who wasn't overly protected by promoters, and in Basilio's case, the mark of someone who was getting better, who was learning his trade. By 1955, when his next shot came along, Basilio was ready, knocking out Tony DeMarco in Syracuse for the world title. He lost the belt to Johnny Saxton on a controversial decision in 1956, then won it back later the same year with a knockout.

Basilio then decided to move up in weight from the welterweight to the 160-pound middleweight division, and challenge the reigning world champion, Sugar Ray Robinson. His victory in September 1957 at Yankee Stadium, a 15-round decision despite a terribly cut left eye, was the peak of his career.

Robinson beat Basilio badly in the rematch the next year, closing his left eye early in the fight and applying a systematic beating. That began the boxer's familiar spiral downward. Basilio was knocked out twice by Gene Fullmer in 1959 and 1960, challenging for the middleweight crown, and finally in April 1961, lost a decision to the reigning champ Paul Pender.

The dawn of the 1960s signaled the beginning of radical changes to the boxing business. The Kefauver Committee would expose the sport's links to organized crime, severely tarnishing its image. What had been a glut of televised boxing on the networks would erode the sport at the local, club level. The ring death of Benny "Kid" Paret in his fight with Emile Griffith in 1962, with a national television audience looking on, made many question the morality of the sport. When television viewers began to tire of the product, and even the *Friday Night Fights* finally drew to a close, little that resembled the boxing business of the '30s, '40s and '50s was left intact.

And the talent supply was drying up as well. Those waves upon waves of poor kids looking for a break, willing to take the hard, hard road for a chance at fame and glory, had been reduced to a trickle. There wouldn't be any more Canzoneris or LaMottas or Grazianos or Marcianos coming down the line.

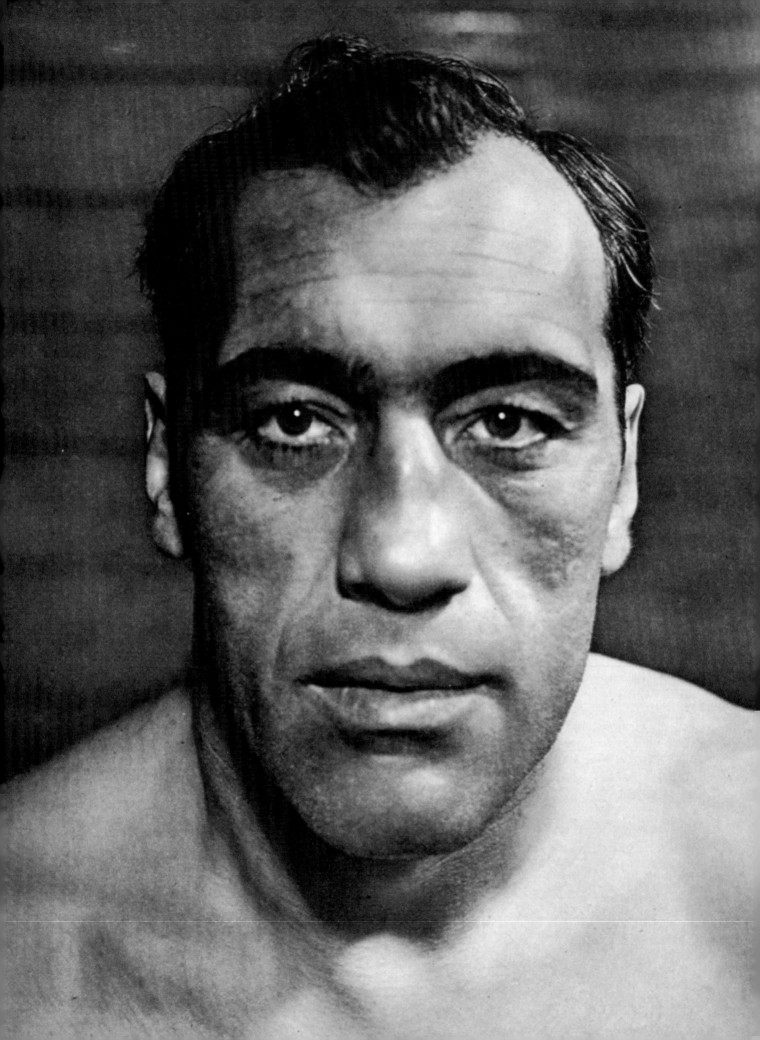

THE EARLY DAYS

THE STRANGE
CASE OF CARNERA

BY JACK SHER

FROM *SPORT*, FEBRUARY 1948

The title of this tale is pitifully inadequate. No single phrase or sentence can possibly capsule into a few words the incredible career of that giant-sized figure, part hoax and part hero, who stumbled blindly into the world sport scene in the Year of Our Lord, 1928, and who, curiously enough, is still part of that scene.

The story of Primo Carnera, the uncommon, outlandish giant of the 20th Century, will be a difficult one for future generations to believe. Even now, well over a decade since the most brutal episodes took place, a reporter delving into Primo's past needs a strong stomach not to be sickened by the facts he uncovers—the filth, the greed, the depravity. This is not, in essence, a sport story, but the tale of a gargantuan, simple, and yes, courageous man who was preyed upon by all the known varieties of human lice.

Those in the fight game who have read Budd Schulberg's best-seller, *The Harder They Fall*, recognize it as a thinly disguised novel of Carnera's life. It etches a sharp and sordid picture of conditions in Cauliflower Alley in the '30s. It throws a harsh light on the thugs who, through violence and skullduggery, made this helpless giant the heavyweight champion of the world. It shows how they then cheated, befouled, and degraded him, and left him at the last a battered, paralyzed wreck, friendless and without hope.

Everyone connected with the ring knows the shameful details. No one knows them better than Primo. "That book, yes, I have read it," he said, nodding his huge head. "It is all true." Then he spread his tremendous, ham-like hands. "But I wish he had come to me. I would tell him so much more."

Carnera could. For, although the novel tells what happened to Carnera on the American scene, although it exposes the gangsters, gamblers, politicians, bankers, bums, fighters, trainers, and petty crooks who infected his career, it does not tell the complete story. It could not tell it completely, because the story has not yet ended. It is still being lived by Primo Carnera. And it will not end, as the novel did, on a note of despair. The story, in its entirety, is not only one of man's inhumanity to man, but one that reveals the dignity of the human spirit, and shows the courage of a pitiful creature who refused to stay down.

Nobody in the fight game likes to talk about Carnera's ring career. Even those who were in no way responsible for it give their information grudgingly. They say it would be best if it were forgotten. The only one who will talk about it honestly, completely, is Primo Carnera himself, the one man who has nothing to hide, the one man who has done nothing of which to be ashamed. Of the dozens of people, the decent and the dirty, who contributed to this document, none gave so much or so freely and fairly as Carnera. At times the simple dignity of his words gave you a choked-up feeling in the throat. His lack of bitterness, where bitterness should have been, created an anger in the listener. Primo Carnera told his story from the beginning. It is the only way it should be told. It is the only way the events which took place can be wholly understood, seen in their proper light against the confusing, chaotic, shifting background of treachery

Left: Primo Carnera, 1948

Primo Carnera demonstrating his stance for Amelia Earhart aboard the Isle de France, 1932

and rapaciousness. It is impossible to understand the forces that act upon a man, unless you know what he is, what conditioned him, how he became a thing that could be shaped, twisted, deceived, and tortured.

This is the story, from birth to now.

A birth is a most commonplace occurrence on this spinning earth, but it is always a thing of wonder. No man is a replica of another, nor will he ever be repeated. And so, perhaps, the wonder of birth is that into the world comes not only flesh and blood, another to take its place among the billions of shapes, but something new and different.

The child, born on October 26th, 1906, in the village of Sequals, in the North of Italy, weighed, at birth, 22 pounds. It was a most uncommon weight. But the mother, Giovanna, was not aware of that when she spoke to her husband, a stone-cutter named Sante Carnera, saying, "Since he is our first child, I shall call him Primo." The word Primo in Italian means first, and the out-sized baby with the strange name was to be the first in the world in many ways—first and set apart from others, looked upon as a freak because of his tremendous proportions.

Carnera's parents were of average weight and height, as were the two brothers who followed him into the world. The family was extremely poor. They lived in a hut-like structure in the foothills of the towering Alps. Sequals is a place of some 3,000 people and Primo's father, Sante, eked out his existence in the manner of most men of the village, fashioning intricate mosaics in stone. The artistry of the craftsmen of Sequals, though poorly paid, earned them a reputation throughout Europe.

Primo and his brothers were taught stone-cutting almost as soon as they could stand. The brothers are still practicing that time-honored craft, one in Newark, New Jersey, the other in London. It would have been much happier for Primo if he had been allowed to stay at it. But the extraordinary man, the giant, has little chance of living an ordinary life. He is singled out, gawked at, prodded, exhibited, and forced along paths not of his choosing.

This pattern began early for the boy who was as large as a man, the mountainous Primo. His parents went to Germany to seek work, and the six-year-old boy was left with his grandmother. At eight, he was man-sized and apprenticed to a cabinet-maker to learn that trade. He became quite skillful at this work,

attended school spasmodically, and proved to be of average intelligence.

"My childhood was miserable, very miserable." It is an adjective Primo uses quite often. "We were always hungry. I worked very hard, extremely hard. At school I was not happy, I was too large to be accepted. Miserable. It was miserable." He smiled. "I did not take part in the sports then. I was too large and clumsy. It was a bad time for me, this childhood time."

This is the way Carnera spoke. Anyone who sits down with him for extended periods of time, who gets him over his initial shyness, is usually amazed by his manner of speech. Once you become accustomed to the booming, deep-toned voice, it is easy to follow what he is saying. His vocabulary is extensive, his choice of words intelligent.

During the time Primo was touring tank-towns in America, belting over set-ups, the sportswriters had a field day ridiculing this guileless, friendly foreign giant. Stories were circulated that he was as stupid as he was large. At the time, his unfamiliarity with the English language was offered as proof of his mental backwardness.

"What do you think of Hollywood?" a reporter was supposed to have asked him. "I knock him out in the second round," Primo was reported as saying. It is possible that he did say it. An American, not familiar with the Italian language, might easily have made just as ridiculous an answer. It is a fact that Primo learned English very rapidly and, besides his native tongue, he also speaks French and Spanish fluently. The endless stories told to humiliate him did not go unnoticed, as many believed. They hurt, but Carnera took them without complaining, never losing his temper, always conducting himself with dignity.

Harry Markson, the press agent for the Twentieth Century Sporting Club, who sees more than the muscular surface of fighters, said: "Primo was a nice guy and a very sensitive guy. I remember," he went on, "how he came in to Jimmy Johnston's office one day. He took Murray Lewin the sportswriter aside and said, 'Please, Mr. Lewin, call me anything you want, but do not call me Satchel Feet any more.' He was very sweet about it and there was something pathetic about it, too."

In talking about his childhood, Carnera did not try to play on sympathy, or exaggerate it. It would be hard to exaggerate. His parents, who had gone to Germany, were interned when World War I broke out, and were placed in a forced labor battalion.

They returned to Italy in 1918, when Primo was 11 years old. The war had had the usual devastating effect, and for a year the family was close to starvation. Carnera's father finally set off for Cairo, where he had the promise of a job. When he began sending money back home, Primo decided it was time to get out on his own.

He was now 12 years old. He was around six feet tall. He looked like a man and people took him for a man. Carnera said that he had a miserable childhood. Actually, he had no childhood at all. At 12, almost penniless, he hoboed into France. For the next five years, the boy with the giant frame worked at everything he could to keep alive.

"I worked very hard," he said, "so hard I was often weak and food was scarce. I did laborer's work. I carry cement bags, lay bricks. I worked for a time at my father's profession, the stone-cutting. I did all sorts of work. I could not go back. What for? There was nothing at home for me. The years were bad. I was an innocent," he smiled. "How do you say it, an ingenuous child?"

At 17, the ingenuous child stood 6-foot-5, had a 50-inch chest, arms and legs like tree trunks. He weighed 250 pounds and was stalking through the streets of Paris hungry, with no job prospect in sight. In desperation, he appealed to the manager of a traveling circus. Here is a body, the boy said; do what you will with it, put it up for people to stare at, make jokes about, exhibit it for the world to see, do this to me, but food is necessary if I am to stay alive—and I wish to live.

The circus man did not need a sharp eye to see money in the form of the huge boy. He was the first to wring profits from the giant from Sequals, to play upon his freakishness of size, to realize that a trick nature had played could bring francs into his pocket. It was the circus that started Primo on the career that would eventually rob him of pride and self respect and place his body on the rack.

The curious, jostling throngs that crowded around the booth where Primo was on display were treated to all sorts of wild theories, mystical explanations of Carnera's size. It was not discovered until many years later, long after Primo had been in the ring, that he was afflicted by acromegaly, a tropic disease that makes giants.

Primo hated the circus life. "It was no good," he said. "It is no life to live. I feel foolish and I am very lonely most of the time. I am paid very little, which I do not realize at the time, and the work is hard and the conditions bad. I get very homesick many times, when I am with the circus, more than when I was a laborer."

Under a variety of names, Carnera was billed first as a freak, then as a strong man, finally as a wrestler. He could, at 17, snatch a 350-pound weight into the air and hold it over his head. He often wrestled as many as 10 or 12 men a day, taking on all comers. In the beginning he was a poor wrestler, but it was good business for the circus when one of the town locals could best the giant.

When circus business was slow, the manager would stage a special wrestling match. He'd paste posters around the town announcing that "The Terrible Giovanni, Champion of Spain," would be seen in an exhibition match. As Giovanni, Primo would perform against experienced mat men. He often made miserable showings, but his size pleased the crowd. He stayed with the circus three years and, toward the end, actually became a fairly competent wrestler.

Eighteen years later, in 1946, it was the things he learned about wrestling in that small-time circus that were to save him, bring him out of obscurity, give him back the self respect and the fortune that had been denied him as a fighter.

The circus, after traveling all over Europe, wound up in Paris in 1928 and disbanded. A second-rate heavyweight pug named Paul Journee, walking through a park one day, came upon Primo sprawled disconsolately on a bench. Journee marveled at his size. He sat down and began to talk to him. It was this simple action that started Primo Carnera on his fabulous ring career. Here began the blood, sweat, frame and fix that, in six short years, was to see him crowned heavyweight champion of the world.

"If I had not been broke that day," Carnera said, "if I had not been so miserable, I do not think I would have gone with Journee to talk to this fight manager, Leon See."

The fight game has had few characters of such clashing temperament as Leon See. He was a strange mixture of a man—at once sentimental and shrewd, tough and learned, a diminutive, kindly charlatan, who had earned a degree at Oxford, been a fighter, promoter, gambler, and referee, a hanger-out in the subterranean dives of Paris, rich one day and poor the next. From the first time he laid eyes on the shuffling giant, the tiny, energetic man had an enormous affection for him.

Carnera has nothing bad to say about Leon See. "He

Carnera rushing to meet his destiny after felling Jack Sharkey, 1933

was shrewd, you have no idea how shrewd," Primo said, "but we were friends. He was always my friend, even though he did wrong many times. His son is here in America now. I do not know where Leon is now. I talked to his son. It is strange," he went on, "we meet here in the lobby of the hotel and we talk about old times. He is a fine boy."

The bustling Frenchman, who enjoyed posing for pictures standing under Carnera's outstretched arms, was delighted with his new charge. He believed him to be the strongest man in the world, and promptly arranged a fight for him. It was the first of many sad mistakes. The 21-year-old Primo knew nothing about boxing. He had over-developed muscles, and was slow and clumsy. Yet, within two weeks after See signed him, he was matched against Leon Sebilo, a Parisian pug of doubtful reputation. Even See, who loved Da Preem, could not resist the opportunity of making quick money.

Primo kayoed Sebilo in two rounds. Whether the fight was on the level, only See knows, and he has never told. From the moment he took Carnera into his heart, and his training camp, Leon See became a frenzied, driven man. It did not take him long to discover Primo's weakness, which was the fact that a slight tap on the chin by a man 100 pounds lighter would send Carnera reeling. Carnera had courage. He could take blows to the body all day long, but the giant had a glass jaw and

the wily Leon was quick to find that out.

The little manager worked long and frantically to teach Primo the rudiments of defense. At the same time, undoubtedly motivated by a desire to cash in, he tossed the huge Italian into the ring at every opportunity, rushing him through 13 fights in less than a year. Primo won most of them by quick knockouts, fighting in Paris, Milan, Leipzig, and Berlin.

Whether these waltzes were on the level is highly debatable, but See was wise enough never to allow his big boy to think he was anything but invincible. Some of the fights might have been square, because some of the so-called fighters who went up against Carnera, couldn't have lasted a round with any American tank-town bum. Names like Luigi Ruggirello, Isles Epifanio, Constant Barrick, Ernst Roseman, Jack Humbeek, Marcel Nilles, to name a few, were patted over by Carnera in quick order, or as cynical French and English boxing writers put it, "to order."

The, reputation of Leon See was far from spotless. His connections among the lower depths of Parisian life were solid and extensive. In fact, in those days, there was something of an international underworld linked to the fight game. It was not long before a coterie of mobsters from New York, U.S.A., took a trip abroad to have a look-see at this large-type character who might make them a fast buck. In less than a year's time, the unknowing Primo was being "cut into pieces," parts of him being sold to sharpsters who frequented the shadowy sections of America.

"It is well known," a prominent booker of fights and wrestling matches told me, "that Leon See sold over 100 percent of Carnera before they ever left France."

The noted sportswriter, Paul Gallico, was the first to uncover the machinations of the underworld types who were preparing to use Primo to bamboozle the public into parting with their money. Some six months after Primo started fighting, Gallico happened to wander into a smoky fight club in Paris, mildly curious about the word-of-mouth publicity that had been passing around about the giant. The place was called Salle Wagram and Primo was matched against a 174-pound powderpuff puncher named Moise Bouquillon.

One of the first mobsters to buy into Primo was also there that night. He did a slow burn when he heard about the presence of Mr. Gallico. Later he said to the sportswriter, "Boy, was that a lousy break for us that you come walking into Salle Wagram that night and see that the big guy can't punch! Just that night you hadda be there. We could have got away with a lot more if you don't walk in there and write stories about how he can't punch."

Primo won that fight, taking a 10-round decision. He went on pushing down the pushovers. The only fighter of any reputation he fought before coming to America was Young Stribling. Strib was no world-beater, but he was a fair enough boy with his dukes. The fights, one in London and one in Paris, both ended in fouls. Carnera won the first, Stribling took the second after being struck a low blow. The English scribes were rather indelicate in their descriptions of the contest, implying that both fights were as rehearsed as a Shakespearean play.

Through all of this, Carnera was kept completely in the dark. This may be hard to believe, but Leon See was with him night and day, censoring what he read and thought. Leon's magic tongue worked triple-time, his words convincing Primo that his strength was as the strength of 10, and his punch devastating. Leon even arranged to have Gene Tunney, then visiting abroad, pose for newsreel pictures with Primo, "Europe's challenger for the title." As sincerely as Leon liked Primo, he couldn't ever pass up an angle. "Tunney was very friendly to me," Primo said. "I was just a novice then and he was very nice: I feel he was pulling for me. He said he hoped he would see me in America soon and wished me luck."

If ever a man worked hard and sincerely to become a fighter, it was Primo Carnera. The huge, simple, gullible giant believed with all his heart and soul that he had the makings of a great champion. He believed no man alive could hurt him. He believed that his punch was dynamite and that he had mastered the rudiments of *la box*, as Leon See called it.

"I dreamed of going to America," he said. "It was with me all the time, this wish, this dream. I work very hard and I was sure that I would someday soon be the champion of the world."

Those last few days in Paris, preparing to sail forth on his conquest of the new land, were very happy ones for Primo. The 23-year-old mountain-sized boy was led across the ocean to his eventual triumphs and cruel slaughter in the spirit of the knight on the white charger. Gene Tunney just happened to be down on the dock when the boat, groaning under the weight of the huge Italian, docked. Again he wished Primo luck. The big fellow was all smiles, filled with sweetness and love toward his fellowmen and his newly chosen profession.

It is no credit to us, as Americans, that we can be duped and ballyhooed into believing anything. The very people, even the sportswise, who later sneered and smeared the giant Carnera for his simple-mindedness, for allowing himself to be so blatantly tricked and cheated, were among those who created the legend of his fistic prowess. It was late in 1929, the stock market had crashed, the world was confused and churning, when Carnera came to the United States. He was immediately hailed as "a mighty killer," a "Neanderthal type with a tremendous punch," "a new, giant menace on the American boxing scene."

The lying, shameless, vicious men who pulled a gunny-sack over the eyes of the giant and the public did a masterful job of it. They were quite a collection of tawdry and dangerous individuals. There were Broadway Bill Duffy and Owney Madden, both of whom had spent time behind bars for anti-social acts of a violent nature. There were, in minor capacities, such cute characters as Mad Dog Vincent Coll (later rubbed out), Big Frenchy DeMange, Boo Boo Hoff, and other parties of odious repute. It is still considered not altogether healthy for anyone to poke his nose too deeply into some of the "deals" these charming chaps cooked up while interested in cashing in on Carnera.

The fraud started in Madison Square Garden on the

night of January 24th, 1930, when Primo Carnera was sent into the ring against a built-up, fourth-rate heavy named Big Boy Peterson. The evil faces crowding around Carnera's corner at ringside were a bit anxious about the affair, knowing that if the spectators failed to swallow the hoax, their plans would be knocked into a cocked hat. Not having anything to offer in the way of a fight, they had wisely decided to give the onlookers a "show." It was some show.

Anyone who has ever seen Primo Carnera cannot help but be amazed by his awesome size. The powerful effect of that tremendous figure of a man, as he lumbers toward a ring, is enough to send shudders through even the most hardened fight fan who revels in bloody slaughter. Primo Carnera, coming down the aisle that night, looked like nothing human. This was a deliberate piece of staging. Followed by the tiny Leon See and other carefully picked midget-sized men, Carnera did not wear the usual fighter's bathrobe. Instead, he was dressed in a hideous green vest, a weird, visor-type cap, and black trunks on which was embroidered the head of a wild boar.

The humorous mutterings of the press, which had implied before the fight that it was to be a phony, were disregarded and forgotten by those who witnessed the spectacle in the Garden that night. The massive figure of Carnera, the lumbering tower of might and muscle that pawed at Peterson, somehow pleased the collected gathering. The men behind the scenes knew that they were "in" and could put the show on the road.

It was a fight that deserves little attention. Peterson managed to get his jaw in front of a glove containing Primo's pumpkin-sized hand and fell to the floor. He was counted out in the first round, undoubtedly resting comfortably on the canvas and contemplating the steaks he would be eating for the next several months. Back in the dressing room, Monsieur See was jubilantly bouncing about the room telling one and all about his fighter's glorious future. Primo sat on the table, surrounded by the tough guys, his large, kindly brown eyes dreamy and filled with wonder. That night he proudly sent a cablegram to his parents in Sequals, telling of his triumph.

"It was the first cable ever received by anyone in my town," he said. "It was very impressive."

The gang bundled up their giant and began a cross-country tour, moving from state to state and leaving behind them a trail of fixed fights, intimidated and coerced pugs and managers. Working with gangsters and gamblers, and using threats and violence, they cold-bloodedly staged one outrageous swindle after another. In one year, Carnera watched 22 victims go down under his playful pushes, more frightened by what they saw outside the ring than by the big, helpless man they faced.

In Chicago, the Illinois Athletic Commission proved somewhat more determined than the New York hierarchy. After Primo cuffed Elziar Rioux to the canvas in 47 seconds of the first round, the yowls of the press were so long and loud that the fighter's purse was held up. But the gang pulled strings and Primo was given the green light, Rioux taking the blame for a poor showing.

What Rioux knew was that it was better to do poorly and live than to tag Carnera and die. The men behind the giant were intent on cleaning up and that they did, gathering unto themselves over $700,000 on the tour. If an opponent refused to take the dive, to "talk business," he was shoved about a little by the muscle-men. If that didn't work, he often found himself, just before a fight, staring into the tiny, round opening of a .38 caliber weapon. Does it sound unbelievable? It happens to be the absolute truth.

In Philadelphia, a Negro heavyweight named Ace Clark walloped hell out of Carnera through the first five rounds. Just before the bell called him out for the sixth, a small, icy-faced man slid up against the ropes near his corner and said, "Look down here, Ace." The fighter looked, saw something gleaming and metallic beneath a coat, and performed an extremely believable dive in the next 30 seconds. A Newark pug was visited in his dressing room and treated right roughly when word reached the "crowd" that he might doublecross them and put up a fight. He too melted in the first round.

Out in Oakland, California, a large, classy puncher named Bombo Chevalier was having a lot of fun belting the amazed Primo around the ring. He might have ended the string of faked victories then and there, but midway through the fight he suddenly discovered something had gone wrong with his eyes. One of his own handlers had been bought, during the course of the fight, and had rubbed his orbs with some sort of inflammatory substance. That incident smelled so foully that an investigation followed, but the gang weaseled out of it and went on to the next swindle.

Some of the fighters Carnera bowled over were not bums, but they were all made to see the light. George Godfrey, a large, fast-moving, and skillful puncher, had

Carnera goes down under Max Baer's furious assault in second round, 1934

a terrible time losing to Primo. It was almost impossible for this boy to fight badly enough for the huge Italian even to hit him! He finally solved the dilemma by fouling Primo in the fifth round.

After the fight, several suspicious reporters came into Godfrey's dressing room and began to ask him how hard Primo could hit. "Hit?" the large Negro grinned, "That fellow couldn't hurt my baby sister." The reporters began to laugh and then into the room walked several of the gentlefolk who were handling Carnera. Godfrey's face changed. "That white boy sure has some punch," Big George said, quickly, "I thought the house had fallen on me a couple of times there."

It was that raw. Long before Primo Carnera became champion of the world, the Duffy crowd had given the heave-ho to Leon See. As sharp as the little Frenchman was, even he could not stomach the conniving that was part and parcel of the Carnera buildup. He could visualize the end. He knew that the "fix" could not go on forever, that someone would tag the vulnerable chin of the giant and the inevitable decline would begin.

Leon did not always play square with Primo in the matter of money. But he did try to teach him to defend himself, and he did his best to keep the big fellow from suffering physical harm. After he was ousted by the gang, See took to writing a syndicated column,

exposing the fights Carnera had. He stated outright that on the few occasions when opponents could not be threatened by guns and brass knuckles, then Primo lost.

While Leon See was at Primo's side, life was bearable for Carnera. "He was the one friend I had in America," Primo said, "He did not always do right. He was reckless and foolish in handling my money, but he was my friend."

Carnera saw very little of the juicy sums collected for the 80-odd fights he participated in before winning the title. In California, Leon took a chunk of Carnera's dough and invested it in real estate, buying two homes. In Oklahoma, he sunk a pot full of cash in an oil well that was dry as dust.

"I didn't know what he was doing," Carnera said, shaking his head. "The banks notified me that the homes he had bought for me were no longer mine. I did not pay something or other. The mortgage, that was it. Leon bought many things for me, but I believe he was cheated."

While Leon was with him, Primo at least had someone with whom he could talk, someone to kill the hours of loneliness. See treated him like a son, babied him, became maudlin and sentimental over the giant he knew was going to be taken away from him by the wolves. Carnera idolized the little manager. If he went out to a movie alone at night, he would scrawl a note to Leon telling him at what time he would return. Then he would rush back to the hotel to tell him all about the picture he had seen.

Shortly after Leon See was forced out of the picture, the dazed and unhappy giant was asked how he felt a manager should treat a fighter. By that time, Primo knew (or suspected) that all was not well, that he was not quite as invincible as he had been led to believe. "He who goes slow, goes surely," he said. "He who wants to travel far, is kind to his horse."

It was after the fight against Jack Sharkey on October 12th, 1931, that Primo Carnera knew that he had been tricked and deceived, that he was not the one-punch killer that he had been led to believe since the days in Paris. It was a terrible, humiliating, cruel fact for him to face. It was much harder to take than the beating the Boston gob gave him.

No one who saw that fight in New York will ever forget the look of pain and wonder on big Primo's face as he went down under Sharkey's blow. It was a sharp left hook to the jaw and it dumped Carnera to the canvas with a thud that could be heard in Times Square. He sat there dumbfounded, his eyes glazed. He finally got up on his feet, but when he saw the scowling Sharkey advancing on him, he dropped to his knees, a pitiful, abject, and stunned creature.

Those who crucified him as being cowardly, who taunted him with boos and derisive cries, did not know what was going on inside the huge man. As later fights proved, he was courageous beyond belief. He could take merciless punishment. That night, it was not Sharkey from whom he was cowering. He was hiding from himself, from the realization that he was nothing but a gigantic fraud in the hands of hoodlums, that he had nothing, neither a punch nor a defense.

Sharkey almost lost that fight. When Primo sank to his knees without being hit, the sailor started to jump out of the ring, thinking the fight was finished. It would have disqualified him, but his handlers managed to restrain him. He went on to pound, jab, poke, and cut up the giant for nine more rounds. Primo took it, then tottered down the aisle, his head hanging.

After that fight, Carnera wanted to quit. He was broke, lonely, sick at heart. "It was too late, then," he said. "They had me by the throat. They would not let me quit. Every fight was to be my last one, but it never was. I had no friends in the game, nobody I could talk to

even, or ask advice. Everyone cared for the money, that's all. I knew it, and this is a very lonely thing."

The gang had an answer for everything. After he beat King Levinsky and Vittorio Campolo, they hustled Carnera out of the country until the stench of the upset would blow over. They pushed him into fights in London, Paris, Berlin, Milan. There was quick and easy money to be made in these places. Carnera's string of knockouts in America could be made to look very impressive and the Sharkey thing could always be explained as a fluke.

"After Leon left," Carnera revealed, "they did not even care whether I trained or not. I did the best I could by myself. They did not care whether I was in condition, or what I did. They just made the matches and took the money and that was all."

Eight months in Europe and then the gang led Carnera back to the States again, arranged another tour, and lined up a bevy of such hand-me-down old-timers as Les Kennedy, Jose Santa, K.O. Christner, Jack Spence, Jim Merriott and even Big Boy Peterson again! By this time, even the public was wise to the set-ups, so the mob used a convenient ruse to ride Carnera into the fight for the title against Jack Sharkey.

On February 10th, 1933, Primo kayoed Ernie Schaaf in the 13th round of a fight at Madison Square Garden. Shortly after the fight, Schaaf died. The ugly fact is that Ernie Schaaf was a sick man before he entered the ring that night. A few months before, in Chicago, he had been terribly battered by Max Baer. He should have been in a hospital bed that night instead of a ring. It was not Primo's ineffectual jolts that killed him, but a lax Boxing Commission.

The death of Ernie Schaaf was just the sort of thing that the men who had the giant in chains could use to boot him into a fight for the heavyweight title. It was just the gimmick they needed. They passed the word around that Primo's mighty punch was responsible for Schaaf's demise.

The incident still has painful memories for Carnera. "It was not me who did this to him," he said. "Everyone knows now that it was not my fault. I would not do such a thing. When it happened I felt sick. I told everyone that it was not my fault."

But the mob made use of the tragic accident—their boy was a mighty man again—and they signed him to meet Jack Sharkey for the title on June 29th, 1933, at the Long Island Garden Bowl.

The Boxing Commission closed their eyes and allowed the fight to take place. There were some very queer strings being pulled in high political circles. It was not the first time that top, national figures had been reached to pull the mob behind Carnera out of the fire. The zippy, dark-haired, fast-talking Jimmy Johnston had intervened a few months before to square Carnera with the New York Athletic Commission, going all the way up the ladder to make a pitch to Jim Farley.

The behind-the-scenes knavery was so obvious that when you study the reports of that heavyweight title fight, you sense the shame of the newsmen who were sent to cover it. Few of them came right out and called it a fake and a swindle, but all of them either felt it or knew it. Nat Fleischer, the most renowned ring expert in the country, stated in plain English that he couldn't understand how Primo won. When I talked to him about it recently, he said, "Sharkey should have knocked him out. Carnera won that fight with an invisible punch. I don't hold Carnera responsible though," he went on. "He was built up by set-ups. He was a nice guy and never meant anyone any harm. He just wasn't made to be a fighter."

And Gallico, who had been keeping close tabs on Carnera's ring activities ever since that night in Paris, was another who announced in clear and ringing words that nothing would ever convince him that it was an honest prizefight, contested on its merits. Paul was still feeling hot under the collar about it as late as 1938, when he wrote his *Farewell to Sport*.

"Sharkey's reputation and the reputation of Fat John Buckley, his manager, were both bad," Gallico wrote. "Both had been involved in some curious ring encounters. The reputation of the Carnera entourage by the time the Sharkey fight had come along in 1933, was notorious, and the training camps of both gladiators were simply festering with mobsters and tough guys. Duffy, Madden, etc., were spread out all over Carnera's training quarters at Dr. Bier's Health Farm at Pompton Lakes, New Jersey. A traveling chapter of Detroit's famous Purple Gang hung out at Gus Wilson's for a while during Sharkey's rehearsals. Part of their business there was to muscle in on the concession of the fight pictures."

Primo climbed through the ropes that night looking very unlike a confident, keyed-up challenger rarin' to slug his way to the heavyweight championship. He looked miserable, ill-at-ease, soggy, and listless. Sharkey

scowled convincingly from his corner, but the beefy John Buckley seemed uncomfortable, as though someone had been following him all day.

For five weary rounds, Sharkey scored point after point, bouncing light left hooks off the huge target that floundered around in front of him. Jack was always an in-and-outer, but at his worst, he should have been able to put Primo away in four heats. He had, some 18 months before, hardly worked up a sweat belting Carnera unmercifully for 15 rounds. On this June night, however, his punches had about as much kick in them as a wet sock swung by a ten-year-old. In the sixth round, after a mild exchange of blows, Sharkey went down as though he had been hit by Jack Dempsey.

He was counted out. Manager Buckley, making pantomimic gestures, rushed to Carnera's corner and demanded to inspect Primo's gloves, implying that they must have contained horseshoes or other such implements of iron. The amazed Carnera stood help-lessly in his corner while this farce was being enacted. The entire scene was fragrant with an unmentionable type of odor.

It must have been a sweet night for the gamblers. The odds were in favor of Sharkey, 5-4. Everyone cleaned up. By this time, the vultures who had been cleaning the big bird through 80 fights had cut them-selves in on grosses that amounted to over $2-million. And Carnera? The day after he won the Championship of the World, he had just $360 to his name.

A month after the fight, the bewildered giant filed a bankruptcy suit. He was also being hauled into the courts on a breach of promise case involving a waitress, who claimed the champ had promised her a ring and a trip down the aisle. Primo escaped to Italy for a few months of peace and attempted, among his own people in the tiny village of Sequals, to collect his wits.

In Rome, the Fascisti hailed the giant as they would a conquering hero returning from ancient wars. A match was arranged against Paulino Uzcudun, a tired old warhorse who submitted to Primo's clumsy clouts for 15 rounds. Mussolini stuck his jaw out an inch or so further, pounded his chest, dressed Carnera in military uniform, and sent pictures to the far corners of the earth showing Primo executing the Fascist salute.

It is not to Carnera's credit that he played ball with the Fascist hoods. But he was politically unaware and, by this time, conditioned to take orders from anyone who held the whip-hand. The element he had been dealing

Referee Art Donovan steps between Carnera and Baer to declare Baer's victory by TKO in the 11th round, 1934

with in America had not been a whit more scrupulous or less brutal than the dictatorship to which he returned.

Primo did disobey Mussolini once. It is not very well known, but the massive man had an inordinate love for automobile racing. He would cram his huge frame into a tiny racing car and, with utter fearlessness, give it the gun. The belligerent Benito forbade him to race, but Primo, on the sly, entered the annual 1,000-mile Italian auto race. He didn't have the moola for a car of his own,

so he drove for the Alfa Romeo auto company and placed third.

"When the boss heard, about it," Primo said, smiling, "he called me to Rome to see him and he gave me hell."

When Carnera returned from Italy to America, he brought with him a little Italian banker named Luigi Soresi. How Soresi was able to chisel into a "cut" on Carnera, why the mob allowed him a share of their boy, is something that Primo, to this day, does not know. Soresi conned Carnera into believing that he would protect him. The way it turned out, he was even more ruthless than the others.

Some of the statements Primo gave out to the press in those days were lulus. In Miami, preparing for a defense of the title against Tommy Loughran, in 1934, Carnera told reporters: "I don't pay any attention to money and such things. I am crazy about boxing. The rest I don't give a damn about!"

And the shifty-eyed, sharply dressed group who hovered around him managed to keep a straight face. They were having the time of their lives in Miami nightclubs, spending C notes in huge quantities, tossing lavish parties, and carrying on in a style that was imitative of Capone in his heyday. They paid absolutely no attention to their fighter's training or condition. They set him up, in miserable quarters on one of the back-lots of the town and never even bothered to see him. Primo tried to get in shape for a week or so, then gave up and sat brooding, lonely and filled with despair. He came into the ring against Loughran some 20 pounds overweight.

Carnera is proud of the fact that he won a decision against Loughran. In a sense, he has a right to be. It was one of the few fights he is certain was on the level. Actually, the Carnera crowd knew that they were taking few chances sending their boy in against Tommy Loughran. They knew Loughran was completely honest and could not be fixed, but he was an aging, washed-up fighter. He was 32 years old, had been fighting for 15 years, and had always been a powder-puff puncher. Most of Tommy's reputation had been made as a clever light-heavyweight. Carnera outweighed him that night by a mere 105 pounds!

Actually, the gang desperately needed one honest fight to hold up in front of the public, no matter how uneven the match. Writers like Quentin Reynolds were putting the finger on them in national magazines, stating, "Carnera is directed by very rough characters, who hover about his corner and sometimes the corner of his opponent." The boys did not consider this a very nice way to talk about them. It hurt them right where they lived, in their pocketbooks.

So Primo leaned against Tommy Loughran for 15 rounds in Miami. He was little better as a boxer than when he had started, but Loughran was unable to hurt him, or he Loughran, and he was awarded the decision.

That same year, such whirlwind pugs as Walter Neusel, Johnny Risko, and Jose Caratoli also punched out a decision over the tired Tommy. At that, Loughran managed to whack Primo a couple of times in such a manner as to make his legs wobble. Carnera landed on Tommy's button time after time with right hand uppercuts that had more steam than the one that floored Sharkey and won him a title. Loughran barely blinked.

The characters behind Carnera might have gone on forever lining their pockets with championship gates, but law and order finally stepped in and took charge. The Roosevelt Administration had outlawed the speakeasies, and G-Men were putting the chase on Public Enemies. Mister Duffy took a trip to the jailhouse for evasion of income tax. Others in the select circle who had a piece of Carnera did not consider it quite safe to be seen in daylight and things, in Runyonesque lingo, had become very deplorable, indeed. Max Baer was clamoring for a crack at the title. The public was fed up with poor Primo, and the unhappy giant was badly in need of money. He agreed to meet Baer.

The thing that took place on the night of June 14th, 1934, in Madison Square Garden Bowl, was not a fair fight either. It was a slaughter, an indecent and pitiful thing to watch. Max Baer could hit. He made a bloody mess of the monstrous, defenseless, reeling ex-circus freak and strong man.

"I never liked Carnera before," a rival fight manager told me. "To me, he was nothing but a big, stupid bum. But, by God, I loved and pitied the big, blind ox that night, because I never seen so much guts."

Baer knocked Carnera down three times in the first round. He gave him a worse beating than Joe Louis later gave Max, but the giant got up and kept on taking it. At the end of the 10th frame, his face a grotesque, bruised, and bloody mask, after being knocked down in every round for a total of 13 times, Primo was still in there taking it. Baer never did beat him into unconsciousness. It would have been much more humane if he had been able to do so. The referee stopped the fight in the 11th, to the relief of everyone but Carnera. Primo was too numbed by that time to feel much of anything.

Did the gang relinquish their hold on Carnera then? They did not. There was still the possibility of wringing more blood-money out of the peaceful Italian. There were still sadistic fans who would shell out to see what they considered a monstrosity being hammered into a pulp by a mere, ordinary man. Soresi and company patched Carnera up and carted him off to South America to paw some pesos out of our unsuspecting friends south of the border. For six months Primo wallowed around rings in Argentina, Uruguay and Brazil, earning his backers still more dough.

Citizen Duffy was released from prison, and one of his first acts was to bring Primo back from South America. The boys had arranged an interesting and remunerative little fracas for their sorely battered fighter. They were throwing him into the same ring with a harmless young heavyweight out of Detroit, a certain Joe Louis. After all, the Bomber couldn't kill the big lug, although it is doubtful if that would have made the slightest difference to the men in Primo's corner on that memorable night.

In the first few seconds of the fight, one of Joe's jolts completely smashed in Carnera's mouth. Who among those who saw the fight and knew the story behind Carnera will ever forget the sight of Duffy and the boys shouting angrily into the ears of the bloody giant, shoving him out round after round to what looked like certain death?

The time was 2:32 in the sixth round when the ghastly affair was halted. What a wretched thing was dragged from the ring that night, what a mess of a man! Thus had fate dealt with the uncommon offspring of Giovanna Carnera, who had once said, softly, "Since he is our first child, I shall call him Primo."

Here on a night in June, 1935, was the apparent end of a career that had started because a miserable, giant-boy of 12 had wandered hungrily into France in search of any work that would keep him alive, and had once listened to the words of an old prizefighter who had found him on a park bench.

If ever a man should have been through with the ring, it was Primo Carnera after the Louis debacle. But the jackals who still had him in tow never asked themselves such a humane question as, "How much is enough?" His name would still draw the suckers.

Carnera kept fighting through 1935 and into 1936. A third-rate Negro heavyweight named Leroy Haynes finally administered the coup de grace. He kayoed Carnera in three rounds at Philadelphia. The fight drew a fairly good crowd, so it was repeated just 11 days later in Brooklyn. Haynes hammered, cut, and chopped Primo for nine rounds, beating him so fiercely that one of the giant's legs became paralyzed and he could no

longer stand up to take his punishment. He was hustled from the ring to a hospital. His tormentors then released him.

Listen to Carnera's words. "I lay in the hospital bed for five months. My whole left side was paralyzed. I was in much pain. During all this time, not one of them came to see me. Nobody came to see me. I had no friend in all the world."

When Primo was released from the hospital, he was still limping. He hobbled up a gangplank and took a boat back to Europe. In Paris he stopped long enough to pick up a meager purse in a fight against someone called Tony Duneglio, which he lost in 10 rounds.

A week before Christmas in 1937, on a snowy night in Budapest, Primo Carnera, the former heavyweight champion of the world, was knocked out in two rounds by an unknown Hungarian heavyweight named Joseph Zupan. It was his last fight. The New York newspapers devoted a couple of lines to it.

The world of sport had written the giant off the books. It looked as though that was the way it was going to be.

Primo went back to Sequals, to the village where he was born. His parents had died, but the people of the small town still had great affection for their giant, and he for them. He built himself a house, lived simply, devoted himself to farming. He was married, in 1939, to a girl who worked in the post office in a nearby town.

After they were married, Primo and Pina planned to settle down to a peaceful life in Sequals. They had two children, a handsome, sensitive-faced boy named Umberto, now seven, and a girl, Joanna Maria, now five years old.

But Carnera's peace was short-lived. The war began, and the Nazis moved into Italy. Primo and Pina buried most of their household furnishings in the ground. The Germans put Carnera to work with a pick and shovel, at 20 cents a day. On Carnera's back is a deep, indented scar, fully five inches long, a wound suffered at the hands of the Germans during this time. At night he would scavenge around the countryside, trying to find food for his children.

One day a plane came in low over Primo's house in Sequals and the family hustled to the cellar in terror. When it had gone, Primo went out into the yard and found a huge box had been dropped. "I approach it very carefully," he said. "I poked it with a stick. I thought it might blow up. It was from you—from the Americans.

It was food, all kinds, and canned milk and cigarettes and beer and almost everything. I knew then that it would soon be over."

The GI's finally trudged into Sequals. They shook hands with Primo, stayed in his house, took pictures of him, talked about fights and America. When the war was over, Carnera was broke, but he was no longer a lonely or hopeless man. The world had hit him with everything, but he was still standing upright and thinking of the future. There came offers from the United States. He was not completely forgotten.

At random, Primo chose the offer of a smalltime Los Angeles promoter named Harry Harris. He wrote, agreeing to come to America and work for him, providing Harris would send him enough money to make the trip. Harris called the Olympic Auditorium, owned by the matchmakers Babe McCoy, Cal Eaton, and Johnny Doyle. He got McCoy on the telephone and said, "I've got Primo Carnera. Are you interested?"

"Yeah?" There was a pause. "Where is he?"

"In Italy," Harris said. "Would you put up the money to bring him over and get him started?"

McCoy talked it over with his partners. They decided they could use Primo as a referee at fights and wrestling matches, signed a deal with Harris, and sent Primo the money to come to Los Angeles. On the 1st of July, 1946, 10 years after he had left the United States a crippled and broken man, Primo was back again. He was 40 years old, but even under the careful scrutiny of the matchmakers of the Olympic, the giant looked as powerful and in as good condition as he had been before the sluggers had gone to work on him. They took him to a gym and watched, in amazement, as he wrestled playfully but skillfully with some of their grunt-and-groan boys.

"What the hell," they said, in effect, "we don't have

Joe Louis stands patiently above a bloodied Carnera after one of three sixth-round knockdowns, 1935

to use this guy as a ref. He wrestles better than most of the beefs we're booking."

A month after Primo's arrival, in August 1946, he was matched against Tommy O'Toole in the main event at the Olympic Auditorium in L.A. McCoy and Harris had not the slightest idea how Carnera would fare as a draw or as a grappler. The fact that he had looked good in a gym could mean nothing.

The night of the match, the only cheerful, confident figure was the big Preem himself. Wrestling was something he knew about. He felt he was built for it, fashioned by nature for and would not look freakish at it, the way he had always looked with those big, padded mittens on his fists.

The giant was right. The match was a sell-out. Primo won handily against the burly O'Toole. The crowd loved him. This was the beginning of one of the most amazing and ironic comebacks the annals of sport. In one year's time, Primo Carnera, who fell harder than any prizefighter in ring history, has climbed to the very top of the wrestling business. From the Hudson Bay Territory to New Orleans, from New York to California, the Italian giant is now the biggest drawing card in professional wrestling. The grosses on Primo's matches have gone over the million-dollar mark.

Those who come to see Carnera wrestle generally come back for his return engagements. They may come, the first time, because they expect to see a freak, or to stare at a man who was a former heavyweight boxing champion. But they discover that Carnera has more to offer than the memory of a pitiful past.

It is a wonderful sight to see Primo Carnera striding toward the ring, whether you see him in an impressive auditorium in a large city, or in a smelly, smoky, barn like structure in some of the tank towns where wrestling is staged. Once the enormous red-and-blue bathrobe is unfurled, the huge body is still an awesome thing to behold. But now, in contrast to the flabby opponents he faces, you are struck by the beautiful proportions of the giant. The skyscraper height, the massive shoulders and chest and legs, the powerful arms send a thrill rather than a shudder through the crowds who watch him.

But what is most impressive of all is the new-found dignity of the huge man. You know he understands what it is all about now. You know he feels he has found where he belongs, a place and a profession where he is no longer regarded as a freak.

In the seamy by-ways and smoke-filled auditoriums of wrestling, where a turbaned "Hindu," a self-styled "Champion of Greece," a bearded "Tyrolean Terror" or "Man Mountain" is commonplace, Carnera gives you the feeling that he is playing his new role as straight as his curious profession will allow.

He studiously refrains from the elaborate play-acting, the contortions, the grunts and groans and burps that are as standard with most grapplers as are the mannerisms of the burlesque "stripper."

In the ring, Primo wears a self-deprecating smile that seems to say to his fans: "You and I know what this is all about. But what the hell—you're having fun, and so am I, so what's the difference?"

Against Tony Galento one night in Newark, New Jersey, Carnera put on a performance that would have been ludicrous in lesser hands. Towering over his opponent, he looked as though he could pick him up with one hand and throw him into Market Street.

Instead, he crouched and stalked and clenched his huge-fingered hands and went through an elaborate ritual of holds and spills and falls that at times looked almost convincing.

The crowd booed without restraint, but the jeers were friendly: "Don't worry, Primo! If you lose this one, you'll win next week in Pittsburgh!" The "contest" ended in a draw. The crowd applauded and whistled and stamped and yelled, but their faces were smiling, and they seemed well pleased. They had got what they paid for—a spectacle—a monster of a man rolling on the mat like a big, good-natured bear in a sideshow.

As a private citizen, Carnera is looked upon today as a decent and honorable man.

When you walk with him through the lobby of a New York hotel, people turn and wave at him. They call "Hi, Primo!" They are not just struck by his size; in their faces are the friendliness and respect that he has needed for so many years. For Primo is one of God's most warm and likable creatures, a man who has a deep and genuine affection for people, and who needs the same treatment in return.

With the exception of one month of vacation, Carnera has been wrestling four to six nights a week for the past year and half. He has traveled over a million miles by air and wrestled some 300 opponents. He's lost just one match—in Montreal, when a large, rough boy named Yvon Robert punched him in the jaw. Primo whacked him back, and Yvon went down and out. Carnera was disqualified.

"Carnera is a wonderful trouper," Al Mayer, who books him in the East, said. "He always shows up for his matches. He never disappoints a promoter. The fans love him."

Mayer opened the books and pointed to some of the black figures that indicated how Primo had been drawing. In four appearances in New York, the gross was over $100,000; in Montreal, $64,000 for three dates; in Cleveland, Los Angeles, and Philadelphia, his single-shot dates gathered $18,000 in each city; in Detroit, $17,000 for a night; in Chicago, $16,000; and in Miami $12,000. And so it goes.

And Primo now gets his check every week, on the line. He gets a large and fair percentage of the take, and he handles the money himself. He has bought himself a $30,000 home in the fancy Westwood section of Los Angeles. It is clear this time, no mortgages.

The men now connected with Carnera are a different breed of cat from his associates in pugilism. His personal manager and closest companion is Joe (Toots) Mondt, a former heavyweight wrestling champion. The bulky, genial Toots has the face of a benign Santa Claus. His reputation in wrestling circles is spotless and his devotion for Primo is completely and wholly genuine.

"I've been traveling with Primo for over a year now," Toots smiled, "and I'll tell you that anyone who can't get along with him must have a hole in his head. He's become one of the best friends I've ever had in this world. He is a clean-living guy, an honest man, and I couldn't ask for anyone better to handle."

Mondt gave up a flourishing business as a promoter around Washington and Oregon to handle Primo. Toots was so impressed by Carnera, who appeared in a match Mondt promoted, that he accepted Babe McCoy's offer to train and handle Primo. Toots is making quite a performer out of Da Preem. And Mondt is the man who can do it. He has met them all—Stanley Zybysko, John Friedberg, Jim Londos, Big Munn, and the renowned Strangler Lewis.

"When I took Primo on a year ago," Mondt said, "I never dreamed he would do so well. After all, he was 40 years old. But age doesn't seem to mean anything in Primo's case. He seems to get better as he goes along." In an easy-going, effortless, and un-phony way, Toots Mondt can sit all day long and spin yarns about his friend, Primo Carnera. He likes to tell you about the giant's tiny appetite; how Primo, who actually eats very

little, is always embarrassed by the huge portions he is served everywhere he goes.

"We have a terrible time at parties and dinners," Mondt chuckled. "The host or hostess always gets upset because Primo does not eat much. They think he does not like their food and they never believe it when I tell them that the only time he eats a fairly average meal is at breakfast."

"It is true," Primo chimed in, smiling, "I do not eat much."

It is constantly amazing to Mondt how easily Carnera makes friends and how many of them he now has. As a fighter, he was undoubtedly the loneliest figure in ring history. As a wrestler, Primo is constantly surrounded by admirers and friends. He gets innumerable invitations to parties and affairs in every city in which he appears.

"He likes people," Mondt explained. "I never knew a man who liked to be among people so much. I can't understand it when he tells me he was once afraid of them and lonely. Now, he is happiest when he is among people. In towns where he has not appeared before, he will strike up friendships with people in the lobby of the hotel, even with strangers he meets on the street, and invite them to our room.

"Milwaukee!" Mondt exclaimed, throwing up his hands. "He is always after me to get a match for him in Milwaukee. There are two men in the contracting business there, Andre and Bruno Bertin. Primo knew them in Sequals. They were boyhood friends of his. He gets into Milwaukee and he practically lives with those Bertin guys and their families. It is hard to get him out of the town."

Even the fighters who slugged Carnera insensible are now included among his friends. He is like a man trying to embrace, with a bear-like hug, the whole world. Max Baer, who took the heavyweight championship away from him, who pounded him so unmercifully, is now counted as one of his pals. In Detroit a few months ago, Baer bought front row seats to watch Primo wrestle Joe Dusek.

"O ho!" Primo bellowed happily, "Max was very excited that night. When Dusek took a slug at me with fists, Max jumped up and screamed at him and took off his coat and was going to get into the ring to help me."

Carnera looked wise. "Maybe it was a joke, maybe he was only clowning, but it shows he is for me, he likes me. Afterwards, he invited me to the nightclub where he is playing and I am in the show with him and we make jokes together. I like Max Baer. He's a good guy."

And old Jack Sharkey, the surly gob, another of the sluggers who pasted Primo to the deck in their first fight, has now benefited by the giant's affection. Sharkey was hired to referee one of Primo's matches, a tangle with Jules Strongbow. It was a very different night, financially, from the one when they met for the second time and the Boston gob got the heavy dough in losing the title while Primo wound up with a pocketful of stones. For the wrestling match, Carnera got 40 per cent of an $18,500 gate, while Sharkey got $300 for overseeing Primo's victory.

Everything has changed for the giant from Sequals. The odds which were once so heavily stacked against him have switched. A world that had no place for him has suddenly opened up what must seem like limitless horizons. At this writing, Primo has left for Mexico, to be re-admitted to the United States under a quota and be allowed to take out the first papers that will eventually make him an American citizen.

Pina, Umberto, and Joanna Maria Carnera are on their way across the ocean, hoping to live permanently in their father's big house in Westwood, California. "This," Carnera said, almost reverently, "will make everything completely happy for me."

But Toots Mondt has still another dream for the giant. He wants to make Primo Carnera the Heavyweight Wrestling Champion of the World. This is what he's been shooting at during all the months he has been touring with Carnera back and forth across the country.

The business of being proclaimed the World's Champion Wrestler, as Toots Mondt explained it, is a complicated set-up. There are about half a dozen men, in as many states and subject to as many rules, who claim to be the Champion of the World. Toots wants Carnera to settle it once and for all, by beating all of them. Primo will therefore have to whip Frank Sexton, who some recognize as the champion. He will have to beat Louie Thesz, the St. Louis boy who holds the National Wrestling Association title. He will also have to pin to the mat such heavies as Bill Longston, Whipper Watson of Toronto, Jim Londos, Orville Brown, Bronko Nagurski, and Roughie Silverstein, former Big Ten Champion from Illinois.

"It is my opinion that Primo can beat every one of these men," Toots said, with a completely straight face. "If the officials are fair and honest, Primo will win all these matches. I mean to see that they are honest," Toots concluded, "because I intend that Primo Carnera shall be the next Heavyweight Wrestling Champion of the World."

If this happens, Carnera will be the only man in sport history who has held both titles, the championship of the world in boxing and wrestling. How much or how little the grappling title means, it is still quite a prospect for the once hopeless and crippled, bruised and life-battered giant who hobbled up a gangplank in 1936 headed for oblivion.

Not even those idealistic weavers of words who created ancient tales designed solely to point out a moral could improve the true-life ending of this story. For what has happened to the ruthless, shameless, cruel, and greedy handful of men who tricked and humiliated and bled the giant? Almost to a man, life has repaid them. Three of them are now penniless, two are in ill health, and one frequents the grimy alleys of crime, fearful for his life.

A few months ago, in a large Eastern city, one of them provided us with a thing that is rare in this modern world, a moment of poetic justice. One of these men who had held the giant in bondage for so many years, one of the elite of the once high-riding mob, approached Primo Carnera after a wrestling match and, in our own graceless, work-a-day language, he put the bite on him.

"He looked very bad," Primo said, "but I could not find it in myself to give him money. Instead, I bought him a meal."

EPILOGUE

Five years after buying a meal for his former tormentor, Primo Carnera realized his dream of becoming a United States citizen. He continued to wrestle through the late 1950s—winning the 'world championship'—and also found a third career as a bit player in several movies, including ON THE WATERFRONT *with Marlon Brando. Although he was not part of the cast, Carnera's story was the thinly-veiled subject of the 1956 movie* THE HARDER THEY FALL—*most notable for it being Humphrey Bogart's last film. A weakness for alcohol began to take its toll on Carnera in the 1960s and, in 1967, following a collapse brought on by diabetes and cirrhosis of the liver, he returned to his hometown of Sequals. The gentle giant passed away there on June 29, 1967 at the age of 60.*

TONY CANZONERI: ONE FOR THE BOOK

BY FRANK GRAHAM

FROM *SPORT*, FEBRUARY 1950

In the time just before and just after World War I, the bantamweight champion was a shoeshine boy named Pete Herman out of New Orleans, but Pete went blind—first in one eye and then in the other. Pete's manager was Sammy Goldman, a thin, quiet little man, who had come out of New Orleans with him. The bond was strong between them and when they no longer could operate together because of Pete's blindness, and Pete had gone home to open a restaurant while Sammy remained in New York, Pete said: "Maybe there will be another fighter as good as me around New Orleans some day. If there is, I'll send him to you."

A couple of years later, Sammy got a wire from Pete which read: "Am sending a kid to you. He will be a great fighter some day."

I think that's one for the book because the kid's name was Tony Canzoneri and he became one of the greatest fighters who ever lived, although Pete, naturally, never had seen him but had only heard about him and talked to him. Pete's friends had told him what promise the kid had shown as an amateur and Pete had satisfied himself by talking to the kid that here was one who would work hard and make sacrifices to advance himself. He knew that here was no knuckle-headed kid who would pay no attention to Goldman, but a serious kid with a dream of becoming a champion one day—the same dream Pete had had when he was a kid and had listened to Goldman and never questioned his judgment but did all the things Goldman had asked him to do.

Canzoneri, like Herman before him, had run the streets of the old French quarter of New Orleans and fought in its alleys and backyards and in the back rooms of some of its saloons. He had fought for the sheer fun of it or for small coins tossed to him by the sports. He was, at this time, not yet 16 years old and he wore a cap and short pants when, shortly after his arrival, Goldman brought him around to see me, saying: "This is the kid I was telling you about. The one Pete sent me."

Tony hadn't got through grammar school but had no regrets on that score, since as long as he could read the sports pages and count up to 10, he felt he had received all the education he needed. But Sammy had different ideas on the subject, and so the little Canzoneri went on reluctant feet to school every day and took his boxing lessons after school. When Goldman thought the boy was ready, he put him in the amateurs. This was his introduction to formal boxing—with strictly enforced rules, a ring, bright lights, and a crowd.

"He never was an amateur at heart," Goldman once said of him—and he wasn't thinking of the dimes, quarters, and half dollars Tony had reaped in New Orleans. "He thought and acted like a pro from the beginning. Oh, I guess he got a kick out of the medals he won. But he was in the amateurs only because I had put him there. He would have liked it much better if I had tossed him right into Madison Square Garden."

His first big year was 1926, when he fought 24 times and attracted a lot of attention. In '27, he beat the renowned Johnny Dundee, and the following year he took the featherweight title from Benny Bass—only to lose it to Andre Routis of France. No great puncher, he was a little desperado in the ring and nobody could knock him out. In 1930, he won the lightweight title from Al

Canzoneri gearing up for his title bout with Kid Chocolate, 1931

Singer on a one-round kayo, and in '31 he added the junior welterweight title by beating Jackie (Kid) Berg.

Remember 1930 . . . 1931? They were bad years. Most of the world, having shared in the gold rush that had begun about 1923, had gone broke in the crash of 1929. But Tony, who had got his when the rush was on, still was getting it. People still managed to find money to put on the line whenever he fought, and he was loaded with it. He was enjoying prosperity but it had no softening effect on him. He still trained diligently, fought as often as he could, and still was a little terror

in the ring. But between times he was having fun with his money. He had cars, clothes, jewelry, and a farm just up from Newburgh near the Hudson River. He supported countless relatives and friends. He was the easiest touch on Broadway and there is no telling how many thousands of dollars he gave away.

In 1932, he lost the junior welterweight championship to Johnny Jadick, tried to get it back, and failed. But that didn't bother him. That title didn't mean anything. Only the lightweight championship meant something. He still went fighting around the country, making money, giving it away, losing some of it on the horses. Then, in 1933, he lost the lightweight championship to Barney Ross in Chicago. The limit in Chicago was 10 rounds and Tony wasn't at all discouraged. Ross was young and dazzling fast but Tony figured he would take him back in New York and, over the more accepted championship route of 15 rounds, wear him down. But it didn't pan out that way. When they fought in New York, Ross won again.

Right there you could draw a line across Tony's record and say, "From there on, no matter how desperately he fought against it, the finish was in sight for him."

Yet there were surprising turns along that downward path. For one thing, he regained the lightweight championship when Ross, having won the welterweight title, gave it up, and Tony established himself as the best of the others, then defended his recaptured laurels against Lou Ambers. For another, he made one of his greatest fights on a May night in 1936 in Madison Square Garden against Jimmy McLarnin.

In many ways, I think, it was his greatest, for he had slowed down by now. He was punching harder than ever before because, being slower, he was getting better leverage. He was a little muffin-faced guy now, his nose

Canzoneri drilling Jimmy McLarnin, 1936

flattened and the scar tissue thick on his eye brows. Countless punches had thickened his lips and put a curl in his ears and, that May night, he was in there with one of the hardest hitters, pound for pound, in the ring.

McLarnin, like Canzoneri, had started as a bantamweight and fought his way up through the classes and had been the welterweight champion. He and Ross had had three fights, McLarnin losing the title in the first fight, winning it back in the second, and losing it for keeps in the third. But that third fight had been a little less than a year before and McLarnin, who always had taken excellent care of himself and seldom had been really abused in the ring, still was a tough and extremely dangerous foe.

For almost three minutes, Canzoneri kept out of range of Jimmy's right hand. Then, in a flash, it happened. McLarnin's right thudded against Tony's chin. His knees sagged. His eyes were blank. McLarnin moved in to finish him. He held and, as McLarnin ripped free of him, backed away. McLarnin was stalking him when the bell rang. Tony followed a tortuous course back to his corner as Goldman leaped through the ropes to meet him and guide him to his chair. Goldman, working over him to get him ready for the next round, said:

"What did I tell you? Didn't I tell you not to let him hit you with his right hand? What are you going to do now?"

Tony's head had cleared. He looked up at Goldman and grinned. "What am I going to do?" he said. "What is he going to do when I hit him with my right hand?"

The bell . . . and McLarnin, in his eagerness to wind up the fight in a hurry, was halfway across the ring as Tony moved out of his corner. McLarnin stabbed with his left and threw a right hand at him. Canzoneri blocked the punch, moved around, hooked with his left—and then smashed McLarnin on the chin with his right. Jimmy was back on his heels. Canzoneri leaped at him and smashed him again. McLarnin held, wrestled, broke, dodged, kept moving until the fog cleared from his brain. Then he began to punch back, but Canzoneri punched with him.

They whirled through eight more rounds. They fought as two kids would on a street corner, throwing aside everything they had learned in their years in the ring, intent only on knocking each other out. Neither could manage it but, at the end of the 10th round, the decision went to Canzoneri. With that punch at the start of the second round, he had changed the course of the fight. After that, hard pressed though he had been at times, he had been in command.

He had won . . . but he had hit his last peak. He would fight well after that, but he never would make a great fight again nor win one of importance. He lost the lightweight championship to Ambers. He fought McLarnin again and McLarnin beat him.

He should have stopped there but he didn't. A newspaperman who was—and still is—his friend, said to him one day: "I hear you want to fight again."

"Yes," he said.

"If you do," the newspaperman said, "I will put the blast on you. I will say that if you haven't got sense enough to quit while you still have your health, your marbles, and your money, the Boxing Commission should make you quit."

"I wish you wouldn't," Tony said. "I'm going to fight Ambers again."

"Well, I will," the newspaperman said. "By the way, what's the matter with Goldman?"

"Nothing. Why?"

"Does he want you to fight again?"

"No. He wants me to quit, too."

"All right," the newspaperman said. "I promise you that if you make the match, I'll blast the hell out of you."

Tony shook his head and walked away.

When the Ambers match was announced, the newspaperman fulfilled his promise. Canzoneri, he wrote, had been a great fighter but now he was through and if he didn't know it, he must have it impressed upon him by a refusal on the part of the commission to approve this contemplated fight with Ambers. What, the newspaperman asked, did the guy want? He had money. He had a restaurant on 49th Street, an apartment in New York, a farm near Newburgh where he raised fruit and vegetables and had a hotel for the summer vacationists. Most important, he had his health and a clear head. Did he want to wind up broke, walking on his heels and hearing funny noises? What good would his money be to him then?

Nobody paid any attention to the piece. Canzoneri went into training for the fight. One day the newspaperman met Goldman.

"You're right," Goldman said, "but there is nothing you or I can do about it."

"What does he want to fight for?" the newspaperman asked.

"Money," Goldman said.

"Money? I thought he had all he needed."

Goldman shook his head.

"But," the newspaperman said, "how about his restaurant? How about his farm? How about . . ."

"Who eats in his restaurant?" Sammy asked. "Nobody except his friends, whose checks he picks up. What does he raise on his farm? Fruits and vegetables. Who eats them? Friends and relatives. Who stays at his summer hotel? Friends who don't pay. He bets on the horses. As soon as they hear he has a bet on them, they get tired. I don't care what he tries, he can get rid of money faster than anybody I ever saw. And how can he make money? Only by fighting. I hope this Ambers fight will be his last. But I don't know. I can't promise you . . . only . . ."

"What?" the newspaperman asked.

"Don't knock him again," Sammy said. "Please. He knows you're right but he can't help himself."

Ambers beat him badly. That was in May of 1937. He didn't fight again until October of 1938. Then Eddie Zivic beat him in Scranton. He was back where he had started. Fighting in the small clubs. Fighting nobodies. Scranton . . . Jersey City . . . Camden . . . Denver . . . San Francisco . . . Poughkeepsie . . . Long Branch. Winning most of his fights . . . but losing to Eddie Brink. Losing to Harris Blake.

They were bringing a new kid along. Al Davis, out of Brownsville. A tough kid who could belt out anybody he could hit. They were looking for a name to put in his record. A name that would mean something. So they matched him with Canzoneri for Madison Square Garden. Tony's friends stayed away from that one. They knew what would happen and they didn't want to see it. Davis belted him out in the third round.

Funny about things like that. Davis, by belting him out, did more for him than all his friends put together, for Tony never fought again.

EPILOGUE

When he left the fight game after the Al Davis knockout, Tony Canzoneri seemed to have a lot going for him. There was his 144-acre spread in upstate New York, with a producing orchard and the horses and goats he raised. There was, for a while, a clothing store, a song-and-dance nightclub act and a part interest in Tony Canzoneri's Paddock Bar and Grill, on Broadway near 50th in New York. Over time, though, everything came unraveled. On the evening of December 10, 1959, Canzoneri was found dead by a maid in a $21-a-week room in the Hotel Bryant in New York, just a few blocks from the bar that still bore his name. At 51, he had been a permanent resident of the hotel for a year and had no other assets. The medical examiner attributed his death to a heart attack and believed he had been dead two days when his body was found.

CHAPTER THREE

GUGLIELMO PAPALEO

THE RETURN
OF WILLIE PEP

BY BARNEY NAGLER

FROM SPORT, MAY 1949

Once again the world feather-weight champion, the kid had come home to Hartford. And now, in the State House of Connecticut, the Governor and his chief deputy, legislators and officials, ladies and gentlemen, had gathered in the executive chamber to pay homage to the boxer.

Willie Pep fidgeted. Nervously he fingered a button on his double-breasted gray jacket. And, of all the thoughts that might have been his at the moment, the strangest of all went through his mind. "Good thing," he thought, "I bought this suit in St. Louis or I'd have to wear an old one."

Yet, this was proper reflection, for the symbolism was deep indeed. Here was Willie Pep being honored in the inner sanctum of the officialdom of the Nutmeg State, where only short years before he had stood up in a police court and paid a $25 fine as a common gambler.

Here was the son of an Italian immigrant being honored by the sovereign State of Connecticut, where only weeks before the cynical had whispered that he had lost the featherweight championship to Sandy Saddler in a fixed fight.

The Governor, Chester Bowles, who had once been concerned with fixed prices rather than fixed fights, spoke to Willie as the crowd in the chamber pressed forward. "We are proud of you," the Governor said. "I listened to the fight on the radio and it was wonderful. I've got a little present for you."

The Governor extended a statuette of an athlete holding aloft a victory wreath. Willie took it in his hand and read the inscription:

"Willie Pep—a great world's champion. From his fellow citizens of Connecticut. State Capital, February 15, 1949."

Willie's eyes filled, but nobody could see the tears because he wore dark glasses to hide the wounds he had sustained in his title-retrieving bout with Saddler five days before. He fumbled for words. Then he said, "Thanks an awful lot, Governor."

There was applause and then a woman pressed forward. She was Mrs. Winifred McDonald, Connecticut's Secretary of State. "I just want to touch you," she told Pep. "I want to go home tonight and tell everyone that this hand touched Willie Pep."

Another member of the Governor's official family, also a woman, screamed at Willie. "I want to shake your hand," she cried. "I think you're wonderful. I won $10 betting on you Friday night." Pep had recovered his composure. "Let's split it," he proposed.

It was an unbelievable scene. A mere prizefighter, a great one at 126 pounds, but a much maligned lad, had taken over a State capital for a day. And it was not enough for some merely to see him. They had to touch him as well to assure themselves a rightful niche in the cult of hero-worship. Not seeing it, it becomes difficult to believe. But it happened, and in happening it became the climax of a story.

It's strange indeed that all this should have happened in Hartford, a city which by now should be accustomed to world featherweight champions. Two before Willie Pep, the great Louis (Kid) Kaplan and Bat Battalino, came out of that section, and yet the citizens of Connecticut will not accept Pep's situation as commonplace.

Left: Willie Pep, 1953

They shouldn't, either. Nothing that ever happens to Pep can be called ordinary. He served in two branches of the Armed Forces, the Army and the Navy, during the war, whereas one was enough for most mortals. And when Willie was involved in an accident 28 months ago, it wasn't one of those usual things like getting conked by a car or run over by a wheelchair. Not Willie Pep!

He fell from the skies in a plunging airliner in a forested area near Midvale, New Jersey, on January 5, 1947. When they picked him out of the wreckage, he had a smashed left ankle, two fractured vertebrae, and an undying compulsion to get back into the ring.

Wrapped in a plaster cast in a Jersey hospital, Pep vowed that he would fight again in a defense of his world featherweight championship. Those who reckoned without the restless spirit that had changed the name of Guglielmo Papaleo to Willie Pep were a altogether wrong. Six months after the accident, Willie was back in the ring, winning a decision in 10 rounds. No mere airplane crash could keep him down.

That's the way Pep does things—never half-way. It's the same in the ring. When he runs up a winning streak, he does it on a grand scale. He scored 62 straight professional victories before Sammy Angott wrestled him to defeat in Madison Square Garden in 1943. Then he went without a setback in 73 straight until Saddler upset him, on a knockout in four rounds, at the Garden last October 29.

It was then that the skeptics said "I told you so," insisting that Pep had tossed the match as the main figure in a betting coup which roped in all the innocents abroad. But in his dressing room in the Garden, Willie sat on a stool and bemoaned his fate.

"I let everyone down," he sobbed. "I let everyone down." The tears came slowly, and the cynics said Willie cried not because he had lost the championship and the bets of thousands of supporters—but because he had lost his good name by throwing the fight.

His manager, large Lou Viscusi, an agent with a deep affection for his meal-ticket, was stunned. "I can't believe it," he muttered. Neither could the public. Sandy Saddler hadn't been given much of a chance, although a large surge of betting money had sent the odds down to 13-5, Pep favored.

They scheduled the return fight for this past February 11. Perversely, the betting men who had cried thief the first time now made Saddler the favorite, by a slight margin. They were saying now that Pep was as washed up as the beach at Coney.

Pep didn't say much beyond insisting, "I was over-confident the first time. I didn't move and he grabbed me fast and held and hit. I'll move a lot this time and he'll never be in a position to score." It must have been that Willie's Hartford followers wanted to see for themselves, for an estimated 6,000 came down to watch.

Willie wasn't trapped this time, except if you count the 10th round, when he was staggered and hurt. But he moved on wispy legs, like the Pep of old. At 26, he turned in his greatest fight, and he regained his title by a unanimous decision. Hardened fight writers who had picked Saddler went into paroxysms of unfettered praise. The 19,097 fans who had paid a record indoor gate for featherweights, $87,563, went away convinced that never again in their days will they ever witness such a demonstration of consummate cunning and ring trickery. Yes, once again, it was Willie the Wisp.

When the unanimous decision went to Willie, 220-pound Viscusi surged into the ring and embraced his champion in a bear-hug. He lifted the boy aloft and kissed him. Pep's face, covered though it was by blood from cuts and bruises under both eyes, across the bridge of his nose, and on the brows, was bathed in a smile. He was the champion again.

That was the way Willie Pep, winner 136 times in 139 fights, regained his title—and his honor. Not coldly and with the precision of a machine, but warmly and with the cunning of a fox and the speed of a whippet. It was Pep doing things differently from all the others who had come before.

It was like the time Viscusi was to sign up Pep nine years ago. Large Lou waited in his gymnasium for Willie to come around with his father, Salvatore, a construction worker who was semi-invalided with a stomach ailment. Viscusi waited and waited, for he knew Pep was a fine prospect, having won two State amateur championships although he was only 16 years old.

Willie didn't show up, but the next day his father came to the gym and told Viscusi, "My boy, he's in hospital with appendicitis." Viscusi visited Willie, a wan-looking, skinny kid who was totally unimpressive as a potential professional fighter.

Some months later, Pep was ready to begin his professional career, launched with a victory over James McGovern at Hartford. Willie was nervous and fidgety, picking at his nails and stroking his hair. As Viscusi sat and watched Willie in the dressing room, he thought,

"Wonder if this kid ever sits down and rests?"

He found out, as the months passed, that Pep did neither. He moved about constantly and only when engaged in ring combat did he settle down to the job at hand. As a matter of downright fact, Viscusi became totally aware of Willie's finicky ways through a sad experience. For 29 fights, Pep appeared satisfied with the manner in which he was being handled by his manager. Then, suddenly, the kid left town and headed for California. It happened as quickly as this is written. Viscusi wondered about it. Then he learned that Pep was dissatisfied because he wasn't being shown enough attention and respect.

At the time, the big fellow in Viscusi's stable was another Hartford featherweight, Bobby (Poison) Ivy, who already was a main-eventer. "I was nobody to them," Pep told sportswriters on his return from the Coast. "Everything was Ivy this and Ivy that. What's the matter with me? I ain't got poison ivy."

On the Coast, Pep won a four-rounder at Los Angeles. When Viscusi wheedled his return, it was with the assurance that Willie would be the big fellow at the party. And he was—but he did it all with his own little fists. In his 48th fight, he was matched with Ivy, who no longer was a member of the Viscusi barn. Pep blasted Ivy in 10 rounds, ripping him from the vine and showing that he wasn't as poisonous as before. It was a big moment in Willie's career.

All this time, Willie was showing the same inability to sit and think things out, to rest. He would visit one corner hangout and stay for five minutes. Then he'd breeze off to another spot. He began dressing sharply, although his suits were tailored without the zooty abandon that was the fashion of the mob.

Money was coming in fast. In five fights at Hartford, he had drawn $70,000, which was real gate money at the time. America was at war, but workers in the munitions plants in Connecticut clamored for the chance to see Willie work in the ring.

"It was a real problem," Viscusi recalls. "I had to move Pep's fights up to 9:15 at night, instead of 10, so the workers could get to their plants on time."

Willie's streak was attracting attention all over the country. Right after knocking out Ivy, he was called down to New York to fight Frank Franconeri in a semi-final eight-rounder at the Garden. He knocked out his foe in one round. Eyebrows were lifted. Nat Fleischer, editor of *Ring Magazine*, sang Pep's praises.

"Never," he said, "in the 200 years of boxing records has a fighter run so impressive a streak." Pep had won 53 in a row. Then the inevitable came to pass. The clamor for a championship chance for Willie bore the right matchmaking fruit. He was paired with Chalky Wright, an aged slickster who not only knew every trick in the ring but had invented some, in a 15-round featherweight championship clash, New York State version, at Madison Square Garden.

It was incredible. Up until the time the Wright match was signed, Pep had boxed only nine rounds in the Garden, all in preliminaries. But there he was fighting for the championship, and Hartford and all of Connecticut answered the call. More than 19,000 customers paid a new indoor featherweight record gross of $71,868 to see Pep take the championship from Chalky.

The fight was something less than thrilling. Willie, hewing to the pattern set by his trainer, Bill (Silent) Gore, stabbed and moved. "If he did anything else," Gore recalls, "I promised to hit him over the head with a stool. I remember I put up a sign in the gym which said, 'Don't Lose Your Head!' That was for Willie in the fight. He worked it just like we wanted."

The fight produced Pep's first big purse, some $7,000. The year before winning the title, he had been earning $48 for a fight. Since then, he has picked up $450,000 in gross receipts, an average of more than $50,000 a year. He made $50,000 in his two struggles with Saddler and, if plans materialize, he can double that in an outdoor bout with Sandy this spring or summer.

Oddly, money hasn't brought too much happiness to Pep, a swarthy lad with an ample nose and the aspect of a person constantly on the search for some place to sit down and think things over. He never gets to do this.

Perhaps the answer lies in the fact that, at 26, he can look back on at least 11 years of manhood, but on no days as a youth. He was 15 when he started boxing as an amateur. He has been doing it ever since. Once, when he was courting the girl he married and later divorced, somebody asked him if he knew how to dance. "No," he replied. "I never had time to learn."

He has been supporting his family ever since he was 16, after leaving Hartford High School to sell newspapers on a street corner. Soon after he was married in 1942, he bought a duplex home in the South End of Hartford. He occupied one floor, while his father, mother, sister, and brother occupied the other.

It was a good thing too, for Willie needs the home now. Two years ago he divorced his wife. She got $12,500 in a settlement. He got custody of their two children, Mary, five, and William Patrick, three. Mary, coincidentally, was born on January 16, 1945, the very day on which Pep was inducted into the Army after being discharged from the Navy because of a punctured eardrum.

"What a birthday present for my daughter," Pep moaned. But he didn't stay in the Army very long. Only 16 days later he was discharged. The Army announced he had a punctured eardrum. It seems the Army and the Navy weren't on speaking terms in those days.

Willie's nervousness brought him some damaging publicity two years ago, shortly before he survived the plane crash which cost the lives of several other passengers on the Miami-to-New York run. It happened when a friend asked Pep to go with him on a walk.

"Okay, I got nothing else to do," Pep said. He walked down toward the river bank with his friend and together they came upon some other pals who were rolling dice. Pep stopped to watch and soon, they say, he was shooting the bones himself. Well, the law came upon the gamblers and Willie was in the clutches.

In court, Willie faced a police judge named Cornelius Moylan. The stern arbiter looked down upon him and, in scathing terms, upbraided Pep. "You are supposed to set an example for the youth of our city," the judge said. "This is disgraceful."

Pep paid a $25 fine, but later, when Cornelius Moylan was running for mayor of Hartford, a championship prizefighter posed with him for campaign purposes. The fighter's name? Why, Willie Pep, of course.

Willie always is getting messed up in this fashion, and sometimes on higher levels, financially speaking. When he speaks to a gambler in Hartford the word goes out immediately that he is to lose his next fight. When he doesn't, the boys agree they were wrong, only to repeat the rumor the next time out.

Joe Cassano, a Hartford fight writer, tells a revealing story. Recently, he heard rumors that Pep was on the town in Hartford, running around in his big convertible Lincoln and paying constant court to women of doubtful background. In this regard, Cassano was tipped off one night that Pep was in a nightclub with one of these women. "How do you know?" Cassano asked his informant, who replied: "Why, Willie's car is parked outside the club."

Cassano checked and found that Pep wasn't within 10 miles of the nightclub. He'd simply lent the car to a friend, who was making a night of it.

Willie's itchiness extends across the length and width of the land. In 1947, on the night he defended his featherweight championship in Flint, Michigan, by knocking out Jock Leslie in 12 rounds, he was paid upwards of $25,000 for the night's work. Instead of waiting around town to pick up his purse, he took a night train back to Hartford. "You pick up the money," he told Viscusi. "I want to get home."

Another time, after whipping Chalky Wright in a non-title 10-rounder in Cleveland, he rode the day coach all the way home because he wanted to leave immediately after the fight and couldn't make connections on a plane or sleeper.

Even after regaining the championship from Saddler, Willie wanted to rush home to Hartford. Only the necessity for medical treatment kept him in New York overnight. The next day, he was whisked by auto to the Connecticut State line at Greenwich, where he was greeted by the Mayor of Hartford, who had provided an automobile escort back to the Insurance Capital.

Willie isn't awed by his position. He takes it all in his stride. He speaks softly, his dark brown eyes peering intently as though he were fencing with an opponent in the ring. He has few hobbies, but the one which he enjoys most is listening to recordings of jazz tunes. He has no special favorites. One orchestra is as good as another in his book.

He prefers to speed when he's at the wheel of his Lincoln, but he is not reckless. It's the same in the ring. Time and time again he has been willing to permit an opponent to hang around so long as the opponent doesn't have delusions of grandeur.

Substantial proof of this was offered soon after Pep first won the championship recognition by beating Chalky Wright. Until that time, Pep had always addressed Bill Lee, sports columnist of the *Hartford Courant*, as Mr. Lee, who believed it was time to doff the mask of caste.

"Willie," Lee told the new champion, "now that you're champ, it would be nice if you call me Bill instead of Mr. Lee. It's more democratic that way."

"SAY, ISN'T THAT WILLIE PEP IN THERE?"

BY FRANK GRAHAM

FROM *SPORT*, JUNE 1956

This was away back in February of 1949 and Willie Pep and Lou Viscusi, who managed him, were on a train taking them from Hartford to New York, where Willie was going to fight Sandy Saddler for the second time. Sandy had knocked Willie out the first time around and now as the train neared the big city, Viscusi said: "We've had a long ride since we've been together, Willie. And even if this is the end of it, we've got to say it's been a good ride."

And Willie said: "That's right, Lou."

It's been a longer ride than they could have dreamed then. Willie has been up and down and all around the fight beat and it isn't a good ride any more. The road has taken him back through the small fight clubs from which he emerged, on his way to greatness, 14 years ago. He's fighting the nobodies again as he did when he, too, was a nobody. In Bennington, Vermont, and Holyoke, Massachusetts and Detroit and Miami Beach and Bridgeport and San Francisco. Fighting kids who are in awe of him at first and are baffled by his sleight of hand, but who, with youth on their side, frequently press him hard in the closing rounds and put welts on his slender body and reopen old cuts on his seamed and hemstitched face. And even though he wins, he has given blood for dollars again.

Millions see him on television but they see him fighting before only hundreds huddled around the dusty rings, where once the crowds that surged to see him packed Madison Square Garden, the Polo Grounds and Yankee Stadium. Once—it was for the third of his four fights with Saddler—his share of the gate was $92,889, the biggest check ever taken down by a fighter below the lightweight division. Now he is fighting for walking around money.

What makes Willie fight? What made Sammy run? In each case, the answer is the same: desperation. He's broke and he has to eat. He has to have a place to live, however humble, and because he has never worked at anything but the bruising trade, how else is he to get the money? What became of the hundreds of thousands of dollars he earned when he was featherweight champion of the world and his name first was linked in history with the names of George Dixon and Abe Attell? Ask the dice-shooters, the bookmakers and the mutuel clerks. Ask the dames.

Another featherweight champion—Chalky Wright, from whom Willie took the title—went broke against the dice. Chalky didn't have the patience to bet on the horses. "You bet on a horse," Chalky said, "and you have to wait to hear how you come out. The dice tell you right away."

Most of the news the dice have to tell Willie is as it was for Chalky. But Willie had to go with horses, too. And the dames. The fact that he seldom has been good never has discouraged him. Dice have taken crazy rolls. The horses have been beaten by anything from a nose to a dozen lengths. The romances, including two marriages, have caused him all kinds of trouble. But, true to form, he tried it again this year for the third time. Why does he always keep going back for more? There must be a fever in him.

And so, in his quest for funds with which to live,

gamble and to caper by candlelight, he goes on his dreary way, fighting the likes of Merle Olmstead and Jimmy Ithia and Andy Arel, who used to be his sparring partner. He has lost only two fights in two years. One, in 1954, was on a knockout to Lulu Perez, but Willie plainly was play-acting then and you can put quotes around that knockout. The other, last year, was on a decision to one Gil Cadilli, but when they met again, he took care of the young man.

There are nights, though, when you still can see flashes of the Pep of whom Abe Attell, who blandly describes himself as a conceited fighter, once said: "He's the greatest featherweight since Attell."

On such nights Willie wheels, spins, feints, blocks and punches with the almost incredible speed and grace of old. "You got to get hit once in a while," he tells young fighters, "but don't get hit on purpose. Don't fight with your face. That's what you got hands and feet for. Stay close enough to the other guy to hit him, but when he gets tough and starts to hit back, move around. And when you're hurt, use your noodle."

Sometimes, on these nights, Willie gets hurt when his wind grows short and he's "walking in mud," as the Spanish fighters say when they are leg weary. When that happens, he uses his noodle, calling on the great reserve of tricks he has learned in more than two hundred fights. That's when you see him, however briefly, as he used to be.

On one of these nights, a year or so ago, he was fighting a kid whose name escapes me and he was giving a good show and winning. Then, early in the eighth round, he got tired and the kid nailed him and he was hurt. He still had nearly three full rounds to go and he didn't know whether he could make it or not. He launched an all-out drive, whirling in on the kid and smashing at his head and body, hoping for a quick knockout. But the kid was tough and game and wouldn't go down and Willie, pulling back, turned and looked pleadingly at the referee.

"What sportsmanship!" the TV announcer at the ringside shrieked. "Willie is asking the referee to stop the fight to save his opponent from further punishment!"

A couple of hundred miles away, one who knows Willie and was watching the fight on his set, laughed out loud. "Sportsmanship, my eye!" he said. "Willie has punched himself out and he's trying to con the referee into stopping the fight to save HIM!"

Which, of course, was true. But the referee, who also knew Willie, signaled him to continue and, somehow, he managed to do it.

His fight with Arel at Miami Beach, the last he made in 1955, was another of his latter-day classics. Again he was well out in front, this time going into the ninth round, when Arel ripped open the scar tissue over his left eye. This must have given Willie a feeling of panic, but if it did, he recovered in a split second. Through the remainder of the round, he counter-attacked sharply, and in the 10th, he unloaded punches on Arel that overwhelmed him, and so, on the brink of defeat, he wrapped up another victory.

That was the way he won his greatest fight of all— the one in February of 1949 in which he regained the title from Sandy Saddler. There had been some question about the honesty of their first brawl, although if the cynics were right and Willie took a dive for Sandy, he did it the hard way, soaking up a frightful beating before he was counted out in the fourth round. At any rate, he was in the ring with Saddler again. He boxed cautiously through the early rounds, giving Sandy the hit-and-run treatment. Then, warming up, he not only clouted the champion but bedeviled him, tying him up, spinning him, grabbing him and throwing him into the ropes. Of the first eight rounds, he won seven. But in the ninth, Saddler almost brought him down with an explosive right cross, and the 10th was a ghastly round for him. Saddler's punches tore the flesh over and under Willie's eyes and it seemed impossible for him to escape being knocked out. But, twisting, turning, clutching and back-pedaling, he survived.

To those looking on, it seemed that his resourcefulness under such cruel fire must serve only to prolong his agony, for surely Sandy would destroy him in the 11th. But as that round opened, Pep charged from his corner, carrying the fight to his tormentor. Now, suddenly, it was Saddler who swayed toward oblivion as Willie whipped punches to his chin. Sandy, lasting out the round, lost the 12th as well, but by this time Willie had little left to throw at him, and through three rousing rounds to the end of the fight he was constantly in peril of being flattened or so hopelessly punished as to cause Eddie Josephs, the referee, to stop it. But at the final bell, though his face was a grotesque mask from which blood dripped to the canvas, Willie Pep was champion of the world again.

How did he become the fighter he is? Where did he learn all the dodges he knows? Well, he became that kind of fighter because there was no other way he could get to the ring or, having got there, advance beyond the preliminary ranks. He was, and he remains, the end product of Benny Leonard's pattern for greatness in the fine art of breaking noses. "To be a great fighter," Benny said, "it is necessary to be a little scared."

As a skinny kid on the mean streets of Hartford, Willie was a study in fear. There was a reason for this unhappy circumstance. The bigger, tougher kids used to lie in wait for him to beat him up. If he saw them first, he would run, and if he saw an open door, he would run into the house—any house—and slam the door behind him.

"Every time I see you," an older boy living on the block said to him one day, "somebody is punching you or banging your head against a wall. Why don't you go down to the gym and learn how to fight?"

So Willie did. The first few days, the man who ran the neighborhood gym chased him out, but his persistence finally won him the right to remain and take free lessons from fighters who were short on sparring partners. Now and then, one of them

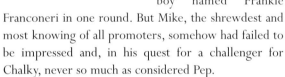

Willie Pep, 1967

would slip him a couple of dollars and, naturally, he liked that. It was better to take punches for pay than for nothing. But he soon learned that if he were to fulfill his new-found ambition to become a fighter, he would have to have more in his repertoire than a left jab, a right cross and a left hook. Besides, some of the terror of the streets remained with him. He was scared every time he put on the gloves. He didn't want to be hurt and he had to find a way to avoid it.

He studied the ways of the artful ones in the gym, the ones who could land a punch and get away and move in again and out and around and make use of the full dimensions of the ring. He noted the tricks they knew and copied them and made up some of his own. With a mind as agile as his body, he soon became proficient and he entered the lists of the amateurs.

Viscusi saw him in the amateurs, signed him to a contract and turned him over to Bill Gore, one of the

wisest of trainers and soundest of instructors. "I learned from Bill," Willie says, "and from a couple of fighters, Red Guggino and Jimmy Leto, who trained at the gym. Leto was a good body-puncher and tried to make one out of me, but I wasn't good at it and he was smart. He told me to stick to my style and he showed me some moves. Guys you fight teach you things without knowing it. The first time I boxed Chalky Wright, he mixed me up a couple of times by feinting with his legs. After he feinted, he didn't do anything but I didn't do anything, either, because I didn't know what to expect. I never saw anybody feint with his legs before, but I liked it, so I copied it."

It was Eddie Walker, Wright's manager, who was responsible for getting Willie the bout in which he relieved Wright of the championship. Willie was enjoying a fantastic success, not having lost a fight in nearly three crowded years as a professional and he had appeared "underneath" on three of Mike Jacobs' cards in the Garden, winning two four-round preliminaries and, on his third appearance, practically shattering a boy named Frankie Franconeri in one round. But Mike, the shrewdest and most knowing of all promoters, somehow had failed to be impressed and, in his quest for a challenger for Chalky, never so much as considered Pep.

Then, on an October day in 1942, Eddie Walker dropped into his office in the Brill Building, headquarters of the Twentieth Century Sporting Club. "I got a guy for you, Mike," he said.

"Who?"

"Willie Pep."

"Nah!" Mike said. "He wouldn't draw a nickel."

"Ask your matchmaker," Walker suggested.

Mike called in his man, Nat Rogers, and asked him what he thought of Pep.

"He's the hottest thing in Connecticut," Nat said. "They'll go to see him wherever he fights."

"Listen, Mike," Walker said. "I had Chalky fighting in Hartford and New Haven just a little while ago, and all we heard about was Willie Pep. They think he can beat Chalky. I don't, but if they do and they will pay to see him try it, he's for me."

And so the match was made and Mike wasn't disappointed in the gate receipts, swelled considerably by the mob that packed in from Connecticut. Willie bounced around the ring as though he were riding an invisible pogo stick but, now and then, he paused long enough to pile up a sufficient number of points to take the decision.

Chalky was a little old man of the ring. He said he was 30 years old, but he obviously was at least five years older. He was an excellent mechanic and he could punch, but he never got a real good shot at Willie. He had held the title for little more than a year, and he hadn't made much money with it, but he accepted defeat gracefully.

"I wouldn't want to win the big one the way Willie did," a disdainful reporter said to Chalky in his dressing room.

"I would," Chalky said. "If I was a young fellow like him, fighting an old fellow like me, I would fight just the way he did."

Willie made many subsequent appearances in the Garden. The only one to beat him there or anywhere else, for that matter, until Saddler caught up with him, was Sammy Angott, then the lightweight champion. It was a 10-round bout at catchweights, no title at stake, and Angott, known in the trade as Sammy the Clutch, not only tracked down fleet Willie, but held him fast, and at the end of a dismal fight, the bored judges gave him the nod. It wasn't the only invitation to slumber in which Willie figured, however. There was a period in which his very name on the Garden marquee kept large numbers of fans away. But they came back after a while and learned to appreciate the artistry of the little man and to enjoy his escape act when he was hard pressed by a bold challenger.

Willie was a busy champion, fighting all over the country, frequently putting his title on the line. After he had lost it to Saddler and won it back, he defended it three times before disaster, in the form of the spindly Saddler, struck again. One who tried in vain to take it from him was Ray Famechon, featherweight champion of Europe. Their meeting was in the Garden and Willie actually reduced the Frenchman to tears by his elusiveness over the 15-round haul. But that was Willie's last brilliant full-length show. In his third fight with Saddler, he quit, claiming a dislocated shoulder, and in the fourth, he simply quit, although he was in front.

"I hate Saddler," Willie said not long ago.

"Why?" someone asked.

"I hate him because he took my title," Willie said, his eyes smoldering.

Sandy did more than that to Willie. He wrecked him. No man can remain champion forever and Willie had a good run with it and once retrieved it after he had lost it. But Sandy was the only one to strip him of his dignity and of his wits, to cause him to quit shamefully, to hold him up to the scorn of those who for so long had been proud to follow in his train.

When Saddler had done with him, he not only was an ex-champion but a vagabond on the lonely trail, his gloves for hire at small wages because he needed the money. His pride was gone. In his sorry state, he could be accommodating to those he once would have brushed out of his way. How else can you explain his knockout by Tommy Collins in Boston in 1952 and his equally strange performance with Lulu Perez in 1954?

But that phase of his life happily has passed. Meager as his returns may be as he wanders through the sticks, at least, he is trying again. It must be that he said to himself: "If I have to go on fighting, at least I can show these young punks that they can't lick me—or buy me either."

His luck with the horses hasn't changed, however. Only recently, he demonstrated that he can lose even when he doesn't bet. One day when he was going to the races in Miami, his pal Jake LaMotta gave him 50 dollars to bet on a daily double. But Willie, not sharing Jake's enthusiasm for this particular combination of horses, held the bet. When the double clicked at a staggering price, Willie grabbed a plane for New Orleans and, on his arrival, called Rocky Graziano in New York, asking him to pacify Jake who, he sensed, would strike him dead on sight. Rocky must have been very persuasive. Within a week, Willie was back in Miami, making the rounds with Jake.

You'll see him around for a while yet, especially if you follow the fights on television faithfully. You'll see a familiar slim figure with quick legs and quicker hands; you'll see him stick and move, and something about him will remind you of a fighter you used to be crazy about. Maybe, then, you will turn to your neighbor and say, wonderingly, "Say, isn't that Willie Pep in there?"

And the saddest part of the whole Willie Pep story is that it will be.

Great Rivalries:

WILLIE PEP
VS.
SANDY SADDLER

BY STANLEY FRANK

FROM *SPORT*, MAY 1970

They fought four times for the feather-weight boxing title, and each return bout was dirtier and more vicious than the one before it. After the second brawl, referee Eddie Joseph complained that his instructions were ignored all night. After the fourth fight, referee Ray Miller was entitled to an even greater complaint: he had been flung to the canvas while trying to pry the fighters apart.

That was the kind of rivalry Willie Pep and Sandy Saddler had going, one with no holds barred, and quite a few invented during the heat of the action. Little men of the ring rarely command much attention, but the public sensed that the savagery of the Pep-Saddler battles was the pure essence of boxing. As a result, their duels in the late '40s and early '50s were as eagerly awaited as those of Graziano and Zale, Louis and Walcott, Robinson and Cerdan.

Today, 19 years after their last fight, each professes great respect for the other man's style. There is only one remaining remnant of the bitterness they once felt for each other, and it is held by the winner of three of the four fights, not the loser: at times Saddler cannot hide the resentment he feels toward Pep's more enduring hold on the public.

Willie's popularity is and was easy to understand. In the good times he was generous with both his time and money. In the bad times he didn't change, and didn't

brood. He shrugged it off and always seemed eager to look on the bright side of things. It isn't surprising that even his memories of the Saddler fights are filled not with alibis but with kind words toward his opponent.

"I had 241 fights as a pro and maybe 100 in the amateurs and I think more of Sandy than any guy I ever met," Willie said recently. "People thought he was strictly a puncher, but he was smart in his style. Not clever, you understand, but smart. I should know." Willie smiled in self deprecation.

"The writers said the one time I beat him was my greatest fight, but even then he busted me up pretty good. I had to have 11 stitches around my eyes and face. There was hardly a mark on Sandy, while I, the world's champion, looked like I'd walked into a meat grinder.

"He was an awful rough customer in the ring, but out of it he's a gentleman. Two years ago they gave me a big testimonial dinner in Hartford (Willie's hometown) and Sandy paid his own expenses to it and made a nice speech about it. It's natural for friction to build up between guys fighting for the title, but that's all past for Sandy and me."

When you talk to Saddler about Pep, he comes off just as affable at first as Willie. We talked to him at the National Maritime Union gym in New York City, where he is the physical director. He was in his working clothes—a gym suit—and from time to time he'd make a point about Pep's moves by jumping up and shadow boxing.

"Pep was well loved for his ability," Sandy said. "He was the cleverest boxer of the last 40, 50 years. He pulled the damndest trick I've ever seen in the ring. It happened the night he defended the title against Chalky Wright in '44, four years before my first fight with him. Chalky could knock you dead with one punch, but he couldn't lay a glove on Pep, who had taken the title from him. Chalky kept stalking him for one good shot and he finally trapped Pep in a corner. Chalky cocked his right to throw a bomb and Pep ducked through his legs and got away. That's right. Pep ducked right through Chalky's legs."

Sandy was silent for a long moment. "I never forgot that," he said finally. "It was the damndest thing I've ever seen."

Sandy began talking about the times he had to go to Latin America to get fights when Pep first dominated the featherweights. And then Saddler's pent-up anger and frustration erupted as suddenly as the devastating left hook he threw in the ring.

"Pep was the great man who made everybody look like a sucker and along came little me and knocked him out in four rounds," Sandy said shrilly. "I licked him in three out of four fights. I made him quit in his corner twice. He knew he'd never see the day he could whip me, but he was elected to the Hall of Fame seven years ago and I haven't come close yet.

"What kind of a lousy joke is this?" he said, his fury mounting. "Why haven't I been named to the Hall of Fame? I'll tell you why. They won't give a black man the credit he deserves. Everybody says Pep was the greatest featherweight of all time, so what does that make me? I knocked him out three times. My punches took the heart out of him. He's in the Hall of Fame and I'm left out in the cold, like I never existed.

"It's the same old story. Keep the black man down. Don't give him a decent break, and that's how it's gonna be in the article you're writing."

I mumbled something to the effect that he surely would be elected to the Hall of Fame in time.

Sandy threw up his hands in disgust. "When? When?" he demanded. "Thousands of people die every day. I want the recognition that's due me while I'm still around to enjoy it. I'll never get it. Sweep the black man under the rug and he'll be forgotten. That's how the stinking system works."

He glared at me, his face and body taut with tension, and then, like a fighter shaking off a damaging punch, he tried regaining control of himself. He changed the subject abruptly and spoke in a normal tone, but the fallout from his bitter outburst hung over the rest of the conversation.

Sandy is right, of course. He belongs in the Hall of Fame if Pep is there, but the chemical, almost mystical, appeal of Willie the Wisp cannot be discounted. Pep was barely 20 years old when he won the featherweight title, the youngest man in 40 years to win a world championship. After turning pro he won 134 out of 135 fights. His only defeat was to Sammy Angott, the lightweight champion, in 1943. Willie wasn't outclassed; he made it close for 15 rounds and lost only because of Angott's superior weight and reach.

Willie seemed to have been born with an intuitive flair for all the classic moves. To be sure, he had a respectable punch, scoring 65 knockouts. But he delighted in showing off his boxing prowess and he frequently held back the finisher to bedazzle an opponent with his footwork and feints.

After World War II, a favorite subject for debate was whether Louis, Robinson or Pep was the best fighter, pound for pound, in the business. When asked for his opinion of the other two, Louis answered: "I don't see no difference between 'em. I think Pep and Robinson are the best boxers around anywhere, any time."

Willie tells an amusing story, which might have been true, explaining how he perfected his elusive style. "I was a skinny runt all the other kids beat up on street corners. One day a fella said to me, 'You're taking a licking every day. Why don't you go to the gym and sign up for the amateurs and at least get five dollars for getting kicked around?' I couldn't believe the guy. 'Holy cow!' I said. 'Five bucks to take a beating and I've been doing it for nothing.'

"So I went to the gym and the man chased me home. I was 15 years old, but I looked closer to 12. The next day the same man chased me out again, but I told him I had to make five bucks. He told the locker room attendant, 'Teach this kid how to hold up his hands and maybe I'll throw him in there.' I worked out a couple of months and began fighting in the amateurs. Everybody laughed at me because I looked so scared and weak. One night a kid chased me around the ring for four rounds trying to tag me with just one punch. He never caught up with me. His name was Walker Smith—later changed to Ray Robinson."

Willie appeared to be at his peak in 1948 when he

The first of 36 classic rounds over four fights, October 29, 1948

THE ITALIAN STALLIONS

FIGHT ONE

Pep vs. Saddler

MADISON SQUARE GARDEN, NEW YORK
OCTOBER 29, 1948

signed for the seventh defense of his title against Saddler, a tall (5-foot-8) converted southpaw, in Madison Square Garden. The challenger had an impressive record of 63 knockouts in 93 fights, but he was a stand-up boxer, the type that was a set-up for Willie.

Although Saddler was raised in New York, he was so obscure that he never had fought a main event bout in his hometown. It wasn't entirely his fault that he had no reputation. His manager was Jimmy Johnston, a colorful old-timer known as the Boy Bandit of Broadway. Johnston had been the matchmaker at Madison Square Garden until he was forced out by Mike Jacobs, the promoter who rose to the top of the heap with Joe Louis. Jacobs hated Johnston and refused to book his fighters into the Garden and other major arenas Jacobs controlled, compelling Saddler to go out of the country to get any action.

In the course of his travels Sandy hit more obscure places in Latin America and the Caribbean than a banana boat. He knocked out the featherweight champions of Venezuela, Bolivia, Cuba, Trinidad, Mexico and Panama for purses that barely covered his expenses. The chance he had been waiting for finally came after Jimmy Johnston died. Jimmy's brother Charley was on better terms with Jacobs and landed a title shot for Sandy on October 29, 1948. The challenger's cut of the gate was a mere 10 percent.

Pep was a solid 3-1 favorite with few takers. A sportswriter observed that the proper odds should have been 135-1 in view of Pep's record. There was little speculation about the fight until rumors of a fix suddenly were heard around town. The whispers were so persistent that Eddie Egan, chairman of the New York State Boxing Commission, called both boys into a private conference at the weigh-in and warned them he would hold up their purses if he saw anything peculiar.

At the opening bell, Willie bounced out prepared to take charge as always by befuddling his opponent with clever combinations, then making him look bad by slipping punches. But he never had a chance to unfold his plan. Sandy threw the first punch, a jab that snapped back Willie's head, then landed a right uppercut in a clinch.

"I felt the uppercut in my right shoulder," Sandy recalled. "I knew it was a good punch and I knew I had the fight when Pep fell into a clinch and sagged against me. When the referee separated us, Pep got on his bicycle and ran away. I don't think he tried to hit me with a real punch the entire round."

In the second round Willie tried to hold off his tormentor with weak jabs, but the mercury in his legs had turned to lead. Sandy belted him around the ring in the third round and muscled him into a corner. Willie did not duck through Sandy's legs as he did against Chalky Wright four years earlier. He was too far gone even to duck the long left hook that caught him on the chin. He went down for a count of nine and was decked again by a right cross before the bell saved him.

But at 2:38 of the fourth round it was all over. Willie was knocked out for the first time in his life by a wicked left hook to the chin. There was a faint murmur instead of the wild, exultant yell that usually explodes when a title changes hands. Most of the 14,685 people sat there in stunned disbelief, as shocked by Willie's inept performance as they were by the result.

Reports of a fix were rehashed, but even the most suspicious parties conceded that if Willie indeed had taken a dive he would have done it with more subtlety and a lot less pain. A more prevalent story was that Willie had not fully recovered from the injuries suffered in an air crash the previous year. Willie was flying from Miami to New York in an old DC-3 when the plane crashed at Middleville, New Jersey. Six passengers were killed. Willie was pulled from the wreckage with six broken vertebrae in his back and a shattered leg. For several weeks it was uncertain if he ever would fight again, but five month later he beat Victor Flores in 10 tough rounds and went on from there, apparently as good as ever. Until he collided with Saddler.

"Nah, the plane crash had nothing to do with losing the title," Willie said in reviewing the fights. "It was simply a case of underrating an opponent. I wasn't ready mentally for a tough fight. I'd won 73 in a row and I'd gotten out of the habit of psyching myself for a fight."

In the next few weeks Pep took on five fights as a warmup to his rematch with Saddler. He won them all, four by knockout. Three and a half months after he had lost his title, Pep felt he was now "mentally ready" to regain it.

The rematch brought the Garden its first sellout in three years, and it seemed that at least half the crowd had come down in special trains from Hartford to see their boy Willie. They were roaring from the beginning, when it was obvious that this was going to be a grudge fight. As referee Eddie Joseph would say later, "I knew it was going to be a rough night when Saddler refused to shake hands before the opening bell."

Willie proved he'd learned his lesson from the first fight and assumed the offensive from the start. He kept the challenger off balance with his jab, stepped inside smartly with sharp hooks and got out before Sandy could retaliate. The first round was all Pep and the second began that way too when suddenly the bout assumed the ugly nature of a waterfront brawl with baling hooks. Each corner later claimed that its boy had been thumbed by the other. Whatever the cause, the Marquess of Queensberry rules were forgotten. Pep stepped on Saddler's feet, grabbed his shoulders and jerked him off balance, almost wrestling him to the floor several times. Saddler charged back like an enraged bull, but Pep was too fast for him. In the clinches he grabbed Saddler's lethal left hand and did his best to tie his opponent's arm into a pretzel.

Willie, sticking and moving, yanking and twisting his man, won seven of the first eight rounds. One more and he would be home free—if Saddler did not tag him with a carbon copy of the punch that had unhinged him in the first fight. But in the ninth round Saddler almost did. Willie was relaxing, coasting on his big lead, when Saddler nailed him with a vicious right cross that buckled his knees. Sandy, releasing his frustration from the early rounds, tore into Willie with undisciplined fury—and lost the chance to save his title. In his anxiety to put his man away, Sandy missed wild punches and floundered in pursuit of Willie, who still had enough savvy to duck and run.

Willie fought strictly from memory in the 10th, circling in the center of the ring to avoid getting pinned into corners, hanging on in the clinches when he was rocked by Sandy. The champion seemed to tire from his effort and toward the end of the round Willie was putting together flurries of combinations that protected him from disaster.

Quite improbably, Willie took charge of the situation again in the 11th and carried the fight to Sandy. He stayed inside, giving Sandy no leverage for his jolting left hook, and the same tactics took the 13th round. Now Sandy could win only on a knockout and he knew it. Using his superior height and reach, he began to bombard Willie at long range. Willie was playing it safe. Too safe.

In the last minute of the 14th, Sandy connected with a murderous hook that spurted blood from Willie's right eye, but it was too late in the round to capitalize on the break. In the final round Sandy stormed all over his man and punished him cruelly, but Willie had just enough guile and heart to stay upright.

The unanimous decision, nine rounds to six in favor of Pep, must have looked like robbery to anyone who judged the fight only by the appearance of the principals. Saddler didn't have a mark on him. Pep's face was a bloody mask and he might have collapsed if his manager, Lou Viscusi, had not picked him up in a bear hug. Saddler's camp denounced the referee for letting Pep get away with murder but Sandy did not join in the criticism, then or now. "A man is in there to win any way he can," he said impassively 20 years later.

They met for the third time on September 8, 1950, at Yankee Stadium before a crowd of 38,781 that nearly doubled the previous outdoor record for a feather-weight title fight. If Pep had given Saddler a post-graduate course before in back-alley brawling, Saddler at least proved an apt pupil. He opened up by hitting on the breaks after clinches, and when the referee warned him to back off cleanly, Sandy responded with two words, one unprintable. "A man's got to protect himself in there at all times," he told me. "Lots of fights are lost by getting clipped on the chin when the referee calls for a break. He should step between the fighters to make sure neither guy throws a sneak punch. I wasn't taking any chances with Pep."

Sandy roughed up Willie on the ropes, clamped half-nelsons on him in the clinches, continued punching after the bell. He was winning the roughhouse but Willie was winning the defense of his title in another brilliant display of hit-and-run, stick-and-slide tactics. Sandy connected with a long left in the third round and Willie went down for a count of nine, but he retreated nimbly without further damage.

Willie won four of the first six rounds and was well ahead in the seventh. Then, just before the bell, Willie was bobbing and weaving on the ropes. Sandy landed a good hook to the body, then grabbed Willie's left arm in the ensuing clinch. Willie felt something pop in his shoulder, but no one else was aware of it.

To everyone's astonishment, Willie did not come out for the eighth round. He sat stolidly in his corner while Viscursi signalled to the referee. Dr. Vincent Nardiello, the Boxing Commission physician, climbed into the ring, spoke briefly to Pep, then to the referee, and spread his hands in a gesture denoting the fight had ended.

It was announced that Pep had suffered a dislocated shoulder and was unable to continue. The title reverted to Saddler on a TKO. While the crowd milled around in

F I G H T II T W O

Pep vs. Saddler

MADISON SQUARE GARDEN, NEW YORK
FEBRUARY 11, 1949

THE ITALIAN STALLIONS

III

F I G H T   T H R E E

Pep vs. Saddler

YANKEE STADIUM, NEW YORK
SEPTEMBER 8, 1950

FIGHT FOUR

Pep vs. Saddler

POLO GROUNDS, NEW YORK
SEPTEMBER 26, 1951

sullen confusion, Dr. Nardiello told sportswriters at ringside that he had not ordered the fight stopped. Pep had said he could not go on.

"Nardiello made it sound like I dogged it," Willie recalled. "How the hell could he tell I wasn't hurt? I couldn't move my left arm. Do you think I wanted to give up the championship when I had a big lead in points?"

Viscusi bellowed that Saddler deliberately had twisted his man's arm, causing the dislocation. Sandy snorted derisively when I asked him for his version of the story.

"It was a hard shot in the belly just before the bell that convinced Pep he'd had enough," Sandy got up and reenacted the incident. "I had him pinned on the ropes like this and I feinted with my head. I'd gone 26 rounds with Pep and I could anticipate his moves. He thought I was going to throw a right and he started to slide away from it, but he zigged the wrong way. I caught him with a left hook in the gut that went up to here." He pointed to his wrist. "His shoulder didn't go. This did." He tapped his heart. "I punched too hard for him. He'd had enough for the night."

The controversial windup made a fourth fight a natural, and Mike Jacobs let the rancor build for a year before he threw the arch rivals into the pit at the Polo Grounds.

Each Pep-Saddler fight had been progressively rougher, and the final meeting set a new all-time record for that sort of thing. They pulled, twisted, heeled, butted and mauled, and paid no attention when the referee began warning them in the second round to fight cleanly. When they did revert to boxing for brief periods, the action followed the pattern of the previous fights. Willie piled up early points with his fancy footwork and quick jabs and Sandy scored with the heaviest punches. He dropped Willie for an eight count in the second round and by the seventh he had opened a slew of old cuts around the former champion's eyes.

Willie, tiring rapidly, tried something new. He hooked a leg around Sandy's ankle and shoved him to the floor. It was such a flagrant foul that the conclusion was inescapable: Willie wanted to be disqualified and get over his misery.

Sandy stalked him relentlessly, taking five light jabs for every hard hook he landed. Definitely the stronger man, he mauled Willie in the eighth and ninth. Willie's best shot was a butt for his opponent's chin as they came out of a clinch.

Willie was leading, five rounds to four, when referee Ray Miller went to Pep's corner to tell him he would halt the fight and call it no contest if the dirty stuff did not stop. Miller later revealed he intended to issue the same warning to Saddler, but before he could say anything Pep told him: "I can't go on. I can't see out of my right eye."

Again, Dr. Nardiello hopped into the ring and gave Pep a brief examination.

The physician subsequently announced he did not stop the fight. Pep had declined to continue.

Willie, once the idol of the mob, was booed as he left the ring. Red Smith, who had written dozens of columns lauding Willie, bluntly accused him of quitting to escape punishment. The identical harsh judgment was passed by a majority of the sportswriters at ringside. The New York State Commission suspended Pep for unsportsmanlike conduct, an indictment that covered a multitude of unspecified charges.

"I was in bad shape, but I didn't ask the referee to stop the fight," Willie says today. "I would've gone out for another round if he ordered me to, but I'll level with you and admit I'm just as glad he didn't. It was the best thing that ever happened to me. An eye is more important than a fight."

He shrugged. "What's the use of talking? People blamed me for a lousy fight and they were right. I did butt Saddler and I was guilty of a lot of things I shouldn't have done. I went into the fight in a bad frame of mind. Saddler crippled me the time before and I made up my mind that if he roughed me up again I'd give it right back to him. Well, he gave me the business and one thing led to another. I lost my head. If I'd boxed him and followed my plan I would've beaten him, but I got sore."

The excitement and the big money went out of the division after the fourth fight. Sandy, only 25, was at his peak, but there was no serious contender in sight. The following year he was drafted into the Army during the Korean War, a turn of events that ultimately worked to his advantage. He lost some ready money, but he found a new career. The Army sent him to school for physical instructors in Wurtzberg, Germany, and the training he received there helped to cushion the shock of a cruel break.

After his discharge from the Army in 1954, Sandy resumed the successful defense of his title. The next year he was going to the gym to prepare for a fight when his taxi was struck broadside by a speeding car. Sandy, who never had been counted out in the ring, was knocked unconscious and when he came to in the hospital the vision from his right eye was a hazy blur. The eye had been pulled from the socket.

"The doctors told me I could be blinded for good if I was hit in the eye, so I gave up the title," he said. "I could've held it five, six more years, I think, if I hadn't been forced to quit, but there's no sense moaning about the money I could've made. I'm better off than most former fighters."

Pep, of course, continued to fight after his last brawl with Saddler. He won 23 of his next 24 fights, losing only to Gil Cadilli on a decision. He retired in 1959, then came back in 1965 at the age of 43 for a year of fights against kids half his age. His last fight was a six-round loss in Richmond, Virginia, for coffee-and-cake money. When he finally finished, his career had spanned 26 years, the longest of the last half-century.

Sandy and Willie were to have three more meetings in the ring after their fourth title bout. "We boxed a three-round exhibition at a benefit for Barney Ross," said Pep. "This was before I was hustled into making a comeback and I hadn't put the gloves on for a long time. Sandy was working out in the gym every day and I was afraid he'd belt me around just to show who was the boss. 'I'm in no shape,' I told him. 'Take it easy. This is just for laughs.'

" 'Don't worry,' Sandy said. 'We'll just spar and give 'em some fancy feints.' Sandy kept his word. He carried me for three rounds and he did the same thing in two other benefits. A gentleman."

Both men are above their old fighting weight of 126, but there is a difference. With Saddler, it doesn't show; with Pep, it does. "Look at this," Sandy said in the gym. He pulled up his shirt and revealed a rock-hard stomach. "I run three and a half miles four times a week and exercise with the pupils here every day. I weigh 138 pounds."

Pep, meanwhile, goes about 155-160 "about 20 pounds more than I should." But he's not really complaining, because the excess is a sign of the happy marriage he's got going, his first good marriage in several tries. "My new wife cries and doesn't eat herself if I don't put away a big breakfast," Willie said. "I try to tell her I never had more than fruit and coffee for breakfast, but she starts to bawl, so what the hell."

Willie is a referee on occasion now, and it isn't inconceivable that someday he might be in the ring with a boy who learned his lessons from Sandy Saddler. Young boxers with promise come along from time to time in Sandy's classes. He hasn't had any turn pro yet, but if they want to make the jump, and if they have promise, Sandy will encourage them.

"Sure, why not?" he said earnestly. "There are a lot of things more detrimental than boxing. It didn't hurt me.

"Guys who wind up bad have nobody to blame but themselves. They rap their managers and conniving promoters, but the truth is that they stopped working and didn't try to learn a good trade and watch their money. Boxing's a tough racket, but it offers a poor kid more money and a better chance to make a name for himself than any other work with his hands. There are an awful lot of people in the world, but only one in 10-million ever gets to say he was a world champion."

Sandy's surprisingly sentimental attitude toward boxing gave another interpretation to his outburst charging that racial prejudice is keeping him out of the Hall of Fame. It was an expression of a black man's bitterness—but it also reflected his deep pride of profession. Sandy wants to be remembered for his achievements in the ring and at least one man never will forget him. Willie Pep.

EPILOGUE

Sandy Saddler and Willie Pep would step into the ring together on two more occasions—in 1971 and again in 1973—for exhibition matches. Saddler mellowed as the years went by and, in 1990, was inducted into the International Boxing Hall of Fame alongside Pep. He died on Sept. 18, 2001 at age 75. After fighting Saddler for the last time, Pep went on to become a prominent referee and, for a while, deputy boxing commissioner of Connecticut. But there were hard times, too. In 1973 Connecticut denied him a referee's license because some of his associates were being investigated for gambling-related crimes, and in the 1980s a magazine article claimed Pep had helped to fix a fight in the 1950s. The main source for the piece subsequently admitted he was a compulsive liar. Slowly, the little big man's reputation began to heal. In 1999, no less an authority than The Associated Press selected him the greatest featherweight and fifth-greatest boxer of all time. Now 81 and in failing health, he lives in a nursing home in his hometown of Hartford.

CHAPTER FOUR

THOMAS ROCCO BARBELLA

THE IMPROBABLE GRAZIANO

BY REX LARDNER

FROM *SPORT*, JANUARY 1956

Joe Louis, the fightingest heavyweight champion, hated only two fighters—Jersey Joe Walcott and Max Schmeling. Jim Corbett, the conqueror of John L. Sullivan, had cool disdain for anyone presumptuous enough to step into a ring or onto a barge with him. Rocky Marciano shows a kind of impersonal detachment toward the opponents he assaults, pursues and buffets; he is a good-natured, if altogether destructive, robot.

On the other hand, Rocky Graziano, the actor, author, comedian, ex-middleweight champion, night-club singer, television panelist and man about town, hated every opponent he ever fought. Just before the fight and during the fight, he hated them with an all-consuming, fiery hatred. Chewing his nails, throwing quick, practice rights, and reading comics didn't take the edge off his anger. Essentially, when untroubled, a generous and gentle, if profane, young man, Rocky admits he didn't care how he won, so long as he won. He rabbit-punched, he hit out of clinches, he hit fighters on the way down and as they tried to get to their feet, he clambered over the referee to get at groggy opponents and he hit after the bell. In all his years of boxing he stuck to a single pattern; he charged across the ring, threw his arm back, lunged forward and swung. Unless he was paralyzed by a body blow, like those delivered by Tony Zale and, surprisingly, Chuck Davey, he never paused and he never moved back. He was constitutionally unable to block punches, just as he was unable to learn to jab or feint or throw a short punch. His trainers found that instructing him in technique was the most dangerous thing they could do.

Fists, it had been impressed upon him from the age of about five, were for punching.

It was as though his hair-trigger temper and sustained rages were beneficial instincts for survival. It was as though they were things he felt he owed his fans. Certainly the fans appreciated Rocky's efforts to please; he was one of the biggest middleweight attractions the world has ever seen and, for at least two years of his career, he made more money than any other man in the ring. And even today, when the Rock is introduced from a ring, his ovation is three times as hearty as that accorded Jack Dempsey. He is the people's choice. Boxing fans, it has been demonstrated, take a primitive slugger to their hearts more than they do someone who dazzles his opponent with footwork—and after Rocky's knockout of the fast, hard-punching Billy Arnold, Damon Runyon called him the new Stanley Ketchel, Ketchel being, of course, the very symbol of a vicious, destructive puncher. Hearing about it, Rocky said, "Ketchel? Get me that salami. I'll knock the bum out."

Stocky, confident, heavy-muscled, with powerful legs and lungs, a powerful back and tough hands, Rocky had, on his best nights, the ability to concentrate utterly on cutting his opponent down, a concentration shaped by his blind, animal fury. The salami in the other corner was venturing to challenge Rocky's superiority in Rocky's chosen field. (If he wasn't a fighter, what was he?) Fighters are prideful specialists and it is probable no one was more prideful, when he was active, than Rocky. Fighters walk in a buoyant, rolling way, gracefully acknowledge the familiarities of strangers, cheerfully submit to the cajolery of bums and modestly tolerate the

Left: Rocky Graziano, 1949

Trainer Whitey Bimstein puts on Rocky Graziano's gloves, 1949

flattery of hangers-on. With them, pride is a devouring thing that spurs ambition and allows them to go along on the assumption that the head is not a housing for the brain and a few useful sense organs, but a target; that the scraping off of scar tissue around the eye is not a painful process; that hands are best used as rapiers and clubs; that blows on the throat do not affect the voice, that blows to the body do not affect the kidneys, and that blows to the head do not affect the reflexes. Graziano's pride, it turned out, took as many blows as his chin. At various times in his career he was called yellow, crooked, and a double-crosser. For some reason, no person in public life is as much exposed to violent public reactions as a prizefighter. Cries of "What's with the bribe, Rocky?" and "How come you run out on Apostoli, Rocky?" pursued him during the bad days wherever he went. They stung deep. Rocky was proud of his crafts-manship. It brought him money and the noisy accolades of his friends and it seemed to remove him, little by little, from a bitter and unpleasant past. The more opponents he defeated, the further away his beginnings seemed. That was the way he wanted it. He spent, after all, six of his first 20 years in reform schools, was deaf for two years as a result of an automobile accident, had an embarrassing relationship with the U.S. Army and never got beyond the fifth grade in grammar school. He once said, "When I got out of the Army, it was either fight or steal—so I turned into a fighter."

Rocky wasn't kidding about that stealing bit. From clipping nickels and dimes out of the milk-money box on the teacher's desk in school and prying pennies out of the chewing gum machines in the subway, Rocky, when he was a tough kid running with the East Side gangs, progressed to heisting more important loot such as bicycles, cameras, watches and expensive toys. In his remarkable book, *Somebody Up There Likes Me,* which he wrote with Rowland Barber last year and has since sold to the movies, he looked back on those days with a candor that was downright hair-raising. "At Christmastime," he said, "with so much merchandise laying loose all over the place, a guy lost money going to school. There wasn't even time for the usual things—sneaking into movies, shooting pool, shooting craps, playing poker, rolling drunks in the subway, stealing trucks for rides, things like that." Naturally, this kind of boyish fun was frowned upon by the authorities. Rocky was always in trouble. He can still remember the words of the detective who turned him over to his grand-mother after an all-night session on the hard wooden benches of Children's Court: "Well, there goes another little guinea on his way. Good-looking kid. But I can tell his kind. Look in his eyes, you see the devil himself. Ten years from now, the Death House at Sing Sing."

The cop was wrong, but not far wrong. That was the path Rocky was walking on, all right—in fact, he wasn't walking on it, he was running along it as hard as he could run. He became an expert on reform schools and he knew what the inside of the Tombs looked like, too. (Later on, after his trouble with the Army, he became acquainted with Leavenworth.) When he was only 16, he and one of his pals spent a terrible night in the station house refusing to confess to a series of robberies even though a couple of cops beat them methodically and mercilessly with lengths of rubber hose and baseball bats. Rocky can be bitterly funny about it now. "Suddenly they stopped the workout," he said. "It was time for the shift to change, and the cops wanted to wash our blood off them before they went home to dinner."

Some of the budding young hoodlum's adventures were less gory and more honestly funny. Like the time a bunch from "the clique" borrowed some shovels and made a midnight attempt to dig up the body of Peter Stuyvesant because they had heard he had been buried with a silver peg-leg, a gold watch and a diamond ring. But there was nothing funny about being in jail, Rocky discovered—not even when your cellmates include such distinguished felons as Jimmy Hines, the famous politician; Robert Irwin, the sculptor who murdered the beautiful model, Veronica Gedeon, and Dixie Davis, the notorious gangster mouthpiece. But it took Rocky a long time to, as he puts it, wise up. If he hadn't got into the Metropolitan AAU Boxing Championships and won the New York City welterweight title (he sold the gold medal for "a lousy six dollars"), and thus began the slow switch from stealing to fighting, Rocky surely would have spent most of his life behind bars—and it probably would have been a short life. But he did, finally, see the light. Not so much, at first, that he was eager to stay on the straight and narrow. It was just that he caught on that there was more money, and easier money, to be made fighting than trying to buck the law. Later on, as he began to be exposed to what he calls "legitimate" people, he realized how crazy he had been. He understood, finally, that when you deliberately do something wrong, you've got to pay for it. If not one

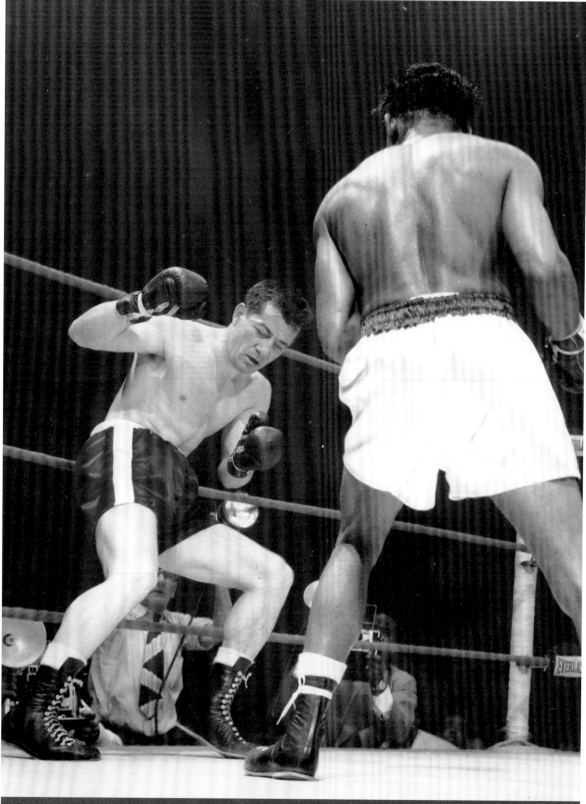

Reeling after a knockout blow from Sugar Ray Robinson, 1952

way, then another.

"When I say the law don't punish you," he has said, "that's what I mean. You got to punish yourself. That's the only way you'll ever go right and make it stick. Until it comes to you, like it come to me one day, that the law ain't your enemy, but you yourself are your enemy, until then you're nothing but a cheap, no-good bum."

That's a man talking, a man who has been here and has been there and has found out a few things about himself as well as about the rest of the world. Rocky wasn't very old in years when he started boxing professionally under Irving Cohen's management while he was more or less in the army, but he was old in experience. And nothing that had happened to him had been able to stamp out the drive, the blind fury, the pure and simple guts of the man. He was never a rookie fighter. Awkward, yes, clumsy and wild. But as soon as the bell rang, he was ready to fight. That was something that had been born in him. He understood that he was in there to beat the other guy, and he wasn't particular about how he did it.

Rocky's most effective maneuver as a civilian fighter—one he was not taught by his trainer, Whitey Bimstein—was holding his opponent's throat with his extended left hand used for leverage on the opponent's windpipe. Despite his superb reflexes, he was crude; it helped his marksmanship when his opponent's head was anchored. So Rocky anchored it the best way he knew how. Rocky had to take four or five punches to land one, and was glad to do it. He had enough confidence in his own punch to consider it a bargain. His pride insisted that he gamble, taking a hard shot in order to pinpoint an opening for his heavy right hand. He was fortunate in that it was just as heavy, when he trained hard, in the late rounds as it was in the early ones. Few ring records are as studded with late round KO's as Rocky's.

Until he forsook boxing for television Rocky was a dependable protagonist in the sport's most popular type of drama—the old faithful wherein the slugger is out-pointed, stung, eluded, hit off balance, tricked, pecked at, chopped up and frustrated by the clever boxer until such a time as he can catch up with his will-o'-the-wisp enemy and land solidly. In 84 fights, some of which were against opponents several pounds lighter than he was (proper casting called for it), Rocky managed to catch up most of the time and land the equalizer. He lost only ten fights. Once he landed the right hard and solid, his opponent was shaken to his heels and his senses were dulled. Rocky was generally as effective a finisher as

Dempsey. He would press in, his head forward, raining roundhouse rights to the jaw, to the jaw, to the jaw, and an occasional left hook to the head or body, lunging, stalking, firing punches without let-up. Finally his opponent would cave in. It is said that Graziano caused more fighters to retire from their profession than any other fighter before or since. Marty Servo, the former welterweight champion, became a barkeeper after his bout with Graziano. After the first Zale fight, which Zale won by a knockout in six rounds, it was Zale who went to the hospital. It was Zale and his manager who vetoed a fourth fight with Graziano—even though Zale had won the third more easily than he had the first. Graziano, who, it developed, had no memory of fighting the second and third rounds of the fight and had a concussion as a result of Zale's punches, wanted Zale again. Zale refused. No more than one-third the fighter he had been, he soon lost the title to Marcel Cerdan.

"When the Rock hits them," his placid, blue-eyed, white-haired manager, Irving Cohen, used to say, "it stays with them. He's liable to hit you on the arm and break it. He throws rocks, that boy."

Rocky's single-minded approach to his work was such that Cohen had to pay his sparring partners higher wages because Rocky was constitutionally unable to take it easy with them during training. He had a compulsion to belt them out. It was such that when he was knocked out by Ray Robinson, considered to be the greatest fighter of his generation, he told Cohen gloomily, "Let's wrap it up. If I can't beat Robinson, I better quit." It was such that, under suspension for not reporting a bribe offer in New York, he refused to let his seconds stop the second fight with Zale, who was tearing his face to ribbons during the first five rounds of their title bout in Chicago. In that one, Rocky came back to his corner virtually in tears from frustration. He couldn't hit Zale because he couldn't see him. His left eye had an inch-long gash under it which Bimstein had covered with carpenter's wax—a substance so dangerous to the eyes if it gets in them that it is used only in championship bouts. The wax had coagulated with the blood and, while Zale couldn't open the cut any deeper, the eye was useless to Rocky. The right eye, from repeated Zale jabs, was swollen to the point where Rocky could hardly see through it, either. Bimstein and Frank Percoco worked desperately over him between rounds. Percoco applied primitive surgery. He pressed a quarter against the swollen part of the eye and broke open the wound, allowing the blood to spurt out. He patched it up before the buzzer sounded and Rocky lurched forward to battle again. By turning his head to the left and peering out of the corner of his right eye, Rocky could see a lithe, dancing Zale within range of his lunges. Rocky took a dozen punches to the cheek, the body and the eyes, and scored a few of his own. Some of them landed sharply. Zale, affected by the heat, arm-weary from the effort of throwing hundreds of punches at Rocky's exposed head, and slowed down by Rocky's roundhouse rights, grew steadily less elusive. The temperature was 113 degrees at ringside. Zale had his championship to buoy him up; Rocky was in disgrace—in New York, anyway—and for him the only way out, no matter what it cost, was to knock out Zale. Zale, several years older than Rocky, felt the heat more. He found himself pinned against the ropes, unable to punch his way out or to escape to either side. Nearly blind, Rocky swung and swung. He hit Zale a hundred times—and Zale would not go down. Rocky was a great finisher of hurt fighters, but Zale would not be finished. Rocky threw two right hands under Zale's heart—probably the hardest two punches he ever threw. Zale would not go down. Then Rocky was being pushed away by the sweating referee. A white blur was between him and his victim. The fight was over. Rocky couldn't see well and his mind was cloudy. Why had the referee stopped it? Because he had kept hitting Zale while Zale was on the ropes? Then the light dawned. It was a technical knockout. He had won. It was vindication. The referee had saved Zale from further punishment. Rocky was champion.

A horde of people crowded into the ring, a robe was flung over him, photographers' bulbs exploded. Rocky's hand was raised, he was kissed by people he didn't recognize, he was dragged from corner to corner and allowed to make the conventional inquiry about the defeated fighter's health. His victory was affirmed by the ring announcer and a microphone was shoved in front of his face. Above the tumult, above the happy cries of the bettors who had taken the short end, an exultant Rocky shouted to the world, "Hello, Ma! The bad boy done it!"

In the steamy dressing room, pushing through the crowd, a reporter shoved his head down next to Rocky's and asked, "How does it feel to be the middleweight champion of the world?"

Rocky had a bewildered look about him. He was happy, but you could see he hadn't grasped the immensity of it. He hadn't begun to fully savor what this victory meant to him, a fighter who was suspended in his home state for failing to report a bribe offer he had refused for a fight that never came off. But he was thinking about it. "I don't know," he said haltingly. "I mean . . . I mean as a kid I . . . I mean I was no good . . . I mean nobody ever thought . . . I mean . . . You know what I mean?"

There were others yelling at him, trying to get stories for their papers. There was one answer they got out of him that summed up Rocky's whole creed as a fighter.

"How did you feel in there when you had him in the corner?" one writer called out to him.

Rocky turned to face his questioner. "I wanted to kill him," he said, and he was very serious. "I got nothing against him, he's a nice guy. But I wanted to kill him."

Rocky received a hero's welcome in New York. Cops on motorcycles and the Mayor's personal representative escorted him to his apartment on Second Avenue. He had made $70,000 for a night's work, the general feeling around town was that the New York commission officials were willing to concede they had been too harsh in suspending him, and everyone agreed that the beating Zale had given him in their first fight was canceled out. Through a gauntlet of congratulations, Rocky beat his way into his home. His daughter Audrey, then four, was in the living-room. She didn't recognize her father. His ear was swollen and bandaged, there was a huge, red lump on his forehead, one eye was swollen and the other was lined with stitches. It hurt Rocky to talk, to walk and even to eat. Audrey asked her father what had happened to him. She knew only vaguely, if at all, that Rocky was a fighter, and he and her mother had kept her from looking at his fights on television. "I fell down in the gutter, honey," he told her.

He spent the night soaking in a warm bath full of Epsom Salts. He was the middleweight champion of the world and he had the scars to prove it.

Rocky Graziano, the 33-year-old television performer and comic personality, has no visible scars. One presumes that the mental ones he developed as an ex-Dead End kid, an ex-convict and an ex-street fighter are now submerged in his spectacular success. A surgeon removed the hardened tissue from over his eyes, and the wounds of his face and body, even after later beatings by Zale, Robinson and Davey, have healed. He is a regular on the *Martha Raye* show. He is the highest-paid panelist on a summertime charades program. He appears as a guest on shows like *Name That Tune, Down You Go, Who Said That?* and

Graziano on the set of the *Martha Raye* show, 1956

What's My Line? He sings, he says, like Jimmy Durante, and he stops nightclub audiences cold with "If I Knew You Were Coming, I'd've Baked a Cake." He poses in boxing trunks with the presidents of television networks and in ballet tights with ballerinas for publicity purposes. He is toying with the idea of starring in his own television show and his aforementioned autobiography, *Somebody Up There Likes Me,* is a gold mine. Rocky now smokes an occasional pipe, gets a haircut more often than he needs it, shaves daily, helps his daughters (the younger, Roxie, is now seven) with their homework, drives a '54 Cadillac which does *not* have his name emblazoned on the sides, and goes over his television scripts with his wife, Norma, in their apartment in Long Beach, Long Island.

"What I love best today," Rocky says, "is just walking down the streets of New York. I can walk down Broadway or First Avenue or even Fifth Avenue, and this

is my town. My name is Rocky Graziano, I had it changed legally from Rocco Barbella, which it was when I was in the can and in the Army, and what's yours? I got a right to ask anybody that, even a cop. Who's a cop to me but some poor guy trying to make a living in a uniform. I'm legitimate, and I'm doing all right, and it's a free country and I'm glad I'm living in it."

I paid a visit to the ballroom of the Henry Hudson Hotel in midtown New York one afternoon recently, to see Rocky at a rehearsal for the *Martha Raye* show. The Henry Hudson, where the New York Giants and visiting French military bandsmen put up, was thick with theatrical atmosphere. Men in tweed coats, cotton polo shirts and scarves, wearing caps and dark glasses, hurried about, showing scripts to one another. A man in a white suit talked over the lessons to be learned from reading Proust with a lady in tight bicycle pants. Men and women with bulky scripts under their arms or briefcases in their hands strolled about the lobby with a purposeful air. The atmosphere was full of Broadway-Hollywood talk: "Be my guest." "When does the integrated commercial go on?" "The typical is prototypical." "I have news for you."

The ballroom, a few yards away, was brightly lit, had a long conference table in the center with a pitcher of water and some glasses on it, a prop coat rack nearby, two prop beds at each end, a line of chairs in one corner, and a couple of pianos near the beds. Another lady in bicycle pants was reading from a script and practicing exaggerated facial expressions. A foreign-looking man in a white waiter's jacket moved across the floor. An exceptionally large lady in a large black skirt and a white blouse poured herself a glass of water. A man in a checkered coat examined the strips of tape that formed right angles and acute angles on the floor, apparently as directional aids for the actors. Martha Raye, dressed in dungarees and a camel's-hair overcoat, came in, followed by a half-dozen distinguished-looking men. Then Rocky Graziano, dressed in a dark blue lumber-jacket, neatly pressed gray slacks, a checked shirt, black shoes and gray socks, walked in. He was followed by a group of large men casually attired. "Hey, cousin!" the largest of the group called. Rocky turned and smiled in a preoccupied way. A man near Martha Raye, who could cackle like a parrot, cackled like a parrot. Rocky waved a hand at the group. "We just come down to see how you was doing, Rocky," the large man said. "Nice to see you," Rocky said. "We thought we would drop by to see how it was going with you," the largest man said. "Yeah, how's things, Rocky?" somebody behind him asked. "Pretty good," Rocky said.

Guys from the old neighborhood, the old gang, from the fight mob, or even guys from what Rocky would describe uninhibitedly as "one of the cans I was in," stop by fairly often just to see how things are going with him. It's interesting, and revealing, to see that to all these faces out of the past, Rocky the television star is the same old Rocky. They may kid him a little, good naturedly, about making love to Martha Raye—"What's Norma gonna say when you get home?" they'll want to know—but their kidding is strictly friendly, between friends. His old pals don't resent Rocky's success, his famous "legitimate" friends, his handsome clothes, his bank account, his improved speech, his confidence as he walks among the greats. They know how he got there,

and they know he never sold out a living soul in order to get there. Which is more than can be said for a lot of the "legitimate" guys.

A dark-haired man in his shirtsleeves called to Rocky that he wanted him to do the picture-frame bit. Rocky waved his hand in a friendly way to his visitors and said, "I'll see you later, huh?" Then he walked over toward Martha Raye, kissed her on the cheek, and sauntered, rolling his shoulders, in the direction of one of the beds. He seemed suddenly expansive, as though he had emerged from an alien element into one he was familiar with. He pretended to throw a left hook at the man in shirtsleeves, who playfully dodged it. "Okay," the man said. "Everybody quiet!"

Rocky shouted in great good humor, "I'm emotin'!" His face took on a world-weary look, and with presence and gestures, he said, "O, wouldst that it couldst have been thee instead of me!" He looked as though he were going to cry. When the scene was over, a lady in a red skirt, holding a script in one hand and a stopwatch in the other, asked him to do it over again for timing. Rocky obliged, looking just as world-weary as before. Then he lit a cigarette and sat down with a newspaper. The man in the white shirt asked him to say, "I love her better than life itself," a couple of times, which he did without a trace of self-consciousness. The man in the shirt appeared pleased. Rocky stuck the lighted cigarette behind his ear and popped a piece of chewing gum in his mouth. The man in shirtsleeves moved off to talk to Miss Raye and I walked over to Rocky. Nat Hiken, who used to direct the *Martha Raye* show and who was the discoverer of Rocky as an acting talent, had told me that Rocky was a thorough study, if not a quick one, that he used to look at his feet when he delivered his lines, and that, like most non-pros, he didn't talk loudly enough—until constant urging trained him to do what the professionals call "project."

Graziano, who thought "free expression" was being allowed to use dirty words and that Stanislavsky was a Russian wrestler, had apparently come a long way. He had made a most difficult jump—from the world of toughs, hoods, spinach-and-lambchops and violence to the world of makeup (for men yet!), theatrical artistry, milking an audience, and memorizing lines; from a world where almost any demonstration of feeling except wrath and cynicism is frowned on to one in which he must play on his emotions like a musician on his instrument. Hiken thought Rocky was a successful

Rocky the style maven for *SPORT*, 1950

actor because, as a boxer, he had learned how to move and because, no matter what he was called to do, the unmistakable Graziano personality showed through.

I asked Rocky if he felt nervous before a show.

"Nervous?" he said. "Never. I'm playing Rocky. I'm doing what comes natural. Before the show, the actors come up to me and fake punches and tell me, 'Don't be nervous, Rocky.' It ain't like you was going out against Zale hooking you to the body. But if somebody had told me eight years ago I was going to make a living acting, I would have said 'You must be crazy.' It was the least thing from my mind. After Robinson stopped me, I thought I was through fighting. But Irving said, 'Well, let's take one more money shot and wrap it up.' So he signed me with Davey and I figured, this guy is a little small welterweight and I'll wrap him up. I wasn't too ambitious for the fight, except for the money, and I couldn't hit him good—he was left-handed—so I lost the decision. Then I was ready to quit, although it hurt me. It was my trade, you know what I mean? So then Hiken saw me on the *Nick Kenny Show* and says he'll give me $1,500 to appear on the *Martha Raye* show. I figured I'd just be taking a bow, which I done plenty, and for $1,500 that's a pleasure. So I see him in his office and he

tells me I'm to say lines, not take a bow. I told him I don't know how to say lines, I hardly know how to read and write. But he has me say, 'I think I'm gonna go out and eat,' the natural way I say it and he says that's great. He says Cagney and Edward G. Robinson and all them guys aren't actors, they just talk the way they talk in real life and they're a big hit. He tried 20 actors for this part, he says, and I'm the only one who done it correct. So I went on the show with Cesar Romero and Martha Raye and Rise Stevens, and it worked out all right. For this, NBC gives me a two-year contract. If I blew a line on the show I would kill myself, and the actors know it.

"I tell you one thing. If I'm ever killed by punches, it'll be by an actor. I was never hit so much in the ring as I am by these actors. They rupture my back with knocks. Even the girl actors. I guess they think it makes me feel at home. It was the least thing in my mind, being an actor, but I done better at it than I done at anything. I like it."

Rocky took his cigarette down from behind his ear and puffed on it. I asked him what he did for exercise these days. "I don't do nothing but play a little golf and run up and down the stairs at NBC," he said. "I used to see these guys play golf when I was doing roadwork out

Larger than life Rocky, 1956

of town on a golf course. I used to say to myself, 'this must be some game if these guys get up at six in the morning and play golf.' So I didn't have no lessons or anything, but I took it up with some friends and I got so I could shoot 85. At NBC I run up and down the stairs, visiting all the different big shots. They ask me in their offices and I tell them stories about the fight game, how Joe Jacobs, Schmeling's manager, used to go around with BB shot in his mouth and peck anybody's head he got the chance at in Stillman's Gym. They didn't know if they were being stung by hornets or what. Or how we used to get a guy's name and announce he was wanted in the phone booth, so when he was in there we would bar it shut from the outside. Nobody is on the phone, of course, and when he tries to get out, he sees he can't. So he's inside there, hollering and yelling and pounding like a crazy man, and nobody pays him any attention. Finally one guy goes over and listens to him, real polite—he's shouting and making motions with his hands—and then the guy makes out he can't understand him and goes away. I never clipped off a guy's necktie with scissors or give out laxatives or anything like that, like some fighters do, but I played some jokes. I know Frank Sinatra pretty good, and one time a kid I know who didn't know whether he should be a boxer or a singer asked me how Sinatra got his voice. So I told him Sinatra goes to a hotel room and takes off his tie and opens a bureau drawer and sings with his head inside it for all he's got. Then he opens up the window and sings out of it as loud as he can. Then he sticks his head inside the drawer again and sings. So the kid goes and does this, with me and a friend looking on, and the manager comes up and throws us all out of the hotel. The kid finally became pretty fair boxer.

"I used to be a real wild kid," Rocky went on, squinting a little, "but I got over it. I wouldn't listen to nobody. I wouldn't manage a fighter because if any fighter done to me what I done to my managers, it would drive me crazy. The only thing that didn't change about me since I got to be an actor is where I get my clothes. I got 20 suits, all mohair, like the rabbis wear, and I get them from Newman Brothers, on the East Side, only now they're tailor-made. Bright, with slash pockets. When I go in there, a bunch of guys come out with tape measures . . ."

"Hey, goombar!" Martha Raye yelled at him in tones that echoed and re-echoed throughout the ballroom. Rocky mashed out his cigarette. "Excuse me," he said. "I got to go rehearse."

On those rare occasions when Rocky had money, he used to buy long-wearing suits, with vertical pockets, from the Newman Brothers at five dollars down and five a week. In those days he and his two brothers and two sisters (five out of the 10 children were all of the family that survived) used to eat doughnuts for breakfast in their tenement kitchen and Rocky was called "Muscles." Rocky was hardy, or he wouldn't have reached adolescence. He was run over by automobiles four times, he fell down an elevator shaft, and once, when he was being chased by two cops for turning on a hydrant, he ran through a plate-glass window in a Chinese laundry shop. Instead of taking him to jail, the police took him to the hospital, where he was sewed up with 56 stitches.

Rocky wasn't the smartest kid in his gang, but, despite these inconveniences, he was the toughest, and when affairs of honor had to be settled man-to-man, it was Rocky who was singled out as the gang's representative. He generally won his fights by knockouts—even against ex-professional or active professional fighters. A good many members of his gang later became prize-fighters; a couple were sent to the electric chair. He was Thomas Rocco Barbella then, and he showed early that he had a devastating sock and that he wouldn't step backward or quit. It was part of the street code—just as it was part of the code, later, to keep quiet about a mysterious bribe offer even though his silence cost him his New York State boxer's license for some 26 months.

Rocky at six was recognized officially as the toughest six-year-old in the park district, at 10 he picked Tony Canzoneri for his special idol, at 15 (having run away from a half-dozen schools) he was beating up the other boys in his yard in reform school, and at 18 he won the Metropolitan A.A.U. welterweight championship. Despite the fame and money that professional fighting seemed to offer, Rocky didn't especially want to become a serious prize-fighter. He didn't like the discipline of training any more than he liked the discipline of school or, later, the Army. He didn't want his face messed up, either. His father had been a boxer known as "Fighting Joe Bob" and hadn't been famous or rich. His uncle enjoyed the same situation. Rocky has memories of them and their friends sitting around the gloomy tenement, swapping boisterous stories about the boxing business over buckets of beer. His father, who got occasional work as a longshoreman, kept boxing gloves around the house and encouraged Rocky and his brothers to fight one another—something they didn't see much profit in, since they felt most of their energies ought to be devoted to bringing in money or raiding pushcarts for groceries.

As he grew older, Rocky forsook the street games of ring-o-levio and stickball for gang fights in parks. He spent more time on street corners and less time in school. He felt his poverty more. Since it was more profitable to fight for gold watches than for free in an alley, he joined clubs and won watches, which he sold at the going rate. He was scouted, naturally enough, by sharp-eyed managers, and finally, getting sick of the diet of doughnuts and seeing no other way to raise his standard of living, he listened to the blandishments of some of them and signed a few contracts. But the rigmarole of training disgusted him and he and his early managers went their separate ways, the latter hoping he would get stiffened when he stepped into the ring with a competent fighter. Rocky finally wound up with Irving Cohen, who had the sense to give him a long leash. Cohen changed Rocky's name from Barbella to Graziano (his grandfather's name) and lined up a fight. Refusing to train much, Graziano nevertheless showed a gang-war, killer instinct and won by a knockout. Other fights were lined up with Cohen trying, in his subtle way, to overmatch Rocky, get him defeated, and thereby show Rocky the value of getting into condition. It was impossible to overmatch him. Rocky kept knocking them over. He even demanded a fight with Sugar Ray Robinson—which, fortunately, he didn't get for a good many years.

He had money in his pockets and he set them up for his friends—their number was growing by the hundreds—in every bar on the East Side. He wallowed in noisy celebrity. He was moving up in the world, at least in the only world he had ever known.

But a fighter's mouthpiece takes funny bounces. The outside world, which he knew practically nothing about, moved in on Rocky. The Germans marched into Poland and the Japanese finally got around to attacking Pearl Harbor. Like many of his contemporaries, Rocky was drafted to push them back. He was sent to Fort Dix, where he was told to pick up cigarette butts. Rocky didn't take to it. A boxer spits when he wants to spit, his friends constantly tell him how he can beat up people, and he sometimes attracts as many customers as the Yankees and the Dodgers draw for a World Series game. It was beneath his dignity. He was sent to see the

captain. The captain called him a wise guy from New York. Yardbird Barbells, after the fashion of his youth and environment, invited him to step outside. The captain made a move, and Rocky, not knowing the captain's plan was to call the MPs, slammed a right hand to his jaw and knocked him out. For once, the old standby was the wrong solution to the problem. You are not supposed to hit your commanding officer in the jaw. If it had been known that Barbells had fought as a pro (professional boxers' fists are considered by law to be deadly weapons), Rocky might still be serving time in Leavenworth. Somehow he escaped a general court martial and was put back at picking up cigarette butts. He went AWOL. Returning to New York, he managed to persuade Cohen that he had been given his discharge, and for four months he won fights—as Rocky Graziano. Then the MPs dropped by and he was shipped to Fort Jay, tried, and sent to Leavenworth.

"I felt lower and lousier every mile the train went west," Rocky says in his book. *"I was leaving the world. I would never see the East Side again. I might as well be dead. Creep town after creep town we went through. They got miles of these here woods and fields between all the creep towns, like it was the reform-school farm stretched out for a thousand miles, which God forbid should ever happen. I knew there must have been some place between New Jersey and Kansas, where my grandfather once worked. But if you had told me there was so much of it and it took three days to get across it, I would have called you a liar . . . I sat hour after hour with my face stuck to the window. I looked out, yet I didn't look out. I seen so much of this sad, lonely country I don't want to see no more. I didn't want to believe that people really lived in such a place, this place with no end to it, and with no river, no movies or pool rooms or candy stores or hock shops or pushcarts."*

Rocky spent 10 months in Leavenworth, and, for a jail, it wasn't so bad. He became the star of the prison boxing team and a pet of the colonel who commanded the post. He also had time to think, and what he was thinking was that he didn't have a hell of a lot to be proud of. Sure, they treated him like a big shot around the prison, but what kind of a big deal is that, being a big shot in the can? Rocky felt even worse when his mother wrote him that his kid brother, Lennie, had been drafted and was overseas with the 69th Infantry Division. Not Lennie, Rocky thought. He's a nice, polite kid. He might get hurt. They ought to send me over to take his place. He even tried to get them to, but they wouldn't. They wanted him where he was, in the can. It made him think some more. It made him realize there was another way to live and maybe he ought to try it.

After ten months, they let him out and gave him a dishonorable discharge. Back in New York, he avoided people—except for a pretty young brunette, Norma Unger, whom he married. They set up housekeeping with Rocky's mother. Rocky just hung around.

One of Rocky's routines when he is a guest member of a television panel goes like this:

M.C.: Tell me, Rocky, what was your toughest fight?

Rocky: Getting my mother out of the house.

But life is different from television scripts. It was Rocky's mother who felt that Rocky should get out of the house—or contribute some rent money. So he looked up Cohen. He submitted to the drudgery of training after Harold Green twice demonstrated that his wild swings could be avoided and he demanded that Cohen line him up a match with the flashy Billy Arnold. Full of misgivings, Cohen did. After taking a terrible beating in the second round, Graziano knocked Arnold out in the third. Afterward, as was often the case with Rocky's foes, Arnold was not much good. "From a $400-dollar-fighter," Graziano says of the Arnold fight, "I became a $50,000-dollar fighter. I could buy some new sweaters, a convertible and some suits with color to them. I done it with my fists."

He also bought a house for his own growing family. It wasn't anything fancy, but it was a nice, solid, two-family brick place on Ocean Parkway in Brooklyn, with a hedge out front and a garden in the back. It was a big day for Rocky when he walked in with Norma and stood there while the moving men carried in their furniture and their other possessions. "It was my own house," Rocky says. "If I wanted, I could lock the door and tell the whole rest of the world to beat it. If I wanted, I could have a ball every single night and take my shirt off and start a crap game and nobody could stop me. Most important, this place belonged to Mr. Graziano, and you better call him Sir on account of he's a husband and a father and it ain't every jerk who can own a house in Brooklyn."

Few people in public life have had so many damaging blows thrown at their solar plexus when they are riding high or have been given so many whiffs of restoring oxygen when they are hanging on the ropes as Rocky has. After working his way up to champion, he was sent into a tailspin when somebody in Washington

made news of his Army troubles. Already barred in New York because of the "bribe" scandal, he was now barred in most NBA states and when, his head full of melancholy thoughts, he skipped out on a fight with Fred Apostoli in California, he was barred in most of the rest, as well as in all the foreign countries where a boxer could make a real buck. The sportswriters protested that it was unfair to hold his past against him, but he was out in the cold until Commissioner Eddie Eagan, acceding to the demands of loyal Graziano fans, and a sizable segment of the press, restored his license to fight in New York. He knocked out Charlie Fusari in 10 rounds. He went to the sticks and piled up a list of unimpressive kayos, including one that was remarkable in that it was a blow to the forearm rather than to the jaw that won it for a badly out-pointed Rocky. When he returned, Cohen got him a fight with Sugar Ray Robinson in Chicago. The super-patriots had finally taken the heat off him everywhere. "I thought he would be over the hill," Rocky says of Robinson. But it was Rocky who was over the hill.

Rocky was down again—and then suddenly he was up. His face, which had been mirroring his emotions for the past 30 years, was in demand on television screens all over the country. People liked to see a tough-talking, square-jawed ex-fighter playing the part of a tough-talking, square-jawed ex-fighter.

Rocky, having finished rehearsing a bit of comic business with Martha Raye, bounced back, tearing open a stick of gum and offering it around. He was friendly with everybody, dodging and throwing playful punches, as much at home as if he were in Stillman's Gym. Charles Laughton in a T-shirt. Why not? John L. Sullivan used to chop wood onstage; Canzoneri and Rosenbloom and the Baer brothers made the jump successfully. So instead of hitting them with your right, you hit them with your personality. Obviously, Rocky has taken it in stride.

"What was your toughest fight?" I asked him when he had a minute.

"Getting my mother out of the house," he said. You could see how naturally the lines came to him.

"This acting racket," he said, "I'm nuts about it. The good food washing around in my belly. The actors calling me Mr. Graziano. I'm a member of a team—you know what I mean? I'm doing something"—he made some abrupt gestures with his hand—"creative."

That's how far Rocky Graziano has come.

ROCKY GRAZIANO REVISITED

BY W.C. HEINZ

FROM *SPORT*, SEPTEMBER 1966

When Rocky Graziano fought you could almost walk on the tension. When he fought in Madison Square Garden you could feel it over on Broadway, and that September night 20 years ago when he fought Tony Zale for the first time and we were driving down with him from Eddie Coco's house in the Bronx you could sense it between the cars jammed along the Grand Concourse, half a mile from Yankee Stadium and two hours before the fight.

So Eddie Coco is still doing time for shooting and killing a parking lot attendant in Miami. The last I heard, Tony Zale was still working for the Catholic Youth Organization in Chicago. Rocky Graziano makes television commercials and public appearances, and I have to think to remember that Emile Griffith is the middleweight champion of the world.

The trouble is that I am now in my middle age and boxing is in its old age, in this country anyway, and Graziano spoiled me . . . the Rock and Joe Louis and Ray Robinson and Willie Pep. They say Louis was the best of the heavyweights since Jack Dempsey, and Robinson was the best all-round and pound-for-pound since Benny Leonard. Pep was the greatest creative artist of the last two decades, and the Rock was the most exciting, certainly the only fighter I ever fell for completely.

You see, I missed Ketchel but those who knew them both said they were alike—exciting just walking down the street, and in the ring the whole embodiment of what boxing is, which is fighting for a prize. Graziano's

prize was the pass to get out of the East Side slum, the broken home and the trouble with the law that were his heritage. For me he put more meaning into a fight than anyone else I ever saw.

Take that first fight with Zale. They had been flattering the Rock with welterweights, and then he ran into this man. At the end of the fifth round they were hollering: "Stop it! Stop it!" They were hoping to save Zale, who in the next round and on quivering legs and with two punches . . . took out the Rock. It remains the best fight I ever witnessed, and Nat Fleischer, who has been watching them for 60 years, puts it second only to Dempsey-Firpo.

Take the second Zale fight. It was 120 degrees under the ringside lights that July night in 1947 in the Chicago Stadium, and the blood was covering the Rock's left eye and his right was closed by swelling. Again it was the end of the fifth round, and this time Frank Percoco took the hard edge of a quarter—two bits—and broke the swelling. In the sixth round the Rock could see again, and the referee stopped it to save Zale's life.

"I wanted to kill him," the Rock was saying in his dressing room minutes later and before he had unwound. "I wanted to kill him. I mean, he's a nice guy. I like him. He's a good guy. But I wanted to kill him."

What I mean is, I don't think there are two people in all of boxing today who have had imposed on them the need to fight like that. That's a tribute to our society, but it's hell on fights.

"How did you get by the doorman?" I was asking the Rock now.

In New York I have this apartment in the 20-storey,

Graziano (left) drinking to the success of *Raging Bull*, the autobiography of Jake LaMotta (right), 1970

white-brick high-rise they erected and opened two years ago on what was the site of Stillman's Gym. The Rock, as a fighter, spent his best working years and I, as a sportswriter, too many of my best working days there. I had wanted to hear Sam Schweitzer, the day doorman and the reincarnation of Jack Curley, who ran the turnstile at Stillman's, say on the house intercom: "Mr. Graziano to see you." Instead, the Rock had rung the bell on my door.

"I just walked by him," the Rock said. "I gave him a wave, and he said: 'Hi-ya, Champ.' He's a nice guy."

"Had you ever seen him before?"

"No, but he's a good guy."

"This reminds me," I said, "of that fireman in Chicago."

I had wanted, sitting on the site of Stillman's Gym, to recall with him what I remember best about it. After all, I remember when New York State banned him for failing to report a bribe offer for a fight that was never held (and a bribe offer that was not accepted). And I remember when the flag-wavers, coast-to-coast, tried to hang him again on an Army rap for which he'd already done his time. Before he had found boxing he had run with guys who were to go to the chair, and for a while there, once the forces for good started to tear him down, it was touch-and-go.

"After the Zale fight in Chicago," I said now, "Whitey Bimstein let me into the shower room. You were resting against the wall of the shower stall, the water just dripping down you, and there was the metal clamp over one eye and the other was almost closed again. There was just you and this uniformed fireman, who was guarding the door, and I had to ask you that newspaper question: How does it feel to be the middleweight champion of the world?

"You said: 'You know, I was nothin'. I mean, I never had . . . The way I grew up I was . . . I mean, I can't . . . You know what I mean?'

"The fireman hadn't said a word, but now he said: 'I know what you mean, Rocky. You're giving a talk on democracy.' You looked at him, and you said: 'You know somethin'? I like you. You're a good guy'."

"I don't remember that," the Rock said now.

"But you do remember Frank Percoco breaking that swelling under your eye with the quarter?"

"Oh, yeah," he said, nodding. "That's a true story."

"I know it is," I said, "and if he doesn't break that swelling you don't win the middleweight title. If you don't win the middleweight title you never fight again in New York State, and if you don't fight in New York you don't fight much anywhere."

"That's right."

"Did you ever hear of another quarter that was parlayed into so much dough?"

"I never did. To tell you the truth, I never did. You know, you're right."

"You had those money fights after that, and then how much did you get for the movie of your life?"

"A quarter of a million."

"How much did you make out of the book they made the movie from?"

"I don't know, exactly, but more than from the movie. I mean, it sold all over the world. It's in 20 different languages, and in Italy it sold the biggest. We still get money from it, but not so much now."

"That annuity you have that pays you for the rest of your life—could you live on it, if you had to?"

"Yeah, just about."

He and Norma, who was from the old neighborhood and married him when he was just a preliminary kid, live in a penthouse in Forest Hills, Long Island. Their older daughter, Audrey, is 22 now and married, and Roxie is 18 and in the theater.

"The night you won the title," I said. "Audrey must have been three years old. She was in the crib at the hotel, and when you got back there she woke up and started crying. You went in to see her, and she took one look at you, with the one eye bandaged and the other swollen, and she said, "Daddy, what happened?"

"That's right," the Rock said, "and I said: 'You see what I mean now? Stay outta the gutter.' That's a true story, too."

They have to be true stories, because no one would believe them otherwise. The Rock, with his own true story, did more to ruin fight fiction than all the bad writers.

"What do you weigh now?" I said.

"He was sitting there in one of the swing-back chairs, wearing a black knitted short-sleeve sports shirt, dark grey slacks and black loafers. I remember when he used to wear an old T-shirt, peg-bottom pants and yellow shoes, and although it is obvious that he can never make 160 pounds again, the weight is well spread through the chest and arms; not all at the waist.

"Right now I weigh 195."

"What do you do for exercise?"

"I play a little golf, but mostly I keep active. I mean, I'm goin' all the time."

"What do you do?"

"I make speeches. You know? Personal appearances."

"Where?"

"All over. I go any place. Dallas, Texas. About two months ago I spoke to the Chamber of Commerce in Albany. The people like me. I mean, the agent's got a lot of ballplayers, but they're not popular everywhere. You take Mickey Mantle or Yogi Berra and everybody likes 'em here, but in Chicago they got their own ballplayers. In Chicago—everywhere—they like me as much as here. Just last week I spoke at Fordham University."

"What did you talk about?"

"Criminology. I spoke to all the kids who were graduatin' and a lot of elderly people, like professors and priests."

"What did you tell them?"

"You know what it is," he said. "I start out, whether I'm talkin' about criminology or juvenile delinquency, and I say: 'You know, I'm so glad my father took the boat, because this is the best country in the world, and if there was another country like this one I'd be jealous'."

Imagining him talking, even as a gag, at Fordham University, I remembered the hearings on the bribe offer when they banned him, ostensibly for life. After they had confused him about the rule book, as it applied to attempted bribes, the one commissioner who seemed to be thinking straight asked him how far he had gone in school and he said: "The fifth grade."

"Then what do you tell them?" I said now.

"I say: 'If you're a juvenile delinquent, two things will solve your problem. All you need is a good alibi and a good lawyer. Then I tell 'em about the guys I knew who went to the chair, and I tell 'em about *Somebody Up There Likes Me*, how they made the movie and about the book."

"Rock," I said, "how much do you see of the fighters of our time? Do you ever see Zale?"

"That's a funny thing," he said. "Everybody always asks me about Zale. You'd think that he was the only guy I ever fought, and I fought a lot of guys."

He had 83 fights, won 52 by knockouts, 14 by decision, one on a foul and drew in six. He was knocked out twice by Zale and once by Robinson in 10 losses.

"But two of the three with Zale were classics," I said now.

"Tony don't come to New York much," he said, "and when I see him he don't say much. He's a very quiet guy."

"I know," I said. "He just used to go in there and fight his fight, and leave the talking to Art Winch and Sam Pian."

"It embarrasses me," the Rock said. "I mean, he was in New York here and we were walkin' down the street. Guys would come up and say: 'Hey, Rock! How are ya? You were the greatest.' I'd say: 'Hey, wait a minute. This here's Tony Zale.' They'd say: 'Yeah. How are ya, Rock? You were great.' I mean, they made me feel sorry for him. I mean, I was embarrassed."

"Do you ever see Louis?"

"Yeah, Joe," he said. "A great guy, too, but I can't figure him out, either. You know? I mean, I make all these appearances and sometimes they want Joe and me. We can cut up $1,500 here, $1,250 there. I try to get in touch with him and he's in the Mombo Islands or Jamaica or someplace and I say: 'Joe, we're booked. We gotta go.'

"One day we're drivin' to Pennsylvania. We're drivin' to—where was it? Oh yeah, Wilkes-Barre. Wilkes-Barre, Pennsylvania. That's it. I said to Joe: 'You wanna go by plane? You wanna go by car?' He wants to go by car, so I pick him up and I left in such a hurry I forgot to get any dough. We're on this turnpike, and I want to get some gas. I say: 'Joe, I forgot my money. Lend me 10 or 20.'

"He don't say a word, sittin' there next to me, but he goes into his pocket and he hands me this fat roll. I get the gas and I look at the roll and there's $400 in it. I pay for the gas and get in the car and go to give him back the money. He says: 'Keep it'."

That's all he says on the whole trip to Wilkes-Barre. 'Keep it.' He's a great guy, but I can't figure him."

"Do you ever run into Robinson?"

"Not much, but four days after he retired at the Garden—they had that thing for him—he called me. He said: 'Rock, what do you call those things you make on TV?' I said: 'Commercials.' He said: 'I'd like to make a few of those. How do you do it?' I said: 'You talk too good.' It's the truth."

"Do you think, at your peak, you could have licked him?"

The Rock would have had to get lucky with the right, and I could never see it. A real fighter always thinks he can lick anybody, though, and before he won the title the Rock kept begging his manager, Irving Cohen, who did a great job picking the opponents, to get him Robinson.

"I always thought I would have had a hell of a shot with him," the Rock said now, "because I think he always was a little worried about me, even that night."

It was the April night in Chicago in 1952 and Robinson was just past his peak but the Rock was well beyond his. In the third round the right dropped Robinson but he came right up and flattened the Rock.

"When I make a talk," he said now, "I tell them: 'I'm one of the few guys had Robinson on the floor. He tripped over my body'."

"How about some of the others?"

"That's a funny thing," he said. "Guys I licked like me. I mean Charley Fusari . . . Tony Janiro. They want me to come over to their places."

"What's Janiro doing?"

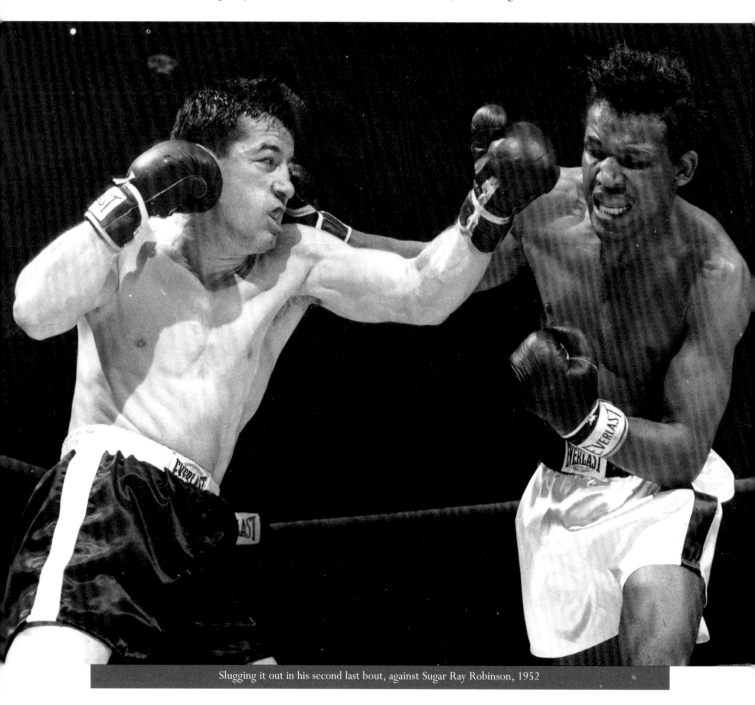

Slugging it out in his second last bout, against Sugar Ray Robinson, 1952

"He's a bartender on 44th Street, between Fifth and Sixth. Everybody likes Tony. You remember Tony Pellone?"

"Very well."

"He's a big man down on the docks."

"How about the fighters out of your old neighborhood?"

"Lulu Costantino's got a bar at 13th and Second Avenue. He's all right. Bozo Costantino's a construction worker. Al Penpino's a longshoreman. Freddy Menna—you remember the flat-nosed welterweight boxed me 4,000 rounds as a sparring partner? He's a shop stewardess at Grumman Aircraft."

"Shop steward?"

"That's right. You remember Terry Young?"

"Yes, one night in the Garden he and Paddy DeMarco fought the dirtiest fight I ever saw. They did everything, and at one point they were actually biting each other. Tommy Holmes, the sportswriter, turned to me in the second round and said: 'These two guys must have learned how to box during an Indian massacre'."

"That's right. Terry Young's a bouncer in the Village now."

"I understand," I said, "that Marty Servo's very sick in Arizona."

"I heard that. A real good guy."

Marty Servo had just won the welterweight title by knocking out Freddie (Red) Cochrane when he fought the Rock, non-title at the Garden. He never defended the title because the Rock ruined him as a fighter in one of the few poor matches that Al Weill, who managed Servo, ever made. I can still see the Rock, holding Servo under the chin with his left hand and beating him with the right with a fury I've never seen before or since in the ring, and after it was over and I got home I couldn't sleep.

"I always liked him," the Rock said.

"I know. When he was tending bar somewhere down here off Times Square you dragged me down there one night to give him a little trade."

"That's right. A good guy."

"What do you think of the fighters we've got today?"

"I saw Emile Griffith and Dick Tiger," he said, and they were fighting for his old title. "A terrible fight. I thought both were washed up."

"What about Cassius Clay?"

"Clay, I think, is a pretty good fighter. If he fought Joe Louis or Rocky Marciano or one of them guys they'd lick him pretty easy, but he's pretty good. I think the only thing wrong with him is he's too wrapped up in his religion. I mean, I give him credit for it, but it gets in the way, I mean, to be a fighter. I think he's one guy really believes that Muslim religion. I start to talk to him about fightin' and he tries to talk me into the religion."

"Why don't we have more good fighters?"

"You know why? We got no poor kids in the whole United States no more. I mean, we got things like relief and welfare and pensions. Today a kid still gets $25 for a four-rounder, but instead of fightin' once a week he's gotta train for a month. Then you've got these guys that own fighters—two, three guys together owning a kid. You give a kid money to live on while he's learnin'; you spoil him."

"Television killed it, too, closing the small clubs."

"That's right, and you know somethin' else? I know a guy's a diamond setter. The diamond setters made a lot of money. They sent their kids to college and they become doctors and lawyers. Now they don't want to be diamond setters, and you got no more diamond setters. You know what that means?"

"What?"

"I tell 'em: 'It's the same in all the uncouth sports-boxin' and diamond settin'. You know what I hear, sittin' here?"

"What?"

"I mean, where the gym used to be. I hear Lou Stillman's voice: 'Get outta here, you guinea . . . ! You don't cop nothin' here, you . . . !'"

"Rock," I said, "how old are you, honest age? When were you born?"

"January first, 1921. In the record book it used to say a year younger, but that was the different Graziano."

He was born Barbella, but when the Army captain challenged him and started to take off his coat the Rock belted him out. Then he went over the hill and took the name and birth certificate, because they used to run together in the old neighborhood, of Tommy Graziano. Under that name, and A.W.O.L., he used to fight for $25 at Fort Hamilton, an Army base.

"Whatever became of the original Graziano?" I said.

"In the can. Doing 20 to 30. He was like a three-time loser. You know?"

I know. It was all there in the way the Rock fought. If boxing were still in the best of its times a lot would have gone out of it for me when the Rock left, but it isn't. It's in the worst of times, I see no out for it, I'm 20 years older and so I end up as the pallbearer for pugilism. I'm sorry.

Great Rivalries:

ROCKY GRAZIANO
VS.
TONY ZALE

BY JOHN DEVANEY

FROM *SPORT*, SEPTEMBER 1969

Rocky Graziano stepped out of the taxi this past May and squinted into the sunshine and smog on Manhattan's Third Avenue. He looked Broadway sharp in an electric-blue suit. He was tieless, his collar open the way it always was when he was 25 years old, the middleweight champion of the world and lived on the lower east side. He was 30 pounds heavier than in his fighting days, that once sleek face as lumpy as a paper sack filled with eggs.

He said hello to the writer who had been waiting for him, and he spoke in that comical ex-pug's growl that has made him rich as an actor in movies and on TV commercials. The writer mentioned several things, including Graziano's three classic fights with Tony Zale. "I hated that waltzin' guy," Rocky said. "I wanted to kill him, you know. Now I'm the best friend he's got." He laughed.

Tony Zale stood with his back to the bar at Gallagher's 33, a restaurant near Madison Square Garden. It was a slack moment during his job as a greeter. He was holding a glass of ginger ale. He does not smoke or drink, and never has. At 55, he has the lean-jawed face of his youth, only a few lines on it, and his trim body has that hardness that made people call Tony Zale of Gary, Indiana, the Man of Steel.

"Those fights with Rocky, they made us famous," he was saying to the writer. "He hurt me in that first one." Tony paused, smiling, his deep-set eyes as dark as bullet holes. "We gave those people their money's worth, didn't we?" he said.

In blood they gave the people their money's worth. In their three brawls—and that's what they were: waterfront brawls and the hell with defense—Tony Zale and Rocky Graziano battered each other from ring post to ring post, smashing each other senseless, the blood flying out of torn mouths and spattering their bodies. Each fight ended suddenly in a knockout and by the third fight you could get 20-1 odds that the fight wouldn't go the limit. In two of the fights, a man seemingly destroyed, staggering and bloodied, suddenly roared out of his corner, fists flying, to win the fight and what was at stake, the middleweight championship of the world.

Some 80,000 people watched the fights two decades ago. They were not televised and there is a movie of only the last one, the least spectacular of the three. From those three encounters the two fighters split well over a half-million dollars.

They met for the first time at a weigh-in at Yankee Stadium on September 17, 1946. Tony Zale, 32, had come out of Gary, where he had worked in the furnace heat of the steel mills. Even when he was middleweight champion of the world, Tony Zale—wearing a square-cut brown suit and a flowered tie—always looked like a steel worker spruced up for a Saturday night date. He carried himself in a stiff, erect way, a quiet man, a confident—almost contemptuous—smile on his bony face. Proud. That was Tony Zale, proud of being champion, proud of what he'd done with his fists.

His father had died when he was two. "He left seven of us," he was saying at the bar in Gallagher's. "He and my mother had come here from Poland. Seven kids. She couldn't speak English. She washed clothes, she took in washing, she worked wherever she could get work. She bought a cow that we kept in the backyard so we would always have milk even if we didn't have money. She was some woman. She gave me my determination.

"I started boxing in gyms when I was 12 or so. My older brothers taught me. I had over 200 amateur fights. After I graduated from high school, I turned professional; that was in 1935. I fought a couple of years, but then I got hurt and I went to work in the mills."

With long poles he plucked white-hot hunks of steel out of open-hearth furnaces. It was a living, but he missed boxing. "I like to work out in the gym," he said. "My trainers had to stop me from overworking. People used to say, 'How can you enjoy fighting?' I couldn't explain it but I used to say that it was easier than working in the mill."

For four years he scrambled up the blood-slippery boxing ladder. He saw all the dirt surrounding the sport, yet somehow he retained the ideals instilled in him by his mother: to work hard, be honest, keep himself clean physically and spiritually.

In 1941 he knocked out Georgie Abrams and Al Hostak to win the middleweight championship. "Then I went into the Navy for four years," he says. "I was stationed in Puerto Rico for most of the war, teaching boxing. I read in the papers about this Rocky Graziano and all his knockouts. I figured I'd be fighting him for the title when the war was over, so I read all I could about him."

The newspapers didn't print everything that could have been written about Rocco Barbella, Rocky's real name. At the age of six he'd run Manhattan's Avenue A like a wolf, stealing buns from bakery wagons for breakfast. At 11 he was behind bars in a reform school. At 16 he was being beaten by cops' billies in the back rooms of precinct houses. At 17 he'd known the screams of junkies and perverts in the cells of the Tombs. At 19, after knocking a captain senseless, he served a year in an Army jail.

"In those days I wanted to kill everyone," Rocky was saying, seated at a glass conference table in an elegant Manhattan townhouse. It is the headquarters of his chain of restaurants—Rocky's Pizza Ring.

Rocky laughed, remembering that wild hoodlum, Rocco Barbella. "Geez," he said, "I knocked out Freddie Cochrane twice, I wrecked Marty Servo—and he never fought again." He paused. "I always felt sorry about that," he said. "Poor Marty."

He grinned, that impish, comic grin. "I was a terror," he said. "Geez, I'd grab 'em by the throats with my left hand and with my right hand I wuz tryin' to knock their waltzin' heads off."

Close to 40,000 people—who had paid $350,000, a record gate for a middleweight fight—came to Yankee Stadium for the first fight. It had been scheduled for June, but Zale came down with pneumonia and it was postponed to September 24, 1946, a cool night in New York. The odds favored Graziano, who at 24 was eight years younger than the champion. Zale was more experienced and the better boxer, but after four years out of the ring there was a question whether he had the quickness of the 1941 Man of Steel.

Rocky, the alley-fighting brawler, knew only one defense—a flurry of swinging fists. At only 154 pounds, he was outweighed by six pounds by Zale. Most of his previous opponents had been welterweights whom Rocky had outweighed by four to ten pounds, and so people wondered how he could hold up against a heavier man's punches.

A minute after the opening bell, the fight assumed the savage character that would make the three Graziano-Zale fights so memorable. Zale stepped in to Rocky, lashing a left hook to Rocky's chin, and Rocky crashed down near a neutral corner, a drunk's look of non-comprehension on his face.

"I looked up at him and he seemed so tall," says Rocky now. "He always seemed tall to me."

The alley-fighter's fury boiled inside Rocky. He got up and tore into Zale. "I wanted to stuff a waltzin' glove down his throat," Rocky was saying, looking down at the glass conference table and seeing Rocco Barbella lunge after Zale.

In the second round Rocky threw a right and saw blood spurt from Zale's slashed lip. He aimed for it again, and twice he slammed padded fists across Zale's mouth and the blood splashed down Zale's legs and spattered his shoes.

Zale ducked a left and Graziano countered with a right. "I saw the right coming," Zale was saying at Gallagher's. "But I hadn't fought a big fight in so long, I was slow blocking it." The punch caught him on the

FIGHT I ONE

Graziano vs. Zale

YANKEE STADIUM, NEW YORK
SEPTEMBER 27, 1946

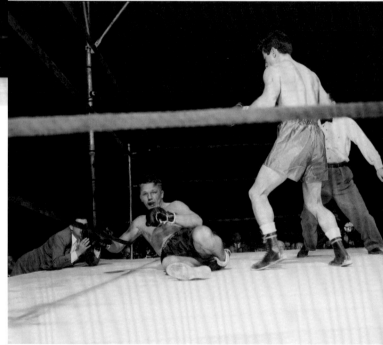

point of the chin, snapping back his head. Zale careened backward, hitting the canvas with the loud clatter of chairs being thrown down stairs.

"I knew where I was and what was going on," Tony says. "I'd been hit harder. Al Hostak, he hit harder. I knew what was going on."

At the count of "three" the bell rang. Zale got up slowly. He started for Graziano's corner, then suddenly shrugged himself erect and walked to his own corner, his face a red smear.

In the third round Rocky chased after Zale, pounding the bleeding face, the champion's eyes rolling crazily up and down. At one point Rocky cradled Zale's bleeding head in his left mitt and flailed it with his right, the beads of blood flying through the air.

"That round I was in bad shape," Zale admits, a rare concession from this proud man. "The pneumonia had weakened me, and after the knockdown, I couldn't seem to bounce back as quick as I usually did."

Weakened or not, the Man of Steel would not go down. At the start of the fourth round he seemed refreshed, charging at Graziano, popping two quick hooks into Rocky's body. "God, he was waltzin' fast," Rocky says, remembering the pain of those hooks.

Zale pounded Rocky in the body all through the fourth round. After fighting Zale, Billy Soose said: "When Zale hits you in the belly, it's like sticking a red-hot poker into your belly and leaving it there."

Zale had learned early the value of sticking those red-hot pokers into an opponent's belly. "I learned to be a body puncher," he says, "in my first fight as an amateur. I had one of my mother's big Polish dinners and then I went to the gym to fight. In the first round I got hit in the solar plexus. I don't remember anything after that until I woke up, vomiting. Right then I decided I was going to be the one who hit other people in the body."

By the fifth round Zale's cuts were sealed and he was moving with his old speed and cunning. He threw a right cross that bounced off Rocky's shoulder and pain flared all the way up to his elbow. "I'd broken a bone in the hand," says Zale, "and after that I couldn't use the right very much."

He threw two quick lefts into Rocky's body. Rocky fell back against the ropes, grunting. With a minute left in the round, he seemed trapped and vulnerable.

Again the alley-fighting fury rose inside Rocky. He drove back Zale with a rain of punches to the head. His right hand aching, Zale covered up; suddenly he was the

hunted instead of the hunter. Rocky ripped a right hand through the leather shield and blood spurted from Zale's torn mouth.

The champion staggered backward on unsteady legs. Rocky came after him, right hand cocked. The bell rang.

Zale's handler, Ray Arcel, mopped the blood off the champion's mouth. "He told me I had to start punching," Zale remembers. "He told me I was losing my title."

Arcel was right. Referee Ruby Goldstein and the two judges had Graziano ahead, three rounds to two. "Arcel told me to concentrate on the body," says Zale. "I told him I would."

Rocky, in his corner, was getting much the same advice. "Whitey Bimstein told me Zale's head was as hard as a watermelon," Rocky says, lighting a cigaret. "He said I should go to the body, but hell, maybe that was a mistake. I wuz never no body puncher."

At the start of the sixth, Rocky looped a left into Zale's abdomen. The champion bent over, elbows dropping to his trunks. Rocky wheeled a right to the head, then a left and now he had the champion trapped in a crossfire.

The crowd was standing, screaming, the roar floating up into the night sky and mixing with the billowing cigaret smoke. Rocky hammered Zale's bleeding face with a half-dozen lefts and rights. "Then I made a mistake," he says. "I leaned forward to throw a body punch like Whitey had told me to do."

He opened up his middle and Zale, crouching, saw the opening to the solar plexus. Standing now at the bar in Gallagher's, the old champion smiles, remembering. He assumes a fighting pose, fists clenched, and then he drives that rock of a right hand toward his listener's belly, and the writer senses the awesome power of that punch 23 years ago.

"Right in there I put it to him," Zale says, a cold smile hanging on his thin lips. He tapped the pit of the writer's abdomen. "Right in the solar plexus."

As Zale's fist plunged into him, Rocky's mouth popped open, sucking for air. He sagged against the ropes. Zale launched a left hook that slammed into Rocky's chin.

"It was like I had no feet all of a sudden," Rocky says. "I couldn't feel the ground under me no more."

He landed on the canvas on his haunches, his back against the ropes. He sat there, staring across the ring with hypnotized eyes.

Goldstein was counting above him. At "six" Rocky leaned back and grasped the middle rope. At "seven . . . eight" he was rising and at "10" he was straightening his body, but Goldstein waved his arms, ending the fight.

Rocky rushed at Zale, but Goldstein and Whitey Bimstein pulled him back. "He shoulda given me the credit of the doubt," Rocky says now. "It was close whether I was up at 10 or not."

Zale was besmirched with blood, Rocky was hardly marked. "Hell," says Rocky, "he looked like the loser and me the winner." The crowd was booing.

Zale's dressing room was closed for 15 minutes. When the reporters entered, they saw the champion sitting on a table, his right hand soaking in ice water. "Clean livin'," he muttered, staring into the ice water. "Clean livin'."

A reporter asked him a question. Zale did not answer. His handlers picked him up and carried him into the shower, his legs trailing behind him. Even while the water poured down on him, Zale went on muttering: "Clean livin' . . . clean livin' . . ."

Zale grins, embarrassed when he is reminded of that scene in the dressing room. "I don't remember much of it," he says. "I was exhausted. You got to remember it was my first hard fight in four years. And I was still weak from the pneumonia."

Graziano, talking about that first fight, smiles ruefully at what might have been. "Hell," he says, "I had that fight won. Then I got careless and he drove the wind out of me."

A writer reminds him what he said after the fight: "There is only one way to lick that Zale. You gotta knock him dead."

"Yeah," says Rocky, shifting in his chair, "he was tougher than any guy I ever fought in my life."

The next day Rocky padded down Avenue A, looking for his pals. They crossed the street to avoid him. Rocky heard what they were saying: that he had stayed down for the count because he had been paid to stay down. "I knew there wuz only one way I wuz going to stop that talk," he says now. "I had to win that second fight."

For the first time in his life, Rocky trained in earnest for a fight. Whitey Bimstein, remembering how Zale had collapsed Rocky with a blow to the body, hurled 100-pound medicine balls into Rocky's gut a hundred times a day. "I wuz in the best shape of my life for that fight," Rocky says. "We worked to improve my left hand. We knew that Zale would be watching my right

and he'd be open for lefts."

On the sultry night of July 16, 1947, in Chicago some 19,000 people—including J. Edgar Hoover and Frank Sinatra—crowded into the indoor Chicago Stadium for the second fight. Despite Rocky's training, Zale was a 13-10 favorite. The heat and the packed arena pushed the temperature at ringside to a steamy 102 degrees.

At the bell the two rivals dashed together with the rapacious hunger of spiders trying to dismember each other. Zale planted a right into Graziano's mid-section, the same blow that had crumpled Rocky a year earlier. But a thousand medicine balls had hardened Rocky's gut and he did not bend.

He snapped two rights to the side of the champion's head, Zale's flesh rolling up under the pounding, and Zale reeled backward, as though yanked by a rope.

The crowd roared, standing, smelling blood and a sudden ending. But Zale steadied, bounding back at Rocky, lashing Rocky's ribs with three left hooks, then stabbing him over the left eye with a right hook.

Blood cascaded down Rocky's face, blinding him. "All I could see of Zale was a red blur," Rocky says.

Rocky tried to wipe away the blood. Zale hammered him in the other eye, and a purplish egg began to balloon under that eye. Between rounds Bimstein sealed the cut over the left eye but Zale diced it open again in the second round with short, vicious chops. Blood sheeted down Rocky's face. "Then he started hitting me in the ribs and belly," Graziano says, "and it was so hot, I couldn't catch my breath. I had pain in both my eyes, and Zale was this red blur that came at me and went away from me."

At the start of the third round Zale switched back to the head. "I knew he was in bad shape," Zale says, "I wanted to finish him off as quick as I could with a good punch to the jaw."

He drilled a right to Graziano's jaw and Rocky flew halfway across the ring, crashing to the canvas.

"I remembered how I hadn't heard the count in the first fight until six and it wuz too late to get up," Rocky says, lighting a cigaret. "I jumped up before the referee could start counting."

Zale swarmed over him, pounding Rocky around the ring, the blood a red cape down Rocky's side. But Rocky stayed on his feet. "I didn't want nobody saying what they said about me after the first fight," Rocky says.

At the end of the third round referee Johnny Behr looked at Rocky's eyes and winced. "One more round

II
F I G H T   T W O
Graziano vs. Zale
CHICAGO STADIUM, CHICAGO
JULY 16, 1947

THE ITALIAN STALLIONS

III

F I G H T   T H R E E

Graziano vs. Zale

RUPPERT STADIUM, NEWARK
JUNE 10, 1948

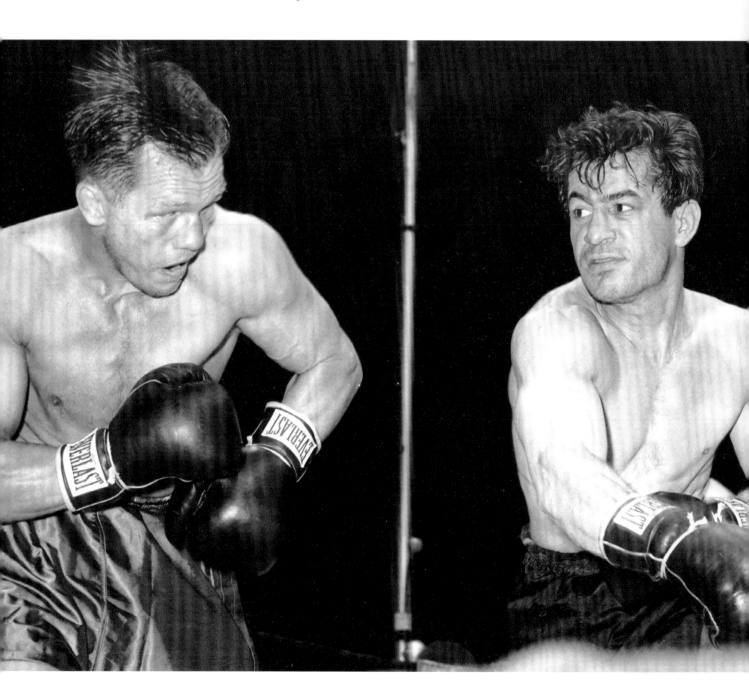

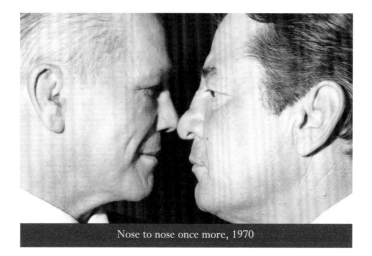

Nose to nose once more, 1970

and if he doesn't come out of it I got to stop the fight," Behr told Bimstein. "If this wasn't a championship fight, I would have stopped it already."

"I wanted that championship real bad," Rocky says. "I thought I should've won it in New York. Now, I thought, 'I'm so close, I'm going to lose it again. I'll go back to being nuthin' on Avenue A.' I remember I yelled at the referee: 'You . . . don't you stop it'."

In the fourth round a furious Graziano ripped into Zale. The left eye was no longer pouring blood, but it had been knocked out of focus. He stood sideways so he could see Zale through the slit that was his right eye. "You know," Graziano says, "that stance made me a better puncher with my left hand, it gave me more power."

In the fifth, Graziano staggered Zale with three straight rights and a left hook. "I couldn't get organized any more," Zale says. "In that fifth round, I remember, I was so exhausted I missed with a punch and fell on my face."

At the start of the sixth, Zale summoned all his remaining strength. He charged at Rocky, winging lefts and rights into Graziano's body for half a minute. Then he backed away, nothing left.

Graziano threw a right that drove Tony against the ropes. He grabbed the champion by the throat with the left hand and pounded his right fist into Tony's face. Tony sunk to the lowest rope. Rocky threw a volley of lefts and rights, a final right spinning Zale upward onto the middle strand, where he hung, head down. The referee pulled Graziano away.

"I remember cursing and trying to climb over Zale to hit him again in the head," Rocky says, smiling at the

memory of himself. "Then someone—Whitey Bimstein—slapped me across the face and he was saying, 'You're world champion, world champion.' I remember I yelled into the mike, 'Ma, Ma, your bad boy done it, he's world champion'."

Zale, hardly marked, stared across the ring at the bloodied Rocky. "I knew what was going on, he shouldn't have stopped the fight," Tony says. "You should never count out a champion until he is flat on his back."

An exuberant Rocky rode back to New York and a hero's parade down Avenue A. Tony Zale went off to the woods of Wisconsin to prepare for the third fight. "I knew I would win back the title," he was saying in Gallagher's. "In that second fight I saw a look on Rocky's face during that third round. He knew then that I was the boss."

Some 21,000 people filled Ruppert Stadium, a minor-league ballpark in Newark, New Jersey, for the third fight on the night of June 10, 1948. They paid $306,000; with the radio rights, Graziano's cut came to $120,000, Zale's to $60,000. In the three fights they had split, almost equally, close to $600,000.

At the bell Zale hammered Rocky toward the ropes, then snapped a left hook, and down toppled Rocky, beginning to pay the price for a year of the lush life. "After I became champion," Rocky says, a rueful grin on his face, "I went the way of all fighters—drinking, smoking, having a good time until all hours of the night, you know. I was the king of the world, I don't think there ever wuz a more popular champion than me except Joe Louis."

At the count of "three," Rocky rose and charged at

Zale, that alley-fighter's urge rising within him. But the full viciousness was gone, lost somewhere between Avenue A and the plush apartment on Ocean Parkway in Brooklyn, where he now lived. He backed off, uncertain about himself.

At the start of the third round Zale crashed a left hook onto Rocky's chin, staggering Graziano against the ropes. Two left hooks nailed Rocky to the ropes and a right cross dropped him.

Rocky was sitting on the canvas, legs outstretched. He heard the referee counting. He crawled along the canvas, grabbed the rope and tried and tried to rise. He was the champion and he couldn't lose this title because he had nothing to go back to except Avenue A.

He rose at the count of six. Zale stepped forward and threw the last left hook he would ever throw in anger at Rocky Graziano. Rocky toppled backward, his head slamming the canvas with the finality of a hanging judge's gavel.

His handlers went up to carry him out.

Zale stood in a neutral corner. He had become the first middleweight champion to regain the title since Stanley Ketchel in 1908. The Man of Steel looked up at the black sky, an expression of thanksgiving and joy on his face.

Rocky woke up in the dressing room. He didn't recognize friends. A doctor said he had a concussion. Rocky stared at the ceiling. "It was," he said 21 years later, "the lowest point in my life."

Later in 1948, Zale defended his title against Marcel Cerdan. Hampered by bone chips in his elbows, he lost to Cerdan and retired. Three years later, after being knocked out by Sugar Ray Robinson and Chuck Davey, Rocky retired.

Graziano fell back on his comical pug voice and made himself rich in movies and commercials. "I always looked up Tony when I wuz in Chicago to make an appearance at a convention," Rock says. "I'd tell the guy who was running it, 'How would youse like Tony Zale and Rocky Graziano together?' and they'd say 'great,' and Tony would pick up a thousand dollars easy for just standin' there while I told jokes. When he opens a restaurant in Chicago in about 1958 he called me up and I flew out there to appear at the opening."

The restaurant went under, carrying much of Tony's money with it. For several years he coached boxing in Chicago. Last year he got a $200-a-week job as the greeter at Gallagher's. "I drop in once a week or so,"

Rocky was saying, getting up now from his chair at the conference table. "We talk old times."

"Who was the better fighter?" the writer asked.

"I wuz," Rocky said in his growling voice. "Every fighter thinks he is the best waltzin' fighter . . ." He paused. "But Zale was one hell of a fighter, he was mean . . ."

"Better than Rocky Graziano?"

Rocky smiled and in a low voice he said: "Yeah, he wuz better."

Tony Zale and Rocky Graziano were standing at the bar in Gallagher's, talking of their daughters, grown now, and of Tony's grandchildren. Then they went downstairs to pose for pictures. When the photographer was done. Rocky said: "I don't know of any ex-fighters who are as close as Tony and me."

"We respect each other," Tony said. "I know what he can do and he knows what I can do." He smiled.

Rocky said he had to rush off to tape the Merv Griffin TV show. He mentioned a movie with Jane Russell he was making.

Tony listened, a smile frozen on his face.

"See you soon," Rocky said, shaking Zale's hand. Then he ran up the staircase to the main floor at Gallagher's where his retinue waited to escort him to the bright lights of TV.

Tony watched him go, that smile stuck on his face.

He said goodbye to the writer. He walked slowly up the staircase, his shoulders square, walking in the erect way he always had when he was the middleweight champion and everyone knew who was boss.

EPILOGUE

Tony Zale lived quietly, passing away at the age of 83 on March 20, 1997. Rocky Graziano, for his part, continued to parlay his colorful delivery and manipulation of the English language into guest shots on television variety shows and small movie parts through the 1960s, and maintained a lively career afterwards as a speaker and a spokesman for various businesses, including a casino. His health began to fail in the late 1980s and, in April 1990, he suffered a stroke. He passed away three weeks later, on May 22, 1990 at age 69. Honored in June 2003 by Ring 8, a charitable organization to benefit old boxers, Graziano's award was graciously accepted by his wife of 47 years, Norma Graziano.

WILLIE PEP AND ROCKY GRAZIANO DISCUSS BOXING—PAST, PRESENT AND FUTURE

BY THE EDITORS OF *SPORT*

FROM *SPORT*, SEPTEMBER 1962

Though it seems such a long time ago when boxing spawned and fed its fighting and colorful champions, it really wasn't. You need go back only to the late 1940s to recall the grinning, mouse-marred faces of Rocky Graziano and Willie Pep. They wore their middleweight and featherweight crowns a little tilted, perhaps, because they wore them with flamboyance and with style. They were the proudest guys in the world and if you were going to take away their crowns, you had to do it while they were lying flat on their backs in the ring.

Because they represent an era that exists no longer, and because, even after their fighting days, they possess a still-burning love for their old profession, the editors of *SPORT* asked them to discuss the way boxing was, is and probably will be.

Willie arrived first at our offices one hot, sticky day in June. He was dressed comfortably in a blue, open-necked sport shirt. The thick curly hair millions of older boxing fans would recognize was still there, though it had moved back a few inches on the forehead. An hour and a half later Rocky came in, apologizing for the delay caused by a luncheon date with Garry Moore. He laid down a copy of the stage play "Separate Rooms" which he would soon be doing in summer stock. After a few playful jabs and insults, the two fighters settled into

their chairs and the recorder began grinding away.

EDITOR: If you had it all to do over again would you do it the same way, would you both become fighters?

PEP: Well, I'd do the same thing only I'd save a little money. That's the only thing different I'd do. I'd try to save a little money.

EDITOR: Would you do it all over again, Rock?

GRAZIANO: I certainly would. I miss it right now. I really honestly do.

PEP: He misses making that two hundred thou.

EDITOR: What do you miss besides the money?

GRAZIANO: Actually, besides the money I miss the thing of training and I was more of a celebrity. Everybody says I'm doing OK as an actor and that kind of stuff, but as a fighter I think I had some of the greatest moments of my life.

PEP: You meet so many nice people. The food is good and the hours are short, too.

GRAZIANO: And the training was good. Remember when you were in shape, Willie? When you were in shape there was a certain thing you felt that was fantastic.

PEP: Yeah, you felt good.

GRAZIANO: You were in good shape, eh Willie? He had to be 'cause he couldn't punch. He never knocked a guy out in his life.

PEP: I didn't punch hard but I punched often.

GRAZIANO: But really, the fight business was a wonderful thing for a guy like me. And for the colored people and the Spanish people now, it's a good thing for them. Years ago it was the Jews and the Irish. And the rough guys on the street—the only thing they could do was become fighters.

EDITOR: Did you, save any money, Rocky?

GRAZIANO: Yes, I did. Not as much money as I shoulda 'cause when you're a young guy and you're a big celebrity you're paying bills for this here and all your friends are broke. You're the only one who makes it. You come from a neighborhood on the East Side and all the guys you've known all your life are broke. And if you don't do somethin' for them and help them out you're just a mean sonofagun and Willie and I, we're not like that.

EDITOR: You lost a lot of money that way, didn't you, Willie, giving it away?

PEP: Well, that's the way I was. I couldn't say no. And I gambled a little bit. Of course I had three old ladies and that made a big dent in my bankroll.

EDITOR: How much did you make in your career?

PEP: Gee, I don't know. I couldn't tell you. Close to a million, I guess. Rocky made over a million.

GRAZIANO: 'Bout three, four, five million.

PEP: See, Rocky, big guys make big money, which is all right. You know, you fought tougher guys. Of course, you're more colorful and you'd knock a guy dead with a punch.

EDITOR: What happens to fighters like Johnny Saxton and Johnny Bratton? What goes wrong with kids like that?

PEP: It's the idea of being a champion and then not being a champion and havin' no money. It's the money.

EDITOR: That's the toughest problem, isn't it? Adjusting after your career is over? You too are good examples.

PEP: Rocky adjusted himself well. He's makin' a good livin'. It was a little tougher for me. I didn't adjust myself too well.

EDITOR: Why should it be that he does well and . . .

PEP: Because he's hustlin', he's doin' somethin'. Tomorrow I could go to work and make $125 a week in construction work. My friend's a boss. Gee, you know, that's a big letdown. I wouldn't do it.

GRAZIANO: It's a real drag. Now I'm talkin' about guys who were really good fighters; I'm not talkin' about the guys who were nothin'. Listen, you've been a famous guy for 20 years and all of a sudden, bang! You can't take a job for $20 a day. That's the right thing to do but, you know, it's very, very hard.

EDITOR: Was it the fame and glory that meant a lot to you as well as the money?

PEP: Oh, yeah, it's great to be recognized; it's wonderful, nothin' wrong with that.

EDITOR: What about Floyd Patterson as a fighter?

GRAZIANO: Patterson, for what's around, is a good fighter, I don't knock him. He's an awful nice kid and he means well, up-and-up, but, you know, I still think he's a light-heavyweight—a big, blown-up light-heavy-weight, but he's got a lot of guts. But Sonny Liston will knock Patterson out in a couple of rounds. No question about it. And I'll tell you somethin' else—I think if Patterson loses this fight he's gonna retire. He's *nice* boy, you know what I mean? But he's got his little idiosyncrasies about him; his ways of thinking are like a fella knockin' off.

EDITOR: You think Liston will win, too, Willie?

PEP: I like Liston. Why? Because he's fought all the leading challengers—Eddie Machen, Zora Folley—he knocked out Cleveland Williams twice and no one knocks out Williams. On paper and everything, Liston figures to be the winner.

GRAZIANO: It's just a shame that there's so few good young kids. That's why we got the colored kids, the Spanish kids—they're going hungry, they're starvin'.

EDITOR: What's going to happen when these groups reach the general status and everybody's equal? There aren't going to be any more fighters then, right?

GRAZIANO: That's why the fight business is going out of business. Would you go see two colored guys or two Spanish guys fight, unless they were real good fighters? It's a shame—I'm sorry. I happen to like colored guys. We slept together, ate together, was incarcerated together.

EDITOR: Do you think that's the real reason boxing's going bad, just because of that?

GRAZIANO: There's another reason. There's no clubs. Name me another club in New York, right now, besides the Garden.

EDITOR: Is that only because of television?

GRAZIANO: Well television hurts quite a bit. Everybody stays home and watches the fights on the set.

EDITOR: Does television do it alone?

PEP: Only if a fight's a natural will they go out of their way. But how many good fights are there, or good fighters?

GRAZIANO: The kids today . . . Like I was at a synagogue the other day—I go around speaking, you know—it was a father and son dinner and the kids were getting their little plaques they won in sports. I say to myself, "There's not one kid here who's got . . ."—you ever see these Spanish guys and the colored guys, they

got thin waists. Us Italian guys—I have a 26-inch waist. These kids today, they're not, they're not—I don't know what it is but there's somethin' missing.

EDITOR: Maybe they have it too easy.

PEP: They drink a lot of milk—we never had any milk. Never took vitamins.

GRAZIANO: Look at us Italian kids—you know how I became champion of the world—I ate pastafazool every night. The will to fight, the will to be successful. Somebody up there likes me. Willie says to me, "Rock, I'm glad your old man took the boat because this is a hell of a country," and he says if there was another America he'd be jealous and want to be there.

EDITOR: You're really talking about heart, then?

GRAZIANO: Well, you know, the toughest kid on the street or in school, that's the guy who becomes a fighter—a wise guy. That's what happened to me. I was the best fighter on the street and a guy says to me, "Hey, you wanta become a fighter?" and I says "Yeah." So I went up to the gym and I met Whitey Bimstein.

PEP: You and I ended up in the hands of a pretty good guy. A lot of guys don't get that break.

GRAZIANO: But we could have gone the other way, know what I mean? When a kid is 18, 19 years old, especially when he's a rough tough kid, you give him a taste of the night clubs, show him a few dollars, and he says, "Yeah, man, I ain't gonna work for a livin'—I'll be a fighter."

EDITOR: How do you revive the fight game now? Is there any hope for it at all?

GRAZIANO: I personally think that they're gonna outlaw the fighting in New York 'cause they turned down Sonny Liston and now they just didn't give Joey Giardello a license. He's a good fighter, Joey, and they just turned him down—this kid ain't doing nothin' wrong. Just because his manager is some wise guy.

EDITOR: Do you think there are any mob guys in the fight business now or is it all talk?

GRAZIANO: No there isn't, not at all. Carbo's in jail and Blinky's in jail. They've done a helluva job of cleaning it up and that's it.

PEP: And this I want to put in: You see, all these commission jobs—they're all political. The commissioner here is a political appointment—he's a *lawyer*. He may be a good lawyer but he's not a boxing commissioner. Why don't they put a fella in who knows boxing, which they never do. They have one in Connecticut, a fella called Dinny McMahon, he's the commissioner—

that's the only right guy I know of.

EDITOR: You saw the last Griffith-Paret fight, Rocky. What do you think went wrong?

GRAZIANO: I don't think there was anything wrong with the fight. I think Paret wasn't physically equipped. I think he got hurt from the Fullmer fight. Fullmer banged his doggone brains in.

EDITOR: Do you think his manager should have had him fight Griffith so soon?

GRAZIANO: Nah, you can't blame nobody. What the heck, he got a good payday. How was anyone to know?

EDITOR: Willie has his own ideas.

PEP: Yeah, I got my own ideas. Let me tell you what I think. See, Rocky, I've reffed a few fights, a few championship fights. Now when you referee a fight with heavyweights, great—they're heavy, they're slow moving—but with featherweights, lightweights, welter-weights you gotta be on top and you can't be on the other side of the ring and this fella—I don't say it's his fault, he don't wanta get in anybody's way he's so worried about TV—he was on the other side of the ring and this guy's bouncing and banging Paret over here. The ref don't know what's goin' on. How can you know what's goin' on in back of a fighter? And then in New York State I find there's a rule: If a guy's body is outside the ring it's a knockdown. He should have been over there countin' the guy out. Then the guy would have had four or five seconds rest before he started fightin' again.

EDITOR: Is there any way to make it safer? Any rule that you could put in to lessen the possibility of someone getting killed?

PEP: They've made it just as safe as they can.

GRAZIANO: I'll tell you the truth, since they put in eight-ounce gloves that's pretty safe. You look at the fighters now they don't get as many cuts as they used to. Look at all the cuts Willie had and I had. I had plastic surgery, you know. I had over 200, 300 cuts on my eyes from six-ounce gloves.

PEP: Yeah, they've got an awful lot of precautionary measures. You gotta take an eight count, bigger gloves, and the referee usually stops it even if they just seem to be in trouble.

EDITOR: Either of you guys punchy?

GRAZIANO: Oh, do you think so? I kinda think Willie is.

PEP: Rocky acts that way all the time so you can't tell.

EDITOR: Why do they talk about punch-drunk fighters all the time?

GRAZIANO: I'll tell you, that's another thing that stems back from the old days. Fighters then, some of them did get punch-drunk. They talked with that Maxie Rosenbloom style, you know.

EDITOR: Are there any great fighters left today?

GRAZIANO: I think Gene Fullmer is a pretty good fighter. I think he's a rough tough kid and got plenty of guts. He's not a good-looking fighter to watch—he can't fight too good—but he wins pretty often.

EDITOR: Rocky, you said a couple of years ago in this magazine that for $50,000 you'd fight any of them. You still say it?

GRAZIANO: Yeah, I'll fight Fullmer right now for $25,000. I'd have a chance. If I got in shape for about six months I'd give him a helluva fight. Any fighter I could hit I could hurt. But if I couldn't hit him I'd be in bad shape. That's how I used to fight. I boxed a kid named Tony Janiro, I couldn't hit him for 10 rounds, I hit him once I knocked him out. Who else? I boxed Fusari, Charley Fusari. For 10 rounds I lost the fight, I hit him in the 10th round I knocked him out.

EDITOR: You're giving us names now—Janiro, Fusari—these fellows weren't champs but they were good fighters. Today you can't go down six, seven, eight names and get fighters like these. What would the fellows in today's main events be fighting in your day?

GRAZIANO: Six rounds. Years ago I was champ of the world so old-time champs like Canzoneri (Tony) would say they were better than we were and we weren't nothin'. But now I don't know. Now there's two champs here sayin' that these young guys today are the same way. Maybe we're wrong but I think now I'm right. Of course I hate to knock any fighter because I really know what he goes through.

EDITOR: What can we do? Is there any way to get the good fighters back?

GRAZIANO: I think fightin' has had it. I think it's had it 'cause my old manager—Irving Cohen—they just took St. Nick's away from him. Now he's looking to open a club. People used to come to St. Nick's as a steady diet. The Garden don't fight every Saturday. They fight every once in a while. But there's no regular crowd. Take a look at the Golden Gloves of this year. There was the worst crop of fighters I ever saw in my life. But what I say about boxing, I really honestly mean it. I think they're gonna outlaw it in New York and New York, I think, is the biggest little country in the world. And everybody's gonna go along with New York. New York makes presidents. That's New York, man. I think the average guy just wants to see a television show. Wants to see wrestling on TV. Lots of people believe that wrestling on TV is true. I know it's full of baloney. And a lot of people come over to me and say, "Hey, you guys don't really bang each other, do you?" I'm talking about guys 20 years old who never saw me fight. They heard about me. They say, "You guys don't hit to hurt each other?"

EDITOR: What do you tell them when they say that?

GRAZIANO: What am I gonna tell them? Anybody that asks me a stupid question I give them a stupid answer. I say, "Sure, it's only in fun, you kiddin'?" But fightin' is the toughest sport in the world, don't care what else you say. They can get killed in these sports car races, too. But still, fighting is tougher.

EDITOR: Does this apply to the mental aspects as well?

GRAZIANO: Sure, you kiddin'? How would you like somebody like me comin' at you looking to knock your brains in? You know you got a chance of gettin' hurt, gettin' licked, gettin' cuts, gettin' hit on the arms, in the tummy, in the kidneys. You think of

all these things. I got knocked out by Tony Zale in Jersey and for three days I didn't remember the fight, I didn't know what the hell happened and in the first round I got hit on the chin which I saw from the pictures. From the sixth round I didn't know what happened. I got a slight concussion on my head and went to the doctor.

EDITOR: If you had a son would you let him fight?

GRAZIANO: If he really wanted to fight, I say this again, I would really make him fight. I swear on anything that's holy.

PEP: Rocky, you said before the business is no good no more. Why would you make him fight?

GRAZIANO: I said that if one kid was a good colorful fighter, he could make, for one fight, $5 million. This is if he's a good fighter.

PEP: What happens before he becomes a good fighter? It's a long, long grind.

GRAZIANO: You'd know what to do with the kid and so would I. He'd have the best shots and the best opportunities with us.

EDITOR: Do you think managers get too much of a cut?

GRAZIANO: Definitely.

EDITOR: Do you think fight managers should get 33-1/3 percent of the fighter's purse?

PEP: It worked all right for me because my manager was very very honest and it worked out good. He took care of all the expenses. If I took a friend to dinner a couple of times a week he still paid for it out of his income. Sure it's an awful lot, but he was all right.

EDITOR: Rocky, you said you wouldn't cut a four-round fighter. When Patterson was starting, Cus D'Amato took that attitude. He wouldn't cut him and was good to him in that respect. Do you think D'Amato was a good manager?

GRAZIANO: I think Cus D'Amato was the best manager that ever lived. He really started that kid. This kid couldn't fight that good. Cus put his whole life around this kid. He really helped this kid. Gave him money, fed him.

EDITOR: Do you think Cus is bad for boxing, though, by his sheltering Patterson? You said before that Liston is the only one who's fought the top contenders. Now Patterson hasn't. A lot of people say this is hurting boxing as much as anything, that the heavyweight champ has been held back. What do you think?

GRAZIANO: You can see that now 'cause there's only a handful of fighters. Years ago there were like 50 heavyweight fighters so you couldn't see it. But now it's so obvious because now there's only Patterson, Liston and a coupla others.

EDITOR: You think this was going on all the

time, then?

GRAZIANO: Oh sure. When I was fightin' my manager wouldn't make me box a coupla guys who were damn good fighters. No, what D'Amato has done for Patterson is the greatest thing around.

EDITOR: What did you do before you started fighting, Rocky?

GRAZIANO: I never held a job in my life. I was a bum.

EDITOR: How about you, Willie?

PEP: I worked in a wallpaper company when I was 16 or 17. I didn't make much dough. I was boxin' amateur while I was workin'.

EDITOR: Was it tough getting used to training and the routine in the beginning?

PEP: No, I liked it. I ate three squares a day; it was pretty nice. And I liked to run anyway. Rocky's a tough guy but I was very skinny and I needed the training. He gets hit with a punch he shakes it off; I get hit with a punch it knocks me down, so I had to be in much better shape than Rocky.

EDITOR: Would you like to be 20 years old and just starting in the fight game?

GRAZIANO: I'd love to be 20 years old again. I'd be a millionaire in three years. By just fightin'.

EDITOR: Could you make that kind of money now as a middleweight?

GRAZIANO: When me and Tony Zale was fightin' as middleweights we outshined the heavyweights. We hold the record right now for the biggest indoor gate of all time and I don't think they'll ever break it. When we get pay TV—not closed circuit, but pay TV—a real good fight will make $30 million, $40 million.

EDITOR: Could Liston and Patterson make that kind of money if pay TV was in now?

GRAZIANO: Sure. Wouldn't you put in a half a buck to see it?

EDITOR: Rocky, you're 20 years old and you're going to make a million dollars in three years—how do you start? What's your first move? Would you be aiming for that big pay TV fight?

GRAZIANO: Sure. Just like when I was a young guy I was lookin' to get into Madison Square Garden. I wanted to get into that doggone Garden so bad. My first big fight in the Garden was Billy Arnold. Knocked him out. I'm glad I knocked that sonofagun out! I knocked him right into President Truman's lap.

EDITOR: Did you two ever spar with each other?

PEP: No.

GRAZIANO: I woulda killed him.

PEP: Rocky, you couldn't hit me with a handful of stones.

EDITOR: Didn't Jake LaMotta box with you once, Willie?

PEP: Rocky put him up to it.

GRAZIANO: One day I says "Go ahead, Willie, work out with Jake in the gym." So they get in the ring and Jake brings his glove all the way back and Bang! He couldn't touch Willie at all.

PEP: He was dead tired, though. He had boxed six, seven rounds with somebody else. He used to box eight, nine rounds a day. That's what I liked about Jake. He said to me one morning, "Come on, Willie, let's do roadwork." I met him at Wolfie's in Miami Beach. He ordered some orange juice, he looked around and then put some brandy in the glass and drank it. So we run. So the next day I met him again, he looked around and put the brandy in his orange juice and drank it. So I says "Jake, what is this stuff?" He says, "Willie, I don't run good but I'm the happiest guy in the world."

GRAZIANO: He was an animal—very strong. And, you know, I was Jake's downfall. Like everything I done, he always came in second. Even with stealin'. I swear to God. The first job he done he got arrested. Now he's tryin' to become an actor. He's doin' not great, but he's tryin'.

EDITOR: Do you have any regrets at all?

PEP: None that I can think of. Boxin' was very good to me. I'd still be boxin', it was so good to me. The food was good and the hours were short.

EDITOR: Is there anything you would have done differently, Rocky?

GRAZIANO: I had a very successful career. There were a lot of knocks and bumps but I was a guy who could stand it. Before I was a fighter I was all messed up. I was out in Kansas and these two commissioners are tellin' me they're takin' my license away. It didn't mean nothin'—nothin'—it hurt me, but I could take it 'cause of my rough background with the war which taught me it's better to be straight than crooked. I really mean it.

EDITOR: Both of you have historic places in boxing now. Do you think history will be good to you in the future?

PEP: Well, they'll read about us. But, you know, fame is fleeting. Who'll remember us? Just the kids in our era. Fathers will know us but their kids won't.

CHAPTER FIVE

GIACOBE LAMOTTA

THE STORY
OF A CHAMPION

BY BARNEY NAGLER

FROM *SPORT*, FEBRUARY 1950

On May 18, 1949, a dark-eyed, pretty, 16-year-old lass named Marie LaMotta sat in a classroom in the Christopher Columbus High School in New York City and put her thoughts down on paper.

"To the world of boxing," she wrote, "Jake LaMotta is a fierce, outstanding figure, known by many titles in all parts of the United States, such as 'The Atomic Bomber,' 'Concrete Chin,' 'Human Dynamo,' and 'The Bronx Bull.' But to me, he is just my brother."

Thus, simply and innocently, in the words of a schoolgirl, Marie LaMotta began to write about the complex fist fighter who is her brother. It was a classroom chore, nothing more, but out of the pure purpose of her writing there emerged a basis for sociological study.

"Little do sports enthusiasts," she continued, "know of the struggle he and his family had to go through before he skyrocketed to fame."

These were challenging words: they cried out for investigation. For, of all the characters playing their roles in the grim drama of pugilism, none comes so sharply into focus as does Jake LaMotta, who unexpectedly became (and if Robert Villemain continues to wield a hex over him, may not long remain) the middleweight champion of the world. The burly, literally big-headed Bronx fighter is the pugilist most often accused and abused in a craft in which double dealing and malfeasance are considered tools of the trade. Mud sticks to Jake LaMotta as it does to a

peasant's boot. I've often heard it said that if the late Ring Lardner were casting about today for a model for his fiction masterpiece, *Champion*, he might be tempted to select LaMotta rather than Stanley Ketchel.

Jake's first manager, slim, slight Mike Capriano, claims LaMotta slugged him during a quarrel over their contract. Jake's first wife, red-haired Ida Geller LaMotta, accused him of beating her. He has been charged with engaging in a fake fight, against Billy Fox in Madison Square Garden, on November 14, 1947. The finger has been leveled at him time and again.

The most disconcerting aspect of LaMotta's place in boxing is that he should have become a world champion despite all the arrows aimed at him. He has been a target for potshot artists of all stripes and inclinations, yet he has managed to overcome the wounds so inflicted. Most have believed he has been his own worst enemy, and yet . . .

You can check in the darkest recesses of boxing's blackness for words of praise for LaMotta. There are few to be found, precious few. Mostly, the denizens of Stillman's Gym, where the fight men collect in New York City, have this to say about him: "He was a great fighter. Too bad he got the raps he did, but he was a great fighter."

Those who know him intimately put a twist on this estimation of Jake. "Got himself in too much trouble," they say, "but one thing about LaMotta. He's good to his family, real good. You can't hate a guy for that."

Even Mike Capriano, LaMotta's first manager, the man who claimed Jake had slugged him, had to say it. "I want to tell you one thing," Capriano said. "Even at 18, LaMotta was good to his family. His father wasn't

Left: Jake LaMotta, 1949

around to take care of the four other kids, and Jake was like a father. He wore an old pair of pants and an old coat and sweater, but his two sisters and two brothers, they were dressed okay."

As Capriano said this, I thought of Marie LaMotta, Jake's younger sister, the schoolgirl who had written of how little the world knew about her brother's struggle up the ladder. I had met Marie some days before, in her brother's home in the Pelham section of the Bronx, the northernmost borough of New York City.

Driving over the Whitestone Bridge from Long Island, I recalled clearly my first encounter with LaMotta, in a plane flying between Cleveland and New York. It was October 21, 1941, the day after LaMotta had fought Jimmy Reeves, a capable, hard-hitting veteran campaigner, in a 10-round fight at the Cleveland Arena. That had been LaMotta's 18th fight as a professional and only his second away from the New York area. It had proved disheartening. Jake had lost. And now, in the plane returning him to New York, LaMotta was deathly sick. The bumpy air ride was doing tricks with his innards. I sat with him for a few minutes and tried to console him. He wouldn't listen. He was wrapped up in his own woe.

I wondered how he would greet me now, eight years later, in the fastness of his own home. I found the house easily enough in the middle-class section of the Bronx. It is a bungalow-type brick building, with a street-surface apartment in which his mother, Mrs. Elizabeth LaMotta, lives with her son, Albert, and with Marie LaMotta. The main floor of the house, reached from the sidewalk by a flight of stone steps, is occupied by Jake, his pretty wife, Vickie, and their two children, Jack, Jr., two years old, and Joseph, one. The front door to the lower apartment bears a green-crusted brass plate with the words, "LaMotta Residence." On the upstairs door, which leads to Jake's apartment, another brass doorplate says, simply, "Mr. J. LaMotta."

I pressed the upstairs doorbell, but before I even heard the ring, a gray-haired woman wearing a starched house dress opened the lower door and called me in. "My son's down here," she said. "He's been waiting for you."

Jake was there, seated on a divan in the living room of his mother's downstairs apartment. "Hey, how do you like the smell of garlic in here?" he called as I entered. "Ma, I told you the garlic was too much in the steak."

His mother laughed. "Come on upstairs," Jake said.

"I'll sit with you in my parlor until my steak gets ready. You can join me eating it."

He led the way up the stairs and I followed. His living room was square. The walls were painted a dark green and the main piece of furniture was a 14-foot semi-circular couch of modern design. Across the room were two pink easy chairs. These flanked a television set.

Jake smiled as he sank into the pink easy chair. "Nice joint," he said, "ain't it? I got four and a half rooms up here and my mother's got four rooms downstairs. We're happy here, but I'm trying to tell Vickie what I need is a farm more than anything else. I want to get away and live in the country, away from the people. I don't need people to be happy. I spend most of my time with my kids."

LaMotta eyed me closely. "So you want to write about me," he said. "Do you want to tell the whole story, like it hasn't been told before?"

"Exactly."

"Okay, shoot," he said. He began speaking, placing one of his heavy legs across the arm of the pink chair. It was an incongruous picture. The big-headed fellow, his bashed face topped by a lush growth of hair, seemed out of place in the atmosphere of this modernistically furnished parlor.

Jake was born on the lower East Side of New York, at First Avenue and 10th Street, July 10, 1922. His father, Joseph, an Italian immigrant, was a fruit and vegetable peddler and had been married a year before. The marriage was never a happy one. The LaMottas were separated time and again, but four more children were born—Mrs. Ann LaMotta Ramaglia, now 26; Joseph, Jr., 24; Albert, 20; and Marie, 16. The family was torn apart because of the incompatibility of Jake's father and mother.

At one time the family moved to Philadelphia, where the father took up his trade of peddling fruits and vegetables, but even this failed. Jake recalled his father as he sat in the parlor chair. "He was selfish. He thought only of his own belly," Jake said. "My father never showed any love for his children. I can remember a beating he gave me. It was terrible. He hit me with a whip that had nine leather thongs. I can still remember it."

Just then, Jake's mother came up the stairs, turned from a little anteroom, into the parlor, and underlined Jake's story. "I remember when that happened," she said. "Jake was seven years old. We were living near a church and my husband said Jake had to be in the house when the bells in the church rang at six o'clock. This

Zapping Fritzie Zivic, 1943

night, Jake was a little late, just a little late. My husband beat him so bad with the whip, I'll never forget it. He was a wicked man."

All the while the LaMottas lived in Philadelphia, one son, Joey, who later was to become a fighter, just as Jake did, remained back on New York's East Side, living with his maternal grandfather, Joseph Merluzzo. Finally, in the depth of the depression, the LaMotta family was reunited. They were brought together again in the squalor of an apartment on Washington Avenue near 169th Street, in the Bronx. The rent was $26 a month. The father wasn't living at home. Mrs. LaMotta was on her own, with five young, yawning mouths to feed.

"I paid $26 a month for the flat," Mrs. LaMotta recalled. "It was four rooms and it had steam heat."

There was one consolation. The LaMottas would not be dispossessed from this flat as they had once been from a flat in Philadelphia. They were on home relief and their rent was guaranteed by the city. The LaMotta family received $64 a month for rent, food, clothing, and other necessities. It was tough.

Jake remembered his days in this area of the Bronx vividly. "I was going to school, even graduated from the ninth grade in P.S. 55, but was I tough!"

His mother interrupted. "You'd better go in and eat the steak now," she said, "or it'll get cold."

Jake arose from his chair. "C'mon," he said. "Let's dig in." He led the way into the kitchen of his apartment, a large, sunny room whose fittings were painted a canary yellow. Mrs. LaMotta brought in the steak on a large platter. The steak was eight inches across and six inches wide. It was smothered in onions. The piece of beef must have weighed three pounds. She placed a plate of cooked carrots and raw celery on the table.

"Dig in," Jake said. He didn't wait, however, but went right to work. Jake cut triangular pieces out of the steak and chewed them lustily. "I always eat like this when I'm in training," he said. "Fighting Villemain December 9, you know. I'll beat his brains in this time, so there'll be no trouble."

Which proves Jake is not a champion prophet. Villemain trounced him decisively in their 10-round non-title bout.

Just as Jake was scoring a victory over the steak, a dark-eyed, brown-haired girl of five walked into the kitchen. "Come over here, Jackie," Jake said. The pretty little girl walked to him and rested on his lap. "This," he said, "is my daughter, Jacqueline. She's my daughter by my first wife, Ida. You knew her. I get Jacqueline every Sunday and, boy, does she like to come here. Don't you?"

The child nodded and smiled. LaMotta cut a piece from the steak and held it aloft, on the fork's tip: "Want some?" he asked Jacqueline. "Sure, daddy," she said. She pulled it from the fork with her hand.

"I remember my father, that's why I love my kids so much," Jake said. "They're going to have every chance, not like I had. You know, when we lived in the Bronx, we did anything!"

He smiled and the crescent scar alongside his left brow stretched as he did so. "I remember, when we came to the Bronx from Philadelphia, we was on our own. Joey used to start fights and I'd finish them. Once I hit a man so hard with a left hook he fell from Park Avenue—you know, where the train runs—right into the railroad cut. I had plenty of trouble. When I left school I never had a job. I shined shoes and I fought with other kids for places to work with my box. Then I got into trouble when I was about 16."

There was silence. I wanted to know what the trouble had been. His brother, Joey, had told me. "Jake never talks about what the trouble was, but it was robbing a jewelry store or something. Jake never was a good thief. I was better. You know, he's ashamed to talk to me about how he got caught."

Jake was caught, however, and he was sent away, to the New York State Vocational Institution at Coxsackie, New York. His term was one to three years. As he sat with me at the kitchen table, his daughter by his side, and devoured the steak, he recalled his life at Coxsackie, a correctional institution for juvenile delinquents.

"I had a lot of time to think when I was up there," he said. "I kept to myself . . . quiet . . . always thinking. I had a burning determination. No matter what course I would have taken when I came out, I would have been successful at anything.

"I picked boxing. I was up there with another kid who wanted to be a fighter, Terry Young, and we boxed a lot in the gymnasium. I found it was a way of expressing myself. Terry Young came from the East Side, where I was born and where my grandfather lived and I boxed a lot with him."

The year and a half spent at Coxsackie doubtless conditioned LaMotta for life. He began reading books up there. "Always read non-fiction, the truth, not that bunk fiction."

While LaMotta was at Coxsackie, he learned one

day that another neighborhood boy, Rocco Barbella, had been brought into the institution. "That was Rocky Graziano," he recalled, "and when Terry and I heard about Rocky, we sent him books and stuff, but he was there only two months—always in quarantine. He got out, maybe for a new trial, or something."

The steak was finished by now. LaMotta got up. He walked back into the parlor, his daughter by his side.

He continued speaking about Coxsackie. "I developed my stamina up there," the windmill-type fighter said. "I used to put my pillow into the window— they had letdown windows, like—and I would punch the pillow for an hour or more at a time. I was determined to be a fighter when I got out."

He had reached this point in his story when his mother came back into the parlor. With her was Marie, wearing a plain dress, and a willowy blonde wearing black slacks and a faded rose-colored-sweater. She could have been a beautiful Hollywood sweater girl. She was Jake's wife, Vickie.

Vickie didn't join in the talk beyond saying hello. She sat on the curved green couch. Jake pointed to Marie. "That's my sister. Pretty, ain't she?"

Marie blushed. "Know what," Jake said, "she's got a composition she wrote in school about me. She called it, 'Champ.' It's good. Read some of it."

Marie went downstairs and came back with the composition, which had been marked in pencil by her teacher, Mrs. Phillips. It said, "A—a good, sympathetic picture."

"Go ahead, read some" Jake said.

Marie picked a passage. "I never really got to know Jake in those days," she read from the composition, "because from the time I was old enough to understand, Jake got into trouble with some of his friends and I never saw him for two years after that. Mother told us he was at college and we let it rest at that."

"Boy, it was college all right," Jake said.

Marie smiled. "I remember when he came home," she said, "Jake was skinny. And it was the day after Thanksgiving and we had a turkey, but we saved most of it for Jake. He just grabbed it off the plate and ate the whole thing."

The steak was in his stomach now, but Jake remembered his homecoming. "I was so skinny," he said, "I weighed about 140. I ate like a horse for the next six weeks. I went away up to 185 pounds. All I was doing was eating. I wasn't doing anything else."

By this time, Jake's brother, Joey, had been boxing at an amateur club named the Teasdale A.C., which was run by a man named Mike Capriano. One day, Joey suggested that Jake go to the Teasdale, which had its gymnasium in a loft on the second floor of the Blenheim Theatre, a movie house.

"I knew the Blenheim Theater because it was right on the corner, where we lived on Washington Avenue, and I used to sneak in there all the time without paying admission," Jake said.

He decided to join the Teasdale, if only for the purpose of taking off weight. Back in his mind was the vow to become a fist-fighter, but the first problem was to reduce.

Jake worked out in the Teasdale gymnasium for eight months. Capriano had supplied some boxing equipment for him, plus some other paraphernalia that he had obtained from an uncle. Once, Jake even told Capriano he had gotten a job as a plumber's helper. "I remember he went away one morning and later came back to work out in the gym," Capriano recalls. "I asked him, 'What about the job with the plumber?' He looked at me and said, 'I cased that job. That's too tough for me'."

In the parlor of his home, Jake recalled the job that he could have had with the plumber. "I guess," he said, "I wanted to be a fighter." At any rate, the moments he had spent with the plumber came in handy. When Jake filled out his membership card in the Metropolitan Amateur Athletic Union, he scrawled in the space reserved for occupation: "Plumber's Helper."

Jake did not have to pick his brains too deeply to reconstruct his days at the Teasdale Gym. "I really worked hard there. Guys wouldn't box me, I was so rough. I was there for eight, nine or 10 months before I had a fight. Some guys even told Capriano and Jimmy Murray, who was training me, that I'd never fight. They wondered why Capriano and Murray bothered with me."

Finally, LaMotta entered the amateur ring. He had been a southpaw when he came into the gym, but Capriano and Murray had "turned him around" and had taught him to fight in the orthodox fashion, with his left hand extended. But having been a lefty, his left fist was the more powerful. Jake had 21 amateur fights and won them all. He floored most of his victims with left hooks to the stomach. He won the Diamond Belt Championship in the light-heavyweight division. Jake had worked himself down to 170 pounds.

"I was in good condition," Jake said in the parlor. He

Reeling—but nöt for real—against Billy Fox, 1947

turned to his wife, Vickie. "Bring my scrapbook from the kids' bedroom," he said. "I want to show Barney a picture of me when I was an amateur."

Vickie came back with a large, black, cloth-bound scrapbook. It contained more than 200 pages of newspaper clippings. It was as impartial a scrapbook as any athlete ever kept. It contained stories of Jake's victories, his defeats, the accusation that he had taken a dive for Billy Fox, pictures of his visit to the Grand Jury which investigated the Fox fight, and stories of the charge by his first wife that he had beaten her and that he had obtained a phony Mexican divorce to marry pretty Vickie.

Jake went back to the first page. He pointed to a picture of himself when he won the Diamond Belt Championship in a tournament sponsored by the Hearst newspapers. "Handsome, wasn't I?" he said.

Vickie laughed. She turned to leave the room. "I got to see if Jo-Jo—my little man—is still asleep and if Jackie is playing okay outside." She left the room and Jacqueline, Jake's daughter, trailed after her.

LaMotta started turning the pages of the scrapbook. He stopped at one page. "I could have entered the Golden Gloves, but I wanted to start making some

money. I was supporting the family by selling the watches I won in the amateur tournaments, but it wasn't enough. I became a pro and Capriano was my manager. I was down to 170 pounds now."

Vickie came back into the room, carrying one-year-old Jo-Jo with her. He was a big boy, with a large, round face, cast in the LaMotta fashion, and saucer-like brown eyes. Jake put him on his lap. "They call me names in the papers," he said. "What would they say if they could see me now with my family?"

He handed Jo-Jo back to Vickie. "It's like I was saying," he said. "I turned pro and fought Charley Mackley in my first pro fight, at St. Nick's. I got $25 for the fight, but I didn't have much left after paying my manager and for my license."

The results of his early fights were marked by agate lines of type in the first pages of the scrapbook, but by the time he had won his first 12 professional fights in a row the fight writers were taking notice of his talents. His 13th professional fight, at the outdoor Queensboro Arena in Long Island City, just across the Queensboro Bridge from Manhattan, was a key one. It was against a fighter named Joe Baynes, who was managed by Joe Gould, the man who piloted Jimmy Braddock to the

Missing with a right early against Marcel Cerdan, 1949

heavyweight championship of the world. Baynes was big and strong and considered somewhat of a tyrant in the ring. Other managers wouldn't permit their fighters to get close to him, much less to climb into the same ring with him for gloved combat.

By the time Capriano signed for the Baynes fight, the clippings showed, LaMotta was training at a gym for professional fighters called Gleason's. It is run by a fight manager of long experience, Bobby Gleason.

It was a fight to remember for Jake. "I got down low that night," he said, "and I punched first to the body and as I arose I hit all the way to the head. I think it was a good showing because everybody thought I would get licked."

Capriano remembers it the same way. "I knew my fighter. Jake was great then. And in wonderful condition. Nobody knew too much about him. I wasn't worried about him."

Others in the fight business think otherwise. "The guy was thrown in with the lions," one fight manager

says now. "Take how he got his next important fight, only the 16th in his career, with a guy named Jimmy Reeves in Cleveland."

This is how Jake believes it happened: A couple of fight men, Billy Brown and Tommy Conti, were sitting in Brown's office in the Forrest Hotel in New York. A telephone call came in from Larry Atkins, the matchmaker at the Arena in Cleveland.

"I got to have a guy to fight Jimmy Reeves here September 24," Atkins told Brown, who blanched immediately. Reeves had the reputation of being something of a killer at the time. What New York manager would take the chance of putting his fighter in with Reeves?

Brown, however, was willing to try. He told Atkins so. Immediately, he and Conti went to work. They checked the list of available middleweights. "I got it," Brown spluttered, finally. "Let's call Capriano about LaMotta. He thinks he's got a fighter. He'll put him in." Brown was right. Capriano apparently was willing to permit his fighter, Jake LaMotta, to face the possibility of a black-and-blue beating. He took the fight, took it for a $300 purse.

It was a long trip for Jake, but it was an experience that has given him a lot to remember and he checks back on the incident with prideful ease, just as he did in the living room of his Bronx home. "We went out to Cleveland together, Capriano and I, on the train," Jake said. "I was sick on the train . . . you know, like car sick. I didn't care who I was going to fight so long as it was for money. I wanted money, nothing else."

In Cleveland, Jake found he wasn't in the main event, even if he was scheduled for 10 rounds. The spotlighted bout at the Cleveland Arena was a heavyweight match between ill-fated Lem Franklin and Tony Musto. But Jake learned one thing that night . . . fight fans are sporting in inverse ratio to the ethics of the boxing business.

His fight with Reeves was a thriller. For seven rounds, Reeves bounced power punches off LaMotta's head. At the end of the seventh round, when LaMotta came back to his corner, Capriano warned him, "You've been trying to hit this guy with your left and he knows it. Why don't you try to do it with your right? Look, your right eye is closed. What a shiner! Now, go out and do as I tell you, or I'll stop the fight. I can't let you take it."

LaMotta remembered that he blew out like a fuse. "Don't stop it or I'll kill you!" Jake warned Capriano. "I'm going out and get this guy!"

LaMotta did just that. He forgot about his left hand, concentrated on working with his right. In the next three rounds, he floored Reeves 10 times. The fight ended with Reeves on the floor, being counted out. But when the decision was announced, it was Reeves who was the winner.

A fight fan is the least inhibited of America's sports customers. He gives vent to his feelings at the drop of a decision and on this night of September 24, 1941, amid the red, white, and blue decor of the Cleveland Arena, he was at his apoplectic best. He was rip-roaring mad. Chairs flew, sundry noggins were bashed, and Tris Speaker, the old baseball hero who was serving as the city's boxing commissioner, got a rousing kick on his gray pate for his trouble. The fans didn't like the decision for Reeves, and they were registering their resentment in the only way they knew—riotously.

The ringside riot put Jake LaMotta in the spotlight. Nobody bothered wondering how Lem Franklin made out against Tony Musto.

"Yes," LaMotta says now, "it was wonderful, but when I got home I found I had gotten only $100 for the fight. I was supporting the family. We moved to a new apartment, on Webster Avenue and 169th Street. It was the same kind of an apartment as the one before, but we were a little happier."

A month later, Jake fought Reeves once again in Cleveland. This time, he again lost the decision and was saddened by the fight business, but it was getting close to Christmas and LaMotta wanted to buy presents for the kids in the family and for his mother. He wanted as many fights as possible.

"I told this to Capriano, and just before Christmas of 1941 he got me a fight with Nate Bolden in Chicago. He got me a fight all right. Nate Bolden was a light-heavyweight who had fought heavyweights like Jimmy Bivins. I was just a 160-pounder, but Capriano was brave. Look, when I fought all these guys they were good."

Jake's daughter, Jacqueline, came into the room and sat on his lap. "She's going to have everything she needs," he said. "I pay her mother $50 a week for her, but I wish her mother would move to a better place. I don't like where they live."

He went right back to reminiscing on the Bolden fight. "I didn't care about Bolden. I just wanted to make my family happy for Christmas. We went out to Chicago and I fought Bolden in Marigold Gardens. What a fight! He was tough. I got home from Chicago with $40 in my pocket. I hoped for a Merry Christmas. We couldn't do much with $40 with all the kids in the family. It was tough."

But the tough fights performed one valuable function for LaMotta; they elevated him to the status of a main-bout fighter in New York City. During 1942, he averaged between $75 and $100 a week in income. He was eminently successful, losing only two fights during the year. One loss was to Ray Robinson.

Most important, however, was the psychological effect all this had on Jake. No longer introverted, he was able to speak out, and did. He developed opinions and attitudes. He was meeting better people, all, oddly enough, through the much-maligned business of boxing. In a boxing phrase, he was getting smartened up. He began buying better clothes and developed a concern about his appearance.

His sister, Anna, brought girl friends to the LaMotta home now, and her friends were intrigued with the thought of knowing a top-notch prize-fighter. One of these was Ida Geller, a shapely girl who was smitten by Jake. It was a two-way proposition. "You know how it was," Jake remembers. "She was coming to the house and I saw a lot of her and before long she was my girl. That's how it was."

Ida was among those who saw LaMotta fight Jimmy Edgar in Madison Square Garden, August 28, 1942. This was a crucial fight. LaMotta hadn't yet fought a 10-rounder in Madison Square Garden. Edgar was managed by John Roxborough, Joe Louis' co-manager. He had come from Detroit heralded as a great fighter. LaMotta upset Edgar in a thrill-filled 10-rounder.

LaMotta's sister, Marie, sat listening to all this. "You got to be big then, Jake," she said. "I remember how all the kids acted to me then, and I was only nine years old. I didn't know whether they wanted to play with me or be near me 'cause I was your sister."

This talk pleased Jake. He doesn't express conceit, but rather exudes it. It is implied rather than expressed. "Sure," Jake said to Marie, "I know that the Edgar fight got me a Garden match with Ray Robinson, first of the five I had with him. I lost that one, but in January, 1943, I went to fight Jimmy Edgar in a return in Detroit."

"You won, didn't you?" Marie asked.

"Sure, and I was a big man in Detroit."

Detroit proved to be a lucky spot for him. He made money there—real money. The purse for his next fight in Detroit was more than $10,000—a fight the boxing racket will never forget. Ray Robinson furnished the opposition, amazing Ray Robinson, who hadn't lost in 129 amateur and professional fights.

Ray was a 3-1 choice, even though Detroit was rooting for LaMotta. A crowd of 18,923 packed into the Detroit Olympia and matchmaker Nick Londes beamed with the thought of the profit. The gross gate was $47,280. That was a lot of money in any league. LaMotta was wonderfully efficient that night. He smashed Robinson to the canvas, punished him about the midsection, tormented him in close-quarter fighting. It was Jake's fight from beginning to end. Robinson's streak had been broken.

Most fight men couldn't believe it had happened. LaMotta knew it had. He came home from Detroit a happy, delirious fellow. It must have been so. He decided to move his family out of the old neighborhood and he was attracted to the house in which he now lives. In addition, he was keeping company with Ida Geller. But he was suspicious. He didn't want to make a move

without legal advice. His uncle, Frank Petrollo, knew a lawyer named H. Jordan Lee, who had an office opposite the Bronx County Building.

"Let's go to see him," LaMotta's uncle said.

Harry Lee, the lawyer, was much impressed with LaMotta the first time he met him. "LaMotta was so quiet," Lee remembers. "He had little to say. He had his brother, Joey, and his father with him. You know, his father had been taken into the Army for a year because he wasn't supporting his family, and he was out now, and Jake was trying to patch him up with his mother. That's why he wanted the house."

The lawyer went to look at the house, at 994 Neill Avenue, in the Pelham section of the Bronx. The price was $14,000. It was a two-year-old house and Lee advised Jake to buy it.

"But I only have $14,000," Jake said.

"Put it in the house," Lee told him. "You can't go wrong."

"I think he needed advice," Lee said to me, "but he didn't trust anybody."

LaMotta bought the house and the entire family, including his father, went to live there. The LaMotta family was a happy one, united by the power of Jake's fists. However, Jake didn't seem to trust anybody. He told the lawyer he needed advice against the people in the fight business. The lawyer told him, "If you need legal or business advice, I will give it to you." This must have impressed Jake. For sure, it did, because he is willing to admit it.

"After the Ossie Harris fight in Pittsburgh in 1943," Jake looks back, "I had $9,000 in cash. I gave it to Harry Lee and he put it in the Bronx County Trust Company in my name. The only thing, Lee kept the checkbook. I trusted him."

Meanwhile, LaMotta fought Robinson again, and this time the officials voted against him. "I didn't care, although I thought I won," Jake smiled, recalling the fight as he sat in his parlor. "I never bribed anybody to win a fight. I went in there on my own and fought on my own. I wanted to win that way."

The loss to Robinson didn't mean much. Jake could have had all the fights he wanted. He had bought himself an automobile—a LaSalle—and he was in love with Ida Geller. "In one of my weak moments," he says now, "I drove up to Greenwich, Connecticut, one day in 1943, and we got married. Just the two of us, Ida and me, and we came home married. I had been putting my

Cerdan hurt his shoulder in this first-round crash to the canvas

career ahead of marriage until then, but I did it anyway."

Ida came to live with Jake at the home now occupied by his second wife, Vickie. A year later, in 1944, Jacqueline was born.

During the same year, it became apparent that LaMotta's father couldn't get along with his mother. "He was a selfish man," LaMotta says. "I had to do something. I put $5,000 down on a big apartment house on Webster Avenue in the Bronx. It had 18 or 20 furnished apartments. I handed the deed over to my father. This was his. He went to live there. He still is running it. He's on his own."

By late 1944, LaMotta was aware of what was going on in the fight business. His brother Joey was with him all the time and, seemingly, Jake wanted to take care of the kid. But he was paying Mike Capriano, his manager 40 percent of his purses, with Capriano paying all expenses. One day, while LaMotta was in Detroit to fight George Kochan on November 3, 1944, he awoke early. Jimmy Murray, who was sleeping in the same hotel suite, was awakened too.

"Where're you going?" he asked Jake.

"Go back to bed," he told Murray, his trainer. "I just want to go out for a walk." That was all. He said nothing beyond this.

That morning, however, he visited the office of the Michigan State Athletic Commission. He thought he had a contract with Capriano which expired the next February. At the Commission offices, he found a contract on file which tied him to Capriano for eight more years.

He and his brother Joey rushed from the Commission offices and put a call through to Harry Lee in New York. "I'm not going through with the Kochan fight," Jake told Harry. "That Capriano's got me tied up for life—eight years."

The lawyer placated him. "Go through with the fight. Don't do anything until you come back from Detroit," he advised.

Jake went through with the fight. Back in New York, he met Capriano in Harry Lee's office. Out of that meeting came the first newspaper campaign against LaMotta.

Lee insists that the argument between LaMotta and Capriano was fiery, that LaMotta once approached Capriano, but did nothing more than to seize his coat lapel.

Capriano contends that LaMotta struck him with the usual "blunt instrument" and tossed him down a flight of stairs in order to get him to sign a release on the eight-year contract.

"That's silly," Jake said in retrospect as his mother, sister, wife, and kids sat by. "After Capriano signed, we went across the Grand Concourse to the Concourse Plaza Hotel and had drinks. We drank to the release Capriano had signed. And, what's more, I met Capriano the next day and paid him his share from the Kochan fight."

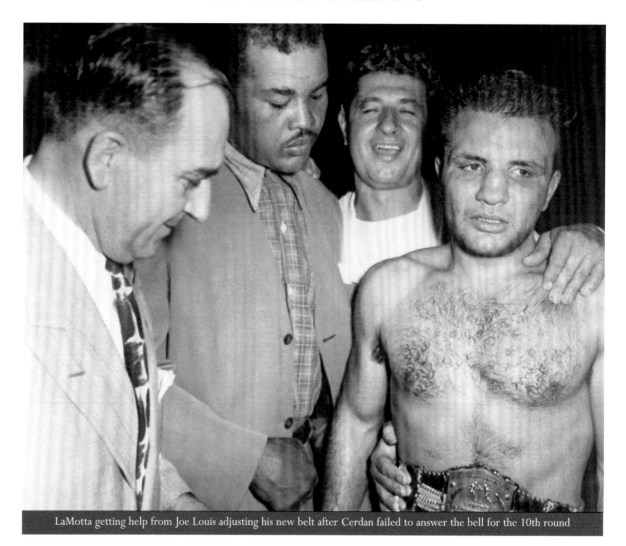

LaMotta getting help from Joe Louis adjusting his new belt after Cerdan failed to answer the bell for the 10th round

That wasn't the way Capriano described the incident. His description was so vivid, he was able to obtain a warrant for LaMotta's arrest on a felonious assault charge. Jake was released in Bronx Magistrates Court on $500 bail and the case was given to the Grand Jury. All involved testified in the case. Lee spent several hours before the Grand Jury. So did Jake. So did Capriano. No true bill was returned. Jake was cleared.

Now he was faced with the problem of getting a manager. There was one drawback. He was determined not to pay any manager 33 percent, the legal fee, or the 40 percent which Capriano had been receiving. Lee suggested that Jimmy Murray be retained as manager and trainer.

"Okay," said Jake, "I'll pay him 11 percent."

The deal was closed and Jimmy Murray became LaMotta's manager. But Jake was wise now. "I don't need

a real manager," he said. "They threw me in with the wolves before. All a manager needs is a rubber stamp for me. I fight anybody. I don't like managers. Look what Capriano did. He says I signed a contract for eight years. I think I signed it, but it was with a lot of other papers while we were getting a drink at a hot-dog stand."

Instead of giving Murray 33 percent, the new manager received only 11 percent. Jake had decided he needed the extra money to pay the expenses of supporting his wife, his child, his brothers, sisters, and mother. The contract with Murray was drawn for only two years. LaMotta had an option to cancel it at any time.

He was happy now. The first fight made for him by Murray pitted him against Robinson for the fourth time. This one was in Madison Square Garden, February 23, 1945. It was a bruising struggle. The officials voted

Robinson the winner; the public thought Jake was the winner. It didn't really matter. For the remainder of the year, except for another losing struggle with Robinson in Chicago, LaMotta went undefeated. He was rated the outstanding middleweight in the world.

More important, Jake was earning large, wholesome chunks of money. Each Robinson fight brought him more than $20,000. He should have been a happy man, but he wasn't. His trouble was domestic. He spoke frankly of his difficulties with his first wife as his second wife sat by his side.

"After our quarrels, when she'd wake up two hours later, she would throw her arms around me and tell me she loved me and I was the best husband in the world. I couldn't stand it, the fighting. I had to make a break. I started going out on my own."

Vickie smiled.

It was during 1945 that Jake's brother, Joey, took up fighting. For a time he was successful, but he lasted less than 20 months and had to quit the ring because of a nasal ailment. During 1945, Jake also became the owner of a fight arena—the Park Arena, in the Bronx. It was symbolic that Jake should own the Park Arena, because the fight club was housed in the old Blenheim Theatre, the very movie house into which Jake had had to sneak to see a picture when he was a kid.

Harry Lee developed the deal which made Jake a young capitalist, or a rookie capitalist, as one sports columnist called him. The entire building was purchased for $65,000, with $15,000 in cash required to swing the deal. LaMotta put up half of the $15,000. Lee put $3,000 into the pot, as did an automobile dealer named Sam Brahms. The remaining $1,500 was put up by Jimmy Murray. The property was subject to two mortgages, one for $44,000, the second for $6,000.

That was only the beginning. The corporation had to put up $40,000 to renovate the building so that it could be used as a sports arena. Each of the partners had to dig deeply for the money. Jake had to go deepest. But just when things looked dark, a propitious fire in the factory loft above the theatre proper brought $20,000 in insurance money. The Park Arena opened up and Jake was not only a fighter now, but also a promoter. For two indoor seasons, 1945-46 and 1946-47, the Park Arena made money. It seemed like a profitable business, but it wasn't. Soon the partners began squabbling. The building could have been sold for $125,000, a move which would

have been profitable to all. The partners couldn't agree. Lee and LaMotta started quarreling over the 2,000-seat arena and before long Lee sold out his shares. Few stockholders were brought in. The Park Arena was in bad shape. It was a burden to LaMotta, but that wasn't all.

In the Spring of 1946, under the guidance of a new lawyer, Irving Tell, LaMotta purchased a piece of land across the street from the Yankee Stadium for $65,000. He named it Jerome Stadium. This one was never successful as a fight club, but now LaMotta isn't worried. "I own that thing lock, stock, and barrel, and it will make money for me. It's my insurance when I quit the ring."

This is why: The Jerome Stadium can be used as a parking lot for Yankee Stadium baseball and football games. In addition, it can be operated as a soda pop and hot dog concession. Jake is looking forward to running this enterprise.

As for the Park Arena, that's gone. The corporation recently sold it to an automobile sales firm for $60,000. It was a headache from beginning to end and may have been responsible, in part, for many of LaMotta's troubles.

In 1946, while he was still the No. 1 middleweight, although Tony Zale and Rocky Graziano were playing footsie with the 160-pound championship, thereby freezing Jake out, LaMotta was a disheartened fellow. "What chance did I have?" he insisted. This was reflected in his personal life. He was quarreling more than ever with the first Mrs. LaMotta. He had met Vickie and, inevitably, decided to marry her. To do so, he obtained a divorce from Ida, a Mexican-type divorce.

Vickie and Jake were married, but while he may have been happy romantically, he was fistically unhappy. One problem followed another. He quarreled with Jimmy Murray, his manager, in March, 1947, and they parted. He hired another trainer-manager, Al Silvani, the man who kept Frank Sinatra in shape for years, and paid him 11 percent. Silvani was just a figurehead, albeit a handsome one.

LaMotta was discouraged. It did not seem that he would ever get a championship chance. Each Tuesday night, fight night at the Park Arena, he would stand in the lobby and ask this writer, over and over again, "Do you think I'll ever get a title shot? I think I will. I'm destiny's boy."

He repeated this so often I almost came to believe him, but not quite. He may have been "Destiny's Boy" but the cards seemed stacked against him. If it wasn't one thing, it was another that was keeping him from a championship chance, even though he admittedly was the outstanding contender. He was making money, surely. For one bout, against Tommy Bell, in Madison Square Garden on March 14, 1947, he earned $21,000. He was hard-pressed, but he won it. As a matter of fact, some believed he was taking it easy so that he would not be rated a giant-killer and, possibly, trap the champion into fighting him.

All he did was snare a young welterweight from Ohio, Tony Janiro, into a Garden fight. Janiro's manager, eager to take a shortcut toward the middleweight title with his boy, forced LaMotta to post a $15,000 forfeit. LaMotta would have to make 155 pounds for the bout. It was absurd. Jake was a bulky 160-pounder.

The bout was under a spell from the beginning. LaMotta, who has never trained in big-time Stillman's Gym in New York, preferring one further uptown, worked hard enough to get down to 154-1/2 pounds. He was trained superbly by his so-called manager, Al Silvani. But, on the morning of the fight, the District Attorney's office in Manhattan, which had been investigating boxing for a long time, purportedly intercepted a telephone conversation between a New York bookie and a gambler in Youngstown, Ohio, Janiro's hometown. "The fight's fixed," one said to the other. "Janiro can't lose."

Janiro's manager, Frankie (Jay) Jacobs, was grilled, as the headline writers say, by the District Attorney. He could shed no light on the so-called fix plot. LaMotta went into the ring, weak as he was at 154-1/2, and routed Janiro, although the kid fought bravely.

It was the first time the fingers were pointed at LaMotta. Until that moment, nobody would dare suggest that Jake would be involved in anything shady in the prize ring.

Nobody knows why, but LaMotta lost his next fight, to a has-been boxer named Cecil Hudson, in Chicago. Perhaps he had been weakened by the weight-making ordeal for the Janiro bout. Perhaps he was just discouraged.

"I guess it was both," Jake says. "Anyway, I didn't think I lost to Hudson."

A few weeks after losing to Hudson, on September 3, 1947, LaMotta was booked to box Tiger Billy Fox in Madison Square Garden. Fox was a Philadelphia light-heavyweight who had rung up a long streak of knockouts—knockouts of doubtful origin. At best, Fox

had scored over a string of hambones who should not have been permitted into the ring in the first place.

Nobody gave Fox a chance, although he had every advantage of height and reach. LaMotta was considered too strong, too seasoned, too rugged. Jake's never-stop-punching style, his ability to fake when he was tired, his sense of pace underlined him as the choice. Ten days before the bout, however, this writer was informed, via a bookmaking source, that LaMotta would lose to Fox. I went to Jake and told him of the rumor. He laughed. "You know me," he said, "I don't throw fights. I'm in there to win. Don't believe it."

The story was picked up in the Metropolitan press. Somehow, while the fight writers wrote about the rumor, they couldn't come to believe it.

That is why the writers flew into high dudgeon when they saw LaMotta get knocked out in four rounds. Mind you, Jake was not floored in that fight. He simply was hit often enough to send him into a dizzy, backward dance. He sat on the ropes, took Fox's blows, didn't fight back. The bout was stopped in the fourth round.

Edward Patrick Francis Eagan, chairman of the New York State Athletic Commission, was at the ringside that night, but when the writers asked him to comment, he said, "Why, it looked all right to me." It didn't appear that way to the reporters. They cried "Fake! Fake!" the next day.

Eagan was forced to take action because of the pressure of the gate. After all, 18,340 fans had paid $102,528 to see the fight. LaMotta's purse came to more than $20,000. Had the customers seen a fight?

"I did the best I could, the way things were," LaMotta explained. "From the second round on, my legs and arms were without strength. I felt clammy and sick. He hit me a good punch in the left side early in the first round. It gave me a shock, but the thing paralyzed me kind of gradually and I didn't really feel it until between rounds."

Beyond this, LaMotta produced a certificate from Dr. Nicholas Salerno, a Bronx physician, who said that LaMotta had suffered a hemotoma of the spleen when he was struck by a blow in a sparring bout on October 13, a month and a day before the Fox fight.

The State Athletic Commission was on the spot. What would it do? Happily, this was the way out. Eagan and Co. fined LaMotta $1,000 and suspended him indefinitely. Later, under threatened legal pressure by Jake's lawyer, Irving Tell, the suspension was lifted. Jake

Facing Sugar Ray Robinson for the sixth—and final—time, Valentine's Day, 1951

had been on the shelf for seven months.

At this point, LaMotta's chance of becoming the middleweight champion was dark indeed. You wouldn't have bet your best friend's toupee on it. As a matter of downright fact, New York promoters were fearful of employing his services lest the customers object. So Jake went down to Washington, D. C., seven months after the Fox debacle, and fought a fellow named Ken Stribling. He scored a knockout in five rounds. Next, he came back to the Park Arena, which was still in operation as a fight club. He was the promoter, after all, and it was natural that he should put himself to work. He was slow-moving against a fair kind of a second-rater named Burl Charity. Jake scored a knockout in six, but he lacked his old luster.

About this time, cynical observers began linking his name with underworld characters. Jake laughed about this. "If they want to do it, it is okay. After all, I do not read the papers. I read books. I know too much about

writers and reporters to believe what I read in the papers. After what I went through with newspaper guys, you expect me to read newspapers?"

Finally, the 20th Century Sporting Club, late property of Mike Jacobs and predecessors of the International Boxing Club as ring operators at Madison Square Garden, offered LaMotta a bout at the St. Nicholas Arena. They put him in with a pushover named Johnny Colan, who had once been a bright boxing prospect, but was now past his day. LaMotta scored a 10-round knockout.

Now he was purified, ready for the big temple. He was matched with Tommy Yarosz, a clever-hitting Pittsburgh lad. LaMotta had to hustle to win, but hustle he did. He was back in good standing.

By this time, Marcel Cerdan, the Frenchman, had captured the middleweight championship from Tony Zale. The prospect was for Cerdan to defend his title in June of 1949, either against Zale, if he wanted the shot,

En route to relinquishing the title to Robinson

or against Ray Robinson, the welterweight boss, or Steve Belloise, another Bronxite. Jake didn't have a chance. This was especially so after LaMotta lost his next fight. This one took place in Montreal and Jake's tormentor was Laurent Dauthuille. "I lost," he now says, "because my eye was cut and I just wasn't right."

Fate's perversity played another trick on LaMotta in his next fight. He won this one, but perhaps it would have been better if he had lost. This writer, a ringside observer, was the only one who believed LaMotta defeated Robert Villemain, the Frenchman, in Madison Square Garden last March 25. This reporter, that is, plus two of the officials, Harry Ebbets, the referee, and Harold Barnes, one of the judges. They gave the fight to LaMotta after 12 rounds.

Eagan, a noted Francophile, flew off the handle. Villemain, the Parisian, had been wronged. Most everybody agreed on this. But Eagan couldn't find fault with LaMotta. He had performed to the best of his ability. So had Villemain. Who was to blame? Why, the officials, of course. In an unprecedented actions the two officials were suspended indefinitely. Both lashed back at Eagan. They had seen the same fight he had, they said, and LaMotta had been the winner. Certainly, however, this latest episode put Jake behind the eight-ball insofar as a championship fight was concerned.

He went out to Detroit after that and pushed over O'Neill Bell, a woebegone figure, in four rounds. It wasn't an important victory—not on the surface, at least.

Then, however, the pot of pugilistic politics began boiling. Tony Zale decided to retire. He wouldn't fight again. Marcel Cerdan was released from the task of defending his title against him. Who would get the chance? Robinson's name was mentioned. So was Belloise's. The late unlamented Tournament of Champions, Inc., to which Cerdan was beholden, had to put on a Cerdan fight in June. Who would be the opponent? Nobody thought of LaMotta. Then, suddenly, his name was mentioned. But, no, 10 times, a 100 times, no. It couldn't be Jake.

Finally, the Tournament of Champions decided to put Steve Belloise into the ring with Cerdan. The fight was to be staged at the Polo Grounds, which the Tournament of Champions had seized from the 20th Century Sporting Club by plunking down $50,000 in cash right in front of Horace Stoneham, owner of the Giants. It was cut and dried, that's what. Belloise, who had knocked out somebody named Jean Stock in Paris, hurried home from Europe to sign. He was a little late. No sooner had he come home than the International Boxing Club bought out the assets of the Tournament of Champions. Included was a middleweight champion, one M. Cerdan, late of Casablanca.

Kingpin in the IBC was Jim Norris, who had been promoting in Detroit's Olympia Stadium, where LaMotta had made his best efforts. "LaMotta's my man," Norris said. Jake smiled. Suddenly, it was announced that the International Boxing Club's first promotion would be a middleweight championship fight between Cerdan and Jake LaMotta in Detroit in June.

I asked LaMotta how he felt when he learned of the good news, as we sat in his green-painted parlor. He sneered. "You know," he said, "somehow I knew it would happen, especially when I heard Jim Norris was taking over. Detroit's my lucky spot."

Jake thought for a moment. "It's funny, too. Back in 1946, after I fought Jimmy Edgar in Detroit and they called it a draw, I burned up. I said, 'I'll never fight in Detroit again—long as I live.' And it was in Detroit that I won my title."

Jake wasn't accorded the slimmest chance against Cerdan. Only his brother, Joey, who had become his nominal manager, cheered him on.

There was only one barrier to the fight with Cerdan. Several days before the championship fight was signed, Joey LaMotta had signed a contract for Jake to box Joey DeJohn at the Syracuse Fair Grounds on May 19, just a month before the title match. DeJohn is a fine puncher, if not too sturdy, and many feared that LaMotta might be clipped by the young upstate New York hammerer. The IBC fretted, the LaMottas fretted, everybody who wanted to see Jake fight Cerdan fretted.

In Syracuse, Jake holed up at the town's best hotel. He talked and talked and talked, first to Joey, then to me, and then to a few local friends. He chattered constantly about the Detroit match with Cerdan. "I've waited too long for this chance to lose to a guy in Syracuse," he said. "And I'm going to be champion."

His determination to win was apparent from the opening gong. He never was better conditioned, never as relentless in assault. LaMotta took some powerful blows to the head, but never faltered. He mince-stepped after his quarry, punching fast and furiously as he had done in days before. On this night, apart from all other recent nights, LaMotta didn't drop his hands and feign punch—brought pain in order to trap his adversary or, possibly; to ensnare himself. He simply moved in and fought his fight. He knocked DeJohn out in the eighth round. He came out of the fight unscathed. The next stop was Detroit and M. Cerdan, the middleweight champion of the world.

The morning of the fight, which was held in Briggs Stadium, unfolded a cloud-filled sky. Jake was up early, in his suite at the Book-Cadillac Hotel. He had come a long way from the fighter who, on his first visit to

Detroit, had taken his breakfast in a greasy spoon on Skid Row. But he was to go back to Skid Row that day.

Al Silvani was in Detroit with LaMotta and he awoke early, too. Al insisted that Jake sneak over to the Commission offices to weigh in before the official weigh-in which was set for noon. It was then nine o'clock. Stealthily, Jake left the hotel. He was being watched by gamblers, hoodlums, and plain fans for any tell-tale signs. After all, Cerdan was the favorite and it would be nice to know what was going to happen in the bout.

When LaMotta stepped on the scale at the Commission offices, he was stunned. He was 161-1/2 pounds, a pound and a half over the middleweight class limit. What would he do, with the official weigh-in only two hours off?

Silvani went into action immediately. He rushed Jake out of the Commission offices, down the elevator and into a taxi. "Take me to a Turkish bath," he ordered the cab driver. They drove to one on Skid Row. Silvani registered LaMotta at the Turkish bath as "Vito Perez." He used the alias to avoid suspicion. For more than an hour, LaMotta sweated in the steam room. Silvani rubbed him down several times. Finally, after 90 minutes, Jake stepped on a scale in the bath. He was down below 160.

"Okay," ordered Silvani, "let's get dressed now."

When LaMotta weighed in that noon, he hit 159-1/2 he had made the weight. The visit to the Turkish bath was kept a secret from the press.

Jake was very confident as he sat in his hotel suite awaiting the fight. Visitors who came to see him ignored him completely. Jake's pretty wife, Vickie, was there, wearing an off-the-shoulder blouse. The visitors paid her attention.

Later that afternoon, it started to rain. At about 5 o'clock, Jim Norris postponed the fight. Now, the question was raised as to whether there should be another weigh-in the next day, when the fight was to be held. Nobody on the Michigan Commission seemed to know the rules. First they ordered that no weigh-in should be held. Then, in a hectic official session, the solons reversed themselves. They ordered a weigh-in, obviously a hardship on LaMotta. Cerdan had made the weight easily.

Jake demurred. "Why should I weigh in again?" he demanded. "You've got to," he was ordered. He sat in his hotel suite and sulked.

Finally, late on June 15, the original date of the bout,

Jim Norris came to visit LaMotta at the hotel. Jim was accompanied by Nick Londes, nominal matchmaker for the IBC in Detroit. I was there, too, along with Al Silvani. The five of us gathered in Jake's bedroom.

"You've got to weigh in," Norris told Jake. "We can't put off the show and the commission insists on a weigh-in."

LaMotta, who had been doing some shadow-boxing, sat on the bed. He was wearing several sweaters and the sweat rolled down his nose. He wiped the perspiration from his face. Then he smiled, knowingly.

"Tell you what," he said, "I'll weigh in tomorrow, but it must be at 10 o'clock in the morning, not at noon."

Everybody wondered. "Okay," said Jake, "tell you why. I'll have to do some more shadow-boxing to get down to weight, but if I have the extra two hours, from 10 to noon, it will give me a chance to recuperate my strength."

"It's a deal," said Norris.

He left the room and went into conference with Lou Burston and Sammy Richman, Cerdan's American representatives. They wondered about the 10 o'clock weigh-in. It was unheard of. They sensed a plot, but they were trapped. "Okay," said Burston, "make it at 10:30. Let's compromise."

Norris called Jake on the phone and told him of the compromise. "Okay," said Jake. He turned from the phone. "I'm going to bed," he said. He picked up a fat book from the dresser in his bedroom. "Guess I'll read a little," he said.

I took the book from his hand and read the title. It was the *Psychoanalysis of Leonardo da Vinci* by Sigmund Freud. I asked him, "Jake, do you always read things like this?"

"Sure," he said. "I even read the Microbe Hunters."

The next morning, at the weigh-in, LaMotta scaled 158-3/4. It was less than he had weighed the day before. The witnesses at the weigh-in ceremony gasped.

I spent most of the day with LaMotta and that night, as he entered the ring, he noticed me in the working press section. He winked. I smiled. He went back to his corner.

Jake LaMotta won the middleweight championship of the world that night, June 16, 1949, in Briggs Stadium, Detroit. He won it by taking command of the fight from the opening gong. He rushed Cerdan, beat him with a left hook, and punched him about generally. Jake was so strong, he tossed Cerdan to the ring floor

when their arms locked. The knockout came in the 10th round, with Cerdan sitting on his stool in his corner and unable to continue. Jake jumped around deliriously. Cerdan was a dejected, beaten figure. The elevator muscle in his left shoulder, he said, had rendered the arm useless from the first round, when he had been tossed to the canvas by LaMotta. No matter what, Jake LaMotta was the world middleweight champion. Destiny, he believed, had given him the championship

As he sat on a rubbing table in his dressing room at the stadium, Eddie Eagan, New York's boxing boss, entered the room. Everybody had waited for this. Would New York recognize LaMotta as champion after all the disturbances he had created, first in the Fox fight and then in the Villemain bout? Eagan had frowned when LaMotta had been given the chance to fight Cerdan.

Eagan walked right up to Jake, extended his hand, and shook Jake's hand. "You're the champion all right," Eagan said. "It was a fine job."

As I sat with LaMotta in the living room of his Bronx home, with his family seated around him, I reminded him of Eagan's visit.

"You know," he said, "I like Eagan. He's the only fellow who didn't claim he got me the fight with Cerdan. Everybody else claims it. Everybody wants to get into the act. Everybody did me good, even Jim Norris. I did most of it myself.

"I paid plenty to get the title. I lost money on the thing. They all say they did this and they did that. They did nothing. They even say they suggested the early-morning weigh-in for the postponed fight. Well, that's not true. I did that myself . . . all by myself."

As we talked, Jake took me in and showed me his clothes closet. There were four or five suits there, that's all, but hanging on the rack were about 25 pairs of slacks. "I like slacks," he said. "I wear them with sport things. I'm conservative. I paid about $15 a shirt for white on white. Got a lot of them." He pulled open a dresser drawer. There were about six shirts, a dozen pairs of shorts, and a dozen or two socks.

"Guess all my stuff is at the laundry now," he said.

He pushed his two hands into his pants belt and pressed against his abdomen. It was a gesture of contentment. "I'm a happy guy," he said. "I grossed about $500,000 in purses, but I spent a lot. I gave my first wife a $13,000 settlement when we settled everything."

We walked back into the living room. I asked him if he had any cash.

"Everybody thinks I do. They say, 'I wonder what he got out of the Fox fight.' I got nothing. I haven't much cash, but my title will bring me about $150,000 in two fights. That's going into annuities. You can bet on that."

He leaned back in the pink easy chair. I thought about the book he had been reading in Detroit, *Psychoanalysis of Leonardo da Vinci* by Sigmund Freud. I asked him, "Did you ever finish it?"

"Sure," he said. "I lent it just now to my friend Pete Petrello—he's a former fighter who now is foreman of a construction job—and he gave me another book in return." Jake walked into his bedroom again and came back with the volume he had borrowed from Pete Petrello. It was *The Basic Writings of Sigmund Freud*. It was heavy and impressive.

I asked Jake if he understood all that he read.

"I read it very slow," he said. "I get stumped once in a while. I just pass it up. I have an idea of the meaning. I read in bed before I go to sleep. It's a good outlet."

I asked him if he ever wanted to write himself, just as his sister, Marie, had written about him.

"When I write my story, it'll blow up everybody," he said, smiling. "You got a good story yourself now. You're the only one I would give it to."

He walked over to the scrapbook and started turning the pages. "You know, I got pictures of Cerdan in here, with his wife and his two kids, when he was in this country. I even got pictures of the crash."

It was the first mention of Cerdan, who went to his death in a plane crash in the Azores while flying here for a return bout with LaMotta at Madison Square Garden. I hadn't mentioned him because I didn't know how LaMotta felt about Cerdan's death. Fate had played a trick on Cerdan. Originally, he was scheduled to fight LaMotta at the Polo Grounds in September, but Jake had claimed injury to a neck muscle. The fight had been called off. After much dickering, during which Cerdan made several false starts for the United States from France, the championship return finally was scheduled for the Garden December 2. Cerdan emplaned for the United States. He never got here.

"I wanted to fight in September," Jake explained. "I even had the doctors give me injections and everything, like a jerk, but it hurt too much."

His wife, Vickie, said, "I was sick when Cerdan died."

"Yeah," said Jake, "he was a nice guy. You don't find many like him in boxing."

Jake sat back in the pink chair. "The real men," he said, "will not come out until I give up the middleweight class. I have been weakened making the weight. I want to fight as a light-heavyweight and if possible a heavyweight. How'd I do with Freddie Mills?"

The reply was noncommittal. Looking at Jake, all 5-foot-7 of him, I wondered. He insisted on going out into the sun porch, forward of his living room, to weigh himself. He stepped on an upright scale. The indicator stopped at 182. It was a month before his slated return fight with Robert Villemain at Madison Square Garden, December 9, and Jake had to get down to 166 for that one—which may be why he lost so decisively.

"I'll make it," he said. "I'm destiny's kid, ain't I?"

He assuredly wasn't on the night of December 9, when Villemain licked him. And a lot of the experts will tell you destiny is through with him, that the busy little Frenchman is going to take Jake's title the next time they meet. But with LaMotta, you never can be sure. He's still cocky, still grinning, still saying:

"I'll beat his brains out. I'll murder him this time. I'm destiny's kid, ain't I?"

EPILOGUE

Putting the loss to Robert Villemain behind him, Jake LaMotta successfully defended his title twice in 1950—against Tiberio Mitri and, in a great fight, Laurent Dauthuille—but, in February 1951, surrendered it to Sugar Ray Robinson on a 13th-round TKO. It was LaMotta's fifth loss in six fights with Robinson. LaMotta fought just 10 times over the next three years, then hung up the gloves and moved to Miami where he opened a cocktail lounge and liquor store. After spending time in prison for corrupting the morals of an underage girl, he moved back to New York where he tried, among other things, stand-up comedy and working as a bouncer at a topless bar. His making—or re-making, perhaps—was the 1980 release of the Martin Scorcese film RAGING BULL, *starring Robert DeNiro as LaMotta. No feel-good* SOMEBODY UP THERE LIKES ME *or* ROCKY, *the movie is widely considered the best boxing—and maybe sports—movie ever made, mostly for its seeringly honest portrayal of the ugliness of the fight game in general and the darkness of LaMotta's own nature in particular. Six times married and now 81, LaMotta is still feisty as ever, living with his fiance in New York.*

CHAPTER SIX

ROCCO FRANCIS MARCHEGIANO

THE BLOCKBUSTER FROM BROCKTON

BY ED FITZGERALD

FROM *SPORT*, JANUARY 1953

There wasn't much a bored soldier shipping out for England could do to kill time on the crowded decks of the Mauretania. Private Rocco Marchegiano of the 150th Combat Engineers didn't have any money in his wallet so he couldn't even get into one of the non-stop games of chance; all he could do was stand around restlessly and watch others shuffling the cards and shaking the dice. Finally, he couldn't stand it any longer. He borrowed a quarter from a pal and got into a penny-ante game of blackjack. He won eight dollars and moved on to a poker game where the stakes were considerably higher. He won $50 more and, feeling hot, bought into the "big game" on the ship, a wide-open crap game. Riding a phenomenal streak of luck, and riding it for all it was worth, he quickly ran his stake all the way up to a bulging bankroll of $1,200.

It was the first time anything like that had happened to him in all his life, but it wasn't to be the last. Half a dozen years after he got his Army discharge, with his name shortened to the more colorful Rocky Marciano, the iron-muscled Italian kid from Brockton, Massachusetts, climaxed a brief career in the prize ring by slugging Jersey Joe Walcott unconscious before a half-million-dollar house in Philadelphia's Municipal Stadium to win the heavyweight championship of the world. The only man in the recorded history of the heavyweight class to win the title without suffering a single professional defeat, Rocky had hit the jackpot just as spectacularly as he had broken the troopship crap game. But this time the stakes were even bigger. By the most conservative estimate the pot held a cool million dollars, and if Rocky's luck stayed with him, he would make his million five times over.

He intends to hang on to what he makes. As plain as an old shoe, Rocky has inevitably learned to like a number of the things money can buy—especially anything you can eat—but he isn't likely ever to become a playboy. He's a neighborhood kid who married a neighborhood girl and who thinks the old hometown is the greatest place in the world. He'll live well but he won't build any bonfires with the dollar bills he has earned by the toughest means known to man.

"I think I learned a good lesson when I won that money on the ship," Rocky said in his noticeably New England accent. "I was the only guy in the company who had any money when we landed in England, and naturally the fellows all wanted to go places, so it didn't take long before I had it all loaned out. I never got it back." Rocky grinned reflectively. "I don't know what ever happened to that money," he said. "But it wasn't put to good use." You get the impression that he intends to take better care of his boxing money, which is a good idea because there is going to be an awful lot of it.

It is no surprise to the fight mob, which has been saying it for at least three years, but there is scarcely an adult newspaper-reader in the United States who does not now know that Rocky Marciano is a human gold mine. The heavyweight championship is almost always an exceedingly profitable commodity. In the right hands, it coins money almost as fast as the U.S. Mint. Rocky's hands are obviously going to rank him right up there with Jack Dempsey and Joe Louis, the

Left: Rocky Marciano and daughter, Mary Ann, 1954

money-makingest heavyweight kings in history. The Rock has everything. No Fancy Dan boxer, he throws technique to the winds when he climbs between the ropes. He fights as though his very life were at stake; he pursues the enemy with an implacable fury that raises the hackles on the backs of the customers' necks. Rocky is not in there to outpoint anybody in an exhibition of boxing skill. He is in there to kill or be killed. He is a primitive fighter who stalks his prey until he can welt him with that frightening right-hand crusher. You can, as with an enraged grizzly bear, slow him down and make him shake his head if you hit him hard enough to wound him, but you can't make him back up. Slowly, relentlessly, ruthlessly, he moves in on you. Sooner or later, he reaches out and clubs you down. He isn't graceful, as Joe Louis was, and he isn't smart, as Jack Dempsey was, but he can hit at least as hard as either of those legendary punchers—and maybe harder. The crowd doesn't ask for anything more.

In addition to the truckload of box office appeal he carries in his shy grin, his infectious good humor and his tigerish style of fighting, Rocky has another major asset in his campaign to haul a few million dollars in honest loot back to the town where he once worked eight hours a day, five days a week, with a pick and shovel. He is in virtually on the ground floor of the giant television boom. No man alive can tell how much money Rocky may be able to command for a title defense a few years from now. Theater television already is outstripping its wildest claims as a money-making medium for headline fights; subscription television, with every set-owner able to tune in the fight by paying a modest fee, could conceivably make a million dollars just a fair take for the champion's end of a purse. The imagination is staggered by the enormous riches plainly within the grasp of this powerfully built son of an immigrant shoemaker.

Judging from the murderous impact his Sunday punch has on the men he faces in the ring—he has scored 38 knockouts in his 43 fights, all of which he has won—Rocky is going to remain champion long enough to do the first truly thorough job of exploiting TV's possibilities as a boxing income-producer. Despite the fact that he is one of the easiest fighters in the ring to hit, as old Jersey Joe proved when he knocked him to the mat in the first minute of their September title fight, Marciano carries the equalizer in his right hand and can put the fear of the Lord into anyone who has the temerity to slug it out with him. If anyone beats him in

the next few years, it will be a lightning-fast boxer, a big Ray Robinson, someone who can take full advantage of the Rock's clumsiness and do to him what Gene Tunney did to Dempsey 26 years ago in Philadelphia.

Charlie Goldman, the wise old trainer who harnessed Marciano's raw power, says the only thing that will beat Rocky is his unbelievably prodigious appetite. Charlie watches him like a hawk to keep him from eating too much but it's a thankless job. All kinds of stories are told about Rocky's feats at the table, and most of them are true. His father, Perrino, tells one of the best. "One time," Papa Marchegiano says, "Mama had some people coming to the house so she made a roast chicken and put it in the refrigerator to slice up later. Then she went out. When she come home she look for the chicken but no chicken. Nothing. Then Rocky comes home and she asked him. At least, he told the truth. He ate the whole thing. He was hungry."

There is a wealthy Italian tomato grower named Jimmy Cereglia who commutes between Atlanta, Georgia, and wherever Marciano happens to be at the moment. He lavishes affection upon the fighter. "Jimmy Tomatoes," as Rocky calls him, once gave a party for Marciano at Greenwood Lake, New York. He kept after Rocky to eat, begged him to eat and enjoy himself, to have a good time. Rocky ate some lasagna, an Italian staple of noodles and meat and cheese, which has more calories per cubic inch than you could count. Then he ate a big bowl of minestrone, Italy's entrancing version of vegetable soup. Ready for some serious eating, he demolished a five-pound steak and, still not quite full, tapered off with two orders of filet mignon. He economized on calories by turning down all dessert offers except a bowl of ice cream. Goldman says disgustedly that he was probably looking for a snack in the refrigerator an hour later.

Rocky laughs sheepishly as Charlie gives him the needle about his astonishing appetite. He defends himself mildly. "Sure," he says, "I like the eats, but Charlie's always laying it on. I ain't that bad."

Maybe not, but he comes close. One night during his long training grind before the Walcott fight, Rocky got up from in front of the camp television set and stretched his weary arms. "Guess I'll hit the sack," he said, and started across the hall to his bedroom. Goldman looked after him suspiciously. "What'd you stash up there tonight?" he demanded. "You been out buyin' some salami or somethin'?" Rocky looked

Nailing Joe Louis (left, 1951) and Lee Savold, 1952

pained. "What's the matter, Charlie?" he said wistfully, "ain't you ever gonna start in trustin' me?" He was still a little pained, one of his buddies said, when he sat down on the edge of his bed, reached under the pillow, hauled out a two-pound roll of salami and bit into it, shaking his head in a puzzled way.

Like many another great fighters before him—Joe Louis, for a recent example—Marciano is a split personality. An out-and-out killer in the ring, instinctively swinging for blood on every punch, he is the mildest, friendliest and most loyal of men outside it. The pal whose faith in his ability got him started on the road to the heavyweight championship is still at his side, sharing in every new stroke of good fortune. Al Colombo, who lived next door to Rocky and talked him into setting out on the glory road, will be on the champ's payroll as long as he wants to be. The same goes for Nick

Sylvester, another old friend from Brockton. Rocky says he keeps Nick around because he can murder him at table tennis but they both know better than that. Rocky is a man who sets great store by family and friends. He thinks his two biggest victories in 1952 were knocking out Walcott and getting his 58-year-old father to quit the shoe factory after more than three decades of unremitting labor—and Rocky isn't so sure they ought to be listed in that order.

Even his opponents become Rocky's friends. He has never been known to utter a disparaging remark about any man he has fought in the ring. The good, the bad and the indifferent, the brave and the cowardly, they all get kind words from Rocky. One man, Carmine Vingo, who almost died from the numbing effects of a Marciano knockout blow, has become a bosom buddy of the champion. Rocky blasted young Vingo into unconsciousness in the sixth round of a Madison Square Garden fight on December 30, 1949. Partially paralyzed and intermittently out cold, Vingo was carried into St. Clare's Hospital in New York and barely escaped with his life. He has recovered completely, although he can never fight again, and is working in a defense plant. Rocky sends him ringside tickets to all his big fights and Carmine is a familiar figure in Marciano's dressing room. Nobody ever told Rocky he ought to do it; it's just his way.

There is no telling how seriously Marciano's career might have been affected if anything had happened to Vingo. Only the people who live with Rocky know how shocked he was by the nearly fatal accident. A Catholic, he prayed constantly that Carmine's life might be spared. He didn't draw an easy breath until a week or 10 days after the fight, it was clear that the boy would live. Rocky has no lurid notions about the striking force of his gloved fists but he never approaches a new fight without a silent prayer that no action of his may cause permanent harm to another man.

Temporary harm is another matter. Rocky knows he is no master boxer and he knows the only safe course for him to follow in any fight is to go for a knockout. As Charlie Goldman says, "They all look better than he does as far as the moves are concerned, but they don't look so good on the canvas."

For a long time, Marciano's succession of knockout victories was taken with a large grain of salt by ring fanciers. They made jokes about his smashing wins over such as Johnny Pretzie, Harry Haft, Phil Muscata, Eldridge Eatman, Gino Buonvino and Johnny Shkor. "Roundheels," they termed them sneeringly. Whenever Rocky was evaded for the full 10 rounds by a Don Mogard, a Ted Lowry or a Red Applegate, the raspberries were even fruitier.

There can be little doubt that Rocky's swift and smooth rise to the top of the boxing world disproved the old ring axiom that you can't learn the trade by knocking over stiffs. Almost everyone agrees there was little danger of his being upended by any of the solemn clowns he fought in his first few years. "Sixty percent of them guys Marciano licked," one old-time fight manager said, "didn't know from nothing. They got a call to go up and fight. They went. They got knocked out. Nobody got locked up and a lot of guys got paid off." That's a cynical but honest appraisal of the way Marciano's reputation was nurtured.

But Rocky was no Primo Carnera. Even though he was tossed in with a parade of ineffectives, he managed to find out what it was all about. Little Charlie Goldman kept whispering the word into his ear, and just by being in the ring and swinging his meat-axe at the selected victims dug up by Al Weill, he picked up a little here and a little there. He learned what his punch could do and what he had to do to exploit it. He learned how to move around, not like Sugar Ray or even like Ezzard Charles, but purposefully enough to line up his heavy artillery and get it on target. He didn't need to do anything more.

The jeers of the fight mob were inspired by something more than a professional scorn for the quality of Marciano's opposition. Rocky was (and is) managed by Al Weill, one of the shrewdest, most successful, and most hated men in the game. When they mouthed their cruel witticisms about Rocky's lack of style, the Jacobs Beachcombers were simply giving vent to their dislike for Weill. After Alphonse ascended the throne of matchmaker for the International Boxing Club, and, in order to comply with the regulations of the New York State Athletic Commission, turned over the managership of Marciano to his stepson, Marty Weill, the catcalls grew even louder. The Weill-haters had what they needed, an issue they could get their teeth into.

It was against the rules for Al to hold down his $20,000-a-year job as IBC matchmaker and manage a fighter at the same time, but everyone knew he was doing it. The managers, trainers, boxers, writers and hangers-on who did not belong to the Weill inner circle did their level best to beat his brains in. Scarcely a week went by that some columnist did not angrily demand an investigation. Young Rocky Marciano, running his roadwork faithfully, belting out the fighters they put in the ring with him, and being his naturally amiable self to everyone he met in the course of the job, found himself squarely in the middle. Entrenched in the seat of boxing power, Weill was safe from the slings and the arrows. It was easier to put the slug on Marciano—with tongue or typewriter, that is—and it soon became fashionable to speak of the Brockton boxer as a clumsy amateur whose heavyweight pretensions were just flights of the Weill fancy.

Five times Rocky had to meet this persistent calumny head-on. Five times he destroyed it. So deeply ingrained was the Weillphobia that provoked the smearing of Marciano's reputation that the dragon was resurrected after each new slaying and Rocky had to do the job all over again. But he never faltered. His fighting heart and his fearsome punch more than made up for his technical deficiencies. One by one he answered the big questions. He outpointed Roland LaStarza on March 24, 1950. He knocked out Rex Layne in six rounds on July 12, 1951. He knocked out the great Joe Louis in eight rounds on October 26, 1951. He knocked out Harry Matthews in two rounds on July 28, 1952. He knocked out Jersey Joe Walcott, in 13 savage and melodramatic rounds on September 23, 1952.

Weill was, incidentally, openly in Marciano's corner for the first time in three years the night the Rock won the title. He had resigned his IBC position in midsummer and had put a stop to the fragile fiction that Marty Weill, who saw the fighter a few times a year, was Rocky's manager. The contract Marty had filed with the New York State Athletic Commission was withdrawn and torn up. Rocky signed a new two-year agreement with Al and the old firm was officially back in business. "Marty," Rocky grinned when he was asked about the contract switch, "was bought out."

But overnight, in fact, in the single shattering second it took for that destructive right hand to explode flush against the black stubble of beard on Joe Walcott's jaw, nobody seemed to care much who was managing Rocky.

What difference did it make? Brother, did you see the way Walcott went down when the Rock let him have it? The Brockton Blockbuster was the heavyweight champion of the world, a slugging successor to John L. Sullivan, Jim Corbett, Jack Dempsey and Joe Louis. There were no jeers now, only cheers, cheer upon volleyed cheer flung into the night sky over Philadelphia and finding an echo in every city and town in America where the most ancient and lustiest of sports had a single follower.

Rocky did it the hard way. Fate selected an extraordinary roundabout way for him to make his boyhood dream come true. As a sports-crazy kid, in his private dreams of glory he was always the heavyweight champ, taking on all comers and knocking them out with a single roundhouse right, but it was only a boy's fantasy. It wasn't a serious ambition, even though he used to tell his father jokingly that he'd take care of all his troubles when he grew up and won the title. Years later, when he was a man grown, working for a living with his strong arms and back, or soldiering in the Combat Engineers, or a veteran on the City of Brockton payroll as a

pick-and-shovel man, he wouldn't have given a dime for his chances of following through on the old vision. Life was very real and very earnest to Rocco Marchegiano.

Things had never been easy for Rocky. He was the first of five children born to Perrino Marchegiano and his wife, Pasqualena. His father had served with the AEF in World War I and had been gassed during the Argonne fighting. He was able to go back to the shoe factory when he returned home to Brockton but he never was the same man physically and his earning power was sharply limited by his disability. As a result, the Marchegianos were just about able to make ends meet; there never was any money left over for "foolishness."

Rocky's father, who can hardly restrain his immense pride when he stands quietly in the background and talks about his famous son, likes to tease Rocky in a heavy-handed way about his thriftiness as a boy. "Mama," he says, "used to give him a quarter sometimes to go to the movies. Like on Saturday afternoon. He would put it in his pocket and go out. That night after he got in bed she would be hanging up his clothes and the quarter would fall out. He didn't spend it." The old man shook his head affectionately. "He always hated to spend money, that boy. He was always working for a dollar. His pleasure was giving money to Mama."

When he wasn't running errands or sweeping out stores for nickels, Rocky was playing ball. Baseball, if it was warm; football, if it was cold. The gang from the neighborhood used to hang out in Edgar Playground when the weather was decent and it never took long to get a game going. Everybody always wanted Rocco on their side; he was the best athlete in the gang. He generally was a catcher in baseball and a center in football, although he also played some first base for a couple of town teams in later years. Except for the usual number of kid fights, he did his first boxing on a punching bag his Uncle John Piccento installed for him in the cellar. "Uncle John gave me my first gloves, too," Rocky said, "and he took me to my first fight, down at the Brockton Arena."

Uncle John had a great deal to do with the shaping of Marciano's career. He not only provided the first boxing equipment Rocky ever had but he was the one who talked the boy into quitting high school during his second year and making a serious start in the world. "Uncle John knew I wasn't much of a student," Rocky says candidly. "He grabbed me one day and told me it wouldn't hurt for me to get out and get a job. The folks could use a little help, he said. So I did. I worked in a shoe factory for a while, then I got a job in a candy factory. I had all kinds of jobs. I worked for a landscape gardener and I worked clearing land for the city and the state both. I liked the pick-and-shovel work a lot better than being in a factory. I couldn't stand being cooped up all day. I had to be out in the air."

In his spare time he kept on playing ball. "Sometimes," he said, "in one week in the summer I'd play as many as eight games. I played for the Sons of Italy, the Ward Two Social Club, the Italian-Americans, for all the teams that asked me. After all, I was still only 17, 18. I was out for a good time when I was off the job."

But the job, whatever it happened to be at the time, was the big thing. The money he was making helped Mama Marchegiano set a better table for her hungry brood and still lay away a few dollars for a rainy day. There was, in those days, no thought in Rocky's mind that things ever would be any different. He had a brief surge of hope once when his Uncle John, thinking the boy might have the makings of a prize-fighter, took him down to the Knights of Columbus for a workout.

"I got in with the local pro for a couple of rounds," Rocky said, "but I didn't get any encouragement." He grimaced. "The guy didn't even let me throw a punch. He was all over me. I guess he told Uncle John to forget about it."

Fortunately, Uncle John kept up a sporadic interest in Rocky's boxing. "He had a bad left arm himself," Rocky said. "He couldn't straighten it out. So he was always after me to learn how to do everything with both arms, in case anything ever happened to one. He wanted me to bat lefty as well as righty. He wanted me to throw with both hands. He kept after me all the time to punch the bag with both hands and get used to punching with either one. That couldn't have done me any harm."

Al Colombo, who lived in the house next door, was Rocky's best pal. Nick Sylvester, who is still with him, and his brother Gene were his friends, too. Their life in the years just before the war was typical of the existence led by hard-working young men in factory cities all over the country. Their interests all lay outside the job. Baseball was their first love. Boxing was their second favorite. Rocky and Allie, as he has always called Colombo, were Joe Louis fans. Their hangout was the Ward Two Social Club. They didn't have steady girls but they liked to go to a dance once in a while. The weeks went along and became months and the months merged into years and there was no reason to suspect things ever would be any different. Then the war came.

Rocky, who was born on September 1, 1924, was 18 years old when he pulled his induction notice out of the mailbox in March, 1943. He felt no particular pain at the prospect of becoming a buck private. It was

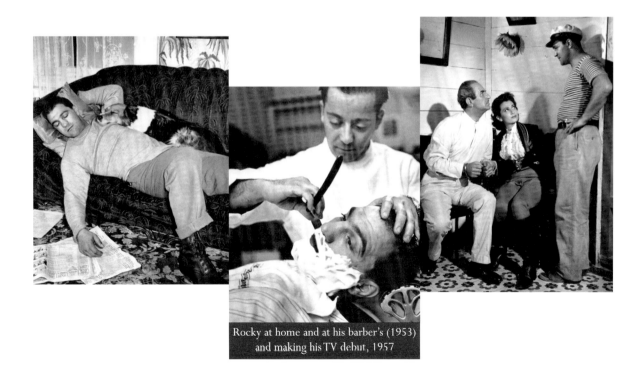

Rocky at home and at his barber's (1953)
and making his TV debut, 1957

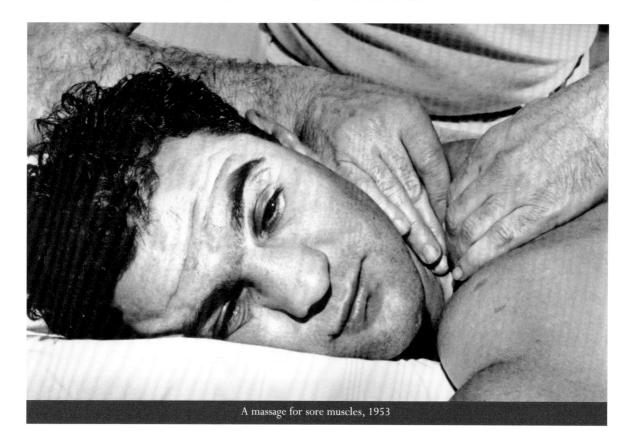

A massage for sore muscles, 1953

another job, and from what he had heard, he wouldn't have to work half as hard as he had been doing. "But they must have taken one look at my thick neck," Rocky said, laughing, "and said to themselves, 'Here's a guy we can work.' Because right away I was in a brand new Combat Engineers outfit, the 150th. And, boy, they made us sweat. We were just ditch-diggers in uniform."

It didn't take Rocky long to find out that when the outfit was in a garrison status he could make life a lot easier for himself by playing ball and boxing. That way he got off a lot of work details, and Rocky would rather get in the ring for a couple of rounds than do KP any day in the week. The accepted story is that his buddies first discovered his punching prowess when he flattened a big Australian soldier who tried to bulldoze some of them in a British pub. Actually, Rocky had started his army boxing at Fort Devens, Massachusetts, before he went overseas, and he kept it up on the other side whenever the opportunity presented itself. When he got back to the States, he fought in an Army tournament and went all the way to the finals at Portland, Oregon, before he was outpointed by a Boston sergeant named Judge DeAngelis.

His success in Army boxing gave new life to Rocky's old longing to be a professional fighter. It still wasn't an all-consuming ambition, but it was there. "Actually," he says, "I was more interested in baseball, but I got cured of that in a hurry. Ralph Wheeler, a sportswriter for the *Boston Herald*, arranged for five of us from the Ward Two club to get a tryout with the Fayetteville, North Carolina club. That was a Chicago Cub farm. I went down there with big ideas, I guess, and I was pretty disappointed when I didn't make it. My arm was dead. I couldn't throw. But I hated to go back home. Everybody in town knew I'd gone down for the tryout and, well, I don't know, I was just ashamed. Allie's cousin, Vince Colombo, had got himself situated with an independent club called the Goldsboro Bugs in Wilson, North Carolina, so I went over to visit him for a while. I told him how I didn't want to go home and he said his club was short of catchers so he got me a job with them. I played for a couple of weeks, maybe three altogether, and I got my hits, but I still couldn't throw. The manager finally told me I'd better go home."

Back in Brockton, with no money in his jeans, Rocky got a job working for the city, clearing land for a new housing project. He worked at that for a couple of months and then, at Al Colombo's urging, began boxing again. "I had about seven amateur fights for the AAU in the Mechanics' Building in Boston," he said, "and I did real good. Then they started the Golden Gloves over in Lowell and I had four fights there and won them all. That qualified me for the All-Eastern and I went all the way to the final. Coley Wallace beat me."

"It was a bad decision," Colombo, who was listening, interrupted. "Eddie Eagan, who used to be the Commissioner in New York, came to see Rocky when he was training for Walcott, and he said he had seen the fight and he thought Rocky had beaten Wallace."

Rocky nodded. "I thought I beat him," he said. "But I didn't get the decision and that's what counts."

Just the same, Rocky had done well enough to agree with Colombo that he might have a future in boxing. He had even made a few dollars out of it. Not much, of course, $15 here and $25 there. Then Al got him a "bootleg" fight in Holyoke for $50. He fought under the name of Rocky Mack and his opponent in the four-round preliminary was another amateur named Lee Epperson. Rocky knocked him out in the third round and had no objections to offer when Al said he was going to write a letter to the famous New York manager, Al Weill, and ask him to take Rocky in hand and make a professional out of him.

Weill still has that letter. It said, in part, "there are quite a few handlers around Boston who are interested but we are dissatisfied with a Boston setup for Rocky. We are interested mainly in a manager in New York who has the contacts to take care of a very promising young heavyweight properly. Believe me, he has tremendous possibilities. You will see he's good enough to go to the top."

With that letter began the gradual transition of Rocco Marchegiano, part-time pick-and-shovel man and part-time amateur boxer, into Rocky Marciano, heavyweight champion of the world. The in-between phase is mostly Charlie Goldman's story.

"Weill turned the letter over to me," Charlie said, "and I wrote Colombo the usual thing. I invited him to bring the boy down for a tryout and I said at least with us he'd get an opportunity to learn the trade. Colombo wrote back and made a date with me. But when the day came they didn't show up. Then the next day they were there. What happened was they didn't have any money and they found out they could bum a ride down on a truck that was headed for New York; but they'd have to wait a day. So they waited. When they finally got there, they met me at my office and I took them down to the CYO gym. There wasn't anybody around for Rocky to box with so I had him punch the big bag. One of the CYO coaches was around, and I'm the kind of a guy that always likes to get somebody else's opinion when I can, so I asked him what he thought of the boy. He told me, 'You'll never make a fighter out of that guy.' But it looked to me like he had a big, strong body and a good, strong punch. You have those things; it's a short cut. I figured I had nothing to lose taking a chance, and Al agreed with me."

Charlie pointed out that one of the main handicaps he had to consider was Rocky's age. "He was 23, going on 24, when I first saw him," the wizened trainer said. "That's old for a fighter starting out. Most good fighters get started as early as 15 or 16. By the time they're in their twenties, they're well on their way. With Rocky it was different. You see, there's nothing much on a young boy's mind except fighting, but the older fellows have to worry all the time about making a living right away, and that makes it tough."

It made it tough for Marciano, all right. Weill advanced him nothing. He had to struggle along as best he could until Goldman thought he was ready to begin fighting—and even then he couldn't hope for more than minimum purses. Fortunately, he had a little money put away, and so did Colombo. They pooled what they had. Then, when things were beginning to get rough, the Mayor of Brockton came to the rescue by putting him on the city payroll for six weeks. That gave Rocky a chance to hold out until Goldman and Weill felt he could give it a whirl.

On July 12, 1948, in Providence, Rhode Island, Rocky had his first professional fight of record. He stiffened one Harry Bilazarian in the first round. One week later he was fed a gentle opponent named John Edwards. He, too, succumbed in the first round.

"He was very awkward," Charlie Goldman says. "He was crude. Right-hand crazy. He had that good right hand, but the way he looped it, it was always telegraphed. Anybody could've seen what was coming when he got ready to throw it."

But Weill was too smart to let Rocky get in with anybody who was likely to take advantage of his inexperience. His opponents were not picked haphazardly. Weill wasn't out to make a quick dollar with his new boy; in fact, Rocky testifies, "he didn't even cut me that first year." What the shrewd New Yorker had in mind was nothing less than the biggest prize of them all. Right from the beginning, he was shooting for the heavyweight title.

The knockouts continued, one after another. The names of the upended "opponents," the trade designation for non-entities who serve as chopping blocks for more favored fighters, meant nothing then and mean nothing now. Bobby Quinn, Eddie Ross, Gil Cardione, Bob Jefferson, Gilley Ferron, James Walls . . . there were 15 of them, all in a row, all twisted and quivering masses of human flesh stretched out on the unfriendly canvas, human sacrifices to Al Weill's Machiavellian design and Rocky Marciano's inevitable destiny.

The name Rocky Marciano, incidentally, was Al Weill's idea, too. He told his white hope that Rocco Marchegiano would never do for a ring name. Too long, too hard to say and too hard to spell. Al Colombo suggested the old pseudonym, Rocky Mack, but Rocky didn't like the idea. He didn't think it sounded like him. But when Marciano was suggested, he went along right away. "At least," he said, "it sounds Italian."

Rocky's uninterrupted string of knockouts was finally cut short in Providence on May 23, 1949, by Don Mogard, an undistinguished journeyman heavyweight who stood on his feet for the full 10 rounds even though he lost the decision. After three more knockouts, Rocky was held to a decision again by Ted Lowry, another club-fighting heavyweight of small skill but stout heart. But he was still unbeaten and he could boast of 21 knockouts in 23 fights as the year 1949 drew to a close. Weill decided to risk showing him in New York.

Carmine Vingo was a vigorous young man the night of December 30, 1949, when he stepped into the ring at the Nicholas Arena to box Rocky Marciano in the 10-round main event. He was much older after the fight was over. He was almost at the end of his life. The doctors who worked tensely around the clock to keep the heart beating inside his big body had to contend with a fractured skull, a concussion of the brain and a damaging blood clot on the brain. It wasn't until a week had passed that they were willing to predict with confidence that he would live. It was a week of hellish torture for Rocky. Nobody outside of Carmine's immediate circle of loved ones was more relieved than Rocky when it was known that Vingo would live. Along with his prayers, Rocky sent his victim a check for $2,000 to help pay his hospital costs and later added $500 more to give the beaten boxer a boost as he set

out to look for a new way to make a living. Their affection for each other today is a warming thing to see. Since Carmine can no longer fight in the ring, Rocky's career has to serve for both of them. Carmine was as wildly happy the night Marciano knocked out Walcott as if he had belted the old champion to the floor himself.

Weill didn't send his tiger back to the wars for almost three months after the Vingo scare. He wanted to make sure Rocky had pushed the episode into the back of his mind. When he did make another match for him, it was a big one. As Rocky had been climbing the ladder in New England, edging ever closer to the charmed circle of legitimate heavyweight contenders, a young college boy named Roland LaStarza had been doing the same thing in New York. Not so savage a puncher as Marciano, but a more skillful boxer, LaStarza had attracted a considerable following among the experts as well as the fans. A meeting between the two was a natural.

The Madison Square Garden battle between the two serious, gifted young heavyweights took place on March 24, 1950, almost three years ago. It is still hashed over, round by round, still the theme of a thousand vehement arguments. It was decided by the narrowest margin allowable in New York State. It was a fight to remember, a crucial fight of heavy implications.

LaStarza, winner of 37 straight as against Marciano's 26 in a row, showed the crowd of 13,658 some fancy counter-punching in the first three rounds as Marciano wasted no time swinging to the attack. By far the largest percentage of Rocky's punches were wild, and the cleverer, more stylish LaStarza was making a good impression at Marciano's expense.

But Rocky kept swinging. Even when the crowd laughed coarsely at some of his worst misses, he showed no outward signs of discouragement. As the fourth round got under way, a few of his long, looping rights to the head began to land. Then, just before the bell sounded to end the round, Rocky smashed a right-hand punch through LaStarza's guard and knocked the broad-shouldered CCNY student off his feet. Bewildered and hurt, but not out, Roland was getting to his feet at the count of eight when the bell broke it off.

Rocky caught LaStarza with a few more good ones in the fifth and, for a while, it looked as though he might wrap up the fight. But Roland came back strong in the sixth and seventh and tightened it up again. In the eighth, Rocky, still swinging freely and showing no signs of tiring, made a costly mistake that almost lost him the

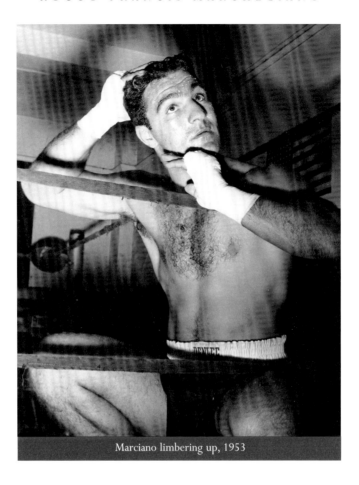
Marciano limbering up, 1953

fight. Throwing right hands as fast and as hard as he could, he let go a low blow that resulted in the referee awarding the round to LaStarza. The ninth and tenth were both close rounds. The crowd roared with pleasure as the two obviously classy rookies pounded each other with punches that hurt. Rocky fooled the cautious LaStarza several times with a powerful left hook, a punch he hadn't tried at all in the earlier rounds. They were slugging at close quarters, each desperately striving for a last-minute edge, when the fight ended.

The Garden was in an uproar as the crowd waited for the decision. Everybody knew how much the fight meant to the two youngsters and the almost universal dislike of Weill lent spice to the suspense. The noise died out quickly as Johnny Addie, the Garden announcer, stepped to the microphone lowered over the ring. Addie gave the result piecemeal. Judge Arthur Schwartz had scored five rounds for Marciano, four for LaStarza and one even. Judge Arthur Aidala had it just the other way around, five rounds for LaStarza, four for Marciano and one even. You couldn't hear a sound except heavy, tense breathing as

Addie said, "Referee Watson scores five rounds for Marciano, five rounds for LaStarza. Points: six for LaStarza, nine for Marciano! The winner, Marciano!"

Wild cheers were mixed with angry boos as the big crowd began to file out of the hall. A quick poll of the working press section showed that most of the boxing writers thought LaStarza had won but that it had been a close fight and it didn't matter much, anyway, because now they could have a terrific return match. In the bowels of the Garden, under the emptying stands, Al Weill, now the matchmaker of the International Boxing Club and officially separated from the managership of Marciano, walked into LaStarza's dressing room to congratulate him on a strong showing. Wild with rage, Roland's manager, Jimmy (Fats) DeAngelo, threw him out and slammed the door in his face.

Weill was to get even by slamming the door in LaStarza's face for the next three years. The much talked about return bout never happened. Weill had other plans. He was pointing the Brockton Blockbuster, as the papers were already beginning to call Rocky, onward and upward. As far as Weill was concerned, LaStarza was just another inevitable casualty. Al couldn't be bothered mourning his hard luck and, not being the sensitive type, he wasn't at all disturbed by the ceaseless needling of the fight writers who thought it something less than kosher for him to play such flagrant politics while supposedly looking out disinterestedly for the best interests of the IBC and the boxing public in his well-paid capacity of matchmaker.

The Marciano saga moved into a new phase. Rocky was firmly established as a contender now. Not the top contender, but a real one nevertheless and a contender who could boast the rarest of all heavyweight commodities, gobs and gobs of color. There was something about Rocky that made even the Weill-haters tingle inside. Your pulse jumped and the sweat oozed out of your armpits when Rocky, black hair flying, muscle-ridged back glistening and magnificently carved arms driving, threw science out the window and crashed into an opponent with the undisciplined violence of a young bull. As did few other fighters of his time, Rocky satisfied the primitive blood lust that lured the customers through the doors.

He went back on the stiff patrol while the master mind in the IBC office searched for the next opening. They flocked to see him in Providence, in Boston and in Hartford, and he seldom disappointed them. He had five fights between June and December, and he won four of them by knockouts. In the fifth, he out-pointed Ted Lowry, the second time Lowry had refused to bend before the Rock's withering fire.

Rocky had a long way to go before he got into the really big money but he was doing well enough. The LaStarza fight, with a $53,723 gate, had been his first big strike. Rocky, who had been going steady for almost three years with Barbara Cousens, the big, blonde daughter of Patrolman Lester Cousens of the Brockton Police Department, wanted to get married. He put it up to Weill, who had so far discouraged the step. Weill agreed reluctantly that Rocky was solvent enough, and had progressed far enough in his trade, to marry. So, on December 31, 1950, Rocky and Barbara were married. Al Colombo was best man. A party at Cappy's Restaurant in Brockton saw Rocky go for his whole end of the LaStarza purse entertaining 550 friends and relatives in the gayest wedding party Brockton had seen in a long time. It was a celebration worthy of the great John L. Sullivan himself, and there wasn't a man,

woman or child in the crowd who wasn't convinced that Rocky Marciano was the living image of John L., the new Boston Strong Boy.

Rocky and Barbara had a short honeymoon in Miami—very short. Then it was right back to the training grind and, on the night of January 29, back to the wars. Keene Simmons was led out to the Providence chopping block and the hero of all New England demolished him in eight rounds. Rocky was back in business.

Another big test was building up for Marciano. Rex Layne of Lewiston, Utah, touted by Jack Dempsey as the best young heavyweight around, had out-pointed Jersey Joe Walcott and knocked out Bob Satterfield in the course of winning 36 out of 37 fights. Only Dave Whitlock had been able to beat him and Rex had taken care of Whitlock in a return bout. Big and strong, he was the picture of a heavyweight fighter. But, before a crowd of 12,565 that paid $73,190 into the Garden box-office, Rocky exposed him as a willing but clumsy amateur.

"It was a contest of long-ball hitters," Jesse Abramson wrote in the *New York Herald Tribune*, "and Marciano came up with the home run."

Crouching, weaving and bobbing, crowding Layne so the big Mormon scarcely ever had elbow room in which to work, Rocky appeared to have parked his left hand in an Eighth Avenue garage. But his right was in Layne's ribs and face all night. Rex began bleeding from a gash over his left eye in the second round. His knees buckled and he almost went down in the third. He was dropped for no count in the fourth. He survived the fifth without any noticeable difficulty but the sixth was as far as he could go. Rocky was obviously determined to come up with the big one as he hurried out of his corner at the start of the sixth round. He threw a few punches, shifted his feet and exploded a short right just above Layne's blood-smeared left eye.

Rex stiffened, rocked, then plunged face down to the floor. He lay motionless, his big body rigid. The seconds running to his aid looked frightened. A lot of the spectators stood transfixed, wondering if it was going to be the Vingo fight all over again. But after a minute or so, Rex came to. He had been knocked out for the first time in his life.

"There I was, on my face," he told the reporters in his dressing room. "I heard the count from one to 10. I kept telling myself that I simply had to get up. But I couldn't move. I couldn't make myself move. It was the strangest feeling."

It was a strange feeling that had become Rocky Marciano's trademark. They said it after the Layne fight, and they've been saying it ever since. When he hits them, they stay hit!

Brockton turned itself upside down for the Marcianos, man and wife, as they drove home in triumph. A big motorcade met them at Providence and Rocky and Barbara were put in the back seat of an open car. Two drum majorettes strutted in front of the VFW band. The Cosmopolitan Club sent a band, and every member of the Ward Two Social Club who could get leave from his job was in the joyous line of march. Horns blew and sirens wailed. Confetti poured down, turning Rocky's thick black hair snow white. Mayor Melvin B. Clifford gave the fighter a huge cardboard key to the city. His mother spoke haltingly into the microphone after she kissed him and patted him affectionately on the shoulder.

"I'm very proud of my son," Mrs. Marchegiano said nervously. "He is beautiful . . . I love him very much."

All Brockton loved him, and always will. He put the city on the map; he gave its citizens a new interest in life. Just as Carmine Vingo had been able to do, all the boys from Brockton identified themselves with their champion, and his victories became their victories. They took as much pride and satisfaction in his rich purses as if they were spending the money themselves. Above all, they rejoiced that success hadn't taken Rocky away from them. He still lived among them, still walked among them as he had done when he was drawing his $35 or $40 a week from the city for swinging a pick.

As a matter of fact, up to this point Rocky didn't even own a car. The Ward Two boys took up a collection and bought him one—a 1951 DeSoto—as a token of their esteem. He didn't even have a license, so they pulled a few strings and got one for him the day they gave him the car. Fortunately for the public safety, he doesn't drive much; he lets Barbara take care of that detail. "I don't guess I've put more than 500 miles on the car," Rocky says. Walking has always appealed to him more than riding. His idea of a little walk is five miles out and five miles back after a meal. It keeps his legs in shape and, besides, it perks up his appetite. Charlie Goldman swears he isn't kidding when he says the only time he has any trouble with Rocky about roadwork is when the Rock is doing too much of it. "You turn your back on him for five minutes," Charlie says, "and he's gone for a five-mile trot." Rocky, in turn, argues that "all the old-time fighters, they'll all tell you the most important thing is roadwork. I think it's the big thing." Rocky will run alone if he has to but he likes to have somebody along to talk to. "I start out with Colombo," he said, laughing boyishly, "then when he's worn out, Sylvester comes in to relieve him." The platoon system works well. It isn't only his persistent running that keeps Marciano in top shape. He doesn't drink or smoke or stay up late. After one of his big wins, Al Weill threw a party for him in a New York hotel and made him drink a glass of champagne. Rocky almost choked on the bubbly stuff. He's perfectly willing to stick to milk; for him, Coke is plenty strong enough when he wants something different.

Rocky likes to read, and, spending as much time as he does in training camps, he gets plenty of opportunity. He goes for sports stories and adventure yarns and whodunits. One of his favorite magazines is *True Detective*. He's not much of a movie man but he regards a Broadway musical comedy as a real big night on the town. "I like 'em all," he said, "but I guess you'd have to say, for me, *Guys and Dolls* was it!" He doesn't rule out straight plays, though, and, in fact, thinks *Stalag 17*, the drama about a prisoner-of-war camp in Germany, was one of the best plays he ever saw. He's an ardent television fan and will sit watching the screen hour after hour. His favorite show is Ed Sullivan's *Toast of the Town*, on which he already has made two well-paid guest appearances.

In Brockton, Rocky's social activities are confined largely to entertaining friends and relatives at home, or making the rounds of their houses, and to the Ward Two Club and the Seville Council, Knights of Columbus. The priests and nuns of St. Colman's parish, where he worships, call on him again and again to serve as a model for their lectures to the neighborhood kids. They've given him two good-luck charms, a St. Anthony medal and a St. Rocco medal, both of which he wears in his bathrobe every time he steps into the ring. (You aren't allowed to wear anything except regulation equipment on your body.)

Rocky doesn't have an especially large wardrobe but neither is he sloppy about his appearance. He realizes that people are watching him closely and he takes pride in making a good impression. He isn't ashamed to ask for advice from the men around him, whether to help in selecting new clothes or to find out exactly how he should act in strange surroundings.

He finds it hard to believe he is a celebrity in his own right and he gets as big a kick out of meeting other celebrities as any ordinary person would. One night when he was training for Walcott, his retinue got a telephone call asking if it would be all right for the Prince of Siam, who was a guest at the Grossinger Hotel, to drop over to the airport a few miles away, where Rocky was training, and have a chat with the challenger. Rocky leaped into action. "Gee," he said, "I figured I'd better work fast. There the Prince was comin' over and I was just layin' around in a T-shirt, watching television. I hadn't even shaved all day. I hustled up to the bathroom and took a quick shave, and I changed my clothes, and listened to everybody tellin' me how I ought to talk to the Prince. Charlie even put on his bow-tie. We were all set. Then he never showed up. They told us after he had to catch a plane for somewhere." He laughed. "Back to Siam, I guess."

One of Rocky's press agents distributed a story to the effect that an aide to the Prince had called back and said protocol demanded that Rocky go to the hotel, where the Prince would receive him. This version carried the punchline that Rocky's camp sent back a polite but firm refusal, to wit: "Tell the Prince he already has his title, but Rocky's still got to win his and he's too busy to go anywhere." It made a funny story but nobody who knows Rocky would believe it. It would be more in character for him to lose half a night's sleep in order to avoid the slightest possibility of appearing rude or "upstage."

Rocky is so good-natured, and so fearful of hurting or embarrassing anyone, that, in all the hundreds of rounds he has boxed preparing for his bouts, he has never once knocked out a sparring partner. That may seem to be a small matter but most big-name fighters take great delight in belting out the working stiffs who go up against them in the camp ring. It makes them feel good; it builds up their confidence. Rocky's confidence is of a more durable and more substantial nature. He knows what he can do with a well-aimed punch and he doesn't demand constant reassurance.

Virtually the last skeptic disappeared from view after Rocky whammed Joe Louis out of the ropes and turned out the lights for keeps on the marvelous old champion's active career. Louis was in the middle of a big comeback in the fall of 1951. Walcott, whom Louis

A home-cooked meal and time with the buddies, 1953

had beaten twice, was the champion, having stunned the boxing world with a midsummer knockout of Ezzard Charles. Louis hungered for the chance to prove he was still as good as either Walcott or Charles and therefore a logical contender for the title. Most insiders suspect he never was especially eager to tangle with the young, powerful Marciano, but he was conned into it by Al Weill, who was willing to risk everything he and Rocky had built up together on his judgment that the aging Brown Bomber couldn't survive the younger man's ruthless punching.

Weill was dead right. His gamble proved to be no gamble at all. Rocky became the first man to knock out Louis since Max Schmeling had done it way back in 1936. Showing absolutely no fear of Louis' vaunted right hand, he harassed the former champion repeatedly with a wicked left hook and got in a steady stream of winners with his own right. It was the left that did the real damage in the climactic eighth round. There was about a minute and a half of fighting time left in the round when Marciano drove a left hook to the point of Louis' chin. Joe lurched backward and sank slowly to the floor. He wasn't out but he was in trouble. Up at eight, the ex-champ appeared to have control of himself. He began to back away from the onrushing Marciano. But as soon as Louis started to move, it was obvious that he was hurt. He tried to stand off Rocky with a few cautious punches but they had no steam or direction. He was dazed. Rocky bulled him against the ropes and the crowd set up a chilling roar. They knew what was coming. Rocky hit Louis with another wicked left hook and Joe began to sink. The Blockbuster from Brockton took no chances. Fighting with the wild intensity that always characterizes his finishing rushes, he fired a killing right that knocked Louis through the ropes and onto the ring apron. It was there, sprawled in a pitifully undignified heap outside the ring with his legs sticking through the ropes, that the great Brown Bomber was counted out.

As is even more clear now than at the time, one boxing era had ended and another had begun. Future historians of the sport are likely to disregard the Charles-Walcott period as a mere hiatus, a recess time in which mediocrity reigned. But the handwriting was on the wall for all to read; the Rock was coming and he would not be denied.

Rocky had one more test to pass before they would let him take the final examination. He didn't look at all

impressive beating veteran Lee Savold in Philadelphia in mid-February, 1952. He cut Savold's face to pieces, leaving it a bloody mask when the referee put a stop to the fight in the sixth round, but he couldn't knock him off his feet, and the fans jeered his awkwardness. The papers took him apart. The Weill-haters had their first chance in a long while to say "We told you so." Something had to be done to restore the Rock's slightly tarnished prestige. Weill decided to take another calculated risk. He sent Marciano against the stridently ballyhooed boxing master from Seattle, Harry (Kid) Matthews, in an outdoor match at Yankee Stadium. Matthews' manager, the shrewd and loquacious Jack Hurley, had been screaming that the monopolistic IBC had blacklisted his fighter and arbitrarily refused to give him title consideration.

It was a deft maneuver by Weill. In what figured to be a good money match, anyway, Marciano could kill a couple of his manager's birds with one stone. If he could put Matthews away, he would not only reestablish himself in the eyes of the fans but at the same time get the troublesome Hurley off Weill's back and make the IBC look good in the process.

Rocky came through on all counts. He clouted Matthews with a left jab in the middle of the second round and followed through tigerishly with a pair of rapid-fire, cruel left hooks. Matthews collapsed like a house of cards, sinking, ironically, in a helpless heap in his own corner, right at Jack Burley's feet. At last, Rocky had a clear track to the title shot. There was no one left to dispute his claim. Barbara Marciano was waiting for her husband when he walked out of the Stadium a few minutes after midnight and pushed his way, grinning happy, through the little crowd of autograph hunters that had waited patiently for him to appear. Rocky hurried up to the blonde girl who spends so much of her time waiting for him. He kissed her while the people on the sidewalk clapped. "This one," he told her, "was for you and the baby." Then they got into a taxicab and rode to a victory party at the plush Hampshire House. Two small-town kids, the shoemaker's son and the policeman's daughter, they were sitting on top of the biggest city in the world.

The next day, Rocky stopped in at the IBC office and picked up a check for $51,512, which is nice pay for approximately five minutes' work. Al Weill, of course, gets one-third of Marciano's purses as his manager's end, and the U. S. Government gets approximately the same.

Rocky shadow-boxing, 1954

But there is still an attractive bundle left for Rocky, and he and Barbara aren't scattering it to the winds. The habits of thrift which Rocky developed in his boyhood are still with him. He lives far more plainly than most fans would believe. The baby that arrived two months after he won the title probably will change that somewhat, but not too much. Rocky wants his kids to have it easier than he did but he doesn't want to overdo it.

It is unlikely that Rocky's children ever will carry the name their father made famous in the prize ring. He never has legally changed his name. He is still Rocco Marchegiano, and he expects to remain so. "It's a touchy thing," he said earnestly when asked about the question. He motioned toward his grey-haired father, pouring a cup of coffee in the kitchen across the hall. "I wouldn't want to do anything to hurt Pop's feelings. He's liable to figure, it's my name, what, am I ashamed of it? And there's my two brothers, it's their name, too. Why should they change? I don't know, I don't think so."

Rocky took very little time off after the Matthews fight. It was a foregone conclusion that he would be going for the brass ring in September, and Al Weill wanted him to think about nothing but the fight, to do nothing that wasn't part of the business of getting ready for the fight. The Rock was already training at Grossinger's Hotel in the heart of New York State's mountain resort area when the match was officially made. He rode down to Philadelphia to sign the papers and pose for the photographers, then went right back to

work. He meant to be ready for this one.

He was ready, all right. He collected the last full measure of interest on the long, hard days of training he had put in. Hit hurtful blows throughout the fight by the bigger, heavier champion, he had the staying power and the resilience to bounce back from each new wound and lay into his rival with renewed strength and determination. He took punishment that would have broken down almost any heavyweight active today, but he still could summon up the reserve power to get in the last word.

What a lusty, gory, savage brawl it was that they put on under the floodlights of Municipal Stadium in Philadelphia last September! The thick-necked, deep-chested, black-skinned champion and the trim, narrow-waisted, short-armed challenger with the gleaming white skin and the deceptively muscular arms and back. There was no pity in either man, not for his enemy or himself. It was a mid-century throwback to the memorable finish fights of an earlier time. They punched each other's faces shapeless, they slugged each other's bodies into aching, purpling masses of bruises. They fought ceaselessly; they even fought after the bell at least four or five times.

The crowd of 40,379, which had paid $504,645 at the gate, had sat quietly through the inevitable parade of introductions before the fight. They had given a big hand to Joe Louis and a big grin to sleek Sugar Ray Robinson, who showed up in a shrieking evening jacket of red, green and blue plaid with dark blue satin collar and lapels. They had tossed their nickels to the newspaper boys roaming the spacious stands and shouting, "Get your late *Inquirer* here! Don't ruin your good suit on the wet seats! Get your paper here!" If they were out-of-towners, they had stormed angrily at the helpless refreshment-stand employees because there was no beer on sale in the stadium, and had finally settled for cream soda or coffee. They had stared appreciatively at all the handsome showgirl types switching in alongside their invariably shorter, bald-headed protectors. They had grumbled bitterly at the news that the IBC had belatedly shoved back the starting time of the main event from 10 o'clock to 10:30 in order to accommodate the West Coast theaters showing the bout on theater television. They were, by the time the referee sent both men to their corners with their instructions, and the bell clanged and the lights went out everywhere except over the ring, panting for action.

They got it, fast. The usually super-cautious Walcott walked right out to meet Marciano and began pounding him inside. He traded a few rights with Rocky, then knocked the younger man off his feet with a whistling left hook. Rocky sat on the canvas, rolling over on his knees, listening intently to referee Charlie Daggert's count. He was up at four, ignoring Charlie Goldman's piercing demand that he take eight. "I got up fast," he explained later, "because I was more mad at myself than hurt." Walcott waded right in again and, as the champion's fists beat a tattoo on Rocky's head and midsection, a rising murmur of apprehension swept the arena. Al Weill was tight-lipped and pale in Marciano's corner. It looked as though the old miracle man might have the makings of another stupendous upset in his gnarled and experienced fists. But Marciano held on and weathered the storm.

He kept on weathering them, too, but as the fight wore on in all its primitive, shocking grandeur, it began to seem that Jersey Joe had huffed and puffed up enough storms to ride out the battle in style and carry off the booty on points. Rocky did well enough in the middle rounds but Walcott came on again with a vengeance and, as they left their stools for the 13th round, the bettors who had backed the champion were beginning to count their spoils. It was a bloody scene, blood sticking to the fighters' gloves and huge stains of blood disfiguring their satin trunks. Most of the blood was Marciano's, leaking from a dangerous slash high on his forehead. Some of it was Jersey Joe's, coming from a cut over his left eye. Rocky was the more desperate figure of the two. He was losing and he knew it. He had to knock his man out if he wanted to be the champion—and he did want to be, badly.

Rocky charged. Jersey Joe retreated against the ropes. Both men drew back their right hands. Everything they had done to each other in the 12 brutal rounds of fighting had come down to this tense moment. Each was swinging to hurt, and Rocky got his shot in first. It splintered the old man's careful defense and shattered his consciousness. It exploded off his jaw with the force of a blockbuster detonating a squarely-hit target. Jersey Joe was done. He went down slowly, reluctantly, painfully. He fell to his knee and for a second some thought he might hold himself there by the ropes. But there was no strength in his limbs; he sagged and crumpled like an abandoned puppet. His battered features, turned ashen gray by the terrible impact of Marciano's blow, buried themselves in the canvas. One of the most amazing champions in the history of the heavyweight division, the oldest man ever to hold the title, had come to the end of the line.

Rocky, standing like a lion at bay in a neutral corner, jumped for joy as he heard the referee count "Ten!" He grinned a bloody grin and embraced Al Colombo as his old friend came running toward him. Bedlam broke loose. The men of Brockton, 3,000 strong, who had made the long trip to Philadelphia to cheer for their hero, bore down upon him in irresistible waves. The police couldn't stop them. They flooded the press section and danced in the aisles. They jumped up on the ring apron and screamed the word of their adoration to the jubilant fighter. They made it all but impossible for the house announcer to clutch his microphone in the center of the ring and close the frantic occasion on the proper traditional note. But the man in the black tie finally made it. After the timekeeper had banged the bell a dozen times in a futile bid for the attention of the delirious crowd, the announcer bellowed his formal declaration over all the competing racket. His electric words formed the only logical conclusion to the fantastic saga of the iron-fisted Blockbuster from Brockton. There could be no other way to end it; Rocky saw to that.

"The time," the man said, "Forty-three seconds of the 13th round. The winner, and new heavyweight champion of the world, Rocky Marciano!"

You can't top that.

THE REIGN

FIGHT FORTY-THREE

43

Marciano vs. Jersey Joe Walcott

MUNICIPAL STADIUM, PHILADELPHIA
SEPTEMBER 23, 1952

FIGHT 44 FORTY-FOUR

Marciano vs. Jersey Joe Walcott

CHICAGO STADIUM, CHICAGO
MAY 15, 1953

FIGHT FORTY-FIVE
45

Marciano vs. Roland LaStarza

POLO GROUNDS, NEW YORK
SEPTEMBER 24, 1953

FIGHT FORTY-SIX
46

Marciano vs. Ezzard Charles

YANKEE STADIUM, NEW YORK
JUNE 17, 1954

FIGHT FORTY-SEVEN

47

Marciano vs. Ezzard Charles

YANKEE STADIUM, NEW YORK
SEPTEMBER 17, 1954

FIGHT FORTY-EIGHT
48
Marciano vs. Don Cockell

KEZAR STADIUM, SAN FRANCISCO
MAY 16, 1955

F I G H T 49 F O R T Y - N I N E

Marciano vs. Archie Moore

YANKEE STADIUM, NEW YORK
SEPTEMBER 21, 1955

AT THE SOUND OF THE BELL, COME OUT FIGHTING

BY BRIAN GLANVILLE

FROM SPORT, APRIL 1970

In 1969, a Miami promoter named Murry Woroner developed a simulation of an all-time championship fight between Rocky Marciano and Muhammad Ali. In January 1970, SPORT sent their man to a New York cinema to 'cover' the fight.

"You don't have to have guys fighting," said a large and disillusioned artist, emerging from the Cinerama movie theater in New York. "It's like *The Selling of the President.* From now on everything is plastic."

Well, yes, I suppose it is. Yet for a non-event, the Clay-Marciano computer fight was remarkably, perhaps even ominously, successful. It brought in $2.5 million, most of them from customers who paid $5 a seat to watch the "fight"—if that is the appropriate word—in movie theaters throughout America. In the Boston Garden, the main event was preceded by a program of bouts fought by live, flesh-and-blood boxers; the price was $10, and 7,000 willing souls paid it.

There are several more or less objective ways of looking at the entire strange phenomenon. The most pessimistic would probably be to regard it as one further step towards the dehumanization of sport, itself a symptom of the dehumanization of mankind and his society. The Olympic athlete treats his body like an engine and is a sad slave to the stopwatch. The American football player is a creature of rigid tactics and other people's thinking. So, by the same token, the real, live boxer becomes obsolete, redundant. You can have a saleable contest without him. Or rather, he may be there in the person of a plump, middle-aged man with a shiny new toupee and a formidable stomach. The stage beyond that, clearly enough, is to do it with actors.

At the time of writing, there is talk of following the success of the Clay-Marciano . . . thing with a . . . thing between Sugar Ray Robinson and Nino Benvenuti. I could tell you now who would win were the two ever put in the same ring during Robinson's prime, but computers, as we saw at the Cinerama, have ways of their own.

Thereby, perhaps, hangs the real suspense, the sublime, magnetic uncertainty of it all.

A second, rather different way of looking at what happened on the night of January 20 would be to rejoice that the blood lust of boxing crowds can now be happily sated with artificial gore of the kind which flowed in such abundance down Marciano's Mount Rushmore-like features. If spectators are prepared to take it all "for real," and it was evident at the Cinerama that many of them were, two problems have been solved with one blow. New life, of a factitious and celluloid kind, has been breathed into a dying sport, while the old necessity for human sacrifice now goes by the board.

In parenthesis, there is a clear analogy here with professional wrestling, a sport with no inner rationale and little connection with the amateur wrestling out of which it grew. Professional wrestling is what the Italians would call "spectacle"; a kind of theater, a thing of villains and heroes, a vulgar, modern morality play. People go simply to be entertained, and the women, especially, enter into the strange spirit of the thing with hysterical zest. "Villains" are quite often attacked; some have even been stabbed to death. Why, then, should boxing not be turned into the same kind of mere performance, and taken a stage further on to celluloid? In human and sociological terms, after all, the decline of professional boxing can be seen only as a benign symptom, its prevalence as a malign one. It is well enough established that a professional boxer, by and large, comes out of the slums, the submerged tenth, the teeming streets of Mexico City, or the Negro ghettoes. But if it satisfies—or satisfied—the kind of primitivism which was once catered to in the Roman Colosseum, surely it is better by far to cater to it on celluloid?

During the cheers and counter cheers at the Cinerama—the noisy black identification with Clay, the white backlash which brought applause for Marciano— I was reminded of a passage in a novel by the English writer Christopher Isherwood. Set in Germany just before the Nazi conquest of power in 1933, it described the scene in a boxing booth where a "challenger," who has quite openly been chatting with the booth boxer's seconds, comes forward to tremendous applause to fight and beat him. If people were ready to believe in this, thought Isherwood, it did not say much for their powers of political discrimination.

This would be hard to argue in the specific case of Nazi Germany, but there may be a danger in spreading the generalization too wide. People do, after all, want in certain contexts to be entertained. They want to suspend disbelief, whether it be in the Cinerama on January 20, the theater or the cinema. Everyone, after all, knows perfectly well that Hamlet, Macbeth and Lear are going to end the evening a corpse; it does not prevent their going to the theater, and getting swept up by the action of the play.

The day after watching Marciano and Clay go through their antics, I was talking to a producer who had been to see the Broadway musical, *1776*. What surprised him, he said, was not only that such an entertaining show could be made out of such overtly unpromising material as the signing of the Declaration of Independence, but the element of suspense which was engendered. Everybody knew what had

happened—after all, it had happened nearly 200 years ago—but there was still a genuine tension before the vote was lost, won and unanimous. While there was a marked lack of authenticity about the Clay-Marciano film—let us settle on that as the operative noun—the audience was involved from the first. It was fascinating to see and hear just how great a hero and a symbol Clay remains to the black community. "I'm going to punish him!" scowled Clay, no more and no less histrionic than in the pronouncements he made before genuine fights. "Mind you, remember what I say!"

"Yes!" cried a black spectator.

"If I could corner him and knock him out," mumbled the newly toupee-ed Marciano, "and that would perhaps take some doing, I could maybe knock him out." For a man notoriously hostile to Clay, Marciano was generous enough to say, "He'll die of old age unless someone drops a bag of cement on his head when he's walking down the street."

Nat Fleischer, the ancient and indestructible editor of *Ring Magazine*, which is still honest enough to recognize Clay as world champion, struck a discord when he said that Clay still had not proved to him that he was a great fighter. *Boo!* cried the black spectators, while one wondered what Clay would have to do to convince Mr. Fleischer. Knock over the Empire State building? Win a contest against a rogue elephant or two?

The fight, a sort of mosaic pieced together according to the dictates of the computer, was as synthetic as its method of assembly might have led one to expect. If belief were to be suspended, as it so manifestly was among many in that Cinerama audience, it had to be given a most substantial helping hand. In the first place, the sound effects were bewilderingly amateurish. A dull *plunk* of hollow percussion greeted every blow, however hard or soft and no matter where it landed.

Secondly, there was but one clinch to be seen in the whole 13 rounds. Could it be, one wonders, that a computer does not yet understand or assimilate anything as crude as a clinch? Yet the clinch is the very essence of professional boxing, many of whose bouts seem to be spent largely in mutual embrace. This leads one on to another valid criticism. Marciano, not to put too fine a point on it, was perhaps the roughest heavyweight champion of all time. To say that he was wholly without skill would not be quite fair—there were times, as he showed in this film, when he could and

would actually take the trouble to slip a punch. But by and large, anything went, and any vestige of a claim that boxing had to being the noble art of self defense, or any kind of art at all, was scattered to the winds by Marciano's success. He met and beat better boxers in abundance from Jersey Joe Walcott onwards. And if boxing needed one final nail in its depressing coffin, it received it from what we were asked to recognize as "The Computerized Championship of the World," when Marciano was given a knockout over Clay.

For Clay could, and can, box; box beautifully. This, over and above his contentious and complex personality, was what endeared him to so many people, millions of them white. He brought back skill, science and an almost balletic elusiveness to a "sport" whose recent, undefeated champion had been a sublimated back alley brawler, prevailing through sheer brute strength and concrete durability.

Which leads us to two closely related questions: first, what really would have happened had the two of them met when each was in his prime? Second, to what extent is a computer in a position to give us the answer?

Many experts were quite unconvinced by the outcome of the computer fight, pointing out that in Marciano's entire 49-fight pro career only once did he win with a knockout as late as the 13th round—in his first fight against Jersey Joe Walcott. On the other hand, there were many who believe that Clay hadn't the punch to knock Marciano out. This is a moot and obscure point; one which is confused rather than satisfactorily resolved by the mysterious knockout of Sonny Liston in Lewiston, Maine. I myself also have seen Clay badly cut Henry Cooper (but then it was always difficult to avoid cutting the unlucky Cooper) and knock out Brian London with a vicious hurricane of punches at Earl's Court. (But that might well have been seen as a merciful release; London had been fighting with what might charitably be described as an evident reluctance.)

The computer had both men tiring by the end, or, as it put it in its horrible computer language, "both men were well below optimum effectiveness." My own

Ali following computer loss, 1970

feeling is that Clay has always hit a great deal harder than many people give him credit, though his failure to knock out a fighter like Karl Mildenherger suggests that knocking out Marciano would have been beyond him. On the other hand, would Marciano have had enough steam to contrive a knockout punch after 13 rounds of chasing the elusive, floating butterfly? I am inclined to doubt it.

The curious lack of clinches and the absence of fouling meant that the presence of the alleged referee, Mr. Chris Dundee, was virtually irrelevant. Mr. Dundee, embarrassed perhaps by his fraternal relationship to Angelo, Clay's trainer, hovered on the fringes of it all like a timid ghost. This, too, deprived the film of conviction.

On the other hand, the commentators were wholly authentic in their bloodthirsty banalities, and they were matched in turn by the blood lust of the audience in the Cinerama. "Open that cut, brother!" they shouted. "Kill him, kill him!" Cries of "Get me some of that meat!" were counter-pointed by the two commentators: "Ali is really using the meat grinder, now."

When Clay slumped down at the last, hung on the ropes in that 13th round, and was counted out by a come-alive Dundee, a black fan leaped to his feet and cried, "Computer lie!"

Probably it did. Or rather it told the truth to the extent of a heavily circumscribed ability. For a computer cannot yet deal with imponderables, and if it tries, its verdict is no better and no worse than an inspired guess by an informed human being. (I hesitate to say "an expert." The experts, after all, were almost unanimous in predicting that Clay would he crushed by Sonny Liston in their first fight, at Miami Beach.)

The "information" you can feed into a computer about one boxer is amorphous enough; when you feed in information about another, then try to play off one set of facts against the other, you are simply wandering into the realms of the fantastic. There is no mathematical way of working out exactly how Clay's style, his characteristic moves, would have worked against Marciano's, and vice versa. I am convinced that a computer, if its worthless opinion had been canvassed before the first Liston fight, would have made Liston an easy winner. But great champions, especially those like Clay (and less so with Marciano) can adapt their style to the circumstances.

The computer is the mute and soulless god of our generation; it is our oracle, and we appear to believe in its omniscience as profoundly as the ancient Greeks believed in the Oracle of Delphi. We must realize that this is no more or less than an act of faith; a state of mind never more clearly betrayed than by the computer scientist who wrote that in due course computers would simply take things over, and the best we could do was to build into them a sentimental concern for our poor, human selves.

Mr. Murry Woroner, promoter of computer fights, will understandably have none of this. The lack of clinches he defends as wholly realistic, rather than the opposite. He looked, he said, at all the fights each man ever had, and "in 76 fights, I saw only ten clinches. Clay would run, he would never get close enough to clinch . . . (and) every time Rocky grabbed him with his right and hit him with his left." He defends, too, the fact that Clay, most sublimely elusive of movers, was so often cornered on the ropes: "He was fighting a man whose whole career was devoted to getting men on the ropes. If you've ever watched a sheepdog fight, he had that way. Little moves to the left and right. Clay said at the end of the fight it was incredible how often he found himself there. He said it would probably have been the toughest fight of his entire career if he'd had to fight Marciano. Marciano did hurt him, and Clay did hurt Marciano."

Woroner also insists, "If you'll notice, there were several occasions on which Marciano actually landed low blows. Fighting from a crouch and being so much smaller than the taller man, it was rather easy to hit low. He'd hit anything he could reach. He didn't do it deliberately. If you turned 'round, he'd hit you on the back of the head."

There was, he went on, a massive induction of data. Every fight each man fought in his prime was taken to pieces, blow by blow. Moreover, the status and condition of each opponent was taken into account (precisely how, one wonders?). "There were 129 variables per fighter. This ranged from the killer instinct to speed of hands." (How do you measure the killer instinct? How deep is the ocean? How long

is a piece of string?)

Referees and trainers were consulted, the important qualities of a fighter were identified. Other experts—writers and the like—were then consulted to assess the importance of these qualities, and finally, says Woroner, "the individual fighters were rated on each of these items." (Opinions, rather than facts, were at issue here.)

To those who criticize the result of his Computerized Championship, Mr. Woroner retorts, "Our computer handled 4,000,000 statistics a round and had available to it everything the man did, every punch he threw in the prime five years of his career. The finest applied mathematical science. What kind of rules did you use to come up with your decision?

"What is truth?" asked Woroner, and stayed not for an answer.

He might have heard it, had he been there in the Cinerama.

"Computer lie!"

EPILOGUE

By the time the computer pronounced Rocky Marciano the all-time heavyweight champion that January night in 1970, he had been dead for almost five months. He was flying from Chicago to Des Moines for a personal appearance on the night of August 31, 1969 when the small plane in which he was traveling crashed into a cornfield during a thunderstorm near Newton, Iowa. He had been scheduled to return home to Fort Lauderdale the next day, which would have been his 46th birthday, for a joint party with his wife Barbara, who had turned 40 on August 30. While Marciano's reputation remained reasonably intact for many years, a 1993 article in SPORTS ILLUSTRATED *and a more recent Showtime docudrama,* ROCKY MARCIANO, *were more negative in their depictions of the retired champ, characterizing him as being obsessed with collecting money from personal appearances, consorting with underworld figures and enjoying scores of extra-marital relationships. Marciano's brothers and children, Mary Ann and Rocky Jr., who was only 17 months old when his father died and was raised by his sister and grandmother after his mother passed away five years later, refused to help promote the Showtime film because they believed it was an unfair portrayal of Marciano.*

CHAPTER SEVEN

CARMEN BASILIO

CARMEN BASILIO
REACHES
FOR THE JACKPOT

BY ED LINN

FROM *SPORT*, OCTOBER 1957

The lesson for the day, children, is Carmen Basilio, welterweight champion of the world. Great champions traditionally come out of the grand mold. They emerge from the amateur ranks with great reputations and fanatical local followings; they pile up a string of knockouts against a string of nobodies; they pass a few of the first stiff tests and they finally take a good beating from a wise old veteran. The loss leaves them with a healthy knowledge of their weaknesses and limitations, and they return to the gym a little wiser and far more determined. The rest is the climb to the top. The three great fighters of our age—Joe Louis, Ray Robinson and Willie Pep—are directly in that tradition. So, for that matter, is Floyd Patterson, although his defeat by (Joey) Maxim was hardly crushing. (Rocky) Marciano is a little outside it only in that he did not suffer the one defeat that the others did.

Basilio, the only modern fighter who can be mentioned in the same breath (or the next breath anyway) with Louis, Robinson, Pep and Marciano, votes from another precinct. If Carmen reminds you of any modern champion, it has to be the hard man from Gary, Indiana, Tony Zale.

As an amateur, Basilio won the Adirondack Golden Gloves championship but got licked down in New York City. His total record as an amateur was 11 wins and three defeats. Basilio refuses to go along with any suggestion that this record was undistinguished. Since he was fighting guys with 50 or 60 amateur fights behind them, he maintains that he did very well. But in his first three years as a pro, he lost to guys named Connie Thies, Johnny Cunningham, Mike Koballa, Eddie Giosa, Vic Cardell, Lester Felton (who did have a touch of class), Johnny Cesario and Ross Virgo.

None of this roster has, to our knowledge, ever threatened to win the championship.

His first managers, who were really promoters, rarely bothered to put him in their main events even though they were cutting his purse. When they did, he was such a poor attraction that they sometimes had neither the money nor the inclination to pay him. His friends and relatives advised him to quit, and an attack of bursitis finally did force him into a temporary retirement. Through it all, Carmen somehow maintained his complete confidence in himself. Through it all, he kept insisting that he was going to be the champion some day.

"I don't regret anything that happened," he can say today. "Not anything. Some people have to learn everything the hard way. That's me. There's one thing to say about learning that way; I learn hard but I learn good."

Even today, as one of the last big draws in boxing, Carmen's biggest purse was the $69,000 (before managerial cut and expenses) that he earned from the second Tony DeMarco fight. Although he has entered the ring as defending champion in three big fights, that was the only time he got the heavy end of the purse. In

Left: Carmen Basilio, 1955

the coming battle against Sugar Ray Robinson, he is getting only 20 percent; Sugar Ray is getting 45 percent. But don't jump over that figure too quickly. Twenty percent of a million dollars is what?

If Carmen beats Sugar Ray—and Robinson didn't seem awfully anxious to fight him—then the rugged little gentleman from the Canastota mudflats will not only be the biggest draw in the game, he will be able to dictate his own terms. We don't know anybody inside boxing—or out of it—who will begrudge him a dime.

Carmen Basilio, a sharp-featured man who bleeds when he fights, is invariably described as craggy-faced and/or hatchet-faced. The adjectives don't bother him, but some of the alleged statistics and specifics do. "There was a guy from *Ring Magazine* who wrote an article about me without even bothering to call me or talk to me," he says. "He wrote that I'd had over 100 stitches taken in my face and it's been picked up by magazine and newspaper writers all over the country. It isn't true." Carmen was so upset that he wrote the guy a sharp letter. "The worst cutting up I ever got," he told the writer, "was from you."

This is not to say that Basilio denies that his style of fighting has made him hospitable to cuts and bruises, particularly in his earlier days. Like Marciano, he is a very short-armed fighter; he almost always gives away four to five inches in overall reach. "I have to try to go inside," he says, "and when you're in close and heads are moving back and forth, they're going to bump sooner or later. Most cuts don't come from punches, they come from butts. It isn't intentional, it's closer to being inevitable."

There is a huge, spreading scar astride Carmen's right eyebrow, the result of being butted by a guy named Jackie O'Brien five years ago. The Wilkes-Barre doctor who treated him botched the stitching job, the wound became infected, and after it had been reopened and cleaned, it developed a mass of scar tissue that has been cut into fairly frequently in subsequent fights.

He has been cut over the left eye too, and has suffered rather small cuts under both eyes. "For some reason," he says, "I never got cut under the eye until I started to fight for the championship. Since then I've had it happen three or four times."

He hasn't had a serious cut, though, since he was butted by Italo Scortichini early in 1954. These days, he moves in and out—staying out of clinches as much as possible—far more than is generally recognized. After knocking out Johnny Saxton in two rounds this year, he

was combing his hair in front of the mirror. "Can you imagine," he asked the sportswriters, "me looking the same way after a title fight as before?"

If there is a widespread impression that Carmen's face shows the treadmarks of every round he has fought, it arose first because he admittedly can be hit, and secondly, because he was born with a fighter's face. "I can show you pictures when I was 13 and I look as if I'd already had a hundred fights," he says. His cheekbones are so high that they force the ends of his eyes into narrow slits. His nose is flat across the bridge. He can still, however, turn his profile and show an absolutely straight line. "I don't claim to be a matinee idol, now, but one thing nobody can say is that I have a battered nose."

What burns him most of all is when writers make up quotes that make him sound stupid at best and punchy at worst. "There are some writers I can't really blame, though," he says dryly. "They have me talking the same way they talk."

As anyone who knows Carmen Basilio can attest, he is far from stupid either inside the ropes or outside. He is one fighter who has thought very seriously about his trade and about the attitude of others toward it. The original lack of respect for his ability still rankles. Almost from the day he turned professional, his friends and relatives had absolutely no compunction about saying: "Why don't you give it up, Carmen? You're never going to get anywhere." When he persisted, they laughed at him; when he lost, they almost seemed pleased. "They don't seem to think that champions are the same kind of people as you and them at all. They think they're some special kind of people you only read about in newspapers. To impress them at all, you have to be twice as good as somebody from New York or Chicago; you have to be sensational."

There can be little doubt that Basilio did improve tremendously over the past four years. Before the Kid Gavilan fight in 1953 brought him to national prominence, his record was 35-10-5 against fairly spotty opposition. In his last 15 fights since then, against top welters and middleweights, he lost only that very disputed decision to Johnny Saxton. But Carmen is still convinced that he was sold short through the early days of his career. "Sure, I improved," he says. "I improved because I got a chance to fight better fighters. I was underrated for a long time, though. I always fooled them, and they always went back saying the same things about me. Even after I beat some good men, my style made them think I was nothing but a club fighter."

A club fighter, by definition, is a boy who takes more punches than he lands. Carmen says: "I used to take three punches to land one, because I didn't know how to do it any other way. These are things you have to learn through experience. After a while, you find yourself making the right moves to slip punches or to feint a man off balance; you find yourself recognizing the other man's feints and countering certain punches very effectively. It's a hard thing to explain because what you learn is in your muscles and your reflexes as much—and maybe more than in your mind."

Basilio does not take three to land one any more. He still looks easy to hit, so easy that when he first got hot, everybody was anxious to take a crack at him. Those who did get in the ring with him found that he was easy enough to hit with the first punch, but that the second and third punches somehow seemed to go astray.

Although Carmen prides himself on his toughness inside the ropes, he ridicules the idea that he doesn't mind getting hit. "Anybody who doesn't mind getting hit," he says, "is crazy. It's part of the business, though.

A professional fighter accepts it and thinks as little about it beforehand as possible. He just tries to get away from as many punches as he can."

Carmen's early background as an onion farmer has been so well publicized that it sometimes seems that the city of Syracuse is a suburb of the Basilio onion farm. Although Carmen hasn't worked on the mudflats since 1949, his life there was so grinding that it seemed to lend validity to the theory—which has been reiterated so often it is now accepted as fact—that most fighters are now the sons of the desperately poor and that they go into boxing only because it is the only way they can make a decent living. Basilio doesn't go along with that theory. "My parents," he says, "have been in this country for 55 years, and they have done all right for themselves. But when I was eight years old, I was already saying that I wanted to be a fighter. I fight because I like to fight. If the time ever comes when I don't like to fight, I'll stop." And he means it.

Nobody really knows what the little world inside the ring is like, of course, except the men who have lived there. But to those of us who look in from the outside, it

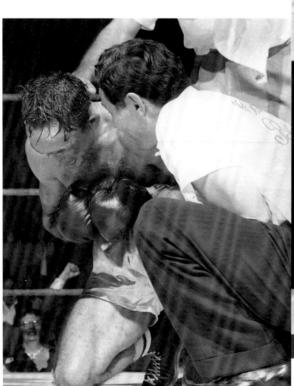

Giving thanks after defeating Sugar Ray Robinson, 1957

sometimes seems as if what is going on is, in some ways, as much a collaboration as a conflict. We had better explain that quickly: At the end of a fight, when the two men who have been trying to club each other to earth fall into each other's arms and almost embrace, one has to wonder whether they are simply following convention or whether the entertainment they have created and the experience they have shared (especially if it was a very good fight) have actually brought them close together. It has even been suggested that the guy who has won seems to feel something close to gratitude or even affection for the guy who has been gracious enough to lose.

As far as Basilio is concerned, it is, for the most part, a matter of convention. "But," he says, "you can gain respect for the other guy. You look up to him. I gained tremendous respect for Tony DeMarco because he was a real tough kid who gave it everything he had. Billy Graham was another tough son of a gun and I always admired him for it. After the first fight, I did become friendly with him. Then I fought him two more times and we became even more friendly. He was no puncher and it was a good thing he wasn't or I'd have never beat him. He had everything else; if he could have hit, he'd have been the champion. He was a hell of a great fighter."

Billy and Carmen run into each other every now and then, and always have a good time together. "We talk about everything," Carmen says, "except fighting."

Unlike his friend Billy Graham, Carmen can hit. His greatest asset, however, is his dedication to training. "Boxing," Carmen says, "is condition," and he is a man who is never out of condition.

"Don't tell me about Marciano or anybody else," says his co-manager, Johnny DeJohn. "This is the hardest trainer there's ever been."

DeJohn had good reason to know about Basilio even before he managed him. During Carmen's early days in the ring, Johnny and his partner, Joe Netro, were managing Joey DeJohn (Johnny's kid brother), a natural fighter who, unlike Basilio, hated the gym. Joey was the darling of Syracuse. The crowd turned out to watch him even against setups; when he faced a name fighter, the arena sold out. For six or seven rounds, Joey DeJohn could beat almost any fighter in the world. But if he hadn't knocked his man out by then, he would usually run out of gas. Carmen was then being managed, to use the term loosely, by Babe and Sam Amos, the local promoters. Since that kind of an arrangement between fighters and promoters is understandably frowned upon

by the New York State Athletic Commission, his manager of record was Tony Amos, their brother.

Basilio and DeJohn both trained at Irv Robbins' Main Street Gym in downtown Syracuse. Carmen would drive in from Canastota (a 50-mile round trip) every day with his own towel, tape and water bottle, and put himself through a rugged training regimen. His managers were never there and they never thought enough of him to provide him with a trainer. Johnny DeJohn and Joe Netro would be there, too, waiting— usually in vain—for their tiger. Every once in a while, the fighter-less managers would look over towards the manager-less fighter, nudge each other and say: "If Joey only had half that kid's determination."

Carmen's heavy training, for all his dedication, did not seem to be doing him an awful lot of good. He was considered a rough, crude fighter, totally lacking in crowd appeal. He discovered that the trouble with having a promoter for a manager was that there was no middleman to collect the money he had coming to him. After he had fought in a main event, Carmen would sometimes be told that the show had lost money and that they would have to "owe" him part of his purse. Once, he was paid off entirely in change.

The one good feature of the arrangement was that he was given a free room at the Kirk Hotel, which the Amos Brothers owned. It was while he was at the Kirk that he met his wife, Kay Simpkins, who was working as a waitress. On their first date, he took her to her first fight. The following week he was fighting the semi-final, so he gave her a ticket and told her to come and watch him. After she saw him score a two-round knockout over Johnny Cunningham, she told him: "You're right. You're going to be a champion." Eleven months later they were married.

Carmen's first heady taste of popularity came not in Syracuse, but in New Orleans. He was matched against Gaby Ferland, a Frenchman from Montreal who was very popular with the local citizenry. Carmen knocked Ferland down five times, forced the fight, and heard the announcer call it a draw. Suddenly, the fans switched loyalties. They booed the decision lustily and cheered Basilio mightily. Three weeks later, before a near-capacity house, Carmen knocked Ferland out in the first round. All at once, he was the biggest thing on the Delta since Captain Billy's Showboat. He fought three more main bouts in New Orleans at $1,000 a throw, the most money he had ever been paid up to that time.

The New Orleans reputation got him a New York television fight against Vie Cardell. With a chance, at last, to let the country know who he was, Basilio broke a bone in his left hand halfway through the fight. He lost a 10-round decision. For the next three months he was out of action. At Christmas, he was broke. A couple of weeks later, his left hand still in a cast, he spent three successive nights shoveling snow from the streets of Syracuse. The $24 he earned was eating money.

When his hand healed, the Amos brothers finally got him a name fighter, Lester Felton. Unfortunately, bursitis was beginning to set into Carmen's left shoulder—and, unfortunately, Felton boxed his ears off. Eventually, the bursitis got so bad that he could hardly lift the arm without pain, let alone swing it. Carmen Basilio left the ring and took a job as a stockman.

Bursitis is caused by deposits of calcium which settle in the joints. The treatment calls for a brief hospitalization, after which a specialist freezes the arm and cranks it around until the calcium deposits have been broken up and set adrift. Carmen didn't have the money for either the hospitalization or the specialist. The most he could afford was a series of shots calculated to dissolve the calcium. Fortunately, it did the trick.

Carmen, who was brought up on a farm, hated the stuffy, enclosed factory atmosphere. But even after he returned to the gym, he did not quit his job. He held on to it for two solid years, working days and training nights. He did not leave until after he had won the New York State welterweight championship from Billy Graham. You do not easily forget the time when there was no money in the house on Christmas.

While Carmen was out of the ring, Tony Amos, his manager of record, had died. Legally, Carmen was a free man. Acting as his own manager, he made a match for himself in Wilkes-Barre. At about this same time, Joe Netro received an inquiry from a Cleveland manager, asking whether Basilio was looking for a new manager. Netro and DeJohn looked at each other and asked, in effect, "Why not us?"

Carmen had already decided to ask them to handle him. They approached each other at almost the same moment and agreed to get together. Joey DeJohn was hotter than ever, so Johnny DeJohn—who knew something about Carmen's troubles with his previous managers—told him: "I can promise you one thing. I'll have the same consideration for you that I have for my brother."

There is every evidence that he has had just that. With Basilio in the gym every day, DeJohn is always there, too. So, as a rule, is Netro. This means something to Carmen. After the years of doing it all by himself, he appreciates that tangible evidence of their interest.

At their own expense, DeJohn and Netro accompanied him to the Wilkes-Barre fight (for which he received the magnificent purse of $142). For a while, it didn't look as if it would be worth their while. At the end of the second round, Carmen returned to his corner and gasped, "If I don't start doing something, he'll take me out." He went on out and began to hit his man (Emmett Norris) some good shots to the belly. By the end of the fight, he had him out on his feet.

There was something peculiarly fitting about the new partnership. DeJohn and Netro, like Basilio, were held in open scorn by the local fight fans. When Joey DeJohn ran out of gas late in a fight, it was blamed not on Joey's own aversion to the training grind but upon his brother's incompetence as a trainer. If Joey had connected with a big New York manager, everybody kept saying, he would have been champion long ago.

If there has been a change of opinion about Basilio, there has been a corresponding upgrading of Johnny DeJohn. "You know," Syracuse fight people say now, almost in surprise, "he's a real good trainer."

Johnny DeJohn, who looks like a cutdown, rough-hewed Barry Sullivan, is the oldest of seven brothers and the only one who never went into the ring himself. Joe Netro, a big, heavy, gray man who generally keeps in the background, has been promoting fights and managing fighters around central and northern New York for years. Like the west coast's Jack Hurley, he has a long mailing list and a sharp pair of scissors; he keeps the mails burning with clippings about Basilio. He also, on the word of DeJohn himself, fans much of the matchmaking and business strategy, even though it is DeJohn who acts as front man.

Says Carmen: "DeJohn and Netro are about the best things that ever happened to me. Without them . . ." DeJohn didn't change Basilio's style; he simply polished Basilio's natural style. He showed him how to throw his left hook, short, fast and inside. He had him come in a little lower than he had been, bobbing and weaving so as to offer the most difficult target possible. Most of all, he impressed upon him the necessity of staying relaxed. Basilio had always been a stiff, tense fighter, a mental condition which contributed to his

Joy after claiming middleweight title from Robinson

awkwardness and drained away his strength. By being relaxed in there, DeJohn told him, he would be able to punch faster and hit harder.

"I didn't really change his style," DeJohn says. "All good fighters have a style of their own. Carmen just got smarter and more confident. Nobody deserves any credit for Carmen Basilio; he did it all himself."

He did it by working harder than anybody else in the game. He trains summer or winter, in sickness or in health, whether there is a fight coming up or not. In the morning, he is out on the road. By one o'clock, he is in the gym. Once, when the main highways were blocked off by a snowstorm, he took to the back roads and somehow made it into the city. "Carmen used to drive 50 miles a day to get here," Irv Robbins says, "while some fighters who lived two blocks away went 20 blocks the other way to keep out of here." Another time, when Robbins told Carmen that the gym would be closed for four days because he was making a trip to Canada, Carmen protested: "I can stand two days off, but not four." Robbins finally had to give him a key to the place.

Sometimes it seems as if Carmen works harder in the gym than he could possibly work during a fight. He will set the automatic bell, work three minutes until it rings, walk around during the minute break (perhaps stopping at the water cooler to wash out his mouth), then swing right back into action as soon as the bell sounds again. He will alternate between shadow boxing around the ring and slamming the heavy bag, grunting out the rhythm of his combinations in either case (uhm, uhm, uhm-uhm). He was originally a one-punch fighter, weak on combinations. But there is nobody in the business now who works better combinations. His favorite is probably a double hook (bangbang) to the body and head.

Carmen has gone as long as two-and-a-half hours (something like 35 rounds), the sweat pouring off him, the breath coming fast. The longer he goes, the more complete his concentration seems to become. His managers' suggestions that he call it a day are angrily shunted aside.

As the time of the fight approaches, Carmen—who is normally an amiable, low-pressure guy—becomes, in his own words, "Mean and grouchy. My wife's word is 'miserable'." Actually, Kay Basilio doesn't pay too much attention to him. "He growls, I laugh," she says. "The more he growls, the more I laugh."

In the gym, he begins to pick on Joe Netro. No matter what Netro says, Carmen snaps back at him. During the last couple of days, Netro stays away from him. If he has anything he wants to tell Carmen, he passes it on through DeJohn.

Carmen is at a loss to explain what comes over him at such times. It isn't worry. The closer he gets to the actual fight, the more confident he becomes. He can't seem to wait to get into the ring.

After the fight, it takes him two solid days to unwind. He wanders around the house, watches television, sometimes even goes out looking for someone to talk to. He loses all sense of time. He has awakened his wife at six in the morning, the day after a fight, and said: "Come on, let's go for a ride."

Although Basilio names the Gavilan fight as the turning point in his career, DeJohn thinks it was the two Pierre Langlois fights. In the first one, which ended in a draw, Carmen tried to fight from outside so that the heavier, stronger Frenchman couldn't lay all over him. Watching the films of that fight while preparing for the rematch, Basilio started a running commentary: "See, I'm standing too far away, my punches aren't getting in. I've got to carry the fight to him and keep him so busy that he can't lay on me." DeJohn kept his mouth shut and let Carmen do all the talking. But in the darkness he was smiling. Now, he was thinking. Now he knows what he's doing.

Most people, upon coming into contact with Carmen, are struck by the remarkable cleavage between Basilio the fighter and Basilio the sensitive, amiable, home-loving man. Just as Carmen always wanted to be a fighter, so he always associated fighting with toughness—a word which, to him, seems to mean a combination of perfect physical condition and utter confidence in his ability to lick any man he looked in the eye. He can talk about this preoccupation with toughness in such a way that he is neither offensive nor

boastful, but simply giving voice to a statement of life that he has come to accept.

He has a habit, too, of ending discussions about the difficulties of the moment by holding up his two fists and saying, "These are all I need." Again, there is no challenge in his voice or conceit in his manner; he merely seems to be giving a simple, honest answer to what he holds to be an unnecessarily complicated problem.

It is not an easy thing to explain; if we have not made it clear here we can only hope that you will take our word for it. The best way to explain his attitude, perhaps, is to say that he does not try to impress anyone with his toughness; his personal satisfaction is the only reward he needs.

If proof is needed beyond our own bald word, however, we can call in the entire population of Syracuse as corroborating witnesses. Basilio has become immensely popular, not only with the fight fans, but with the city as a whole. When he appeared at a local meat market to autograph pictures for the customers, the market's receipts were 25 percent greater than the previous high. He does pretty well on his own account; he is an insurance agent for Prudential and last year his sales totaled $250,000. Irv Robbins was at a wake, recently, when his brother let it be known that Irv was a good friend of Carmen's. Immediately, the solemn purpose of the gathering was suspended while the mourners surrounded Robbins and made him promise to arrange a mass introduction. When they came to meet him, they each brought along a small mob of kids, all of whom seemed to regard Basilio as the most important man in the community.

Their parents, as a matter of fact, tend to agree with them. They know that Basilio is a man who is constitutionally unable to turn down any invitation that involves children, and they know him to be the kind of healthy example that athletes, for reasons we've never been fully able to accept, are supposed to be.

He has been so amiable about making these appearances that, for awhile, it affected his family life and even his fighting condition. When Kay and Carmen celebrated their seventh wedding anniversary last May 1, it was the first time in four years that he hadn't been out somewhere making an appearance.

The demand for him to make these public appearances has been so heavy that he has had to change his telephone number, already unlisted, every couple of weeks or so, because people are continually finding out what the number is and then passing the word along to friends. But even the frequent number changes do little good. Folks have come driving up to his home at two or three in the morning, wanting tickets for his next fight or just wanting to see Carmen. This, he explains, makes it tough for him to stay in condition, what with the considerable loss of sleep.

Although Carmen has no children of his own, he and Kay have been raising her nephews, Eddie and Freddie Thune. They came into their home four years ago when Freddie was one and Eddie six. To see Carmen hug them before they go off to bed is to know that he looks upon them with as much affection as if they were his own. He takes them to the gym with him regularly. Freddie, the younger boy, has his own locker and trunks and when he strides in behind Carmen, he usually orders Robbins to tape his hands. Then he goes into the ring and shadow boxes or stands on a chair and punches the bag.

A cute little kid like that, especially when he's there with the welterweight champion of the world, naturally gets a lot of attention. Photographers almost always ask for a gag picture of Carmen and Freddie, and Carmen, without making a big thing of it, always manages to make sure that Eddie—a quiet boy who keeps himself in the background—gets into a picture with him, too.

For the past four years, the Basilios have been living in Chittenango (six miles closer to Syracuse than Canastota), in a modest six-room clapboard home which he bought with the money from the second Graham fight. The result has been a lively feud between Chittenango and Canastota over who really owns the copyright to him. Carmen, for instance, has always belonged to the volunteer firemen; he loves to jump out of bed at the clang of the bells and go dashing off to the fire. This year, his old outfit in Canastota wanted him to march with them in their field day exercises; Carmen had to turn them down on the grounds that only legitimate members were supposed to participate. But in order that his old friends wouldn't be offended, he promised that he wouldn't march with Chittenango when they had their field day. He then, of course, had to go to the Chittenango officers and carefully explain why he wouldn't be able to participate in their exercises this year either.

He is essentially a home-town boy. He has done most of his fighting in and around Syracuse and his world has remained that little area in and around Syracuse. Although he has received almost all of the important boxing awards—the Neil Plaque from the New York Writers and *Ring Magazine*'s championship belt—the one that means the most to him is the *Syracuse Herald-Journal's* award given in memory of sportswriter Lawrence J. Skinner. A close second is the Pontiac which he received when a Canastota men's club staged a testimonial dinner for him in 1953. The original plan had been to raise enough money to present him with a traveling bag. Within two hours after the appeal for contributions went out, they had enough money to buy the Pontiac.

His friends are still the friends of his struggling years. Recently, he went golfing with some buddies on member-guest day at the Lake Shore Yacht and Country Club. Carmen was the guest of Anthony 'Ninni' Falcone, one of the better golfers in the area, along with two old friends, Red Erwin and Johnny Falcone. Johnny Falcone, who now owns the Kirk Hotel, ran the restaurant where Carmen ate during the tough years. Erwin, a sporting goods salesman, goes back to the same era. When Erwin was in a deep state of depression following the loss of his wife, Carmen insisted that he come to live with him and Kay. This was at the stage of Carmen's career when he was just beginning to get recognition, the Davey stage and he had plenty of worries of his own. But he took Red around with him, taught him enough so that he could work his corner and kept him at his side until Red began to recover. He is, it should be evident by now, a decent, kind and thoughtful human being.

Carmen and his friends do not go to the golf course to break any records; they go to laugh. They play a needling game. The only act considered unsporting is to step up and sink a putt before your opponent has had a chance to make a few sharp and cogent remarks. Carmen was easily the worst golfer in the foursome, but even Ninni Falcone flubbed a couple of shots, as good golfers almost always do when they're playing hackers. One of the sacred traditions of these matches is that Carmen must always throw a club in what purports to be blind anger. Carmen tries to wait until he has flubbed a shot so badly that he can give the others a chance to yell: "Haw, you can throw the club farther than you can hit the ball!"

They played a leisurely nine holes (we shall not reveal the scores on the plea of cruel and unusual punishment), then Carmen had to leave to attend a father-son meeting of the Optimists' Club of Fayetteville, a small town between Syracuse and Chittenango.

Golfer Basilio, like boxer Basilio, is a converted left-hander. Although he does his putting as a southpaw, Carmen goes the rest of the way around the course right-handed. This switch-over affects his game not at all; that is, he is a dedicated and eternal duffer which ever way he slices the ball. But Carmen can enjoy himself on the course, a trick not many duffers master.

Basilio's favorite relaxations are really hunting and fishing, generally in the company of his wife. For a while, he caught the golf bug bad—bought Kay a complete outfit so she could accompany him around the course—and tried to convince himself that it was giving him all the exercise he needed between fights. Eventually, though, he admitted to himself that an afternoon's walk was hardly the best possible way for a fighter to stay in condition and he eventually went back to the gym.

Despite the widespread inclination to write Basilio off as a fighter who wins on power and condition, he has become a very able tactician. He consistently does better against an opponent the second time around. In studying movies or reviewing his fights in his mind, he concerns himself almost exclusively with his own mistakes. If he can fight to the top of his ability, he believes, he can lick anybody he is put into a ring with.

Carmen Basilio is a man of his times in that he is the first champion who owes his original reputation to the little white screen in the parlor. In pre-television days, a fighter's out-of-town reputation meant nothing to the New York crowd. New York is the world's most provincial city; anybody from out of town is presumed to be a club fighter until he has fought a major fight in New York and convinced the syndicated columnists and the wire service reporters that he has something to offer.

When Carmen meets Sugar Ray Robinson in the Yankee Stadium on September 23, it will mark only the fifth time he has ever appeared in the big city. And it will be the first match that could be called a major fight by the wildest stretch of the imagination. Before his battle with Gavilan, Carmen had lost his only two fights in New York and his only two fights in Chicago. In the past, that would have been enough to eliminate him forever as a serious contender. He remained in the welterweight picture only because in his frequent television fights out of Syracuse he captivated the viewers with his Pier Six brawling. Carmen has appeared on television 23 times, only slightly less often than Ed Sullivan. In one way, though, his television fame was a mixed blessing. Carmen succeeded Chuck Davey as the darling of the little old

ladies who enjoy watching the beer and razor-blade commercials. As a result, Carmen and Chuck were lathered by the same shaving brush, as far as the sportswriters were concerned, and the sportswriters had gone so far in damning Davey as a synthetic, built-up 'television' fighter, after the Gavilan fiasco, that it almost seemed as if they thought most of those little old ladies were an even money bet to beat him themselves.

Basilio's managers, far from unaware of the role television was playing in his career, used it with calculated skill to build up his following. Although everybody else wanted to black out the Peter Muller fight, DeJohn—determined not to do anything that might jeopardize Basilio's increasing popularity—refused to go along. The fight was televised and it sold out anyway.

The Syracuse promoter during Basilio's climb to the top has been Norman Rothschild, a young restaurant owner who assumed the Amos Brothers' debts shortly after Basilio returned to the ring and who took over as fight promoter for the War Memorial Stadium. There has been some publicity to the effect that Rothschild, usually billed as an old friend of Carmen's, set out deliberately to get some name opponents. Basilio just shrugs when he is asked about it, leaving the definite impression that he and Rothschild were never more than casual acquaintances.

DeJohn says: "Don't get me wrong. Norman is a dead honest guy. His word is gold. He came along when this town needed a promoter badly; it wouldn't be right to say he didn't help us. He just didn't do some of the things he's been given credit for. What it was, it was a wheel; we all helped each other. Without all three of us, we'd have never made it."

Rothschild's first promotion, Joey DeJohn vs. Robert Villemain, sold out so quickly that he had to put ads in the Buffalo and Rochester papers warning their readers not to come down. Johnny DeJohn then asked Rothschild to get him either Chico Vejar or Chuck Davey for Basilio. Vejar wasn't interested, but Davey's people, who looked upon Basilio as just another local boy, were. At this point, Rothschild—who reminded DeJohn that Carmen had never drawn a house of better than $4,000 in his life—offered him 15 percent of the gate, which must be pretty close to the legal minimum.

"What do you think this fight will draw?" DeJohn asked him.

Rothschild guessed it would do about $15,000.

"All right," Johnny said. "We'll take 15 percent if it's

Going after a different sort of game, 1958

$15,000 or under, but if it, goes a dollar over we'll get 20 percent."

The fight did $26,000 and Carmen took down a purse of better than $5,000, the first real money he had ever earned in the ring.

But the fight did not come off as easily as all that. If Basilio's life before the Davey fight had been a battle for recognition, it became thereafter a long and patient pursuit after the ranking fighters of his division. Just as in the traditional movie chase, there were always handicaps to overcome and barriers to be hurdled before he finally cut his man off at the pass.

The original contract for the Davey-Basilio fight was signed for April 24. A few days later, Davey signed to fight Vejar in Chicago on May 7. Chico was about to go into the Army, and the IBC (International Boxing Commission) wanted to give him—and his manager, Steve Ellis, the IBC radio announcer—one last purse. (A

Vejar-Davey fight, to be fair about it, was a natural culmination of the buildup of Chuck Davey as a challenger for Kid Gavilan's title.) If some sportswriters intimated that a Vejar win would be most surprising in that his value over the next couple of years would be negligible to anyone but his drill sergeant, then let us put it down to the overly suspicious nature of newspapermen. At any rate, Davey's manager of record, Hector Knowles, announced that the Vejar fight was so important that he could not let his boy risk being injured in a prior fight. He signed a contract promising to meet Basilio on May 15, but since Knowles was not licensed in New York, there was some skepticism expressed about its worth. These doubts were confirmed when the first word out of Chicago, after Davey's victory over Vejar, was that he had suffered such serious cuts around the eyes that he could not fulfill his obligation to Basilio. They were not so serious, apparently, that he could not sign to fight Fitzie Pruden for the IBC on May 28.

The howls sent up by the press changed those plans in a hurry. Kid Gavilan took over the Pruden fight, and Davey agreed to come to Syracuse on May 29.

In the end, the Davey run-around was the best thing that could have happened to Carmen. Fight interest in Syracuse is centered pretty solidly in the Italian section on the north side. But the north side had never accepted Carmen; first, in all probability, because Joe DeJohn was their boy, and secondly because Carmen, who was from Canastota, was never really considered a local boy. But when the north side read about the way he was getting tossed around by the New York and Chicago mob, Carmen suddenly became one of their own. (This is one of the reasons why the gate was so much better than had been anticipated.) Norm Rothschild had been taking Carmen around to their club meetings and Communion breakfasts anyway, and many of them had begun to feel that they knew him. And it is impossible to know Carmen without liking him.

The fight itself now belongs to the ages. Davey, who was a 4-1 favorite, bounced around, looking classy, but he didn't have a punch hard enough to make Basilio notice it. Carmen chased after him, landed all the solid punches, and had him bleeding heavily over both eyes. With one-and-a-half minutes left in the fight, referee Joe Palmer (officiating his first main event), stopped the fight. The commission doctor, Charles Heck, overruled him. Half-a-minute later, Palmer stopped it again and raised Basilio's hand in victory. Dr. Heck once again came into the ring, looked at Davey, and ordered the fighters to continue.

When the decision was announced, one judge had it 5-5 on rounds with Basilio ahead on points. The other judge had it 5-4-1 Davey. Palmer had it even on rounds too, but he gave Basilio a two-point edge. For the third time within five minutes, Basilio was declared the winner.

He still, of course, has not won the fight. Half an hour after the bout had ended, Deputy Commissioner Tom Graulty told the writers that although Palmer had given Davey the second and ninth rounds, he had neglected to award him any points. Under those conditions, Davey could have received no worse than a draw. A draw is what Graulty called it, and Commissioner Robert Christenberry confirmed the ruling a few days later.

What burned up Basilio more than anything was the lack of support he got from the Syracuse papers. The

Herald-Journal called it a "gift verdict," and reported that its own card had been 7-2-1 for Davey.

"Syracuse," Basilio says, "is a college town. Roy Simmons, the Syracuse U. boxing coach, swings a lot of weight with the boxing writers, and he was a big Davey fan. Davey was a college man with a master's degree, and we were nothing. We were from the wrong side of town. They came to see Davey win and they couldn't believe they were seeing what they were seeing."

Carmen did get a quick rematch in Chicago, as the IBC moved to salvage its projected Davey-Gavilan fight. This time he lost a 10-round decision—although he broke up Davey's face pretty well. Carmen is convinced that he won that fight too. When the commission doctor came into his dressing room for the routine post-battle examination, Carmen told him: "Go over to the other guy; he's the one who needs you."

"He's all right," the doctor said.

"Sure," Carmen said. "If it had been me that had been cut up like that, you'd have stopped it. It's nice to be on the right side—the IBC side."

Another fight in Chicago resulted in a loss to Billy Graham, a decision that even Carmen is willing to admit was justified. But Carmen is impossible to discourage. On the train back to Syracuse, he told his managers, "Get him back. Next time I'll knock the hell out of him. I know what mistakes I made." When his managers looked dubious, he said grimly: "Never mind, the day's going to come when I'll fight in the Yankee Stadium."

That was Carmen Basilio. When he lost a fight, he would say: "I'll just have to work harder." When he was stalled on one big fight after another, he would say, "All right, this will give me more time to get into condition." When he started fighting, he said he was going to be the champion, and neither hell nor highway robbery ever made him doubt it for a moment.

Graham had kept fooling him by feinting with his left, then jabbing. Carmen studied that move so carefully that he not only learned how to protect himself from the feint and to counter the feint, he learned how to feint very well himself.

Graham had always had a reputation as the best infighter in the business, but in the return bout in Syracuse 10 months later, Carmen went inside with him and just overwhelmed him. Whenever Billy made a move with his left, Carmen would club underneath it with his right. Halfway through the fight, it looked as if Graham had a big red hole in his ribs. When Billy's guard started to come down, Carmen began to throw the right to the head. He won a good 12-round decision.

By this time, Carmen had a big Syracuse following. He had scored a sensational three-round knockout over Sammy Giuliano at the War Memorial, decisioned Ike Williams in what Syracuse writers still call the toughest, bloodiest fight ever seen in their city, and knocked out Carmine Fiore.

After the Graham fight, Rothschild offered Kid Gavilan a $50,000 guarantee to defend his championship against Basilio. (When Gavilan's manager, Angel Lopez, reached for the guarantee, it got cut down to $42,000.) While it was technically billed as a championship fight, nobody really took Basilio that seriously. The newspapers set the odds at 4-l, but unfortunately you can't go down to the newspaper and put in a bet. Where real money was involved, the odds were 6-1. The future looked bright for the underdog bettors when Carmen staggered Gavilan in the second round with a left hook. As the champion gathered himself together and charged back, you could almost see him thinking that he was going to put this local punk in his place. Carmen met him coming in and hit him with 1) a left, 2) a right, 3) a thunderous left hook.

Gavilan landed flat on his back; it was only the second time he had been knocked down in his long career. When he got up, he looked wobbly, but Carmen was suspicious. A badly hurt fighter will invariably look for his corner as he struggles off the canvas; Gavilan, Carmen had noted, had looked straight at him. So Carmen moved in carefully and feinted once or twice to test the Kid's reactions. When he saw Gavilan react perfectly, he knew that the Cuban was putting on an act. His instructions had been to stay even for 12 rounds, then come on over the last three rounds. He did come on at the finish, but two of the three officials did not think he had stayed even before that—despite the fact that he had landed several more good left hooks during the course of the fight. Gavilan got a split decision which most of the writers thought he deserved. The Syracuse fans did not agree with them. Nor, for that matter, did the great majority of the viewers who had watched the fight on television.

Referee George Walsh had to have a police escort back to the dressing room and his car was almost tipped over by an angry mob which surrounded him later in the parking lot.

In Basilio's dressing room, his handlers were screaming and his wife was crying. Only Carmen himself seemed unconcerned. "Gavilan kept his championship," he said later, "but I knew I was going to get all the publicity." In that, he was right. He was confident, too, that Gavilan would have to give him another title fight. In that, he was wrong. It was 21 months before he got another crack at the title. And then he became involved in a crazy round robin of "wrong town" championship fights, with Gavilan defending against Saxton in Philadelphia, Saxton defending against DeMarco in Boston, DeMarco defending against Basilio in Syracuse, Basilio defending against DeMarco in Boston and Saxton in Chicago and Saxton defending against Basilio in Syracuse. When Basilio loses the title, it will probably be to Stan Musial in St. Louis.

New York State's Commissioner Christenberry kept insisting that Gavilan give Basilio another shot at his title. When Angel Lopez and Johnny DeJohn met to discuss it, all Lopez could talk about was Basilio's left hook.

The best Basilio could get in the way of opponents were a couple of middleweight spoilers, Pierre Langlois and Italo Scortichini. When Carmen was held to successive draws against them, Lopez had his out.

A visit to the doctor showed that Basilio's troubles had been caused not so much by Langlois and Scortichini as by a pair of infected tonsils. The tonsils came out, and Carmen took care of both Pierre and Italo in return bouts. He was fighting at this time, for the most part, in bouts promoted by Rothschild and televised over Ray Arcel's Saturday night Dumont network series. When Rothschild offered him Joe Miceli, who was going very bad, DeJohn told him: "Look, we're going ahead, not backward."

The way to get ahead, it was obvious by this time, was to walk arm-in-arm with the IBC. DeJohn, Netro and Basilio went to New York City, discussed the matter with IBC matchmaker Billy Brown, and signed to meet Carmine Fiore.

A few months later, Kid Gavilan—still on the lam from Basilio—went to Philadelphia to keep an engagement with Johnny Saxton, fell among pickpockets, and came home without his title. Harry Markson, managing director of the IBC, announced that Saxton's first defense was going to be against Basilio. He even named the date, April 1, 1955. The hitch was that Saxton's manager, Blinky Palermo, had been denied a New York license because of his criminal record and unsavory reputation. Palermo, well aware of the universal desire to get Basilio his deserved shot at the title, tried to pressure Commissioner Julius Helfand into reconsidering his application or, at the very least, into letting Saxton sign for the fight as his own manager, a subterfuge so obvious as to make the ban on Palermo meaningless.

The innocent victim of all this maneuvering was, of course, Basilio. Norman Rothschild was offering Saxton a $50,000 guarantee, but it was perfectly apparent that no Saxton defense was going to be made in New York. It wasn't made against Basilio at all.

To break the deadlock, Palermo accepted a $40,000 guarantee from Boston promoter Sam Silverman to defend the title against Tony DeMarco, a local boy whom the Saxton forces were able to look upon without terror.

A hurried conference in Boston among the IBC and the Saxton, DeMarco and Basilio camps brought about the firm agreement to give Basilio the next title bout. "You don't have to take my word for it," Palermo told DeJohn. "I'll put it in writing."

Saxton and DeMarco both signed contracts to meet Basilio if they won, but the contract for the fight also contained a clause guaranteeing Saxton a rematch within 90 days if he lost the title.

When DeMarco flattened Saxton, it looked as if poor Carmen would have to sweat it out again. He didn't only because Palermo—either because he was under IBC pressure or because he was trying to prove that he really wasn't such a bad guy after all—agreed to abide by the spirit of his promise to DeJohn and step out of the picture temporarily.

Carmen finally had his crack at his title. In a bruising match, in which he let DeMarco do most of the leading, he scored a knockout in 1:52 of the 12th round. The big money fight was now quite obviously a return bout with DeMarco in Boston. Since Saxton was supposed to have fought the winner of the first bout, he had to step aside a second time. This time, to reward him for his patience, he was given $12,500 off the top of the receipts. The second DeMarco fight was even more rugged than the first. For eight solid rounds, Carmen took a clobbering. Toward the end of the seventh, a long right-hand punch turned his legs to rubber and almost dropped him for the second time in his career. (He was knocked down by a guy named Jerry Drain when he was still a preliminary boy. Carmen insists it was a half slip.) Ignoring his corner's pleas to take a count, Carmen held to his feet by, it seemed, sheer will power.

"Why," he said afterwards, "should I give him the satisfaction of knocking me down?" He had been hit so hard that, his left foot was numb. As the warning buzzer sounded before the eighth round, he jumped up and tried to shake some feeling back into the foot. To the spectators, though, it looked as if he had recovered completely from the blow and was straining to get back into action. Across the ring, DeMarco's mouth fell open. In the eighth, Tony tried desperately to finish him off. He succeeded only in punching himself out. After the eighth, Basilio took complete command. He ended it in 1:54 of the 12th round, two seconds longer than it had taken him to do the job the first time.

The second DeMarco fight was a climax to the years of hard and faithful—and sometimes thankless— training. Not only was Carmen in condition to withstand the best DeMarco could throw at him, but he had hurt his left hand in the second round and had won the fight almost exclusively with his right.

With Helfand still unwilling to fold Palermo in his arms, the Saxton fight went to Chicago. Saxton's legal claim on Basilio—if you can remember back that far— went all the way back to the return-bout clause that had been inserted in the DeMarco-Saxton contract. Basilio, having assumed that obligation, through delay and proxy, had to accept the 30-30 split in the money, too.

Also, since they were already operating under a return-bout clause, there was no comparable return-bout clause in the new contract, even though Carmen was meeting Saxton for the first time. The effect of all this was that when they met in Syracuse for the rematch after Saxton had won the first time by using his strongest weapon—the outrageous decision—Carmen had to take the challenger's 20 percent end. And since Saxton was fighting under an entirely new contract, he did get the return-bout clause: So when they fought for the third time, there was a 30-30 split.

If all this is confusing—and it is—the best way to sum it up is to say that although Basilio was the defending champion in two of the three fights, Saxton came out of the series with $149,000 and Basilio with only $113,700.

In the Chicago fight, 20 of the 27 reporters at ringside thought Carmen had won, but the officials thought differently. One of them only gave Basilio three rounds out of 15, another only four. Carmen thought, quite frankly, that Saxton, who fought one of his typical run-and-hold battles, was "under protection." The referee not only stopped him from fighting inside, he says, but always gave him an extra push while he was breaking them.

In order to give Carmen his chance to fight Saxton again in Syracuse, where Saxton would not be under protection, Helfand finally permitted Johnny to sign his own contract. It was a gesture that Basilio is still grateful for. So much so that one of the reasons he accepted 20 percent for the Robinson fight was the knowledge that Helfand wanted a big September fight for New York.

"Winning back the title was the biggest thrill of all," he says. "Thrilled as I was the first time, I never really realized what it was until it was taken away."

In that second fight, Saxton surprised almost everybody by making a strong stand for two rounds. Basilio had a hunch he might make a fight of it. "After Saxton has fought a man once," Carmen says, "he seems to get a little more confident."

The real reason seems to be that Saxton's camp had come up with the crazy theory that Basilio couldn't fight if he had to move backwards. Saxton tried to move him backwards for two rounds—a job for which he was not ideally equipped—and Basilio just stood there and beat the hell out of him. It was by far the most polished display of fighting he had ever shown. He destroyed Saxton with body punches through the early rounds, then went to the head and split Johnny's mouth open in the seventh round. In the ninth he knocked him cold.

The final bout, in Cleveland, is scarcely worth mentioning. Carmen took Saxton out in two rounds. Bang, bang, and into the shower.

In his upcoming fight against Sugar Ray Robinson, Carmen may be taking the short end of the purse for the last time. For this fight, in which the middleweight champion will be defending his title against the welterweight champion, the Basilio camp originally asked for 30 percent, in the hope that they would get 25 percent. They actually did sign a contract with Jim Norris which guaranteed them the 25 percent. The only trouble with the contract was that everybody signed it except Sugar Ray.

Robinson insisted on 45 percent—the 40 percent he deserved because it was his championship that was at stake, plus five percent he wanted out of Norris' hide for old times' sake.

Normally, the fighters have a maximum of 60 percent to split between them. In this case, Norris agreed to go up to 65 percent, which meant that if Ray

held to his demands, Carmen could only get 20 percent. When he and his managers came to New York to get the matter settled, they offered to split the difference and let Robinson have 42-1/2 percent. Norris called Robinson, but Sugar Ray refused to back off his original figure.

"He isn't going to fight for less," Norris told them. "Let's discuss another fight for Carmen." Basilio had already received a guarantee of $100,000 to fight Indian Ortega in Los Angeles, but he had also received an offer of $75,000 to fight Joey Giardello in Philadelphia. Norris wanted the Ortega fight, and DeJohn asked for a day to think it over.

He, Basilio and Netro went back to their hotel to talk it over. While they were kicking the Ortega fight around, Basilio suddenly said: "What the heck, let's take the 20 percent and fight Robinson."

Twenty percent of a million dollars is, after all, not to be cast aside lightly, even if 25 percent is more pleasing to the trained eye. In addition, a sensational victory by Basilio could make the motion pictures of the fight worth a fortune. And if Carmen wins, he won't have much trouble making up that five percent in the money that will come in from appearances and endorsements. This, at least, was the argument Basilio's managers had to use when the Syracuse folks blasted them for signing their boy so cheaply.

In the old days, when champions took six-month vacations between fights, a fighter was old when he reached 30. Carmen, at 30, is still improving with every fight. "I feel stronger now," he says, "than I ever have. I feel as if I have more energy. A lot of this talk about age is in the mind. Some fighters hit 30 and begin to train less because they feel they're getting old and that their reflexes are going to be slowing up anyway. If they train less, it's only natural that they'll slow down."

It is possible that Carmen Basilio is just entering into the golden years of his ring career, both artistically and financially. Johnny DeJohn likes to say: "Ray Robinson's career is coming full circle. His championship started when he won the welterweight title. Then he moved up and won the middleweight championship, and finally he fought for the light-heavyweight title and lost on a freak. He came back to fight the middleweight champion, and here he is, back where he started; about to fight the welterweight champion again. The circle is closing. It's going to end for Robinson where it began. And then," says DeJohn, his eye on that jackpot whirring on the horizon, "they're all going to have to come to us."

THE BIG FIGHT

BY THE EDITORS OF *SPORT*

FROM *SPORT*, JULY 1958

On the eve of the March 25, 1958 Basilio-Robinson rematch, in which Sugar Ray would re-claim the middleweight title on a 15-round split decision, SPORT *set out to capture the color that typified a major championship fight.*

The show that a championship fight once was has changed and diminished. A big fight used to have the electric charm to excite a city, even the nation, and draw the fight mob to it. But big fights just don't happen often any more; they may even be fading away. The last echo of the old days was when Ray Robinson met Carmen Basilio in Chicago last March for the middleweight title. It is worth remembering—a big fight was on the boards, and people cared again.

The Sugar Ray personality did much of the job. While the ballyhoo of boxing has changed, Robinson hasn't. He still brings his built-in, old-style showmanship with him. There were 17 in the Robinson party that arrived in Chicago a week before the fight—Ray, wife Edna Mae, two managers, one manager's wife, two trainers, a New York detective serving as Ray's bodyguard, a rubdown man, personal physician Vincent Nardiello and his wife, three sparring partners, lawyer Martin Machat, a camp secretary, and a press agent. They took over the sixth floor at the Conrad Hilton Hotel. The rate for Ray's own suite was $100 a day.

A mile away was Basilio, at the Bismarck, in a three-room suite, at $42 a day, with five in the party—Carmen, wife Kay, his two managers, and burly (6-foot-4, 240 pounds) Syracuse friend Jules Isaacson. They were joined later by Carmen's father, two brothers and a Marine buddy.

The 19,400-seat Chicago Stadium was scaled at $40 tops, standard for a title bout, but for the first time in years, sale of the high-priced seats ran behind the cheap ones. (The recession was blamed.) At fight time, there was one unoccupied $40 seat when narcotics agents recognized the ticket-holder as a dope peddler and carted him away. One gate-crasher arrived with a pair of blue-and-gold trunks, claiming they were for Robinson. The ushers threw him out.

The Saturday before the Thursday fight, a rumor spread that Ray had gone to a Turkish bath to sweat off weight. Six hours after the fight, the rumor, still unverified, persisted. At Thursday's noon weigh-in, Ray had to strip (except for his socks) to make the 160 weight. All ladies were asked to leave, but one elderly woman, standing on a chair, remained as Ray mounted the scale in his socks and made weight.

The Broadway-to-Hollywood crowd, a big fight staple, was in fair attendance. Frank Sinatra sat with Leo Durocher. Standbys Joe DiMaggio, Toots Shor, Tony Martin and Don Ameche were there.

The battle showed Robinson as the genius he is at learning from a first fight. He held and boxed in spurts, moved in and out, missed more punches than was once his habit, but scored because Basilio, surprisingly, stood up, took punches and went into his crouch only when hurt. At the end, his left eye looking like abused liver, Carmen knelt and prayed. Later, in his dressing room, loser Basilio retched from swallowed blood.

Robinson's dressing room had been closed to the press, an unusual censorship. Only Edna Mae and Walter Winchell were allowed in.

The next day, the Robinson crowd left town. Basilio remained in Chicago, in a hospital for examination of his eye, with wife Kay still quietly nearby. The big fight—one of a diminishing breed—was over.

FIGHT I ONE

Basilio vs. Robinson

YANKEE STADIUM, NEW YORK
SEPTEMBER 23, 1957

FIGHT II TWO

Basilio vs. Robinson

CHICAGO STADIUM,
CHICAGO
MARCH 25, 1958

Staggered by Gene Fullmer, 1959

BASILIO'S BACK
WHERE HE BELONGS

BY BARNEY NAGLER

FROM *SPORT*, JUNE 1960

One night last winter, Carmen Basilio sat in the living room of his gray clapboard house at 100 Anderson Place, Chittenango, N.Y., and watched the snow blanket his front lawn. Accompanied by howling winds, the snow had been falling for hours, and had forced Carmen to call off a hunting trip. He was unhappy, but not surprised. It had been happening like that all winter. Whenever Basilio made plans, it seemed, something fouled them up.

A few weeks earlier, Carmen had looked forward to another hunting trip. But he caught the flu and never went. Before that, a carpenter had been hired to do some quick and important renovation work on a house Carmen had bought. But the carpenter caught the flu and the work was delayed.

Just about that time, too, the National Boxing Association temporarily blocked Basilio's return to the welterweight division. That setback, of course, hurt most of all.

When Carmen announced early last winter that he wanted to fight Don Jordan for the welterweight title, it had been looked upon as a wise decision. Basilio first punched his way to boxing fame as a welter. He relinquished his 147-pound title in 1957 to go after bigger pay days as a middleweight, and he fought heavier opponents with ample success. He won the title. Right along, though, people had been saying that Carmen had a better chance for long-term success as a welterweight. Nobody in that division can come close to him, they said. He can hang on a lot longer there, because, for one, he won't get hurt.

It wasn't that way in the middleweight division. Carmen was hurt fighting Sugar Ray Robinson, and he was hurt, most of all, in his last fight—the championship bout with Gene Fullmer. Returning to the welterweights to close out his brilliant career was a smart move, but going back where he belongs wasn't easy.

First of all, his managers, John DeJohn and Joe Netro, were barred for life by the New York State Athletic Commission for cutting in an undercover man, Gabe Genovese, on the money they made as Basilio's agents. Then, the National Boxing Association ruled, arbitrarily, that Basilio could not fight Jordan for the title. This surprised both Carmen and Don. They had agreed to fight in Syracuse for the championship.

Patience had always been one of Carmen's virtues, but he began to show signs of wear. He had set his heart on another shot at the 147-pound championship, which he had held twice before and which he had given up after winning the middleweight crown from Sugar Ray Robinson in September, 1957.

Some months before the NBA ruling, you see, Basilio had endured the frightful lacing by Fullmer. Carmen had wept in the dressing room at the Cow Palace in San Francisco and he had talked about retiring. His wife and family agreed. Hang up your gloves, they said. But Carmen reneged. In his mind, he had come up with a sensible compromise. He asked for a chance to fight Jordan, and Norman Rothschild, Carmen's Syracuse promoter, arranged the match.

Without warning, the NBA came out against the fight, even though precedent was on Basilio's side. In recent years, two other former champions who had given up their titles—Joe Louis among the heavyweights and Robinson among the middleweights—had been allowed to fight for their championships upon their return to the ring. Basilio was not granted the same privilege, and he was angry. He described the NBA as a politically motivated group without sanction by any governmental body, federal or state.

Basilio talked about the NBA as the snow fell in Chittenango.

"Boy, I was mad," he said. "I wanted to go over to Providence and punch that Tony Maceroni (president of the NBA) in the nose. But I cooled off. I was thinking of fighting Jordan and having a couple more fights and hanging them up. Now I don't know."

Basilio thought a while, and then he mentioned that he might like to fight Fullmer again. "I said once," he said, "that there was no difference fighting middleweights; that condition could make up for the loss in weight. I still think so."

Basilio had said that in this magazine back in 1957, after he won the middleweight title from Robinson. But now, new elements have been added. Can Carmen, at the age of 33, work himself into sharp enough condition to make up the weight and size he gives away to 5-foot-10, 160-pound middleweights? At 5-foot-6-1/2, Basilio is even shorter than many welterweights. At 156 pounds (the most he's ever fought at), he was sluggish against Fullmer, and he was beaten badly.

"I'm as good as a 33-year-old fighter can be if he is a 33-year-old fighter who has kept in condition," Carmen said. "I've still got it. My reflexes are as good or better than the night I fought Fullmer. I just didn't have it that night."

Indeed, he was telling the truth. Against Fullmer, Basilio had been a standing target and only condition and a stout heart had prevented him from being knocked down and counted out. Instead, the fight had been stopped with a weary Basilio still on his feet.

"Remember that night?" Carmen said.

"I do," the visitor said.

"Remember what happened in the dressing room before the fight? My managers, DeJohn and Netro, weren't allowed to work with me. They weren't even allowed in the dressing room before the fight. The California Boxing Commission and Jack Urch, an investigator, said my managers couldn't work because they were under investigation for giving some money to

Genovese. About that I know nothing."

"I remember," the visitor said, "you cried after the fight."

"I cried before the fight," Carmen said. He was not shamed by the admission.

"Look," he went on, "there was Joe Netro, a big, fat, happy-go-lucky man barred from working with me, and there he is crying. Ever see a grown man cry? It ain't nice. I just broke down. I cried. Then I realized I was going in to fight a tough guy like Fullmer. I just didn't have it."

Basilio's face is marked by his trade. There are scars over both eyes, but when he turns his smile on, he casts a warmth, incongruous with his toughness. Now he was unsmiling, almost pensive, and the one with him knew the fighter wanted to keep talking.

"You know boxing's been my life," Basilio said. "That's obvious. Everything I have I have because of it. I came off a job shoveling snow and got rich in boxing. Wouldn't have made it if I went into growing onions, like my father. Boxing is my job and that's why I'm sticking to it."

"And your family?"

"They'll have to suffer a little longer," Basilio said. "My wife Kay hates it. She's been after me to quit for a long time. She doesn't understand what it means to me. I love boxing. I like training. Other fellows find training the toughest thing; not me. I love to run and to work in the gym. I'm a guy who loves his trade. It's done nothing but good for me. I can't knock it."

Forgotten was the anguish Basilio had suffered outside the ring as well as within the ropes. He had been a qualified challenger for a long time before he got a shot at Kid Gavilan's welterweight crown in 1953. When he finally got his chance, Carmen knocked down Gavilan, but lost the decision.

For more than 30 months, Basilio waited for another chance. Instead, Gavilan blew the title to Johnny Saxton in a questionable fight in Philadelphia. Then, Saxton refused to fight Basilio. Johnny fought Tony DeMarco in Boston instead, and lost his title.

Boxing mills grind mysteriously and Basilio wound up with a fight for the title. He knocked out DeMarco twice within seven months. Later, he fought Saxton at the Chicago Stadium and Saxton won what most people thought was a poor decision.

At this point, promoter Rothschild hired the aforementioned Mr. Genovese to intercede in his behalf with

Taking stock after loss to Fullmer, 1959

Blinky Palermo, a Philadelphian with a police record, who was Saxton's manager. For a fee of $10,000, Genovese delivered the contract for a return bout between Basilio and Saxton. Basilio knocked out Saxton. He was the world welterweight champion again.

He was back on top now, but he was a champion without a challenger. The pickings were slim among the welters and Carmen was looking for the big pay days. So, he started angling for a shot at Sugar Ray Robinson, the middle-weight champion. Sports-writers couldn't put the rap on a guy for trying to make a buck, but most of them felt that Carmen was making a mistake. He's a rugged fighter, they said, but he's not big enough to tangle with Robinson and Fullmer. Even if he does win the title, he won't last long as a middleweight.

Carmen got his fight with Sugar Ray—and he won. Robinson earned $483,666 for his work. Basilio's end was $215,639. Carmen had the title. He could have stashed it away for a con-siderable time, but, instead, six months after winning the championship, Basilio fought Robinson again. It was a close fight, with Robinson the winner.

For more than a year Robinson sat around. A rubber match with Basilio would have packed any arena. Slow to anger, the New York State Athletic Commission finally called a hearing on Robinson's inactivity. It was a fiasco and wound up with Robinson trying to promote the fight himself and then calling Basilio yellow when he refused to go along with Sugar Ray's money scheme.

The NBA would not stand by without taking action, although it was an organization known for procrastination in the past. It shucked Robinson of the middleweight championship. Fullmer beat Basilio to win NBA recognition as the 160-pound titleholder while Robinson later lost the New York State and Massachusetts version of the title to Paul Pender.

The defeat by Fullmer, which marked the first knockout on Basilio's record, came in the 74th fight of his career. It was his worst performance as a front-rank fighter. For weeks he was shattered by the experience and stayed away from his favorite hangouts in Chittenango and his hometown of Canastota, and in the big city nearby, Syracuse, where he trains in a gym run by Irving Robbins.

In time the wounds healed. Carmen began to talk about returning to the welterweights, and he came down to New York to testify when his managers were facing expulsion by the boxing board. He said he knew nothing about Netro's and DeJohn's financial dealings with Genovese. Each manager said the other was unaware that Genovese was cutting in on their end of Basilio's purses. The commission construed their answers as lies and disbarred them.

"It hurt me deep when those two fellows were kicked around by the New York commis-

Tending to young fans, 1960

sion," Basilio said, "but if they stuck their necks out and did something against the laws of New York, they got what was coming to them."

"Does that mean you will not have them with you if you fight in another state, where they are licensed?"

"They were always honest and above board in their dealings with me," Basilio said. "I have a license to fight in Illinois, for example, and they are not under suspension in Illinois. I understand I would be within my rights to let them be with me in a fight in Illinois and to share in my purse. I think I'm right, but I'm not crossing that bridge until I come to it. Right now I'm worried about my new house."

"Is the house you bought new?"

"New? Hell, no. It's just about as old as I am. It's 32."

"You'll be 33 shortly. Why try to cut down your age?"

"Hell, you get to be my age and you're a fighter, you

want to cut as many corners as you can."

"What kind of house is it?"

"Well, it's in Chittenango, over by Route 5. This one we're in now is clapboard. The other house is decorated with natural color shingles. We had to get a bigger house with the boys growing up."

"I thought there were no children in your family."

"The boys are Eddie Thune, who is 12, and Freddie Thune, who is 8. They are Kay's nephews and they live with us. They're like our own kids and it's great having them around. The new house, which isn't really new, like I said, has eight rooms, including three bedrooms. There are only six rooms here."

"How come Kay never got to look upon your fighting as a job, like a man going to work in the morning selling insurance or cars?"

"I think it's because she's been sick, you know, and she liked having me around all the time. If a fellow's a fighter, he doesn't spend as much time home as a guy selling insurance or cars, like you say. And if you're a fighter a lot of people come around and tell your wife you are getting hit too much or your managers are making the wrong matches or other things like that. Makes it tough. She worries."

"Don't you think you have been hit too much in boxing?"

"I think a lot of people think I've been hit a lot. Actually, I've never been hit half as much as people think. Listen, I fought a puncher like Robinson and I came out of it all right. I move a lot under punches, or I slip them, and I bother the guy I'm fighting so that he isn't throwing as much as he should. I've taken care of myself."

"How do you feel about Sugar Ray Robinson now?"

"Sure I'm still sore at him," Carmen said. "He's a greedy guy but it hasn't helped him. They should have taken his title away a long time ago for not fighting. I never trusted him and I don't like the man. With Fullmer, it's different. Gene's a real nice guy. We're good friends."

The visitor looked at Basilio. A great many things had happened to the young man since a night eight years ago, when the visitor saw him for the first time, in a bout with Billy Graham at the Chicago Stadium. Graham had won nine of 10 rounds and had given Basilio an artistic lacing.

It was the second straight loss that Carmen had suffered within five weeks. After four years of fistic ups and downs, Basilio would have been excused if he had decided to quit boxing. But he stuck with it.

Some years later, after Carmen had won the welterweight title for the first time, John DeJohn was asked about that night in Chicago.

"You mean the Graham fight," said DeJohn. "I'll tell you about it. That's when I knew I had a real fighter. Carmen took a pretty good licking that night and kept moving in on Graham. We went back to Syracuse by train and Carmen said, 'Get me that fellow again. I learned tonight I know how to fight. Something happened in there and now I know I'm a fighter.' You know what? I believed him."

A personal epoch has been spanned by Basilio since the Chicago revelation. At the beginning of the boxing bridge is a career as first a hungry, and then a successful welterweight fighter. There is, in the middle, the great glory that Carmen fashioned battling against the odds in the middleweight division. And there may be, at the end, if Basilio can get his way, a bruising finish as a welterweight back where it all began; back where he belongs.

EPILOGUE

Carmen Basilio never did make it back to the welterweight division. He lost a rematch with Gene Fullmer and, in April 1961, a world middleweight title shot against Paul Pender, then retired. That fall, he took a job as physical education instructor at LeMoyne College in Syracuse, where he'd remain for 20 years. "I loved it, it was a lot of fun working with young kids," he recalled in November 2003. In 1970, his nephew, Billy Backus, followed in his uncle's footsteps by becoming, briefly, welterweight champion of the world. In the early '80s, Basilio and wife Kay were divorced, he moved to Rochester to join Genesee Brewery as sports activities director and was remarried, to Josephine. Brother Paul started a successful sausage company using his mom's recipe and his brother's name: Carmen Basilio's Italian Sausages. After retirement in the early '90s, the son of an onion farmer became the inspiration for the creation of the International Boxing Hall of Fame in his hometown of Canastota. Heart problems—he's undergone six bypass operations—have slowed him since, to the point he doesn't do a lot nowadays except "take orders from my wife. She's a tiger, the real fighter in the family."

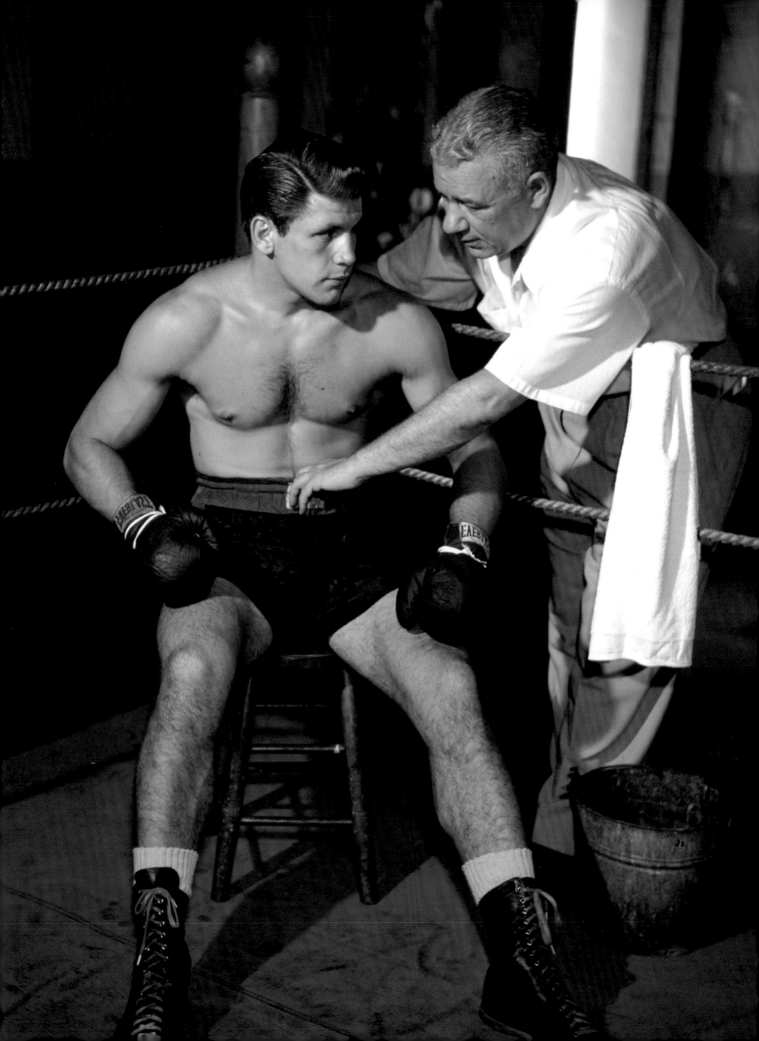

THE END OF AN ERA

A HEAVYWEIGHT
NAMED ROLAND

BY LEWIS BURTON

FROM *SPORT*, DECEMBER 1949

It's morning—any morning—at a nondescript corner grocery in the Italian-populated Van Nest section of the Bronx in New York. The store is the forerunner of the modern super-market, with butcher shop, dairy, packaged foods, vegetable bins all crowded together. Behind a heavily laden counter, a solid-looking young man with rumpled brown hair and alert brown eyes asks, "What can I do for you?"

No matter what you answer, he can oblige. He can do anything from sawing off a T-bone steak to socking your head loose.

This is the young fellow to whom some boxing writers turned their thoughts the June night in Chicago when Ezzard Charles outlasted Jersey Joe Walcott and gained the National Boxing Association's recognition as world heavyweight champion. The next day, one of the more famous, Bill Corum, said in his column which appears in the *New York Journal-American* and elsewhere: "I must feel that a kid in N.Y. named Roland LaStarza would . . . have knocked both fighters . . . flatter than a flapjack."

Suggesting the idea of a heavyweight ruler named Roland is, of course, revolutionary. Jim, John, Jack, Gene, Bob, Joe—yes. But Roland? Maybe yes, maybe no. Probably no. Nevertheless, by that time LaStarza had run up 31 straight victories. Since then, he has added a few more. He is about to graduate from the role of prospect to that of factor. He attained the status of a Madison Square Garden headliner last winter. Generally, he has realized some of the future forecast for him a year ago in *SPORT*.

Can LaStarza, contaminated by two years of college education, become heavyweight title holder, succeed to the throne held by Sullivan, Corbett, Jeffries, Dempsey, Tunney, and Louis but never by a college man? The odds are against it, as they almost always are for heavyweight contenders. Still, Roland demands special study because he is being freely nominated and cautiously handled. Whether he succeeds or fails, there may be lessons future aspirants can learn from him.

Dismiss for a moment the moods and complexes that help make a man, and this is LaStarza: He is aged 22, a son of Italian-born parents, the "baby" in a family of three children. He's a well-proportioned, bulgy-muscled 185 pounds, give or take a couple, and stands 5-foot-10-1/2. He takes care of his body proudly. He's a powerful puncher, fast with both hands. He won 35 of 36 amateur bouts. He is unbeaten in a similar number of pro bouts. He attended the College of the City of New York two years, interrupted by 18 months in the Army. He isn't married and he hasn't got a girl.

I canvassed opinion on his chances. The view I liked best was offered by heavyweight Lee Oma of Detroit, a constantly reforming renegade. Oma, with 16 years experience, is just about as smart in the ring as any fighter to be found. Last spring, LaStarza began a regular diet of boxing with him to pick up whatever he could from the ring-wise Oma's vast fund of tricks. "When he gets through boxing me the first day," Oma complained, "he says, 'Thanks very much, Lee.' What sort of a guy is that? He must have an inferiority complex. He should feel he's better than me if he's any sort of a fighter. He should expect me to come over and say thanks. He don't have to play second fiddle to anyone. What he needs is more meanness. You got to be mean to be a great fighter.

"But he's got enough stuff to beat Lee Savold, Joe Baksi, and Bruce Woodcock. I'll stack him up against Woodcock any time. It'll take a very fast man who can box to beat him. Ezzard Charles is too fast for him—but if this kid keeps getting more ferocious and gets mean and gets over that 'thank-you' stuff, he can be world's champion."

After three months, Oma announced that his pupil's rights over the heart threatened to reactivate an old injury and he decreed that the tutelage was over. LaStarza was able to look back on the post-graduate course in clout with a chuckle of delight. He had learned something of the art of feinting and pushing. When he started with Oma, his first reaction was discouragement. He'd fire away, miss, and wonder why. Then he observed how Oma would tip him off balance with a flick of a glove on the shoulder, and do it so subtly that it went unnoticed by the victim. LaStarza can do that, too, now.

Ray Arcel, an astute man-about-rings who seconded almost half of Joe Louis' challengers, faults LaStarza on two counts: first, he isn't tall enough; second, he hasn't yet developed keen "ring sense." Arcel added that they were handicaps which could be overcome and expressed a belief Roland can surmount them.

The quality known as "ring sense"—resourcefulness, trickery, and the ability to "use the ring"—can be developed only through experience. Some have more to start with than others, and some learn quicker than others, but it is chiefly a product of seasoning. Excellent prospects too often pay the penalty of being rushed into top-flight competition before they've had that essential background. Jimmy DeAngelo, LaStarza's ardent manager, is to be given credit for not making that mistake, so far, in the face of accusations that he's rearing Roland on pop-downs. On the whole, they've been set-ups only because LaStarza made them so.

Although height is a desirable advantage for a heavyweight, Bob Fitzsimmons, champion from 1897 to 1899, measured exactly the same as Roland and was 10 pounds lighter. Tommy Burns, the title claimant between Jeffries and Johnson, stood only 5-foot-7. In more modern days, Mickey Walker demonstrated that ability can be an offset to inches for campaigning effectively among the heavies. But it is true that Fitzsimmons

and Burns have been the only heavyweight bosses since Sullivan to measure less than six feet.

There are people who hold that politeness is an incurable disease for a fist fighter. LaStarza is not among them. As a man exposed to two years of CCNY before turning professional, he has the college student's attitude toward many things. No heavyweight since the days of Gene Tunney has been more systematic in preparation to become a ring success. He believes meanness can be acquired and he is working at it.

For a while, he reserved the possibility of returning to college and completing work for a bachelor's degree in physical education. He reasoned that you go to college to learn how to make a living, but he found his fists doing the trick. In two years up to the start of last summer, he cleared $7,000 from boxing after payment of managerial and training expenses. A $3,600 purse for stopping Gino Buonvino at Madison Square Garden had been his peak gross pay.

With the prospect of much better days in the ring, he gave up thoughts of resuming formal education. He found that ferocity began to come easier because the die was cast. There was no going back. Each opponent suddenly became an obstacle bent on making him a failure—a menace to his future that must be beaten down.

Last June 27, at Coney Island Stadium in New York, he found he actually could hate an opponent. He met Harry Haft, a refugee from an Austrian concentration camp whose fierce determination made up for a lack of ring savvy. To Haft, hardened in a school where death was the price of softness, a fight was a fight. He flew out of his corner and rammed LaStarza with his head. His arms whirled like a windmill. In a clinch, with Roland's left arm out straight, he yanked at the elbow in a manner suggesting he wouldn't mind breaking it.

For two rounds, LaStarza's efforts were paralyzed by his anger. Then he proceeded to rip and tear. By the fourth, when he landed with a stiff left jab, a crunching right cross, and a sharp hook, Haft could take no more. He crumpled, arose at the count of four, and went down again. The referee stopped the brawl. Haft and his manager argued that he voluntarily went down the second time to take full advantage of the nine seconds allowed him. They said they wanted it to continue.

The suggestion galvanized LaStarza. He began to shed his ring robe with the ardor of a kid yanking off his jacket for a street fight. His handlers had to hurry him

out of the ring. The grapevine between dressing rooms brought word that Haft wanted to battle it out in private. Enraged again, Roland was plowing through the door before DeAngelo applied a restraining armlock and pacified him with threats of disciplinary action by the New York State Athletic Commission.

Such a typically Latin display of temper isn't normal for LaStarza. He needs more deep-down villainy, and there's a question whether it can be acquired; since he is a good-natured, disciplined product of a well-ordered home. Actually, he is only one step removed from the delivery-boy days in his parents' store. The day before last Christmas, Manager DeAngelo visited their little market to extend his holiday greetings. They were very busy. Mama LaStarza interrupted a conversation and pointed to a bushel basket piled high with provisions.

"That's for Mr. So-and-so, Rollie."

Mama said. "You better get it right over. You know he always gives you a nice tip."

Roland's head dropped. He twisted and shuffled with the embarrassment of a schoolgirl making her first public recitation.

"Aw, gee, Mom! I can't take that over," he pleaded. "It'd look funny."

"But Rollie, you've got to help us."

DeAngelo put in a tactfully gruff word to ease the situation. "Go on, take it over!" he said. "Are you too lazy to help out?"

When Van Nest's candidate for the heavyweight championship went out the door with the basket on his shoulder, DeAngelo turned to Mama. "Look Mrs. LaStarza," he said. "Roland is 21 years old now. He's getting to be an important man. He isn't a little boy now."

She looked at the manager a moment, nodded her head and smiled. "I guess you're right," she acknowledged.

Two months later, a sense of Rollie's real consequence came home to the LaStarzas. He was matched with Gino Buonvino, an emigrant Italian with a fair record in this country. Gino had been the victim of a first-round knockout by Savold. It was his only defeat in this country, and afterward he resumed winning without interruption, so that the Italian sections of the Bronx again rallied to his support.

The match developed strong feelings in Van Nest. The older folk supported Buonvino. The younger ones—those born in this country—were largely with LaStarza. Neighbors who had never wagered before were now betting $200 and more on the outcome. Money flew out of mattresses. The situation created an intensity of purpose in LaStarza such as he hadn't felt before. Furthermore it was his first main bout in Madison Square Garden. By ring time he knew he was going to—had to—knock out Buonvino.

In the first round, he put everything behind a straight right to the face and blasted Gino to the canvas. Buonvino survived that session and several more, but in the fifth Roland bludgeoned him down three times. As the bell ended that round, a thundering right hammered Gino to the floor—out to the world. He was dragged to his corner and revived. LaStarza had to bomb him only once in the sixth. It draped Gino over the ropes, and the referee called a halt.

A month later, the Van Nest Regulars, a social club, tossed a beefsteak in Roland's honor. The Van Nest Recreation Club was jammed to the doors with winners and losers. They presented him with a $150 wristwatch. That offering is a particular source of pride to the family. In Van Nest, there's no longer a divided opinion on who'll be the next heavyweight champion.

When Roland Edmond LaStarza was born May 12, 1927, on Melville Street, not far from his present home, fate had already begun to shape his future. His father, Marco, a short, stocky man, liked to box with gloves. As soon as his first-born, Jerry, was old enough, Papa LaStarza set up a small ring in the basement of their house. The second child being a daughter; it fell to Rollie to take the beatings that big brother Jerry was daily disposed to hand out.

School, consequently, had its advantages for Roland. It released him from his brother, four years his elder. He graduated from P.S. 34 and then Christopher Columbus High School. In the late afternoons, they'd box. Jerry, who went on to become a Golden Gloves middleweight champion and turn professional, had the sort of pugnacity which Roland admits he could use today. Each session offered a complete excuse far Jerry to knock the sawdust off his kid brother.

If Roland didn't throw punches, Jerry naturally became outraged and beat the tar out of him for his timidity. If Roland did throw punches, Jerry naturally became angry and beat the tar out of him for his temerity. That went on day after day, and Roland sums up his boyhood with brother by saying "It was just boff-boff." To defend himself, he developed an extremely deft left hand. Eventually, at the age of 15, he followed his brother into training at a CYO gymnasium in midtown. Jerry joined the Air Corps and became a fighter pilot over Germany, and Roland was on his own.

He became a busy athlete. He played sandlot football when he wasn't in the gym or fighting. He ran up a string of knockouts. He won the Golden Gloves novice light-heavyweight championship in 1944, the open championship in 1945. In 37 bouts, Al King, a Clevelander, was the only one to beat him legitimately. But there was a decision scored against him by Adolph

Quijano, a Texan, in an intercity tournament, despite a knockdown LaStarza scored in the first round. Quijano was afterward found to be a professional and the bout was voided.

About that time he entered City College. He was so preoccupied with boxing that his classwork fell to a C-minus average. He couldn't play football, but he played varsity lacrosse under an assumed name that overcame eligibility difficulties. All the while, in the back of his mind, was the thought that some day he'd become a pro ringman. The Army snatched him when he became 18, just as hostilities ended, and he served overseas in the Trieste area for a year.

But all the while he was in service, he took care of his body. He didn't smoke nor drink. He exercised and he attended church daily. For gaiety, he played the harmonica. In February, 1947, he was finally separated from the Army, and was already back in class when his discharge came through. Again he began preparation for his ring career, and signed up with DeAngelo, who simply went up and asked. After six months he said farewell to books and the collegiate life.

His Madison Square Garden debut wasn't sensational. He appeared against Jimmy Evans, another ex-serviceman, in a six-round preliminary. He looked smart and skilled for four rounds and then he started to fall apart. Evans batted him all over the ring, but Roland had done enough in the early chukkers to save the decision.

That bout taught him the necessity of roadwork and relaxation. The tightness vanished after his first Garden bout, but the stamina came only through hard work on the roads near home. About a year later, he learned another important lesson, to wit: perfection isn't everything. His foe was a giant Oklahoman, Gene Gosney, with no science whatsoever but a Dempsey-like wallop. His own story of what happened is the best:

"I once fought a perfect fight, and nobody paid any attention to me," he said. "But this time I almost get killed, and everybody raves how marvelous I am.

"I was sleeping up until the fourth round. I was stepping back with my head pulled back, and Jimmy was telling me about it. But I kept doing it. All of a sudden, I felt myself turning over and falling on my right side. I came up and it happened again. Jimmy signaled, 'Shake your head!' I shook it. My head began to clear and I held on till the end of the round. I was afraid if I'd go down again, the referee'd stop it.

"Then I went to work. First I jabbed. Then I began cutting him down from all angles. I had him draped over the ropes with a bad gash over his left eye in the seventh, and the referee stopped it. I was terrible but I was sensational, and the public began taking notice for the first time."

The customers like a killer who can get off the floor to win, but Roland is inherently cautious. He, like many another college man, can't see the need for taking either punches or needless risks.

A common complaint against LaStarza is that he has adopted Joe Louis' patient stalking tactics, without having the advantage of height, weight, and punching speed that the Brown Bomber possessed. Accordingly, Roland's opinion of the retired champion is interesting if not amusing.

"I saw him fight Walcott twice," LaStarza begins.

"He's a terrific hitter, but I don't think he's got much brains. He's strictly a stalker. He didn't have that one-punch knockout. When he hurt you, he was on you. He's slow but he always gets there."

Without any reference to brainpower, it can be said this isn't a bad description of LaStarza so far. Roland is just beginning to feel his fistic oats and sound like a challenger. He's in a hurry to advance himself, while DeAngelo sticks to patience. Recently, Roland took a long series of tests and injections for an allergy which affected his breathing. DeAngelo made that an excuse to tighten the reins on his ambitious warrior.

"Who is there around?" Roland surveys the field. "Bernie Reynolds? He's a good hitter, but in close he's no good. Ezzard Charles is fast but he couldn't punch his way out of a paper bag. I know I can hit harder than him. He's tricky but I know a few tricks myself. I'm younger and stronger than Charles. I'm not afraid of anybody."

EPILOGUE

Well, there was one guy who neither the writer nor LaStarza himself had included in their reckoning in late 1949—a fellow Italian-American named Marciano. A few months later, on March 24, 1950, when LaStarza and Marciano squared off at Madison Square Garden, LaStarza, noted as a defensive specialist, and the power-punching Marciano both had perfect records—37-0 and 25-0 respectively. The fight, a classic, was the closest of Marciano's career. LaStarza was superbly elusive, slipping punches, sliding away and, when the opportunity presented itself, spraying combinations. After 10 give-and-take rounds, one judge had it 5-4-1 for LaStarza, the other 5-4-1 for Marciano. The referee had it 5-5. That took them to the scorecards to count points; Marciano prevailed with a three-point edge.

"Losing the decision like that was a real blow because I was sure I had won the fight," LaStarza remembered 53 years later, in October 2003. "The second time, when we fought for the title, I was so over-trained. When we started training I was 192 pounds. By the weigh-in I was 174. I was helpless." That fight, Marciano's first title defence after his obligatory rematch with Jersey Joe Walcott, resulted in an 11th-round TKO for Marciano.

LaStarza's career petered out after that. He fought just six more times over the next five years, losing four. After

boxing, he moved to California, where he tried acting and worked for a while as a flight instructor—he had earned his pilot's license while still fighting—and then, in the early 1960s, to Florida, where he owned a cattle ranch with his father and brother. But he was diagnosed with heart problems and the required medication grounded him as a flyer. "I used to love flying," he said wistfully.

Jane LaStarza, his wife of 42 years, passed away in 2001, which, along with the heart disease, has made for tough times. He's endured four coronary bypass operations. "I'm supposed to walk every day, 15 to 30 minutes, but I don't do it enough," he sighed.

He thinks Italian-Americans' rise in social status is responsible for thinning out their ranks in the fight game: "Now they can be doctors like my son Mark." He doesn't follow boxing much today but regards his time with fondness. "I look back on it as all a privilege right now," he said. "Having the wherewithal to be a fighter and meeting all those people you meet. There is still pleasure in people recognizing me. I can still walk down the street and people say, 'Hey, Roland, you were a great fighter.' I still get letters, one or two a month. I had a shot. I made it all the way to the top except for the title. I was a nice guy, but I was tough in the ring. My memories are full of boxing."

THE CHAMPION
NOBODY KNOWS

BY GORDON COBBLEDICK

FROM *SPORT*, OCTOBER 1950

"The way I figure it," said Guiseppe Antonio Berardinelli, "God had a reason for puttin' everybody in this world. He put me here to be a fighter."

If this is an accurate interpretation of the Master Plan, there can be no complaint from above about Guiseppe's meek acceptance of his predestined role in life. Nor can he be graded anything less than "A" for the single-mindedness with which he has pursued perfection in his calling.

For Guiseppe Berardinelli, the man you know as Joe—or Joey—Maxim, light-heavyweight champion of the world, has always known that he was intended to be a fighter. He has been fighting more or less formally since, at the age of eight, he hurled the first of a series of daily challenges at the postman. He became an amateur flyweight at 12. At 16, he suffered one of his rare defeats as an amateur when Jimmy Bivins decisioned him in the final bout for the Cleveland Golden Gloves welterweight championship. At 17, he won the Golden Gloves middleweight title. At 18, or as quickly as he could legally do so, he turned professional.

Within a year, he was fighting seasoned middleweights, light-heavyweights, and heavyweights with reckless disregard for the consequences, which, however, turned out to be uniformly good. While still a pro freshman he defeated, among others, Lee Oma, Nate Bolden, and Clarence (Red) Burman, all experienced veterans who outweighed him by plenty.

He is prepared today to defend, at 175 pounds, the light-heavyweight title he won by knocking out Freddie Mills in London last January. Or he will enter the ring at 185 against any heavyweight you care to name.

The one thing he can't do is punch, which makes the more remarkable his success in a profession wherein the ability to knock a man kicking with a single blow is considered all but indispensable. Berardinelli (hereinafter to be referred to as Joe—or Joey—Maxim) early recognized this deficiency in his equipment, and determined to compensate for it by becoming a perfect boxer.

He was fighting Bob Satterfield in Chicago a couple of years ago when Jack Kearns, his manager, stormed into the ring at the end of one of the middle rounds, shouting a threat that if Joe didn't follow instructions, he (the good doctor) would personally belt him on the chops with a right hand. A press-row spectator, overhearing, kiddingly admonished Kearns to pick on someone his own size.

Whirling savagely on his stool, Maxim snarled at the heckler, "You keep your nose out of this! If he wants to hit me, he can hit me."

But in an undertone to Kearns, he added, "You couldn't lay a right hand on me if you tried for the rest of your life."

Doubtless he was right. Most of the world's foremost righthand punchers have been trying without success to tag Joey with right hands for the last 10 years. Curtis Sheppard, the Hatchet Man, did it one memorable night in Cleveland, writing the only kayo defeat on Maxim's record. So convincing was the knockout, and so unlikely did it appear that Maxim would ever get up, that the promoter suffered a heart attack at ringside and the boxing commission doctor, who was still trying to find signs of life in Maxim, was

Left: Joey Maxim, 1950

obliged to abandon that job in order to minister to the stricken impresario.

Three weeks later, still with a concussion of the brain, Maxim stabbed and cuffed Sheppard silly in a return bout.

"A foolish thing," he now admits. "If we'd had the kind of physical examinations then that we've got now, they'd never have let me fight. But I was a cocky kid and not any smarter than I should have been. It never occurred to me to be afraid of Sheppard."

Before, and especially after, the championship fight with Mills last winter, Doc Kearns spouted at great length about "the new Maxim," the killer, the paralyzing puncher, suggesting that he had imparted to his protégé a useful trick possessed in notable measure by one of his earlier champions, a man named Jack Dempsey. The doctor's oratorical campaign made Maxim smile.

"Look," he told me on his return from England in February, "you and I are friends. So why should I kid you? I'm not one of these guys that belt you out with a punch. Never was. Never will be. I punch fast. I punch often. But I don't stiffen guys.

"It's like this: You hit a guy in the mouth two-three hundred times, he gets so he don't like to be hit in the mouth. It hurts him, takes something outta him. I wear him down and stop him maybe, but I don't knock his head off. I don't cave the ribs in."

The number and caliber of opponents Maxim has worn down and stopped isn't impressive. Oliver Shanks, Herbie Katz, Frank Green, Charlie Roth, Jack Marshall, Claudio Villar, Ralph DeJohn, Bearcat Jones, Jimmy Webb, Joe Kahut, Pat McCafferty, Freddie Mills—that's the list.

But the roster of men he has beaten (more often than not in one-sided exhibitions of speed and boxing skill) includes many illustrious names—or what pass for illustrious names in these days of ring impoverishment. He trounced Jersey Joe Walcott in the latter's home city of Camden in 1946, outboxed Jimmy Bivins in 1948, and won the American light-heavyweight title from Gus Lesnevich in 1949.

Bivins previously had beaten him once and Walcott subsequently won two close and disputed decisions from him. Maxim has met Ezzard Charles three times and has lost three times. But two of the fights were so close as to create wide differences of opinion among ringsiders.

His most exciting fights with Bivins, a fellow Clevelander, have occurred in the privacy of various training gymnasiums. The two have carried on a running feud since their early amateur days, having met as featherweights, lightweights, and welterweights before tangling in the professional ring as full-blown heavies. Whenever they fought in the gym, it was always for keeps. They forgot the separate matches for which they were training and often the timer forgot his watch and let them go—four, five, six minutes of bitter, brutal brawling at a stretch. Maxim, as has been indicated, permits himself no illusions about his punching prowess, but he does recall one blow with deep satisfaction.

"It coulda been the best I ever threw," he said later. "I'm working with Bivins in Johnny Papke's gym the day before I left for England to fight Mills. You know that overhand right of Jimmy's? He let one go and I stepped inside and hit him in the mouth with a right hand. It felt good. I stepped back and Jimmy fell flat on his kisser. I got more kick outta that than I did outta stopping Mills."

He shook his head. "A funny guy, that Bivins. In the ring he hates my guts. He butts and thumbs me and hits on the break and trips me and tries to fall on my legs. Outside the ring he boosts me and tells people I'm a nice guy and a good fighter. How you gonna figure him?"

The prophet who never got a break from the hometown rooters had nothing on Joey Maxim. In Cleveland, he is (or was until he came home with a world championship) held in polite contempt by the customers. It has been estimated that those who have stayed away from his fights at home would, if they could be gathered together, fill a stadium twice the size of Soldier Field in Chicago. Fight fans in Cleveland, like fight fans elsewhere throughout the land, love a puncher. And Maxim is no puncher.

In England, on the other hand, he is acclaimed as the greatest thing since Jem Mace. His mastery of the classical stand-up boxing style has made Maxim a favorite across the sea. In consequence, both he and Kearns are content to do the major part of their campaigning in and about London, where boxing interest is at fever pitch and a man can make a buck.

They were both rooting for Bruce Woodcock to defeat the American, Lee Savold, when they fought in London in June for the British version of the world heavyweight championship, believing that the international aspects of a Woodcock-Maxim bout in September would result in a choice payday for the firm.

Savold's victory and the immediate talk of a heavy-

Outlasting Sugar Ray Robinson in 104-degree heat, 1952

weight championship bout between him and Ezzard Charles apparently left Maxim out in the cold. However, business soon picked up for the Maxim-Kearns combine. An invitation to meet Woodcock, despite the lacing he took from Savold, was too promising to turn down. So Maxim will fight the British heavyweight in a London bout on November 14 in the hope that English fight fans are still interested in their slightly damaged Mr. Woodcock.

After Jake LaMotta made a first successful defense of his middleweight crown against Tiberio Mitri in July, Detroit matchmaker Nick Londos started negotiations for a light-heavyweight match between LaMotta and Maxim in Briggs Stadium, where LaMotta has always been a successful drawing card. Naturally, Joey's ears perked up at the first sounds of the proposal, which smelled discreetly but definitely of money.

Joe was born March 28, 1922, in the Five Points section of Cleveland, Ohio. At 28, he is a veteran of more than 300 fights. As an amateur, he quit counting when the total reached 200. As a pro, he has had more than 100, despite a two-and-a-half-year interim in which he served with the Army Air Force.

He can't remember when he first fixed a boxing championship as his life's goal, but neither can he remember a time when it wasn't uppermost in his mind. He didn't want to be the neighborhood tough guy, and had no ambition to lick all the kids on the block. He

wasn't a street fighter, and the Five Points cops don't even remember him as a boy. It was a boxer he meant to be, with gloves and trunks and a trainer and manager.

A man named Vic Rebersak operated a small dry cleaning establishment in Joe's neighborhood. Being a thorough-going ring bug, he also trained a stable of amateur fighters in a makeshift basement gym below the store. Maxim had made friends with Jimmy Bone, a well-known amateur several years his senior. Bone took the 12-year-old to Rebersak's gym one day and Joey was promptly tossed out as a juvenile. He was back the next day and again Rebersak bade him get lost.

But on his third visit, Rebersak came downstairs from his steam irons to find the 100-pound punk, stripped to his undershorts, rattling the light bag like a vaudeville performer (an accomplishment he had perfected by hours of practice in Bone's garage). That time, Joey stayed. Shortly thereafter, Rebersak matched him with a 16-year-old novice flyweight and Maxim boxed the older boy into a state of dizziness.

As a 13-year-old bantamweight, he entered the Golden Gloves tournament conducted by the *Cleveland Plain Dealer*, giving his age as 16, the lowest limit permitted by the rules. He was still 16 the following year when he moved up to the featherweight class, and 16 again when he became a lightweight a year later. By the time he had reached the welterweight finals against Bivins, he was a legitimate 16 and was 17 when he copped the middleweight title. At one stage of his amateur career he spun a string of 69 straight victories.

It was Rebersak who gave him his ring name, which for years appeared in the Cleveland sports pages as Maxin—with an "n." A reporter finally thought to inquire as to the origin of the pseudonym and Rebersak replied, indicating surprise at the writer's ignorance: "'Cause he punch so fast—rat-a-tat-tat-chust like Maxin gun." Since that illuminating explanation, it has been Maxim.

Joe was in the service when Rebersak sold his contract to Kearns in 1945. The reported price was $10,000. It may have been considerably less, but, in any case, the transaction left a residue of strained relations between Maxim and his former manager. Joey received none of the purchase price, an oversight which he still regards as unforgivable in view of the fact that at the time the money changed hands, his wife and infant daughter were living on an allotment from his pay as an Air Force pfc.

Celebrating with wife Mitchie after Robinson fight

However, Maxim's current insistence that Rebersak never taught him anything about fighting is not a by-product of his new disaffection for his first ring mentor. He makes the same statement regarding Kearns, whom he holds in high regard as a man and as a manager. It is his contention that Kearns has no equal as a trainer and conditioner of fighters, or as a boxing business man.

"Doc knows better than any other man alive how to train a guy for a fight," he said recently. "He's a great one for physical condition. He takes charge of the sparring partners when I'm training, tells 'em when to tear into me and when to box and everything to do to me. When he says I'm ready, I'm ready.

"But Doc don't teach me how to fight. Nobody ever taught me anything about fighting. I learned it by working at it. I'm still learning it that way. I study and work at it and that's how I learn."

It has been suggested by some critics that Kearns,

who guided Dempsey and Mickey Walker to lofty pinnacles in the beak-busting profession before becoming Maxim's proprietor, is no man to handle young and high-spirited fighters because he introduced Walker to the illusory delights of champagne and night life and so brought about, or at any rate hastened, the Toy Bulldog's downfall. Maxim is violently intolerant of this opinion.

"Doc never pointed a gun at Walker and made him drink that stuff," he argued. "He never ordered him to stay up all night. He was the same Doc Kearns when he had Dempsey, and Dempsey didn't go sour on him. He never made me drink and he never kept me outta bed when I shoulda been getting my rest. For my dough. he's a great guy and a great manager."

Maxim's own dissipating begins and ends with a glass of red wine with his platter of spaghetti. He doesn't smoke and finds no fun in the night life that has ruined many a fighter. At home he lives quietly with his wife, Micheline, and their daughters, Maxine, seven, and Charlene, four, in a small middle-class house in a quiet middle-class street in the middle-class neighborhood where he was born and grew up. The only thing that distinguishes his house from those of the mechanics and clerks and small storekeepers who are his neighbors is the big Cadillac parked out front. Only the second car he has ever owned, it was bought with his purse from the Mills fight—about $8,000 after taxes. That was the first "big" payday of his career.

He has been a busy fighter, however, and has made a comfortable living. He bought his house before the war, shortly after he and Mitchie, Collinwood High School classmates, were married. They were both 19 at the time. Before entering the Army, he paid off the mortgage and installed some improvements. Now, with relatively big money in sight, he and Mitchie have their eyes on another place—a ranch-type house which he boasts is right across the street from Frankie Yankovic, the "polka king." It isn't that the old neighborhood is unfit for a champ, but only that the kids need more room in which to grow up.

A provident young man in an improvident profession, Maxim confesses some concern over his future. He knows that his ring days are numbered and when they're over he doesn't want to hang around the soiled fringes of the fight game.

"I got these three to take care of," he said, taking in Mitchie and the girls with a gesture. "I don't know anything but fighting. I gotta set myself up so there'll always be some money coming in." He paused. "You wanna know something? I was never much good in school. I never read a book in my life. Sometimes I try, but I find I've read maybe three-four pages and don't know what they said because I keep thinking about fights I've had or fights I'm going to have."

As a means of providing for the future, Joe recently bought a grocery and delicatessen just around the corner from his home on Pasnow Avenue. The place has been a neighborhood institution for 22 years. Joe remodeled the front with knotty pine and installed his older brother, Emmanuel, as manager. It proved to be a happy choice, for Emmanuel is a good business man who works long hours and watches the small change. One night a week, Joey goes behind the counter and dispenses salami and pickles in person. The business is returning a modest but steady profit to the Maxims.

Maxim's father and mother still live in the old neighborhood. His father, John, a cement finisher by trade, has only a parent's interest in Joey's profession.

"He's too chicken-hearted to be a fight fan," the son explained fondly. "He don't like to see anybody get hurt, especially me. I say to him, 'Pa, how'd you like to see me fight tonight?' and he pretends to think it over and then he says. 'I don't think so. The money, you know.' I say, 'Money, nothin'. I got tickets for you.' Then he thinks some more and says, 'I must go to work in the morning. You go and fight. I go to bed'."

But Joe's mother is different. She served as his trainer when he was in the amateurs, rubbing the soreness out of him when he'd come home from a tough fight. She has seen him in several bouts, and once traveled to Pittsburgh to watch him go against Charles.

"She's even got so she tells me what I did wrong," Joe reports. "Once I thought she was going to whip me when I got home after losing an amateur fight to Jimmy Bivins. Said I let Bivins catch me on the ropes too much. Said I ought to be ashamed of myself."

That Joey hasn't let himself be caught on the ropes too often is apparent from the fact that he is virtually unmarked after 16 years in the ring and after more than 300 fights. Not even the characteristic puffed eyebrows of the fighter distinguish him from any young businessman. His good-looking, swarthy face is reminiscent of Jack Dempsey's before the latter's was scarred by his later years of warring.

Today Joey Maxim is that satisfied man who has reached a goal he set early in life. Or maybe not completely satisfied, at that. He has the light-heavyweight championship, but there's the "big one" still ahead. His sights are set on the crown that was worn by Sullivan and Corbett, by Jeffries and Willard, by Dempsey and Tunney and Louis.

And don't forget this: he's got Doc Kearns in his corner. That never hurt a fighter yet.

EPILOGUE

Within seven months of the above appearing in SPORT *magazine, Joey Maxim got his shot at the world heavyweight championship. But the result was the same as the first three times he'd fought Ezzard Charles—he emerged on the short end of a 15-round decision. Twice thereafter, he retained his light heavyweight title, first against Bob Murphy, then in June 1952 against Sugar Ray Robinson. The latter fight was notable for the fact it was fought in temperatures of 104 degrees outdoors at Yankee Stadium, with the first referee, Ruby Goldstein, collapsing and having to be replaced after the 12th round. It was also the only time in 201 career bouts that Robinson, thought by many to be the greatest fighter ever, failed to answer the bell.*

In December 1952, Maxim lost his title to Archie Moore on a 15-round decision in St. Louis. Though he tried twice, once in 1953 and again in 1954, to get it back, both results mirrored the first. Maxim defeated up-and-comer Floyd Patterson in 1954, but would win only twice more in 10 fights before retiring in 1958. He became a greeter for Las Vegas hotels and casinos. After he suffered a stroke in February 2001, his two daughters flew him to West Palm Beach so they could be with him. But he never recovered and passed away on June 2, survived by his two daughters, six grandchildren, four siblings and his 97-year-old mother, Henrietta Berardinelli.

THE JOEY GIARDELLO COMEBACK

BY STAN HOCHMAN

FROM *SPORT*, APRIL 1964

Atlantic City is bleak in December. The boardwalk creaks in the wind, and the waves flop grumpily on the desolate beach. It is a heckuva time and place for a middleweight championship fight, but Joey Giardello, who fought there last December, didn't care. He would have fought Dick Tiger for the middleweight championship in an igloo in Anchorage or in a thatched hut in Nigeria . . . Well, maybe not in a thatched hut in Nigeria, because the last time he got a chance at the championship he wound up in Gene Fullmer's Montana backyard and all he got was a bloody draw.

Giardello had agreed to take 15 percent of the gate. It sounds like a piddling percentage, but Giardello would have fought for a box of taffy or a candied apple, because he knew he could beat Tiger and he wanted the championship.

He also knew he was 33, and before the fight he admitted, "I might not have too many tomorrows left."

But the poignant part of it is that he took the piddling percentage because time was running out on an oath he had made nine years before.

In 1954, Giardello served 4-1/2 months of a 6-to-18 months sentence for assault. While he was at Holmsburg his father died.

"They brought Joey to the wake in Brooklyn," his brother Bob remembers. "The guards stood outside. Joey went over to the casket and swore on it that he would win the championship some day."

It was six years before he got a chance. He fought Fullmer in Bozeman, Montana, which seems like a foolish place to fight a devout Mormon. ("It was on television, and I never thought they'd steal it," Joey said afterward.)

"Before they gave the decision," Bob says, "Joey said he did it for his dad. He thought he had it won for sure. When they announced a draw he couldn't believe it. He never knew if he'd get another chance."

There was nothing in Giardello's history to encourage hope for another chance. Discouraged, he didn't fight for five months. Then he lost some fights he shouldn't have lost, and he broke with his manager of 11 years, and he started having trouble with guys like Wilfie Greaves and an awkward club fighter named Johnny Morris.

People figured he was through, and maybe that's why Tiger's people agreed to the fight. The whole thing was a dream come true.

"I dreamed that fight over and over in my mind," Giardello said afterward. "It went just the way I dreamed it. The guy is a mauler, and I've fought a few maulers."

Tiger never got close enough to maul Giardello. The challenger squirmed out of corners and popped his left hand in Tiger's angry face, and by the 14th round Joey's corner was jubilant.

"I told Joey he was the champion," cornerman Arnold Giovanetti said. "And started to cry."

There was a final flourish. For years people had seen Giardello squander his talents. Nobody thought he could go 15 rounds because he had only gone 15 rounds once before during his 15-year fighting career.

"Let 'em know you're in good shape," Giovanetti told him. "When I holler 'Jersey Joe,' dance around

Left: Joey Giardello, 1954

Training on Philly streets (above, 1954) and celebrating with wife Rosalie after winning the title from Dick Tiger, 1963

him. Give him the fadeaway like Walcott used to do."

"I went out there in the 15th," Giardello remembered, "and I hit him eight punches, beep, beep, beep. Then I danced away a little, because I knew the fight was over."

The fight was over. And afterward Giardello said, chuckling: "When the chips are down, and the money is on the line, bet Giardello."

He was gloating, and he had a right to gloat. He was 33 years old and supposedly washed up. He had negotiated for the title fight by himself, and he took $10,000 of his $11,000 purse and bought his contract from Arman Laurenzi who had held it for one nerve-wracking year.

Despite Giardello's brash confidence, his victory over Tiger surprised a lot of people, and not just the book-makers who made Joey a 3-1 underdog. It

surprised people who knew him best and knew how he had dissipated his skills for years, ignoring advice and shunning training.

"Not many guys fool me, but he did," Joe Pollino said. Pollino trained Giardello for nine years, but has been replaced by Adolph Ritacco. "As far as smartness and being cute, he had it all over the other guy. I thought Joe would win if it was a 10-round fight, but I thought he couldn't do 15 with such a monster."

Tony Ferrante managed Giardello for 11 years before selling his contract to Laurenzi early in 1963. "I thought if Joey was in a fight, he'd be tired when the 15th round came around," Ferrante said. "But Joey was never in a fight. After the third round I knew Joey was gonna win from the way he was moving. I knew the other guy wasn't gonna hit him."

You'd think Laurenzi would be wailing because he

had agreed to peddle Giardello's contract to the fighter before he won a championship.

Nope. Laurenzi talks like a man paroled from a horror house. "My friends tell me I blew this, I blew that." he said wanly. "All I know is I would have had an attack of some kind if I had kept on with it. As for Joey beating Tiger I knew the guy had good legs and knew his way around the ring. To me, he's the last of the great white fighters. But I never dreamed Joey would be dancing in the 15th round. I thought it would be a stop job on face cuts of something."

It was an upset because there was nothing in Giardello's history to indicate he could go 15 rounds if necessary. But it wasn't that startling an upset because Giardello had the essential style of a clever, elusive counter puncher to befuddle and beat the one-gaited Tiger.

Why did it take Giardello so long to get to the top? Why did he have trouble with people like Charlie Cotton and Pierre Langlois when he was younger and stronger? Why did he blow earlier chances with weird antics or lumbering upsets?

"I had natural ability," he says. "Everything came easy for me. Nobody showed me nothing. I'd lay off for three months, and I'd go to the gym and box four rounds with good fighters with no trouble. I wouldn't watch my diet. I wouldn't go to bed early. The next day I'd walk instead of run. Sometimes I wouldn't make the weight until the week before the fight."

Giardello looks like a fighter. He has a fighter's face, crowned by dark, wavy hair. What is left of the cartilage in his nose zigs, then zags. There are little puffs of flesh above his eyes where surgery has healed the scar tissue.

He is sensitive to criticism, restless and easily discouraged. He is seldom alone. "I don't even like to go to the corner by myself," he says. And he is willing to be talked into many things. "I was easily led," he says of his boyhood escapades, but it is a trait that pursued him into manhood.

He doesn't like to look back because his past is cluttered with disappointment. He is vague on a lot of incidents, partly because his memory has been jostled by 124 fights and partly because he just doesn't want to remember.

He was born in the Flatbush section of Brooklyn and he resents the up-from-the-slums stories that followed his victory over Tiger. "We weren't poor," he says. "We weren't rich, but we weren't poor. I had four brothers.

We'd have one baseball glove for all of us. One bike for all of us. We shared. My father worked for the Department of Sanitation. He fought under the name of Eddie Martin.

"Once, when I was 14 or 15 I wanted to fight Golden Gloves. I went to a gym and said my father was Eddie (Cannonball) Martin, the champion. The guy in the gym asked me his real name and when I told him, he chased me.

"I loved all sports. I remember the first big-league game I ever saw, the Dodgers and the Cardinals at Ebbets Field, July 16, 1941, my birthday. I can tell you the lineups of both teams that day.

"I went to Automotive Trades High School but I didn't bother too much with school. I was absent a lot."

Giardello's real name is Carmine Tilelli. A chum named Charley Bonfiglio helped Tilelli get his new name a long time ago in Brooklyn.

Bonfiglio was at Giardello's raucous party after the Tiger fight and he told the story. "We were living in a room in a Turkish Bath," he said. "We decided to join the paratroops. He was 15, so I went down the street and the first guy I saw who looked old enough I asked if he wanted to sell his birth certificate.

"I offered him two or three bucks. It was Joey Giardello. It could have been Joey Goldberg."

Giardello says that isn't the way it happened. "He's telling a lie," the champion insists. "It was his own cousin. And I had to go to the parish priest and ask for the baptismal certificate. The priest started asking about my mother and how he hadn't seen her around lately. I didn't want to lie to a priest, so I cut it short."

Anyway, Giardello wound up with the 82nd Airborne. "I was easily led," he says. "The other guy got stationed away from me because he'd been in the service before or something. I was 15 and left alone, and that's when I realized what I had done."

When he got out of the Army, he visited Philadelphia. "I had had some street fights as a kid, and done some boxing in the Army," he says. "Somebody asked me to take a fight and I did. I was going to stay in Philly a few weeks and I wound up staying 15-1/2 years."

If the origin of his name is hazy, the source of his nickname is also vague. His friends call him "Chubby" although he was a lean, hard 158 for Tiger.

"When I was born I was a big baby," Giardello says. "My family called me that, but they're the only ones who do."

"He was a big, fat sloppy kid when he came into the gym," is the way Pollino remembers it. "He didn't know his left hand from his right. Everything he knows, I taught him."

"Nobody showed me nothing," Giardello says. "I'd box and then I'd stick around and watch guys box. I'd pick up moves just by watching. I never had any amateur fights."

He doesn't remember much about his first professional fight, a two-round knockout of Johnny Noel in Trenton. "After that I fought Jimmy Larkin in Atlantic City one night," he says, "and we drove to Wilkes-Barre and I beat Bobby Clark the next night."

Giardello won 17 in a row before he lost an eight-rounder to Joe DiMartino in New Haven. Like so many of the losses that litter his record, he insists, this one was "robbery."

"I gave him a good beating," Giardello remembers. "But they give him the decision. One of my friends yelled 'The ref should drop dead.' Well, in the main event that night the ref had a heart attack.

"A guy named Reynolds was fighting. The ref got this heart attack in the fifth round, and they had to get a new ref. He didn't die, though."

Jimmy Santore was Giardello's first manager, but he sold his contract for $1,500 to Ferrante and Carmen Graziano in the summer of 1951.

"I lost to Gus Rubinci," Giardello remembers. "I hadn't been training and he started hollering and embarrassed me in front of people. I never could stand that. So I told him I didn't want to fight for him."

Ferrante took over. He had a friend in Jim Norris, and Giardello began to move. "They said I was a mob fighter," Giardello says. "If I was a mob fighter how come I never got a title shot?

"If I had had someone else managing me, I'd have won the title sooner. I was ranked number one and fighting guys I didn't have to fight. I'd win six, seven in a row and he'd keep promising me a shot. Then I'd lose one and he'd scream 'You blew the shot'."

Ferrante is out of boxing now. "Look, I'm glad he won the title and I hope he makes a ton of money," he says. "But he can't knock me. I've still got the signed contracts from the Bobo Olson fight, and he took it upon himself to get in an accident. Then he took it upon himself to get into trouble."

The accident injured Giardello's knee and delayed the

fight. While still using crutches, he got involved in a riot at a South Philadelphia gas station which resulted in the pumps, the windows, and the attendant being battered.

"I don't want to talk about it," Giardello says. "But people who know me, know I didn't beat anybody up. I was there, but I didn't do anything."

The Olson fight never came off, and Giardello did his time and came out chastened and penitent. He had to fight his way back up the rankings and it looked like a losing fight when he lost two in a row to Charlie Cotton.

Then he broke Bobby Boyd's jaw in the first round and knocked him out in the fifth and was back in contention. "That was my best fight as far as timing was concerned," Giardello says.

Ferrante remembers it vividly. "I had to shove him in the ring to fight Boyd," he says. "I never told him how to fight, but this time I told him to come out and throw a right hand at Boyd's jaw. He hit him on the button and the fight was over in the first round."

Maybe Ferrante helped and maybe he didn't. Anyway, Giardello was denied a New York license for "association with unsavory characters." He was surprised. "Undesirables?" he said. "Isn't that all there is, undesirables?"

And Ferrante still grumbles at commissions and their strict requirements. "What do they want," he snorts, "all college kids?"

Giardello finally split with Ferrante. "He lost confidence in me," the fighter says. "I fought Johnny Morris in Baltimore and I looked bad. I was sluggish and had fat hanging over me.

"I weighed 164 and at the weigh-in I told the guys to crowd around me, and someone stuck a finger up my back and lifted me so I could make the 162 pounds.

"After the fight Ferrante blew his stack. Then he wanted me to fight Jose Torres in Puerto Rico around Christmas time. He said he'd get me $7,500. I didn't want to fight around that time and besides, I knew we could get $12,000 from Joe Louis, who was promoting fights.

"Ferrante thought I was burned out, and he was just trying to get all he could out of me, so I got a guy to buy my contract."

The guy was Laurenzi, who qualified because he was a "real good fight fan since he was 14." It was not a happy arrangement. "I never pretended to be a manager," Laurenzi admits.

"He fought Greaves in Jacksonville and we wound

up with $534 for the whole thing. Expenses ate up almost all of my share for the Burford fight. Joey had $8,000 from the Ray Robinson fight, and there was $3,300 expenses out of my share.

"When he got a whiff of the Tiger fight he went to New York for three days and came back with an expense sheet of $1,800, with $500 for steaks. I said I wasn't gonna go for it, and he went to the commission.

"I'd had my fill and after a lot of arguing I agreed to take $10,000. All I can say is it was an experience. It was good because you meet a lot of people, but you also meet some of the world's worst."

Giardello likes the idea of being master of his own fate. "I can't believe some of the offers that came in after I won the title," he says. "I turn them over to Arnold. I've got a lawyer to handle legal matters, and I wish I had had a lawyer four or five years ago."

Troubles flutter around Giardello the way moths flutter around a candle. People will be surprised if he is able to cash in on his championship without something weird happening to him.

His history includes some daffy decisions, like the one with Billy Graham that was finally upheld in the courts. "I beat him," Giardello remembers, "and I'm back in the dressing room and a writer says to me, 'Graham won.' I said 'That's your opinion.'

"He said, 'Oh, no, they changed the scorecards and they gave the decision to Graham.' I couldn't believe it. The way it turned out, though, I got a million dollars worth of publicity out of it, and that fight made me."

Giardello came away with a healthy respect for Graham. "I used to be the greatest five-round fighter in the world," he says. "I would start fast, punch the other guy around and win the first five rounds. Then I'd dance and stick and con him around for the next five. I gave only enough to save the decision. Well, Graham wouldn't let me con him. He gave me no choice to dog it."

A couple of years later his fight with Willie Vaughn wound up as "no decision" because the three officials weren't using the same point system to score it.

The one that rankles him the most is the draw with Fullmer. "He ain't a fighter, he's a billy-goat," Giardello said afterward. "He says he wouldn't fight me again because I'm dirty. Well, he butted me first and he didn't stop until I butted him back. So, who's dirty?"

Giardello fought Tiger twice in 1959, losing the first ("I thought I won that one") and winning the second ("Tiger thought he won that one").

He wasn't the No. 1 contender when Jersey Jones, Tiger's manager, agreed to the title match. "Of all the middleweight contenders," Jones explained, "Giardello is the best known. He's a throwback to the old-time

Moment of greatest glory against Dick Tiger (above, right, 1963), besting Rubin "Hurricane" Carter, 1964

Beating on an aging Sugar Ray Robinson, 1963

fighter. He fought anybody any place and any time."

A lot of the time he was fighting himself, but Giardello says all that has changed. He has a $35,000 home in Cherry Hill, New Jersey, where he lives with his patient wife Rosalie and his three sons.

"She's always after me to quit," Giardello says. "When I won the title she said I ought to quit. I told her we can't eat the title. She always uses my real name. She doesn't like the limelight."

Giardello likes the limelight and wouldn't dream of quitting. "I can go another five years," he says. "And being champ I might decide to fight another five years.

"I can beat any middleweight around. You're only old if you've had a lot of wars. I've had 130 fights, but I'm not old. I've only been knocked down three times in my life.

"I've got the fastest reflexes ever recorded on an IBM machine. They tested us before the Robinson fight and I had the best score they ever had."

But it isn't reflexes and it isn't a stout jaw that have kept Giardello around for so long, long enough to finally win a championship. "I had to be a fighter," he says. "I like the glory of it.

"I loved to go in the ring and box. I liked the idea of trying to outsmart somebody. People think guys got to be dumb to be fighters. I say you've got to be smart to hang around a long time."

EPILOGUE

Joey Giardello hung around as champion for nearly two years, including a successful defense against Rubin 'Hurricane' Carter that was later immortalized on celluloid, but when Dick Tiger came back looking for his title, in October 1965, Giardello surrendered it in a tough, 15-round decision. He fought just four more times, winning twice and losing twice, before retiring in late 1967 and settling into a quite life in Cherry Hill, N.J., under his original name, Carmine Orlando Tilelli.

And then, suddenly in early 2000, Giardello was back in the news again. Norman Jewison's film The Hurricane, *about the imprisonment on murder chargers of Carter, had been released. In a key scene, the film shows a punch-drunk, blood-spattered Giardello being clearly beaten by Carter but winning a racially-tinged decision. Upset at the thoroughly false depiction—he suffered only a small cut in the middle rounds and won what a majority at ringside thought was a clear decision over a listless Carter— Giardello launched a federal lawsuit against Universal Pictures, Beacon Communications and Aloof Films. With a phalanx of boxing figures (including referee Robert Polis, who scored the fight 72-66 for Giardello and deemed the film's portrayal "ludicrous") supporting him, Giardello asked for unspecified damages but also to have a video clip placed at the end of the movie showing actual footage from the fight. Giardello said he had no quarrel with Carter or any of the actors but planned to take on Hollywood and "fight them for what is right." Joined at the press conference by his wife, Rosalie, and their four sons, Giardello added, "I never ducked a tough fight, (and) they made me out a stiff. This is about my reputation as a fighter ... I got*

grown kids and grandchildren who never saw me fight. They look at that (movie), what are they supposed to think?"

Six months after filing suit, Giardello settled out of court for an undisclosed sum and Jewison's agreement to make a statement on the DVD version of The Hurricane *that there was "no doubt" that Giardello was a great fighter. Observed Carter himself, in a televised interview, "Joey clearly out boxed me ... and therefore I did not win the title."*

"We sued, we won the case—it was nothing hard, just something we had to do," Carmine Tilelli recalled in November 2003. At 73, his voice is gravelly and full of gratitude. "I was glad that Dick Tiger gave me a shot; I appreciated it very much," he said. "(The night he lost the rematch) I thought I won, but it was okay. I was 37. I was just happy I had won the title ... for a guy who had fought for 20 years and didn't get a title shot ... I was very happy for my kids and for my family. I enjoyed boxing very much ... I loved to fight. Not that I picked fights or anything. I never had an amateur fight. I was broke and I was in Philly and asked this friend if he could get me a fight, he did and it went from there."

In retirement, the kid from Brooklyn devoted his time and energy to raising his four sons and, among other causes, raising money for the St. John of God School for Special Children, where his son Carmine attended. Now 50, Carmine Jr. works for the city of Cherry Hill: "He went out and got his own job ... I'm so proud of him ... he's my man ... if I keep talking about him I'll start crying."

Of Rosalie, his wife of 53 years, Tilelli said, "she's so beautiful ... I'm a very, very, very happy man."

BATTLE OF GREAT YOUNG HEAVYWEIGHTS
MA
GARDEN
FRI. N
8:30 P.M.
MA
10 ROUNDS
WILLIE
PAS
JOE
RO
JOHNNY DIGILIO
TO
RESERVED - - $2

AFTER THE GLORY DAYS

BY STEPHEN BRUNT

Where have all the Italian Stallions gone? There are still a few who carry on the great tradition, but really the long line has been broken, forever, by the curse of prosperity. The original immigrants struggled merely to survive in America. Their children and grand-children fought to climb the economic ladder, fought for respect, fought just to be able compete under their own names. They helped change forever the image of the Italian-American, with their courage, their passion, their skill and heart.

But succeeding generations didn't have to endure that same struggle, and few fighting fathers, given the choice, would ever wish that desperate life on their sons. Those whose path was made easier by the sacrifice of their forefathers had other options in life. Even those with athletic talent could pursue more genteel, less dangerous sports, following the path not of Rocky Graziano and Jake LaMotta and Rocky Marciano, but of Joe DiMaggio, or Joe Montana, or Phil and Tony Esposito.

By the 1960s, most of the Italian stars had disappeared from the fight game, leaving but a few, isolated heroes, reminders of a time gone by.

Joey Giardello (real name Carmine Tilelli) was in truth a leftover from the 1950s whose late career renaissance carried him into another, very different decade. Born in Brooklyn in 1930, he grew up in Philadelphia, and began boxing as a pro way back in 1948, when he ran up a string of easy victories before coming back to earth—both because he wasn't quite good enough, and because his career was derailed by the criminal element then dominant in boxing. Giardello was persistent, though, and his title shot finally came in 1960, when he fought to a 15-round draw with the reigning middleweight champ Gene Fullmer. After that near miss, Giardello lost four of six and seemed finished. But then he bucked the odds, coming back to upset aged Sugar Ray Robinson in 1963, and that won him a date with the new champ, tough Nigerian Dick Tiger. Giardello beat Tiger by unanimous decision at Convention Hall in Atlantic City and held the belt for most of two years, before finally losing it back to Tiger in what was their fourth fight (they had split the other two earlier in their careers). For today's audiences, Giardello is probably most famous for defending the championship with a 15-round decision over Rubin "Hurricane" Carter in 1964, which was a racist robbery if you believe the movie version of Carter's life, but which the boxing observers of the time regarded as an eminently fair verdict. He fought on until 1967, compiling a career record of 101-25-7.

Willie Pastrano, like that other famous Willie—Pep—was a boxing stylist rather than a brawler, though he could sometimes surprise with his power. After growing up in the tough streets of New Orleans, he turned professional in 1951, and by the time his career finished 14 years later, would compete in every weight class from welterweight to heavyweight. Pastrano was trained by another Italian-American, Angelo Dundee, whose most famous protégé, Muhammad Ali, later acknowledged that he incorporated aspects of the older fighter's style into his own. Pastrano fought and beat a host of top-10 fighters, including heavyweights Brian London, Rex Layne and Tom McNeeley. He also beat Joey Maxim in 1955, and in 1962 fought to a draw with Archie Moore. Pastrano won the light-heavyweight title from Harold Johnson in 1963, and then defended it twice in 1964, knocking out Terry Downes and Gregorio Peralta. Jose Torres stopped Pastrano with

Left: Willie Pastrano, 1956

body shots in 1965 (only the second time in Pastrano's career that he was knocked out), taking the title, and Pastrano retired immediately thereafter, with a record of 63-13-8.

Nino Benvenuti was a handsome, talented fighter, who was born in the Italian section of the Istrian peninsula, making his home in Trieste. He won a gold medal in Rome in 1960—the same Olympics that produced a light-heavyweight champion named Cassius Clay—and was celebrated as a national hero. Benvenuti turned pro after the Games, fighting exclusively in Europe, winning the continent's middleweight championship, and in 1965 won what was then the lightly-regarded WBA light middleweight (154-pound) world championship. His big breakthrough, though, came in 1967, when he journeyed to America for the first time and took Emile Griffith's middleweight title at Madison Square Garden in New York—a bout celebrated by *Ring Magazine* as the fight of the year. That great ring war naturally spawned a rematch, which Griffith won at Shea Stadium, and then a third fight, in which Benvenuti recaptured the title. In 1970, Benvenuti traveled to Australia, for what appeared to be a mismatch, a title defense against journeyman Tom (the Bomb) Bethea, who entered the ring with an unimpressive career record of 8-6-1. But a shoulder injury forced Benvenuti to quit in the eighth round, handing the title to Bethea for two months, until Benvenuti knocked him out in their rematch in Umago, Yugoslavia. Later that year, Benvenuti met his match in the great Argentinian champion Carlos Monzon, who stopped him in the 12th round of their title fight. After being knocked out in three rounds in a rematch with Monzon in 1971, Benvenuti announced his retirement.

Vito Antuofermo was in many ways reminiscent of fighters from a long past generation. He was born in Bari, Italy, and moved to Brooklyn as a 10 year old, where he grew up tough and fearless. As a fighter, there was nothing fancy about Antuofermo, but he was always willing to mix, willing to take a punch to land one, and because of that won a loyal fan following both in America and Europe. In 1979, Antuofermo won the world middleweight title from Hugo Corro. In his next fight, he defended the crown against Marvin Hagler, a rising star from Marciano's home town, Brockton, Massachusetts, who was trained by Italian-American brothers, Pat and Goody Petronelli. They fought to a controversial draw at Caesars Palace in Las Vegas—the

last blemish on Hagler's record until his career-ending, split-decision loss to Sugar Ray Leonard in 1987. Antuofermo lost the championship to England's Alan Minter in 1980, lost to him again in a rematch, and then was stopped by Hagler at Boston Garden. He fought on until 1985, when he was beaten by future world champ Matthew Hilton, and then turned to acting, where he's had small roles in films including *Goodfellas*, and *Godfather III*.

In more recent years, the appearance of new Italian-American boxing stars has always been tinged with nostalgia, as though they were doing their best to follow a familiar, though ancient script. Ray "Boom Boom" Mancini, who won the world lightweight title in 1982, fought for the honor of his father, whose own promising career had been cut short when he went to war. Vinny Pazienza, like Marciano and Pep, a world champion and a product of New England's working-class Italian community, brought a wild flamboyance to the ring, but his greatest quality was a familiar one: the willingness to wade through punches and face down impossible odds. Most recently Arturo Gatti, a native of Montreal who has spent most of his fighting life in New Jersey, has stirred memories of another generation of fighters—especially during his classic three fight series with "Irish" Micky Ward. Every time he enters the ring, he seems to be cut, and to endure tremendous punishment. But never, ever does he surrender, earning the highest compliment possible: There's a throwback for you, a *Friday Night Fights* guy, an Italian kid who would have fit right in with the best, in the old days, and even held his own.

Still, though there may be fewer Italian-Americans in the ring than in the glory days, the fighting image remains potent in the imagination, and in the cultural mythology. That tells you something about how a people wants to identify itself, the qualities it hopes to embody. Boxers, not surprisingly, were the first athletes to be celebrated by the Italian-American Hall of Fame. And a writer/actor named Sylvester Stallone cobbled together the stories of thousands of Italian-American fighters and wound up with an archetype, Rocky Balboa, who audiences would cheer through a series of films. Rocky, like all of those real Rockys, persevered. However daunting the challenge, he just kept on fighting.

The sons and daughters of Italy, the grandsons and granddaughters of immigrants, the succeeding generations rediscovering their roots, could do worse than to see themselves that way.

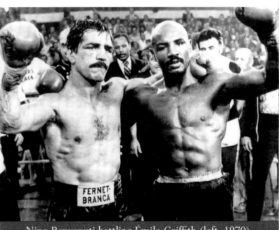

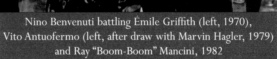

Nino Benvenuti battling Émile Griffith (left, 1970),
Vito Antuofermo (left, after draw with Marvin Hagler, 1979)
and Ray "Boom-Boom" Mancini, 1982

Reflecting on a trilogy for the ages, Rocky Graziano (left) and Tony Zale, 1970

APPENDIX

CARMEN BASILIO

Born: April 2, 1927, Canastota, NY
Record: 56-16-7 (27 knockouts)

1948

November 24	Jimmy Evans	Binghamton, NY	KO 3
November 29	Bruce Walters	Syracuse	KO 1
December 8	Eddie Thomas	Binghamton, NY	KO 2
December 16	Rollie Johns	Syracuse	W 6

1949

January 5	Johnny Cunningham	Binghamton, NY	D 6
January 19	Jay Perlin	Binghamton, NY	D 6
January 25	Ernie Hall	Syracuse	KO 2
February 19	Luke Jordan	Rochester	W 6
April 20	Elliott Throop	Syracuse	KO 1
May 2	Connie Thies	Rochester	L 6
May 8	Jerry Drain	Syracuse	KO 3
May 18	Johnny Clemons	Syracuse	KO 3
June 7	Johnny Cunningham	Syracuse	KO 2
July 12	Jesse Bradshaw	Syracuse	TKO 2
July 21	Sammy Daniels	Utica, NY	W 8
August 2	Johnny Cunningham	Utica, NY	L 8
August 17	Johnny Cunningham	Syracuse	W 8
September 7	Tony DiPelino	Rochester	W 8
September 30	Jackie Parker	Syracuse,NY	KO3

1950

January 10	Sonny Hampton	Buffalo	W 8
January 24	Cassill Tate	Buffalo	W 8
February 7	Adrien Mourguiart	Buffalo	KO 7
March 6	Lew Jenkins	Syracuse	W 10
March 27	Mike Koballa	Brooklyn	L 8
April 12	Gaby Ferland	New Orleans	D 10
May 5	Gaby Ferland	New Orleans	KO 1
June 21	Guillermo Giminez	New Orleans	TKO 8
July 31	Guillermo Giminez	New Orleans	TKO 9
August 28	Eddie Giosa	New Orleans	L 10
December 15	Vic Cardell	New York	L 10

1951

March 9	Floro Hita	Syracuse	W 8
April 12	Eddie Giosa	Syracuse	W 10
May 29	Lester Felton	Syracuse	L 10
June 18	Johnny Cesario	Utica, NY	L 10
September 17	Shamus McCray	Syracuse	W 8
September 26	Ross Virgo	New Orleans	L 10

1952

February 4	Emmett Norris	Wilkes-Barre, PA	W 10
February 28	Jimmy Cousins	Akron, OH	W 8
March 31	Jackie O'Brien	Wilkes-Barre, PA	W 10
May 29	Chuck Davey	Syracuse	D 10
July 16	Chuck Davey	Chicago	L 10
August 20	Billy Graham	Chicago	L 10
September 22	Baby Williams	Miami	W 10
October 20	Sammy Guiliani	Syracuse	KO 3
November 18	Chuck Foster	Buffalo	TKO 5

1953

January 12	Ike Williams	Syracuse	W 10
February 28	Vic Cardell	Toledo, OH	W 10
April 11	Carmine Fiore	Syracuse	TKO 9
June 6	Billy Graham	Syracuse	W 12
June 25	Billy Graham	Syracuse	D 12
September 18	Kid Gavilan	Syracuse	L 15
	(For World Welterweight Title)		
November 28	Johnny Cunningham	Toledo, OH	TKO 4
December 19	Pierre Langlois	Syracuse	D 10

1954

January 16	Italo Scortichini	Miami	D 10
April 17	Pierre Langlois	Syracuse	W 10
May 15	Italo Scortichini	Syracuse	W 10
June 26	Al Andrews	Syracuse	W 10
August 17	Ronnie Harper	Fort Wayne, IN	TKO 2
September 10	Carmine Fiore	New York	W 10
October 15	Allie Gronik	Syracuse	W 10
December 16	Ronnie Harper	Akron, OH	TKO 4

1955

January 21	Peter Muller	Syracuse	W 10
June 10	Tony DeMarco	Syracuse	TKO 12
	(Wins World Welterweight Title)		
August 10	Italo Scortichini	New York	W 10
September 7	Gil Turner	Syracuse	W 10
November 30	Tony DeMarco	Boston	TKO 12
	(Retains World Welterweight Title)		

1956

March 14	Johnny Saxton	Chicago	L 15
	(Loses World Welterweight Title)		
September 12	Johnny Saxton	Syracuse	TKO 9
	(Regains World Welterweight Title)		

1957

February 22	Johnny Saxton	Cleveland	KO 2
	(Retains World Welterweight Title)		
May 16	Harold Jones	Portland, OR	TKO 4
September 23	Ray Robinson	New York	W 15
	(Wins World Middleweight Title; gave up World Welterweight Title)		

1958

March 25	Ray Robinson	Chicago	L 15
	(Loses World Middleweight Title)		
September 5	Art Aragon	Los Angeles	TKO 8

1959

April 1	Arley Selfer	Augusta, GA	TKO 3
August 28	Gene Fullmer	San Francisco	TKO by 14
	(For NBA Middleweight Title)		

1960

June 29	Gene Fullmer	Salt Lake City	TKO by 12
	(For NBA Middleweight Title)		

1961

January 7	Gasper Ortega	New York	W 10
March 11	Don Jordan	Syracuse	W 10
April 22	Paul Pender	Boston	L 10
	(For World Middleweight Title)		

TONY CANZONERI

Born: November 6, 1908, Slidell, LA
Died: December 9, 1959, New York
Professional Record: 137-24-10 (44 knockouts), 4 no decisions

1925

July 18	Jack Gardner	Rockaway Beach, NY	KO 1
July 25	Henry Usse	Brooklyn	W 4
August 22	Henry Usse	New York	W 6
September 5	Ray Cummings	Bayonne, NJ	ND 4
September 12	Paulie Porter	New York	KO 5
October 3	Johnny Huber	New York	W 6
November 7	Henry Molineri	Brooklyn	KO 1
November 12	Harry Brandon	Brooklyn	W 4
November 26	Ralph Nischo	New York	W 4
December 7	Danny Terris	Brooklyn	W 6
December 23	Danny Terris	New York	KO 4

1926

January 13	George Nickfor	New York	KO 4
January 21	Kid Rash	Brooklyn	W 4
January 26	Mickey Lewis	New York	W 4
February 13	Romeo Vaughn	Brooklyn	W 6
February 18	Al Scorda	Brooklyn	W 4
March 6	Bobby Wolgast	Brooklyn	W 6
March 11	Jacinto Valdez	New York	W 4
March 20	Tommy Milton	Brooklyn	W 6
March 25	Mike Esposito	New York	D 6
May 8	Benny Hall	Brooklyln	D 6
May 28	Sammy Nable	New York	KO 5
June 16	Sonny Smith	Brooklyn	W 6
June 21	Willie Suess	New York	W 6
June 25	Archie Bell	Brooklyn	KO 5
July 26	Manny Wexler	Woodhaven, NY	KO 5
August 8	Young Montreal	Woodhaven, NY	W 6
August 14	Buck Josephs	Brooklyn	W 6
August 28	George Mack	Long Island City, NY	D 6
September 20	George Marks	Woodhaven, NY	W 6
October 5	Benny Hall	New York	W 6
November 6	Davey Abad	Brooklyn	L 10
November 13	Enrique Saavardo	New York	KO 5
November 22	Andre Routis	Brooklyn	W 12
December 17	Bushy Graham	New York	W 10

1927

January 12	Joe Ryder	New York	D 10
January 22	Vic Burrone	Brooklyn	W 10
February 4	Johnny Green	New York	W 8
March 7	California Lynch	Brooklyn	W 10
March 26	Bud Taylor	Chicago	D 10
	(For NBA Bantamweight Title)		
April 18	Vic Burrone	New York	D 10
April 25	Harold Smith	Brooklyn	KO 3
May 3	Ray Rychell	Chicago	KO 7
June 24	Bud Taylor	Chicago	L 10
	(For NBA Bantamweight Title)		
July 27	California Lynch	Cleveland	W 10
January 9	Eddie Anderson	Long Island City, NY	W 10
August 17	Pete Sarmiento	Brooklyn	KO 1
August 25	Iowa Joe Rivers	Kansas City	ND 10
September 2	Eddie Anderson	Chicago	LDQ 2
October 3	Tommy Ryan	Brooklyn	W 10
October 24	Johnny Dundee	New York	W 15
	(Wins Vacant World Featherweight Title)		
November 7	Billy Henry	Philadelphia	KO 2
November 22	Vincent Di Leo	New York	KO 1
December 1	Ignacio Fernandez	New York	W 10
December 30	Bud Taylor	New York	W 10

1928

January 30	Pete Nebo	Philadelphia	D 10
February 10	Benny Bass	New York	W 15
	(Unifies World Featherweight Title)		
February 23	Pete Passifium	Brooklyn	W 4
May 28	Claude Wilson	New Orleans	KO 1
June 13	Vic Foley	Montreal	W 10
June 27	Harry Blitman	Philadelphia	L 10
August 28	Bobby Garcia	Newark	KO 1
September 28	Andre Routis	New York	L 15
	(Loses World Featherweight Title)		
October 29	Gaston Charles	New York	W 10
December 8	Chick Suggs	New York	KO 6
December 14	Al Singer	New York	D 10

1929

January 18	Armando Santiago	Chicago	KO 5
February 6	Joey Sangor	Chicago	KO 7
February 26	Ignacio Fernandez	Chicago	W 10
March 8	Cecil Payne	Detroit	W 10
April 9	Eddie Anderson	Milwaukee	ND 10
April 26	Sammy Dorfman	New York	W 10
May 10	Andre Routis	Chicago	W 10
June 4	Ignacio Fernandez	New York	W 10
July 9	Phil McGraw	New York	W 10
August 2	Sammy Mandell	Chicago	L 10
	(For World Lightweight Title)		
September 20	Eddie Wolf	New Orleans	W 10
September 27	Eddie Mack	Chicago	KO 8
October 18	Johnny Farr	New York	W 10
October 30	Estanisla Loayza	Chicago	W 10

1930

January 17	Jackie Berg	New York	L 10
March 4	Solly Ritz	Brooklyn	KO 1
March 14	Estanisla Loayza	New York	W 10
April 1	Steve Smith	New Haven	KO 7
April 8	Frankie La Fay	New York	KO 1
May 5	Harry Carlton	New York	W 10
May 14	Johnny Farr	New Haven	W 10
June 4	Joe Glick	New York	W 10
June 24	Tommy Grogan	Long Island City, NY	W 10
July 21	Benny Bass	Philadelphia	W 10
August 26	Goldie Hess	New York	W 10
September 11	Billy Petrolle	Chicago	L 10
November 14	Al Singer	New York	KO 1
	(Wins World Lightweight Title)		

1931

January 26	Johnny Farr	New Orleans	ND 10
February 25	Joey Kaufman	Jersey City, NJ	KO 1
March 6	Sammy Fuller	Boston	L 10
March 23	Tommy Grogan	Philadelphia	W 10
April 24	Jackie Berg	Chicago	KO 3
	(Retains World Lightweight Title; Wins World Jr. Welterweight Title)		
June 25	Herman Perlick	New Haven	W 10
July 13	Cecil Payne	Los Angeles	W 10
	(Retains World Jr. Welterweight Title)		
September 10	Jackie Berg	New York	W 15
	(Retains World Lightweight and Jr. Welterweight Titles)		
October 29	Phillie Griffin	Newark	W 10
	(Retains World Jr. Welterweight Title)		
November 20	Kid Chocolate	New York	W 15
	(Retains World Lightweight and Jr. Welterweight Titles)		

1932

January 18	Johnny Jadick	Philadelphia	L 10
	(Loses World Jr. Welterweight Title)		
February 15	Lew Massey	Philadelphia	W 10
April 4	Ray Kiser	New Orleans	W 10
May 23	Battling Gizzy	Pittsburgh	KO 5
June 16	Harry Dublinsky	Chicago	W 10
July 18	Johnny Jadick	Philadelphia	L 10
	(For World Jr. Welterweight Title)		
September 29	Lew Kersch	New York	KO 3
October 12	Frankie Petrolle	Brooklyn	KO 3
November 4	Billy Petrolle	New York	W 15
	(Retains World Lightweight Title)		

1933

February 3	Billy Townsend	New York	KO 1
February 23	Pete Nebo	Miami, PA	W 10
April 20	Wesley Ramey	Grand Rapids, MI	L 10
May 21	Battling Shaw	New Orelans	W 10
	(For World Jr. Welterweight Title)		
June 23	Barney Ross	Chicago	L 10
	(Loses World Lightweight & Jr. Welterweight Titles)		
September 12	Barney Ross	New York	L 15
	(For World Lightweight and Jr. Welterweight Titles)		
October 28	Frankie Klick	New York	W 10
November 24	Kid Chocolate	New York	KO 2
December 4	Cecil Payne	Cleveland	KO 5
December 15	Anacleto Locatelli	New York	W 10

1934

February 2	Anacleto Locatelli	New York	W 12
March 1	Pete Nebo	Kansas City	W 10
March 13	Baby Arizmendi	Los Angeles	W 10
June 28	Frankie Klick	Brooklyn	KO 9
August 28	Harry Dublinsky	Brooklyn	L 10
September 26	Harry Dublinsky	Brooklyn	W 10

1935

January 7	Eddie Ran	Newark	KO 2
January 21	Harold Hughes	New York	W 8
January 31	Leo Rodak	Chicago	W 10

February 26	Chuck Woods	Detroit	L 10
March 15	Chuck Woods	Chicago	W 10
April 25	Eddie Zivic	Pittsburgh	KO 7
May 10	Lou Ambers	New York	W 15
	(Regains World Lightweight Title)		
June 10	Frankie Klick	Washington, DC	W 10
July 25	Bobby Pacho	Chicago	W 10
August 19	Frankie Klick	San Francisco	W 10
September 13	Joe Ghnouly	St. Louis	W 10
October 4	Al Roth	New York	W 15
	(Retains World Lightweight Title)		

1936

January 23	Bricio Garcia	New York	KO 9
January 30	Toots Bashara	Philadelphia	KO 3
February 15	Billy Hogan	New York	KO 4
March 2	Steve Halaiko	New York	KO 2
April 9	Johnny Jadick	New York	W 10
May 8	Jimmy McLarnin	New York	W 10
September 3	Lou Ambers	New York	L 15
	(Loses World Lightweight Title)		
October 5	Jimmy McLarnin	New York	L 10

1937

April 5	George Levy	Newark	KO 7
April 13	Frankie Wallace	Brooklyn	W 8
April 24	Joey Zodda	Brooklyn	KO 7
May 7	Lou Ambers	New York	L 15
	(For World Lightweight Title)		

1938

October 17	Eddie Zivic	Scranton, PA	L 10
October 26	Howard Scott	Jersey City, NJ	W 8
November 1	Al Dunbar	Camden, NJ	KO 3
November 22	Howard Scott	New York	W 8
December 10	Jimmy Murray	Brooklyn	W 8
December 30	Eddie Zivic	New York	W 10

1939

January 19	Wally Hally	Denver	W 10
January 27	Joe Gavras	San Francisco	KO 2
January 31	Everett Simington	San Jose	KO 3
February 7	Bobby Pacho	Los Angeles	W 10
March 7	Eddie Brink	Buffalo	W 8
March 28	Eddie Brink	New York	L 10
April 11	Jimmy Vaughn	New York	D 8
May 1	Jimmy Tygh	Phiadelphia	L 10
May 15	Nick Camarata	New Orleans	D 10
June 5	Harris Blake	Buffalo	L 10
July 6	Joe De Jesus	New York	W 8
July 17	Ambrose Logan	Brooklyn	W 8
August 3	Joe De Jesus	Brooklyn	W 8
August 18	Joey Wallace	Long Beach City, NY	W 8
August 26	Gerald D'Elia	New York	W 8
September 19	Eddie Brink	Brooklyn	W 8
November 1	Al Bummy Davis	New York	KO by 3

PRIMO CARNERA

Born: October 26, 1906, Sequals, Italy
Died: June 27, 1967, Sequals, Italy
Professional Record: 87-15 (69 knockouts), 1 no decision

1928

September 12	Leon Sebilo	Paris, France	KO 2
September 25	Joe Thomas	Paris, France	KO 3
October 30	Salvatore Ruggirello	Paris, France	KO 4
November 25	Epifanio Islas	Milan, Italy	W 10
December 1	Constant Barrick	Paris, France	KO 3

1929

January 18	Ernst Rosemann	Berlin, Germany	TKO 5
April 28	Franz Diener	Leipzig, Germany	LDQ 1
May 22	Moise Bouquillon	Paris, France	W 10
May 30	Marcel Nilles	Paris, France	KO 3
June 26	Jack Humbeeck	Paris, France	KO 6
August 14	Jose Lete	San Sebastian, Spain	W 10
August 25	Joe Thomas	Marseille, France	KO 4
August 30	Nicolaieff	Dieppe, France	KO 1
September 18	Herman Jaspers	Paris, France	KO 3
October 17	Jack Stanley	London, England	KO 1
November 18	Young Stribling	London, England	WDQ 4
December 7	Young Stribling	Paris, France	LDQ 7
December 17	Franz Diener	London, England	TKO 6

1930

January 24	Clayton Peterson	New York	KO 1
January 31	Elzear Rioux	Chicago	KO 1
February 6	Cowboy Billy Owens	Newark	KO 2
February 11	Buster Martin	St. Louis	KO 2
February 14	Jim Sigmon	Memphis	KO 1
February 17	Johan Erickson	Oklahoma City	KO 2
February 24	Farmer Lodge	New Orleans	KO 2
March 3	Roy Ace Clark	Philadelphia	KO 6
March 11	Sully Montgomery	Minneapolis	KO 2
March 17	Chuck Wiggins	St. Louis	KO 2
March 20	Frank Zavita	Jacksonville	KO 1
March 26	George Trafton	Kansas City	KO 1
March 28	Jack MacAuliffe	Denver	KO 1
April 8	Neil Clisby	Los Angeles	KO 2
April 14	Leon Bombo Chevalier	Oakland	TKO 6
April 22	Sam Baker	Portland	KO 1
June 5	K.O. Christner	Detroit	KO 4
June 23	George Godfrey	Philadelphia	WDQ 5
July 17	Bearcat Wright	Omaha	KO 4
July 29	George Cook	Cleveland	KO 2
August 30	Riccardo Bertazzolo	Atlantic City	TKO 3
September 8	Pat McCarthy	Newark	KO 2
September 18	Jack Gross	Chicago	KO 2
October 7	Jim Maloney	Boston	L 10
November 30	Paulino Uzcudun	Barcelona, Spain	W 10
December 18	Reggie Meen	London, England	KO 2

1931

March 5	Jim Maloney	Miami	W 10
June 15	Pat Redmond	New York	KO 1
June 26	Umberto Torriani	Buffalo	KO 2
June 30	Bud Gorman	Toronto	KO 2
July 24	Knute Hansen	Rochester	KO 1
August 4	Roberto Roberti	Newark	KO 3
August 6	Armando de Carlos	Wilmington, DE	KO 2
October 12	Jack Sharkey	New York	L 15
November 19	King Levinsky	Chicago	W 10
November 27	Vittorio Campolo	New York	KO 2

1932

January 25	Moise Bouquillon	Paris, France	TKO 2
February 5	Ernst Guehring	Berlin, Germany	TKO 5
February 1	Pierre Charles	Paris, France	W 10
March 23	George Cook	London, England	KO 4
April 7	Don McCorkindale	London, England	W 10
April 29	Maurice Griselle	Paris, France	TKO 10
May 15	Hans Schoenrath	Milan, Italy	TKO 4
May 30	Larry Gains	London, England	L 10
July 20	Jack Gross	New York	TKO 7
July 28	Jerry Pavelec	New York	TKO 3
August 2	Hans Birkie	New York	W 10
August 16	Stanley Poreda	Newark	L 10
August 19	Jack Gagnon	New York	KO 1
September 1	Art Lasky	St. Paul, MN	ND 10
October 7	Ted Sandwina	Tampa	KO 4
October 15	Gene Stanton	Camden, NJ	KO 7
October 17	Jack Taylor	Louisville	KO 2
November 4	Les Kennedy	Boston	KO 3
November 18	José Santa	New York	TKO 6
December 2	John Schwake	St. Louis	KO 7
December 9	King Levinsky	Chicago	W 10
December 13	Big Boy Peterson	Grand Rapids, MI	TKO 2
December 16	K.O. Christner	Omaha	KO 4
December 19	Jim Merriott	Galveston, TX	KO 1
December 29	Jack League	San Antonio	W 6
December 30	Jack Spence	Dallas	KO 1

1933

February 10	Ernie Schaaf	New York	KO 13
June 29	Jack Sharkey	New York	KO 6
	(Wins World Heavyweight Title)		
October 22	Paulino Uzcudun	Rome, Italy	W 15
	(Retains World Heavyweight Title)		

1934

March 1	Tommy Loughran	Miami	W 15
	(Retains World Heavyweight Title)		
June 14	Max Baer	Long Island City, NY	TKO by 11
	(Loses World Heavyweight Title)		
November 24	Vittorio Campolo	Buenos Aires, Argentina	W 12

1935

January 13	Seal Harris	Sao Paulo, Brazil	KO 7
January 22	Bill Klaussner	Rio de Janeiro, Brazil	TKO 6
March 15	Ray Impelletiere	New York	TKO 9
June 25	Joe Louis	New York	TKO by 6
November 1	Walter Neusel	New York	TKO 4
November 24	Ford Smith	Philadelphia	W 10
December 9	George Brackey	Buffalo	KO 4

1936

March 6	Isidoro Gastanaga	New York	KO 5
March 16	Leroy Haynes	Philadelphia	TKO by 3
May 27	Leroy Haynes	New York	TKO by 9

1937

November 18	Albert DiMeglio	Paris, France	L 10
December 4	Joseph Zupan	Budapest, Hungary	KO by 2

1945

July 22	Michel Blevens	Udine, Italy	KO 3
September 25	Sam Gardner	Trieste, Italy	KO 1
November 21	Luigi Musina	Milan, Italy	KO by 7

1946

March 19	Luigi Musina	Trieste, Italy	L 8
May 12	Luigi Musina	Gorizia, Italy	L 8

JOEY GIARDELLO

Born: Carmen Orlando Tilelli, July 16, 1930, Brooklyn, NY
Professional Record: 100-25-7 (32 knockouts), 1 no decision

1948

October 1	Johnny Noel	Trenton, NJ	KO 2
October 10	Jimmy Larkin	Atlantic City	KO 1
November 7	Bobby Clark	Wilkes-Barre, PA	W 4
November 16	Jackie Cole	Trenton, NJ	KO 1
November 20	Johnny Brown	Reading, PA	KO 4
December 16	Johnny Madison	Atlantic City	KO 1
December 30	Willie Wigfall	Philadelphia	KO 1

1949

February 24	Clyde Diggs	Philadelphia	D 6
March 15	Don Ennis	Reading, PA	KO 4
April 7	Bill Montgomery	Philadelphia	KO 1
April 25	Ray Morris	Wilkes-Barre, PA	W 4
April 28	Joe Aurillo	Philadelphia	W 6
May 2	Emerson Charles	Philadelphia	W 4
June 6	Henry Vonsavage	Philadelphia	KO 2
June 20	Ray Haas	Philadelphia	KO 3
July 13	Leroy Fleming	Washington, DC	KO 1
November 14	Mitchell Allen	Philadelphia	W 6
December 5	Jim Dockery	Philadelphia	KO 2

1950

January 5	Johnny Fry	Philadelphia	W 6
January 16	Joe DiMartino	New Haven	L 8
January 26	Johnny Bernardo	Philadelphia	W 8
February 9	Johnny Bernardo	Philadelphia	W 8
March 23	Armando Amanini	Brooklyn	W 8
March 27	Steve Sabatino	Philadelphia	KO 1
March 29	Johnny Brown	Allentown, PA	W 6
April 20	Tommy Varsos	Brooklyn	KO 1
May 4	Hurley Sanders	Brooklyn	W 8
May 17	Carey Mace	New York	KO by 8
August 25	Al Berry	Scranton, PA	KO 1
September 26	Ted DiGiammo	Wilkes-Barre, PA	KO 1
October 16	Bruce Ubaldo	Wilkes-Barre, PA	W 8
October 26	Harold Green	Brooklyn	KO by 6
November 27	Gene Roberts	Philadelphia	D 8
December 18	Leroy Allen	Philadelphia	KO 5

1951

January 6	Freddie Lott	Brooklyn	W 8
February 10	Jan Henry	Philadelphia	W 8
February 22	Hal Sampson	Brooklyn	W 8
February 24	Tony Wolfe	Philadelphia	KO 3
March 15	Roy Wouters	Philadelphia	L 8
March 29	Primo Cutler	Philadelphia	W 8
April 12	Roy Wouters	Philadelphia	W 8
April 30	Ernie Durando	Scranton, PA	W 10
May 25	Gus Rubicini	New York	L 8
August 13	Otis Graham	Philadelphia	W 8
August 27	Johnny Noel	Philadelphia	W 8
September 14	Tommy Bazzano	New York	W 6
October 8	Tony Amato	New York	KO 7
November 13	Rocky Castellani	Scranton, PA	L 10
December 12	Bobby Dykes	Miami Beach	L 10

1952

January 9	Sal DiMartino	Miami Beach	D 10
March 28	Sammy Giuliani	New York	D 8
May 5	Joe Miceli	Scranton, PA	D 10
June 5	Roy Wouters	Philadelphia	W 6
June 23	Pierre Langlois	Brooklyn	W 10
August 4	Billy Graham	Brooklyn	W 10
September 15	Georgie Small	Brooklyn	W 10
October 13	Joey Giambra	Brooklyn	W 10
November 11	Joey Giambra	Buffalo	L 10
December 15	Billy Graham	New York	W 10

1953

February 2	Harold Green	Brooklyn	W 10
March 6	Billy Graham	New York	L 12
April 7	Gil Turner	Philadelphia	W 10
May 30	Hurley Sanders	Newark	W 10
June 26	Ernie Durando	New York	W 10
September 29	Johnny Saxton	Philadelphia	L 10
October 26	Walter Cartier	Brooklyn	W 10
November 23	Tuzo Portuguez	Brooklyn	W 10

1954

January 8	Garth Panter	New York	TKO 5
February 5	Walter Cartier	New York	TKO 1
March 19	Willie Troy	New York	TKO 7
May 21	Pierre Langlois	New York	L 10
June 11	Bobby Jones	New York	W 10
July 7	Billy Kilgore	Philadelphia	W 10
September 24	Ralph Tiger Jones	Philadelphia	W 10

1955

January 25	Al Andrews	Norfolk, VA	W 10
February 15	Andy Mayfield	Miami Beach	KO 8
March 1	Peter Mueller	Milwaukee	KO 2

1956			
February 11	Tim Jones	Trenton, NJ	TKO 10
March 10	Hurley Sanders	Paterson, NJ	W 10
March 27	Joe Shaw	Philadelphia	W 10
May 7	Charlie Cotton	New York	L 10
May 28	Charlie Cotton	New York	L 10
July 2	Tony Baldoni	New York	KO 1
July 26	Franz Szuzina	Milwaukee	W 10
August 28	James Kid Bussey	Miami Beach	TKO 9
September 28	Bobby Boyd	Cleveland	KO 5
November 15	Charlie Cotton	Milwaukee	W 10
December 14	Charlie Cotton	Cleveland	W 10
1957			
February 6	Randy Sandy	Chicago	W 10
March 27	Willie Vaughn	Kansas City	ND 10
May 17	Rory Calhoun	Cleveland	W 10
July 2	Joe Gray	Detroit	KO 6
July 17	Chico Vejar	Louisville, KY	W 10
September 27	Bobby Lane	Cleveland	KO 7
November 5	Wilfred Greaves	Denver	W 10
December 27	Ralph Tiger Jones	Miami Beach	W 10
1958			
February 12	Franz Szuzina	Philadelphia	W 10
May 5	Rory Calhoun	San Francisco	W 10
June 11	Franz Szuzina	Washington, DC	W 10
June 30	Joey Giambra	San Francisco	L 10
November 19	Spider Webb	San Francisco	TKO by 7
1959			
January 28	Ralph Tiger Jones	Louisville, KY	L 10
May 6	Holly Mims	Washington, DC	W 10
June 16	Del Flanagan	St. Paul, MN	KO 1
August 11	Chico Vejar	St. Paul, MN	W 10
September 30	Dick Tiger	Chicago	L 10
November 4	Dick Tiger	Cleveland	W 10
1960			
April 20	Gene Fullmer	Bozeman, MT	D 15
	(For NBA Middleweight Title)		
September 27	Clarence Hinnant	Billings, MT	TKO 3
October 11	Terry Downes	London, England	L 10
December 1	Peter Mueller	Cologne, West Germany	L 10
1961			
March 6	Ralph Dupas	New Orleans	L 10
May 15	Wilfred Greaves	Philadelphia	TKO 9
July 10	Henry Hank	Detroit	L 10
September 12	Jesse Smith	Philadelphia	W 10
November 6	Jesse Smith	Chicago	W 10
December 12	Joe DeNucci	Boston	D 10
1962			
January 30	Henry Hank	Philadelphia	W 10
July 9	Jimmy Beecham	St. Paul, MN	W 10
August 6	George Benton	Philadelphia	L 10
November 12	Johnny Morris	Baltimore	W 10
1963			
February 25	Wilfred Greaves	Jacksonville	W 10
March 25	Ernie Burford	Philadelphia	W 10
June 24	Ray Robinson	Philadelphia	W 10
December 7	Dick Tiger	Atlantic City	W 15
	(Wins World Middleweight Title)		
1964			
April 17	Rocky Rivero	Cleveland	W 10
May 22	Rocky Rivero	Cleveland	W 10
December 14	Rubin Carter	Philadelphia	W 15
	(Retains World Middleweight Title)		
1965			
April 23	Gil Diaz	Cherry Hills, NJ	W 10
October 10	Dick Tiger	New York	L 15
	(Loses World Middleweight Title)		
1966			
September 22	Cash White	Reading, PA	W 10
December 5	Nate Collins	San Francisco	TKO by 8
1967			
May 22	Jack Rodgers	Pittsburgh	L 10
November 6	Jack Rodgers	Philadelphia	W 10

ROCKY GRAZIANO

Born: Thomas Rocco Barbella,
January 1, 1921, New York
Died: May 22, 1990, New York
Professional Record: 67-10-6 (52 knockouts)

1942			
March 31	Curtis Hightower	Brooklyn	KO 2
April 6	Mike Mastandre	New York	KO 3
April 14	Kenny Blackmar	Brooklyn	KO 1
April 20	Godfrey Howell	New York	D 4
April 28	Charley Ferguson	Brooklyn	L 4
May 4	Ed Lee	New York	KO 4
May 12	Godfrey Howell	Brooklyn	KO 4
May 25	Lou Miller	New York	D 6
1943			
June 11	Gilbert Vasquez	Brooklyn	KO 1
June 16	Joe Curcio	Elizabeth, NJ	KO 4
June 24	Frankie Falco	Brooklyn	KO 5
July 8	Johnny Attelly	Brooklyn	TKO 2
July 22	George Stevens	Brooklyn	KO 1
July 27	Randy Drew	Long Island City, NY	KO 1
August 12	Charley McPherson	Brooklyn	W 6
August 20	Ted Apostoli	New York	W 4
August 24	Tony Grey	Long Island City, NY	KO 6
September 10	Joe Agosta	New York	L 6
September 21	Sonny Wilson	Brooklyn	W 8
October 5	Freddie Graham	Brooklyn	KO 1
October 13	Jimmy Williams	Elizabeth, NJ	TKO 2
October 27	Charley McPherson	Elizabeth, NJ	D 6
November 12	Steve Riggio	New York	L 6
November 30	Freddie Graham	Jersey City, NJ	W 8
December 6	Charley McPherson	New York	W 6
December 27	Milo Theodores	Newark	TKO 1
1944			
January 4	Harry Gray	Jersey City, NJ	W 8
January 7	Jerry Pittro	New York	TKO 1
January 18	Phil Enzenga	Brooklyn	TKO 5
February 9	Steve Riggio	New York	L 6
February 24	Manny Morales	Highland Park, NJ	KO 4
March 4	Leon Anthony	Brooklyn	KO 1
March 8	Harry Gary	Elizabeth, NJ	W 6
March 14	Ray Rovelli	Brooklyn	W 8
April 10	Bobby Brown	Washington, DC	KO 5
May 9	Freddy Graham	Washington, DC	KO 3
May 29	Tommy Mollis	Washington, DC	TKO 7
June 7	Larney Moore	Brooklyn	KO 2
June 27	Frankie Terry	Brooklyn	TKO 6
July 21	Tony Reno	Brooklyn	W 8
August 14	Tony Fiorello	Long Island City, NY	W 8
September 15	Frankie Terry	New York	D 8
October 6	Danny Kapilow	New York	D 10
October 24	Bernie Miller	Brooklyn	TKO 2
November 3	Harold Green	New York	L 10
December 22	Harold Green	New York	L 10
1945			
March 9	Billy Arnold	New York	TKO 3
April 17	Soloman Stewart	Washington, DC	KO 4
May 25	Al Davis	New York	TKO 4
June 29	Freddie Cochrane	New York	KO 10
August 24	Freddie Cochrane	New York	KO 10
September 28	Harold Green	New York	KO 3
1946			
January 18	Sonny Horne	New York	W 10
March 29	Marty Servo	New York	TKO 2
September 27	Tony Zale	New York	KO by 6
	(For World Middleweight Title)		
1947			
June 10	Eddie Finazzo	Memphis	TKO 1
June 16	Jerry Fiorello	Toledo, OH	TKO 5
July 16	Tony Zale	Chicago	TKO 6
	(Wins World Middleweight Title)		
1948			
April 5	Sonny Horne	Washington, DC	W 10
June 10	Tony Zale	Newark	KO by 3
	(Loses World Middleweight Title)		
1949			
June 21	Bobby Claus	Wilmington, DE	KO 2
July 18	Joe Agosta	Springfield, MA	KO 2
September 14	Charley Fusari	New York	TKO 10
December 6	Sonny Horne	Cleveland	W 10
1950			
March 6	Joe Curcio	Miami	TKO 1
March 31	Tony Janiro	New York	D 10
April 24	Danny Williams	New Haven	KO 3
May 9	Vinnie Cidone	Milwaukee	TKO 3
May 16	Henry Brimm	Buffalo	KO 4
October 4	Gene Burton	Chicago	KO 7
October 16	Pete Mead	Milwaukee	KO 3
October 27	Tony Janiro	New York	W 10
November 27	Honey Johnson	Philadelphia	KO 4
1951			
March 19	Ruben Jones	Miami	KO 3
May 21	Johnny Greco	Montreal	KO 3
June 18	Freddy Lott	Baltimore	KO 5
July 10	Cecil Hudson	Kansas City	TKO 3
August 6	Chuck Hunter	Boston	WDQ 2
September 19	Tony Janiro	Detroit	TKO 10
1952			
February 18	Eddie O'Neil	Louisville, KY	TKO 4
March 27	Roy Wouters	Minneapolis	TKO 1
April 16	Ray Robinson	Chicago	KO by 3
	(For World Middleweight Title)		
September 17	Chuck Davey	Chicago	L 10

JAKE LAMOTTA

Born: Giacobe LaMotta,
July 10, 1922, New York, NY
Professional Record: 83-19-4 (30 knockouts)

1941			
March 3	Charley Mackley	New York	W 4
March 14	Tony Gillo	Bridgeport, CT	W 6
April 1	Johnny Morris	White Plains, NY	TKO 4
April 8	Joe Fredericks	White Plains, NY	KO 1
April 15	Stanley Goicz	White Plains, NY	W 4
April 24	Lorne McCarthy	White Plains, NY	W 4
April 26	Monroe Crewe	Brooklyn	W 4
May 20	Johnny Cihlar	Brooklyn	W 4
May 27	Johnny Morris	New York	W 4
June 9	Lorenzo Strickland	Woodhaven, NY	W 4
June 16	Lorenzo Strickland	New York	W 6
June 23	Johnny Morris	New York	KO 3
July 15	Joe Baynes	Long Island City, NY	W 6
August 5	Joe Shikula	Long Island City, NY	D 6
August 11	Cliff Koerkle	New York	W 6
September 24	Jimmy Reeves	Cleveland	L 10
October 7	Lorenzo Stickland	White Plains, NY	W 8
October 20	Jimmy Reeves	Cleveland	L 10
November 14	Jimmy Casa	New York	W 6
December 22	Nate Bolden	Chicago	L 10
1942			
January 27	Frankie Jamison	New York	W 8
March 3	Frankie Jamison	New York	W 8
March 18	Lorenzo Stickland	New York	W 10
April 7	Lou Schwartz	New York	KO 9
April 21	Buddy O'Dell	New York	W 10
May 12	Jose Basora	New York	D 10
June 2	Vic Dellicurti	New York	W 10
June 16	Jose Basora	New York	L 10
July 28	Lorenzo Strickland	New York	W 8
August 28	Jimmy Edgar	New York	W 10
September 8	Vic Dellicurti	New York	W 10
October 2	Ray Robinson	New York	L 10
October 20	Wild Bill McDowell	New York	TKO 5
November 6	Henry Chmielewski	Boston	W 10
1943			
January 2	Jimmy Edgar	Detroit	W 10
January 15	Jackie Wilson	New York	W 10
January 22	Charles Hayes	Detroit	TKO 6
February 5	Ray Robinson	Detroit	W 10
February 26	Ray Robinson	Detroit	L 10
March 19	Jimmy Reeves	Detroit	KO 6
March 30	Ossie Harris	Pittsburgh	W 10
May 12	Tony Ferrara	Cincinnati	KO 6
June 10	Fritzie Zivic	Pittsburgh	W 10
July 12	Fritzie Zivic	Pittsburgh	L 15
September 17	Jose Basora	Detroit	W 10
October 11	Johnny Walker	Philadelphia	TKO 2
November 12	Fritzie Zivic	New York	W 10
1944			
January 14	Fritzie Zivic	Detroit	W 10
January 28	Ossie Harris	Detroit	W 10
February 25	Ossie Harris	Detroit	W 10
March 17	Coley Welch	Boston	W 10
March 31	Sgt. Lou Woods	Chicago	W 10
April 21	Lloyd Marshall	Cleveland	L 10
September 29	George Kochan	Detroit	W 10
November 3	George Kochan	Detroit	TKO 9
1945			
February 23	Ray Robinson	New York	L 10
March 19	Lou Schwartz	Norfolk, VA	KO 1
March 28	George Sugar Costner	Chicago	KO 6
April 19	Vic Dellicurti	New York	W 10
April 27	Bert Lytell	Boston	W 10
July 6	Tommy Bell	New York	W 10
August 10	Jose Basora	New York	TKO 9
September 17	George Kochan	New York	KO 9
September 26	Ray Robinson	Chicago	L 12
November 13	Coolidge Miller	New York	KO 3
November 23	Walter Woods	Boston	KO 8
December 7	Charley Parham	Chicago	TKO 6
1946			
January 11	Tommy Bell	New York	W 10
March 29	Marcus Lockman	Boston	W 10
May 24	Joe Reddick	Boston	W 10
June 13	Jimmy Edgar	Detroit	D 10
August 7	Holman Williams	Detroit	W 10
September 12	Bob Satterfield	Chicago	KO 7
October 25	O'Neill Bell	Detroit	KO 2
December 6	Anton Raadik	Chicago	W 10
1947			
March 14	Tommy Bell	New York	W 10
June 6	Tony Janiro	New York	W 10
September 3	Cecil Hudson	Chicago	L 10
November 14	Billy Fox	New York	TKO by 4

(LaMotta later admitted under oath that he took a dive in this fight)

1948			
June 1	Ken Stribling	Washington, DC	TKO 5
September 7	Burl Charity	New York	TKO 6
October 1	Johnny Colan	New York	TKO 10
October 18	Vern Lester	Brooklyn	W 10
December 3	Tommy Yarosz	New York	W 10
1949			
February 21	Laurent Dauthuille	Montreal	L 10
March 25	Robert Villemain	New York	W 12
April 18	O'Neill Bell	Detroit	KO 4
May 18	Joey DeJohn	Syracuse	TKO 8
June 16	Marcel Cerdan	Detroit	TKO 10
	(Wins World Middleweight Title)		
December 9	Robert Villemain	New York	L 10
1950			
February 3	Dick Wagner	Detroit	KO 9
March 28	Chuck Hunter	Cleveland	KO 6
May 4	Joe Taylor	Syracuse	W 10
July 12	Tiberio Mitri	New York	W 15
	(Retains World Middleweight Title)		
September 13	Laurent Dauthuille	Detroit	KO 15
	(Retains World Middleweight Title)		
1951			
February 14	Ray Robinson	Chicago	TKO by 13
	(Loses World Middleweight Title)		
June 27	Bob Murphy	New York	TKO by 7
1952			
January 28	Norman Hayes	Boston	L 10
March 5	Eugene Hairston	Detroit	D 10
April 9	Norman Hayes	Detroit	W 10
May 21	Eugene Hairston	Detroit	W 10
June 11	Bob Murphy	Detroit	W 10
December 31	Danny Nardico	Coral Gables, FL	TKO by 8
1954			
March 11	Johnny Pretzie	West Palm Beach, FL	KO 4
April 3	Al McCoy	Charlotte	KO 1
April 10	Billy Kilgore	Miami Beach	L 10

ROLAND LASTARZA

Born: May 12, 1927, The Bronx, NY
Professional Record: 55-8 (25 knockouts)

1947			
July 7	Dave Glanton	Queens	W 6
July 15	Jack Johnson	New York	KO 6
August 12	Al Zapalla	New York	KO 5
August 25	Jim Dodd	New York	KO 5
September 9	Jim Johnson	New York	KO 1
October 10	Zeke Brown	New York	KO 1
October 21	Matt Mincey	New York	W 6
October 31	Jimmy Evans	New York	W 6
November 11	Lorne McCarthy	New York	W 6
December 1	Matt Mincey	New York	W 6
December 13	Fred Ramsey	Brooklyn	KO 4
December 23	Luther McMillam	New York	W 6
1948			
January 30	Mike Belluscio	New York	W 6
February 14	Frankie Reed	Brooklyn	KO 4
February 24	Jimmy White	New York	KO 2
March 19	Steve King	New York	W 6
April 7	Cluade McClintock	Bridgeport, CT	W 6
April 24	John Holloway	Brooklyn	KO 5
May 4	Freddie McManus	New York	W 6
June 25	Ben Rusk	New York	W 6
July 14	Tony Gangemi	New York	W 8
July 27	Oscar Goode	New York	KO 4
August 17	Teddy George	New York	KO 2
August 30	Mel McKinney	New York	KO 4
September 23	Don Mogard	New York	W 6
October 20	Mike Jacobs	Jamaica, NY	W 6
November 6	Don Mogard	Brooklyn	W 8
December 10	Gene Gosney	New York	KO 6
1949			
January 14	Bill Weinberg	New York	W 8
February 25	Gino Buonvino	New York	KO 6
April 28	Eldridge Eatman	New York	W 8
June 9	Jimmy Corollo	New York	W 10
June 27	Harry Haft	Brooklyn	KO 4
July 29	Jackie Lyons	New York	KO 5
September 2	Joe Domonic	New York	W 8
October 26	Walter Hafer	New York	KO 9
December 2	Cesar Brion	New York	W 10
1950			
March 24	Rocky Marciano	New York	L 10
May 1	James Walls	Holyoke, MA	KO 3
May 13	George Fuller	Waterbury, CT	KO 9
August 25	Keen Simmons	Long Beach, CA	W 8
October 20	Dulio Spagnolo	New York	W 10
1951			
January 15	Tiger Ted Lowry	Providence	W 10
February 5	Curt Kennedy	Providence	KO 6
March 12	Keen Simmons	Providence	W 10
May 4	Vern Mitchell	New York	KO 8
June 11	Gene Felton	Baltimore	KO 3
August 3	Tiger Ted Lowry	Long Beach, CA	W 10
December 21	Dan Bucceroni	New York	L 10
1952			
February 1	Bill Wilson	West Palm Beach, FL	KO 4
February 13	Ralph Schneider	Miami Beach	W 10
April 18	Joe McFadden	New York	KO 5
May 30	Dan Bucceroni	New York	W 10
October 9	Rocky Jones	Akron	L 10
December 1	Rocky Jones	Brooklyn	W 10
1953			
February 13	Rex Layne	New York	W 10
September 24	Rocky Marciano	New York	TKO by 11
	(For World Heavyweight Title)		
1954			
March 30	Don Cockell	London, England	L 10
December 1	Charlie Norkus	Cleveland	L 10
1955			
March 2	Julio Mederos	Miami	KO by 5
1957			
June 11	Jimmy McMillan	Houston	KO 3
October 8	Al Anderson	Holyoke, MA	W 10
1958			
December 1	Larry Zernitz	New York	L 10

ROCKY MARCIANO

Born: Rocco Francis Marchegiano, September 1, 1923, Brockton, MA
Died: August 31, 1969, Newton, IA
Professional Record: 49-0 (43 knockouts)

1947			
March 17	Lee Epperson	Holyoke, MA	KO 3
	(Fought under name of 'Rocky Mack')		
1948			
July 12	Harry Bilazarian	Providence	TKO 1
July 19	John Edwards	Providence	KO 1
August 9	Bobby Quinn	Providence	KO 3
August 23	Eddie Ross	Providence	KO 1
August 30	Jimmy Weeks	Providence	TKO 1
September 13	Jerry Jackson	Providence	TKO 1
September 20	Bill Hurdeman	Providence	KO 1
September 30	Gil Cardione	Washington, DC	KO 1
October 4	Bob Jefferson	Providence	TKO 2
November 29	Patrick Connolly	Providence	TKO 1
December 14	Gilley Ferron	Philadelphia	TKO 2
1949			
March 21	Johnny Pretzie	Providence	TKO 5
March 28	Artie Donato	Providence	KO 1
April 11	James Walls	Providence	KO 3
May 2	Jimmy Evans	Providence	TKO 3
May 23	Don Mogard	Providence	W 10
July 18	Harry Haft	Providence	KO 3
August 16	Pete Louthis	New Bedford, MA	KO 3
September 26	Tommy DiGiorgio	Providence	KO 4
October 10	Ted Lowry	Providence	W 10
November 7	Joe Dominic	Providence	KO 2
December 2	Pat Richards	New York	TKO 2
December 19	Phil Muscato	Providence	TKO 5
December 30	Carmine Vingo	New York	KO 6
1950			
March 24	Roland LaStarza	New York	W 10
June 5	Eldridge Eatman	Providence	TKO 3
July 10	Gino Buonvino	Boston	TKO 10
September 18	Johnny Shkor	Providence	KO 6
November 13	Ted Lowry	Providence	W 10
December 18	Bill Wilson	Providence	KO 1
1951			
January 29	Keene Simmons	Providence	TKO 8
March 20	Harold Mitchell	Hartford	TKO 2
March 26	Art Henri	Providence	TKO 9
April 30	Red Applegate	Providence	W 10
July 12	Rex Layne	New York	KO 6
August 27	Freddie Beshore	Boston	TKO 4
October 26	Joe Louis	New York	KO 8
1952			
February 13	Lee Savold	Philadelphia	KO 6
April 21	Gino Buonvino	Providence	KO 2
May 12	Bernie Reynolds	Providence	KO 3
July 28	Harry 'Kid' Matthews	New York	KO 2
September 23	Jersey Joe Walcott	Philadelphia	KO 13
	(Wins World Heavyweight Title)		
1953			
May 15	Jersey Joe Walcott	Chicago	KO 1
	(Retains World Heavyweight Title)		
September 24	Roland LaStarza	New York	TKO 11
	(Retains World Heavyweight Title)		
1954			
June 17	Ezzard Charles	New York	W 15
	(Retains World Heavyweight Title)		
September 17	Ezzard Charles	New York	KO 8
	(Retains World Heavyweight Title)		
1955			
May 16	Don Cockell	San Francisco	KO 9
	(Retains World Heavyweight Title)		
September 21	Archie Moore	New York	KO 9
	(Retains World Heavyweight Title)		
1956			
April 27	Announces Retirement		
1970			
January 20	Muhammad Ali	(movie/computer fight)	TKO 8

JOEY MAXIM

Born: Giuseppi Antonio Berardinelli, March 28, 1922, Cleveland
Died: June 2, 2001, West Palm Beach, FL
Professional Record: 82-29-4 (21 knockouts)

1941			
January 13	Bob Berry	Cleveland	W 4
January 27	Frank McBride	Chicago	W 8
February 17	Orlando Trotter	Chicago	L 8
April 29	Bob Berry	Cleveland	W 6
July 11	Tony Paoli	Cleveland	W 10
July 28	Johnny Trotter	Chicago	W 8
September 13	Lee Oma	Youngstown, OH	W 8
September 15	Nate Bolden	Chicago	W 10
October 6	Bill Petersen	Chicago	W 10
October 27	Oliver Shanks	Chicago	TKO 5
December 1	Clarence Red Burman	Cleveland	W 10
1942			
January 16	Booker Beckwith	Chicago	L 10
March 11	Herbie Katz	Cleveland	KO 6
March 23	Lou Brooks	Baltimore	W 10
April 20	Frank Green	Chicago	KO 2
May 11	Charles Roth	Chicago	LDQ 2
June 1	Charles Roth	Chicago	KO 4
June 22	Jimmy Bivins	Cleveland	L 10
July 10	Lou Brooks	Wilmington, DE	W 10
July 27	Curtis Sheppard	Pittsburgh	W 10
August 10	Altus Allen	Chicago	L 10
August 27	Jack Marshall	Chicago	KO 8
September 22	Shelton Bell	Pittsburgh	W 10
October 5	Hubert Hood	Chicago	W 8
October 13	Larry Lane	Akron	W 10
October 27	Ezzard Charles	Pittsburgh	L 10
December 1	Ezzard Charles	Cleveland	L 10
1943			
January 18	Clarence Brown	Chicago	W 10
February 15	Clarence Brown	Chicago	W 10
March 10	Curtis Sheppard	Cleveland	KO by 1
March 31	Curtis Sheppard	Cleveland	W 10
April 26	Al Jordan	Chicago	W 10
August 9	Nate Bolden	Chicago	W 10
October 29	Buddy Scott	Chicago	W 10
December 1	Claudio Villar	Cleveland	KO 6
1944			
January 31	Georgie Parks	Washington, DC	W 10
April 28	Buddy Walker	Detroit	W 10
May 29	Bob Garner	Chicago	W 10
June 26	Frank Androff	Chicago	W 10
July 27	Lloyd Marsall	Cleveland	L 10
December 19	Johnny Flynn	Cleveland	L 10
1945			
February 2	Johnny Flanagan	Chicago	W 8
April 16	Clarence Brown	Detroit	W 10
November 26	Cleo Everett	Detroit	W 10
1946			
March 4	Howard Williams	Detroit	W 10
March 11	John Thomas	New York	L 10
March 27	Ralph DeJohn	Buffalo	TKO 1
April 1	Buddy Walker	Baltimore	W 10
April 9	Phil Muscato	Buffalo	L 10
May 7	Charley Eagle	Buffalo	D 10
May 14	Phil Muscato	Buffalo	W 12
August 2	Phil Muscato	Rochester	W 10
August 14	Henry Cooper	Chicago	W 10
August 28	Jersey Joe Walcott	Camden, NJ	W 10
October 10	Clarence Jones	Akron, OH	W 10
October 16	Bearcat Jones	Toledo, OH	KO 5
November 12	Jim Ritchie	St. Louis	D 10

December 3	Jimmy Webb	Houston	KO 6
December 12	Al Velez	El Paso, TX	W 10
December 17	Jack Marshall	Houston	W 10
1947			
January 6	Jersey Joe Walcott	Philadelphia	L 10
January 28	Marty Clark	Miami	TKO 7
May 12	Charlie Roth	Louisville, KY	KO 4
June 23	Jersey Joe Walcott	Los Angeles	L 10
September 8	Clarence Jones	Wheeling, WV	KO 5
September 17	John Thomas	Cleveland	W 10
November 12	Bob Foxworth	Chicago	W 10
December 8	Billy Thompson	Philadelphia	W 10
1948			
January 9	Olle Tandberg	New York	W 10
February 2	Bob Sikes	Little Rock, AK	W 10
February 13	Tony Bosnich	San Francisco	W 10
March 22	Pat Valentino	San Francisco	D 10
April 27	Louis Berlier	Houston	W 10
May 7	Francisco De La Cruz	El Paso, TX	W 10
May 27	Roy Hawkins	Tacoma, WA	W 10
June 7	Pat Valentino	San Francisco	D 10
June 22	Joe Kahut	Portland, OR	W 10
June 29	Bill Petersen	Seattle	W 10
September 28	Bill Petersen	Portland, OR	W 10
October 19	Joe Kahut	Portland, OR	L 15
November 12	Bob Satterfield	Chicago	W 10
December 7	Jimmy Bivins	Cleveland	W 10
1949			
February 28	Ezzard Charles	Cincinnati	L 15
May 23	Gus Lesnevich	Cincinnati	W 15
	(Wins American Light Heavyweight Title)		
October 25	Joe Kahut	Cincinnati	TKO 5
November 30	Pat McCafferty	Wichita, KS	TKO 4
December 9	Bill Petersen	Grand Rapids, MI	W 10
1950			
January 24	Freddie Mills	London, England	KO 10
	(Wins World Light Heavyweight Title)		
April 19	Joe Dawson	Omaha	KO 2
May 12	Bill Petersen	Memphis	KO 6
September 25	Johnny Swanson	Huntington, WV	KO 3
October 10	Bill Petersen	Salt Lake City	W 10
November 22	Big Boy Brown	Moline, IL	W 10
December 11	Dave Whitlock	San Francisco	KO 4
1951			
January 27	Hubert Hood	Indianapolis	KO 3
May 30	Ezzard Charles	Chicago	L 15
	(For World Heavyweight Title)		
August 22	Bob Murphy	New York	W 15
	(Retains World Light Heavyweight Title)		
December 12	Ezzard Charles	San Francisco	L 12
1952			
March 6	Ted Lowry	St. Paul, MN	W 10
June 25	Ray Robinson	New York	TKO 14
	(Retains World Light Heavyweight Title)		
December 17	Archie Moore	St. Louis	L 15
	(Loses World Light Heavyweight Title)		
1953			
March 4	Danny Nardico	Miami	W 10
June 24	Archie Moore	Ogden, UT	L 15
	(For World Light Heavyweight Title)		
1954			
January 27	Archie Moore	Miami	L 15
	(For World Light Heavyweight Title)		
June 7	Floyd Patterson	Brooklyn	W 8
November 24	Paul Andrews	Chicago	W 10
1955			
April 13	Carl Bobo Olson	San Francisco	L 10
June 28	Willie Pastrano	New Orleans	L 10
1956			
September 29	Edgardo Jose Romero	Vancouver	W 10
1957			
January 25	Eddie Machen	Miami Beach	L 10
May 3	Eddie Machen	Louisville, KY	L 10
June 18	Carl Bobo Olson	Portland, OR	L 10
1958			
April 12	Heinz Neuhaus	Stuttgart, Germany	L 10
April 27	Giacomo Bozzano	Milan, Italy	L 10
May 17	Ulli Ritter	Mannheim, Germany	L 10

WILLIE PEP

Born: Guglielmo Papaleo,
September 19, 1922, Hartford, CT
Profesional Record: 230-11-1 (65 knockouts)

1940			
July 3	James McGovern	Hartford	W 4
July 25	Joey Marcus	Hartford	W 4
August 8	Joey Wasnick	New Haven	KO 3
August 29	Tommy Burns	Hartford	KO 1
September 5	Joey Marcus	New Britain, CT	W 6
September 19	Jack Moore	Hartford	W 6
October 3	Jimmy Riche	Waterbury, CT	TKO 3
October 24	Jimmy McAllister	New Haven	W 6
November 22	Carlo Duponde	New Britain, CT	TKO 6
November 29	Frank Topazio	New Britain, CT	TKO 6
December 6	Jim Mutane	New Britain, CT	KO 2
1941			
January 28	Augie Almeda	New Haven	TKO 6
February 3	Joe Echevarria	Holyoke, MA	W 6
February 10	Don Lyons	Holyoke, MA	KO 2
February 17	Ruby Garcia	Holyoke, MA	W 6
March 3	Ruby Garcia	Holyoke, MA	W 6
March 25	Marty Shapiro	Hartford	W 6
March 31	Joey Gatto	Holyoke, MA	KO 2
April 14	Henry Vasquez	Holyoke, MA	W 6
April 22	Mexican Joey Silva	Hartford	W 6
May 6	Lou Puglose	Hartford	KO 2
May 12	John Cockfield	Holyoke, MA	W 6
June 24	Eddie DeAngelis	Hartford	TKO 3
July 16	Jimmy Gilligan	Hartford	W 8
August 1	Harry Hitlian	Manchester, CT	W 6
August 5	Paul Frechette	Hartford	TKO 3
August 12	Eddie Flores	Thompsonville, MI	KO 1
September 26	Jackie Harris	New Haven	TKO 1
October 10	Carlos Manzana	New Haven	W 8
October 22	Connie Savoie	Hartford	KO 2
November 7	Billy Spencer	Los Angeles	W 4
November 24	Dave Crawford	Holyoke, MA	W 8
December 12	Ruby Garcia	New York	W 4
1942			
January 8	Joey Rivers	Fall River, MA	KO 4
January 16	Sammy Parrota	New York	W 4
January 27	Abie Kaufman	Hartford	W 8
February 10	Angelo Callura	Hartford	W 8
February 24	Willie Roach	Hartford	W 8
March 18	Johnny Compo	New Haven	W 8
April 14	Spider Armstrong	Hartford	KO 4
May 4	Curley Nichols	New Haven	W 8
May 12	Aaron Seltzer	Hartford	W 8
May 26	Joey Iannotti	Hartford	W 8
June 23	Joey Archibald	Hartford	W 10
July 21	Abe Denner	Hartford	W 12
	(Wins New England Featherweight Title)		
August 1	Joey Silva	Waterbury, CT	TKO 7
August 10	Pedro Hernandez	Hartford	W 10
August 20	Nat Litfin	West Haven, CT	W 10
September 1	Bobby Ivy	Hartford	TKO 10
September 10	Frank Franconeri	New York	TKO 1
September 22	Vince Dell'Orto	Hartford	W 10
October 5	Bobby McIntire	Holyoke, MA	W 10
October 16	Joey Archibald	Providence	W 10
October 27	George Zengaras	Hartford	W 10
November 20	Chalky Wright	New York	W 15
	(Wins World Featherweight Title)		
December 14	Joe Aponte Torres	Washington, DC	KO 7
December 21	Joey Silva	Jacksonville	TKO 9
1943			
January 4	Vince Dell'Orto	New Orleans	W 10
January 19	Bill Speary	Hartford	W 10
January 29	Allie Stolz	New York	W 10
February 11	Davey Crawford	Boston	W 10
February 15	Bill Speary	Baltimore	W 10
March 2	Lou Transparenti	Hartford	KO 6
March 19	Sammy Angott	New York	L 10
March 29	Bobby McIntire	Detroit	W 10
April 9	Sal Bartolo	Boston	W 10
April 19	Angel Aviles	Tampa	W 10
April 26	Jackie Wilson	Pittsburgh	W 12
June 8	Sal Bartolo	Boston	W 15
	(Retains World Featherweight Title)		
1944			
April 4	Leo Francis	Hartford	W 10
April 20	Harold Snooks Lacey	New Haven	W 10
May 1	Jackie Leamus	Philadelphia	W 10
May 19	Frankie Rubino	Chicago	W 10
May 23	Joey Bagnato	Buffalo	KO 2
June 6	Julie Kogan	Hartford	W 10
July 7	Willie Joyce	Chicago	W 10
July 17	Manuel Ortiz	Boston	W 10
August 4	Lulu Constantino	Waterbury, CT	W 10
August 29	Joey Peralta	Springfield, MA	W 10
September 19	Charley Cabey Lewis	Hartford	KO 8
September 29	Chalky Wright	New York	W 15
	(Retains World Featherweight Title)		

October 25	Jackie Leamus	Montreal	W 10
November 14	Charley Cabey Lewis	Hartford	W 10
November 27	Pedro Hernandez	Washington	W 10
December 5	Chalky Wright	Cleveland	W 10
1945			
January 23	Ralph Walton	Hartford	W 10
February 5	Willie Roache	New Haven	W 10
February 19	Phil Terranova	New York	W 15
	(Retains World Featherweight Title)		
October 30	Paulie Jackson	Hartford	W 8
November 5	Mike Martyk	Buffalo	TKO 5
November 26	Eddie Giosa	Boston	W 10
December 5	Harold Gibson	Lewiston, ME	W 10
December 13	Jimmy McAllister	Baltimore	D 10
1946			
January 15	Johnny Virgo	Buffalo	KO 2
February 13	Jimmy Joyce	Buffalo	W 10
March 1	Jimmy McAllister	New York	KO 2
March 26	Jackie Wilson	Kansas City	W 10
April 8	George Knox	Providence	KO 3
May 6	Ernie Petrone	New Haven	W 10
May 13	Joey Angelo	Providence	W 10
May 22	Aponte Torres	St. Louis	W 10
May 27	Jimmy Joyce	Minneapolis	W 8
June 7	Sal Bartolo	New York	KO 12
	(Retains World Featherweight Title)		
July 10	Harold Gibson	Buffalo	TKO 7
July 25	Jackie Graves	Minneapolis	TKO 8
August 26	Doll Rafferty	Milwaukee	KO 6
September 4	Walter Kolby	Buffalo	TKO 5
September 17	Lefty LaChance	Hartford	KO 3
November 1	Paulie Jackson	Minneapolis	W 10
November 15	Tomas Beato	Waterbury, CT	KO 2
November 27	Chalky Wright	Milwaukee	KO 3
1947			
June 17	Victor Flores	Hartford	W 10
July 1	Joey Fortuna	Albany	KO 5
July 8	Leo LeBrun	Norwalk, CT	W 8
July 11	Jean Barriere	North Adams, MA	KO 4
July 15	Paulie Jackson	New Bedford, MA	W 10
July 23	Humberto Sierra	Hartford	W 10
August 22	Jock Leslie	Flint, MI	TKO 12
	(Retains World Featherweight Title)		
October 21	Jean Barriere	Portland, ME	KO 1
October 27	Archie Wilmer	Philadelphia	W 10
December 22	Alvara Estrada	Lewiston, NY	W 10
December 30	Lefty LaChance	Manchester, CT	TKO 8
1948			
January 6	Pedro Biesca	Hartford	W 10
January 12	Jimmy McAllister	St. Louis	W 10
January 19	Joey Angelo	Boston	W 10
February 24	Humberto Sierra	Miami	TKO 10
	(Retains World Featherweight Title)		
May 7	Leroy Willis	Detroit	W 10
May 19	Charley Cabey Lewis	Milwaukee	W 10
June 17	Miguel Acevedo	Minneapolis	W 10
June 25	Luther Burgess	Flint, MI	W 10
July 28	Young Junior	Utica, NY	KO 1
August 3	Teddy Davis	Hartford	W 10
August 17	Teddy Davis	Hartford	W 10
September 2	Johnny Dell	Waterbury, CT	TKO 8
September 10	Paddy DeMarco	New York	W 10
October 12	Chuck Burton	Jersey City, NJ	W 8
October 19	John LaRusso	Hartford	W 10
October 29	Sandy Saddler	New York	KO by 4
	(Loses World Featherweight Title)		
December 20	Hermie Freeman	Boston	W 10
1949			
January 17	Teddy Davis	St. Louis	W 10
February 11	Sandy Saddler	New York	W 15
	(Regains World Featherweight Title)		
June 6	Luis Ramos	New Haven	W 10
June 14	Al Pennino	Pittsfield, MA	W 10
June 20	John LaRusso	Springfield, MA	W 10
July 12	Jean Mougin	Syracuse	W 10
September 20	Eddie Campo	Waterbury, CT	TKO 7
	(Retains World Featherweight Title)		
December 12	Harold Dade	St. Louis	W 10
1950			
January 16	Charley Riley	St. Louis	KO 5
	(Retains World Featherweight Title)		
February 6	Roy Andrews	Boston	W 10
February 22	Jimmy Warren	Miami	W 10
March 17	Ray Famechon	New York	W 15
	(Retains World Featherweight Title)		
May 15	Art Llanos	Hartford	KO 2
June 1	Terry Young	Milwaukee	W 10
June 26	Bobby Timpson	Hartford	W 10
July 25	Bobby Bell	Washington	W 10
August 2	Proctor Heinold	Scranton, PA	W 10
September 8	Sandy Saddler	New York	TKO by 8
	(Loses World Featherweight Title)		
1951			
January 30	Tommy Baker	Hartford	TKO 4

February 26	Billy Hogan	Sarasota, FL	TKO 2
March 5	Carlos Chavez	New Orleans	W 10
March 26	Pat Iacobucci	Miami	W 10
April 17	Baby Ortiz	St. Louis	TKO 5
April 27	Eddie Chavez	San Francisco	W 10
June 4	Jesus Compos	Baltimore	W 10
September 4	Corky Gonzalez	New Orleans	W 10
September 26	Sandy Saddler	New York	KO by 9
	(For World Featherweight Title)		

1952

April 29	Santiago Gonzalez	Tampa	W 10
May 5	Kenny Leach	Colombus, GA	W 10
May 10	Buddy Baggett	Aiken, SC	KO 5
May 21	Claude Hammond	Miami Beach	W 10
June 30	Tommy Collins	Boston	TKO by 6
September 3	Billy Lima	Pensacola, FL	W 10
September 11	Bobby Woods	Vancouver	W 10
October 1	Armand Savoie	Chicago	W 10
October 20	Billy Lima	Jacksonville	W 10
November 5	Manny Castro	Miami Beach	TKO 5
November 19	Fabala Chavez	St. Louis	W 10
December 5	Jorge Sanchez	West Palm Beach, FL	W 10

1953

January 19	Billy Lauderdale	Nassau, Bahamas	W 10
January 27	Davey Mitchell	Miami Beach	W 10
February 10	Jose Alvarez	San Antonio	W 10
March 31	Joey Gambino	Tampa	W 10
April 7	Noel Paquette	Miami Beach	W 10
May 13	Jackie Blair	Dallas	W 10
June 5	Pat Marcune	New York	TKO 10
November 21	Sonny Luciano	Charlotte	W 10
December 4	Davey Allen	West Palm Beach, FL	W 10
December 8	Billy Lima	Houston	KO 2
December 15	Tony Longo	Miami Beach	W 10

1954

January 19	David Seabrooke	Jacksonville	W 10
February 26	Lulu Perez	New York	TKO by 2
July 24	Mike Turcotte	Mobile, AL	W 10
August 18	Til LeBlanc	Moncton, Canada	W 10
November 1	Mario Colon	Dayton Beach, FL	W 10

1955

March 11	Myrel Olmstead	Bennington, VT	W 10
March 22	Charley Titone	Holyoke, MA	W 10
March 30	Gil Cadilli	San Francisco	L10
May 18	Gil Cadilli	Detroit	W 10
June 1	Joey Cam	Boston	TKO 4
June 14	Mickey Mars	Miami Beach	TKO 7
July 12	Hector Rodriguez	Bridgeport, CT	W 10
September 13	Jimmy Ithia	Hartford	TKO 6
September 27	Henry Pappy Gault	Holyoke, MA	W 10
October 10	Charley Titone	Brockton, MA	W 10
November 29	Henry Pappy Gault	Tampa	W 10
December 12	Lee Carter	Houston	TKO 4
December 28	Andy Arel	Miami Beach	W 10

1956

March 13	Kid Campeche	Tampa	W 10
March 27	Buddy Baggett	Beaumont, TX	W 10
April 17	Jackie Blair	Hartford	W 10
May 22	Manuel Armenteros	San Antonio	KO 7
June 19	Russ Tague	Miami Beach	W 10
July 4	Hector Bacquettes	Lawton, OK	KO 4

1957

April 23	Cesar Morales	Ft. Lauderdale	W 10
May 10	Manny Castro	Florence, SC	W 10
July 16	Manny Castro	El Paso, TX	W 10
July 23	Russ Tague	Houston	W 10
December 17	Jimmy Connors	Boston	W 10

1958

January 14	Tommy Tibbs	Boston	L 10
March 31	Prince Johnson	Holyoke, MA	W 10
April 8	George Stephany	Bristol, CT	W 10
April 14	Cleo Ortiz	Providence	W 10
April 29	Jimmy Kelly	Boston	W 10
May 20	Bobby Singleton	Boston	W 10
June 23	Pat McCoy	New Bedford, MA	W 10
July 1	Bobby Soares	Athol, MA	W 10
July 17	Bobby Bell	Norwood, MA	W 10
August 4	Luis Ramona	Presque Isle, ME	W 10
August 9	Jesse Rodrigues	Painesville, OH	W 10
August 26	Al Duarte	North Adams, MA	W 10
September 20	Hogan Kid Bassey	Boston	TKO by 9

1959

January 26	Sonny Leon	Caracas, Venezuela	L 10
January 27	Announces Retirement		

1965

March 12	Hal McKeever	Miami	W 8
April 26	Jackie Lennon	Philadelphia	W 6
May 21	Johnny Gilmore	Norwalk, CT	W 6
July 26	Benny Randell	Quebec City, Canada	W 10
September 28	Johnny Gilmore	Philadelphia	W 6
October 1	Willie Little	Johnstown, NY	KO 3
October 4	Tommy Haden	Providence	TKO 3
October 14	Sergio Musquiz	Phoenix	KO 5
October 25	Ray Coleman	Tucson	TKO 5

1966

March 16	Calvin Woodland	Richmond, VA	L 6

RING MAGAZINE'S FIGHT OF THE YEAR

1945 **Rocky Graziano** (KO 10) over Freddie Cochrane
1946 Tony Zale (KO 6) over **Rocky Graziano**
1947 **Rocky Graziano** (KO 6) over Tony Zale
1948 Marcel Cerdan (KO 12) over Tony Zale
1949 **Willie Pep** (W 15) over Sandy Saddler
1950 **Jake LaMotta** (KO 15) over Laurent Dauthuille
1951 Jersey Joe Walcott (KO 7) over Ezzard Charles
1952 **Rocky Marciano** (KO 13) over Jersey Joe Walcott

1953 **Rocky Marciano** (TKO 11) over **Roland LaStarza**
1954 **Rocky Marciano** (KO 8) over Ezzard Charles
1955 **Carmen Basilio** (KO 12) over **Tony DeMarco**
1956 **Carmen Basilio** (TKO 9) over Johnny Saxton
1957 **Carmen Basilio** (W 15) over Sugar Ray Robinson
1958 Sugar Ray Robinson (W 15) over **Carmen Basilio**
1959 Gene Fullmer (TKO 14) over **Carmen Basilio**

PHOTOGRAPHS & ILLUSTRATIONS